Regulatory Frameworks and Digital Compliance in Green Marketing

Shamim Akhtar
School of Management,Jiangsu University, China

Prasad Siba Borah
School of Management, Jiangsu University, China

IGI Global
Scientific Publishing
Publishing Tomorrow's Research Today

Published in the United States of America by
IGI Global Scientific Publishing
701 East Chocolate Avenue
Hershey, PA, 17033, USA
Tel: 717-533-8845
Fax: 717-533-7115
Website: https://www.igi-global.com E-mail: cust@igi-global.com

Library of Congress Cataloging-in-Publication Data
Names: Akhtar, Shamim, 1991- editor | Borah, Prasad Siba, 1972- editor
Title: Regulatory frameworks and digital compliance in marketing / [edited by] Shamim Akhtar, Prasad Borah.
Description: Hershey, PA : IGI Global Scientific Publishing, 2025. | Includes bibliographical references and index. | Summary: "The book aims to explain that businesses can use digital tools, platforms, and technologies to drive eco-innovation and implement effective green marketing strategies that align with sustainability goals. Through a series of in-depth analyses, practical strategies, and real-world case studies, this book offers valuable insights for businesses to extract the power of eco-innovation and digital technology to achieve green marketing excellence in all parts and businesses of the world"-- Provided by publisher.
Identifiers: LCCN 2025000189 (print) | LCCN 2025000190 (ebook) | ISBN 9798369398319 hardcover | ISBN 9798369398326 paperback | ISBN 9798369398333 ebook
Subjects: LCSH: Green marketing | Marketing--Technological innovations | Sustainable development
Classification: LCC HF5413 .R44 2025 (print) | LCC HF5413 (ebook) | DDC 658.8/02--dc23/eng/20250404
LC record available at https://lccn.loc.gov/2025000189
LC ebook record available at https://lccn.loc.gov/2025000190

British Cataloguing in Publication Data
A Cataloguing in Publication record for this book is available from the British Library.

Table of Contents

Detailed Table of Contents

This chapter explains transformative relationship between eco-innovation, green marketing, and digital transformation, exploring how businesses can use these elements to address global sustainability challenges. It describes eco-innovation as the development of environmentally friendly products, processes, and systems designed to reduce ecological impact while promoting economic and social benefits. The chapter introduces green marketing, a strategic approach to promoting sustainable products and practices that align with the values of environmentally conscious consumers. The explanations expands to examine the important role of digital transformation in enabling and accelerating both eco-innovation and green marketing efforts. It highlights emerging trends in green marketing and the rise of collaborative digital ecosystems, offering an indication into the future of sustainable business practices.

This chapter aims at focusing on the damage done because of consumerism and its impact on the environment. The chapter emphasizes the need for going green by companies and the consumer to save the environment. Moving forward, the chapter explores how various companies are trying to go green and the overall adoption of those practices by the consumers. The chapter will also focus on the challenges and the barriers faced by the consumer while going through the process of buying a green product.

This chapter examines how digital platforms and gamification strategies foster environmental awareness and promote the UN SDGs and sustainable consumer behavior in response to escalating global ecological challenges. It explores how environmental awareness is enhanced through digital social influence and gamified systems to drive sustainable behaviors and encourage societal shifts toward green consumption. By integrating the persuasive power of social media and the engaging mechanics of gamification, this chapter demonstrates their synergy in boosting motivation and accountability in environmental initiatives. Supported by empirical evidence and case studies, it highlights their transformative impact on green purchasing habits and broader sustainability goals while emphasizing their alignment with the United Nations Sustainable Development Goals (SDGs), including climate action and responsible consumption.

With the advent of the internet, it has become easier for businesses to deliver their products to distant regions. However, this convenience has also significantly increased competition. Now, consumers have access to the entire market in the palm of their hands through mobile phones. With just a few clicks, they can compare businesses and their competitors, evaluating who offers better quality at a lower price. Traditional advertising, where you simply highlight your product's features in an ad, is no longer effective. People no longer have the time or interest to watch conventional 1-2 minute advertisements. The rise of big data has revolutionized sales and marketing. Now, data is being generated every second, and the ability to analyze this data to identify consumer preference patterns has become the cornerstone of strategic marketing.

This chapter explores the integration of Green Human Resource Management (Green HRM) and green marketing as essential strategies to address environmental challenges and foster sustainability. Green HRM encompasses practices like green recruitment, sustainability-focused training, and performance management aligned with eco-friendly goals, while green marketing promotes environmentally conscious products and services, enhancing brand trust. The chapter highlights the synergy between these concepts, showing how Green HRM strengthens the authenticity of green marketing efforts. Case studies of companies such as Wipro, IKEA, and Toyota demonstrate practical applications, innovative solutions, and benefits, including employee engagement programs, gamification, and green KPIs. Challenges like regulatory hurdles, resource constraints, and cultural resistance are analyzed, alongside strategies to overcome them.

The rapid rise of e-commerce has inadvertently triggered an environmental crisis by promoting rapid deliveries, excessive over-packaging, and a "fast fashion" mentality that contributes to resource depletion, pollution, and ethical concerns in production, spurring transportation-related carbon emissions, creating significant amounts of non-recyclable waste. In response to this challenge, this chapter investigates how digital innovations and consumer behaviors facilitate circular economy practices in sustainable e-commerce while also evaluating digital marketing strategies that foster a greener future. Grounded in circular economy and sustainable development principles, the chapter examines how digital innovations and consumer behaviors can facilitate sustainable practices in e-commerce. Utilizing a conceptual framework supported by Patagonia, Etsy, and The RealReal case studies, the analysis explores how eco-friendly product curation, ethical sourcing, supply chain transparency, sustainable logistics, and AI-driven personalization are key drivers for promoting sustainable e-commerce.

Foreword

In a world increasingly defined by environmental crises, digital revolutions, and rising demands for corporate responsibility, the need for marketing strategies that are both sustainable and tech-savvy has never been more pressing. *Regulatory Frameworks and Digital Compliance in Green Marketing* arrive at a crucial moment in history, when businesses, governments, and consumers alike are seeking new ways to align economic activities with environmental imperatives and digital innovation.

This timely volume delivers an essential roadmap for navigating the evolving nexus of green marketing, digital transformation, and regulatory compliance. It offers a comprehensive and interdisciplinary exploration of how organizations can balance innovation with responsibility, ethics with efficiency, and environmental stewardship with market competitiveness. For readers across the globe, whether scholars, students, business professionals, or policymakers, this book offers valuable insights into the shifting paradigms of sustainable and digitally enabled marketing.

What sets this book apart is its capacity to bridge theory and practice through a rich collection of perspectives. Each chapter is a doorway into a critical dimension of modern marketing, addressing eco-consumer behavior, green human resource management, sustainability gamification, big data analytics, and digital marketplace ethics. The authors masterfully integrate academic rigor with practical relevance, offering readers both the conceptual tools and actionable strategies needed to thrive in today's regulatory and environmental landscape.

A central theme running through the volume is the role of digital transformation as a catalyst for green innovation. Technologies such as blockchain, artificial intelligence, and big data are shown not merely as operational tools, but as strategic enablers of sustainable marketing. These technologies are explored in the context of enhancing transparency, driving consumer engagement, and ensuring regulatory compliance, elements that are rapidly becoming non-negotiable for any organization seeking long-term viability.

Moreover, the book does not shy away from complex challenges. It tackles issues like consumer resistance to green products, inconsistencies in global regulatory frameworks, and the environmental implications of e-commerce logistics. By shedding light on these obstacles, it offers real-world solutions informed by case studies from global brands. These examples lend credibility and global resonance, allowing readers from diverse markets to draw parallels and adopt best practices in their local contexts.

Importantly, the book underscores the significance of human capital in driving sustainable changes. With dedicated chapters on green HRM and the strategic alignment of workforce practices with environmental values, the editors remind us that sustainable transformation begins from within. Empowering employees with green mindsets and digital fluency is no longer a choice, it is a competitive necessity.

As marketing professionals and organizations increasingly operate in borderless digital ecosystems, the importance of understanding and adhering to international environmental regulations cannot be overstated. This book provides a forward-thinking guide to navigating such frameworks, offering not only regulatory awareness but also digital tools that can automate and enhance compliance. This dual focus ensures that readers are not just informed but equipped for action.

Above all, *Regulatory Frameworks and Digital Compliance in Green Marketing* is more than a scholarly text, it is a call to action. It challenges conventional marketing approaches and encourages a shift toward practices that are future-ready, socially responsible, and digitally sophisticated. For global readers, it presents an opportunity to rethink and retool marketing strategies for a world that demands more from businesses than ever before. Whether you are a student seeking to understand sustainable business trends, a policymaker shaping environmental legislation, or a business leader steering your company toward greener horizons, this book will serve as a vital companion in your journey. It is with great enthusiasm and confidence in its value that I recommend this volume to all who aspire to create a meaningful impact through marketing.

Komal Khalid
King Abdulaziz University, Jeddah, Saudi Arabia

Preface

The evolving global marketplace has created an urgent need for marketing strategies that are not only innovative and data-driven but also sustainable and ethically grounded. In recent years, increasing environmental concerns, consumer demand for transparency, and tightening regulatory landscapes have brought green marketing and digital compliance to the forefront of academic and professional discourse. This book, *Regulatory Frameworks and Digital Compliance in Green Marketing*, brings together insights from leading scholars and practitioners to examine how businesses can navigate these complexities through eco-innovation, green marketing, digital transformation, and regulatory compliance.

As editors, our aim was to create comprehensive and interdisciplinary reference work that explores how marketing strategies can align with broader sustainability goals. Each chapter examines a unique aspect of this challenge, from eco-consumer behavior and green HRM practices to regulatory frameworks and gamification strategies, providing both theoretical perspectives and practical implications. This diversity reflects the multifaceted nature of modern marketing and the growing importance of digital tools in shaping and enforcing compliance.

The chapters also emphasize the role of digital transformation in enabling green marketing efforts, offering insight into how technologies like big data, blockchain, and artificial intelligence can enhance transparency, optimize sustainability efforts, and ensure regulatory alignment. Whether discussing consumer behavior or sustainable e-commerce, this book highlights how innovation, regulation, and ethics must work in tandem to address pressing environmental and business challenges in the 21st century.

CHAPTER 1: INTRODUCTION TO ECO-INNOVATION AND GREEN MARKETING AND DIGITAL TRANSFORMATION

Author: Shamim Akhtar

Overview:

This opening chapter sets the stage by introducing the synergy between eco-innovation, green marketing, and digital transformation. It defines eco-innovation as the creation of sustainable products and processes that reduce environmental harm while boosting economic and social value. Green marketing is presented as a strategy for promoting such innovations to an eco-conscious market. Digital transformation is positioned as a key enabler, driving innovation and consumer engagement. Emerging trends and collaborative digital ecosystems are also explored, offering a forward-looking perspective on sustainable business models.

CHAPTER 2: GO GREEN: AN ECO-CONSUMERISM VIEWPOINT

Authors: Prachi Wani, Pritesh Somani, Vishwanathan Iyer

Overview:

Focusing on the consumer side of sustainability, this chapter explains the consequences of unchecked consumerism and the urgent call for eco-conscious behavior. It highlights how businesses are shifting to greener practices and how consumers are responding. The chapter also unpacks the challenges consumers face in adopting green products, such as higher costs, lack of awareness, and limited availability, offering insights into bridging the gap between green offerings and consumer adoption.

CHAPTER 3: DIGITAL SOCIAL INFLUENCE AND SUSTAINABILITY GAMIFICATION EFFECT ON ENVIRONMENTAL AWARENESS AND GREEN CONSUMPTION BEHAVIOR

Author: Benard Korankye

Overview:

This chapter examines how digital platforms and gamified experiences are transforming sustainability communication and consumer behavior. It explores how social media influence and gamification enhances environmental awareness and drives eco-friendly purchasing. With references to the UN Sustainable Development Goals, the chapter uses empirical data and case studies to show how technology can inspire accountability and collective action toward green consumption.

CHAPTER 4: MARKETING IN THE DIGITAL AGE: NAVIGATING TRANSFORMATION, CONSUMER BEHAVIOR, AND BIG DATA

Author: Ambreen Shah

Overview:

This chapter focuses on the shifts towards the digital marketing landscape and the pivotal role of big data. The chapter outlines how consumer behavior has evolved in the internet age, making traditional marketing tactics obsolete. It explains how big data analytics empower marketers to uncover trends, personalize offers, and strategically position their brands in an intensely competitive environment where instant information access is the norm.

CHAPTER 5: NAVIGATING ENVIRONMENTAL REGULATIONS IN DIGITAL MARKETING: ENSURING COMPLIANCE WHILE PROMOTING GREEN CLAIMS

Authors: Vishal Jain, Archan Mitra

Overview:

This chapter investigates how businesses navigate the intersection of digital marketing and environmental regulations. It reveals the complexities of ensuring compliance while promoting sustainability claims, especially for SMEs. The role of AI and blockchain in enhancing transparency and regulatory adherence is discussed. The chapter closes with policy recommendations and industry strategies for harmonizing environmental goals with marketing effectiveness.

CHAPTER 6: THE ROLE OF HRM IN SUPPORTING GREEN MARKETING STRATEGIES

Authors: Shuja Iqbal, Aasim Gill

Overview:

This chapter outlines how HRM integrates sustainability into hiring, training, and leadership development. Human Resource Management (HRM) is spotlighted as a key driver of green marketing success. It discusses cultivating a green organizational culture and overcoming internal barriers to change. Emerging trends such as digital tools and cross-disciplinary collaborations are also highlighted for embedding sustainability in the workforce.

CHAPTER 7: HUMAN RESOURCE MANAGEMENT AND GREEN MARKETING: ALIGNING WORKFORCE WITH SUSTAINABILITY

Authors: Brendan Ezeudoka, Charles Igwe

Overview:

This chapter, built on the previous chapter, deepens the discussion around Green HRM, emphasizing its strategic role in reinforcing green marketing authenticity. Real-world case studies from companies like Wipro and IKEA showcase how aligning employee practices with environmental values enhances credibility and operational efficiency. The chapter also explores challenges like regulatory inconsistencies and cultural resistance, offering possible strategies.

CHAPTER 8: SUSTAINABLE E-COMMERCE PLATFORMS: INTEGRATING GREEN MARKETING STRATEGIES IN DIGITAL MARKETPLACES

Author: Tinashe Mangudhla

Overview:

This chapter critiques practices such as over-packaging and fast delivery, focusing on the environmental implications of e-commerce. It explores how circular economy models and digital innovations, like AI personalization and transparent sourcing, can reduce these issues. Case studies from Patagonia and Etsy illustrate how sustainable logistics and ethical product curation can transform digital marketplaces into forces for environmental good.

CHAPTER 9: REGULATORY FRAMEWORKS AND DIGITAL COMPLIANCE IN GREEN MARKET ORIENTATION

Author: Courage Simon Kofi Dogbe

Overview:

This chapter provides a comprehensive look at Green Market Orientation (GMO), detailing its components and drivers such as regulations and consumer demand. It evaluates the role of digital compliance tools (e.g., AI, IoT, blockchain) and major regulatory initiatives (EU Green Deal, FTC Green Guides) that support GMO adoption. With insights from companies like Unilever and Tesla, the chapter presents a roadmap for successfully integrating compliance, innovation, and market orientation in sustainability strategies.

CHAPTER 10: PRACTICAL IMPLICATIONS AND FUTURE OF ECO-INNOVATION, DIGITAL TRANSFORMATION AND GREEN MARKETING

Author: Prasad Borah

Overview:

Concluding the volume, this chapter synthesizes key themes and projects future directions for sustainable business practices. It reexamines the interconnection of eco-innovation, digital transformation, and green marketing, providing actionable guidance for firms to align strategies, invest in green tech, and build consumer trust. Case studies and frameworks offer practical insights for leaders aiming to embed sustainability into core business functions and long-term planning.

Throughout this volume, the contributing authors have provided critical insights and research that shed light on how businesses and institutions can respond proactively to environmental and regulatory demands. Topics such as the influence of digital platforms on green consumer behavior, the integration of eco-principles into HRM, and the implementation of sustainable practices in e-commerce are not just timely, they are essential for shaping the future of responsible marketing. These perspectives are especially valuable for scholars, students, policymakers, and practitioners who are navigating a world where compliance and sustainability are rapidly becoming key performance indicators.

We are particularly proud of the collaborative nature of this work, which spans global institutions and diverse perspectives. From foundational theories to case-based applications, this book illustrates how academic research can serve as a practical guide for organizations striving to meet evolving environmental standards while maintaining competitiveness in digital markets. It is our belief that this volume offers actionable insights and frameworks that readers can adopt and adapt across a range of organizational contexts.

In closing, we would like to extend our sincere gratitude to the authors, reviewers, and contributors who made this volume possible. Their dedication, expertise, and passion for sustainable marketing have greatly enriched the content of this book. We also thank our readers for joining us on this important journey toward a more responsible and forward-thinking marketing landscape. It is our hope that this book not only informs but inspires future research, policy, and practice in sustainable and digitally compliant marketing.

Acknowledgement

We extend our thanks to IGI Global Scientific Publishing for giving us the opportunity to develop the book and present knowledge for the readers around the globe. We also thank the connected team of IGI for supporting during all phases of book completion. Moreover, we acknowledge the contributions of all the authors.

Shamim Akhtar, Prasad Siba Borah

Chapter 1
Introduction to Eco-Innovation and Green Marketing and Digital Transformation

Shamim Akhtar
https://orcid.org/0000-0002-9608-3909
Jiangsu University, China

ABSTRACT

This chapter explains transformative relationship between eco-innovation, green marketing, and digital transformation, exploring how businesses can use these elements to address global sustainability challenges. It describes eco-innovation as the development of environmentally friendly products, processes, and systems designed to reduce ecological impact while promoting economic and social benefits. The chapter introduces green marketing, a strategic approach to promoting sustainable products and practices that align with the values of environmentally conscious consumers. The explanations expands to examine the important role of digital transformation in enabling and accelerating both eco-innovation and green marketing efforts. It highlights emerging trends in green marketing and the rise of collaborative digital ecosystems, offering an indication into the future of sustainable business practices.

DOI: 10.4018/979-8-3693-9831-9.ch001

1 INTRODUCTION

1.1 Understanding Eco-Innovation

Eco-innovation refers to the development of innovative products, services, processes, or business models that reduce environmental harm, promote resource efficiency, and create sustainable value. It blends ecological consciousness with innovation, aiming to address challenges like climate change, resource depletion, and pollution. Eco-Innovation spans various industries, encompassing renewable energy technologies, sustainable agriculture, waste management systems, eco-friendly packaging, and green transportation. Beyond product development, it also includes systemic shifts, such as circular economy frameworks and low-carbon production techniques (Sandionigi et al., 2024).

1.1.1 Components of Eco-Innovation

Eco-innovation involves three main components:

Environmental Improvement: It seeks to minimize negative ecological impacts through energy efficiency, waste reduction, and adoption of clean technologies.
Economic Growth: By creating competitive advantages, eco-innovation fosters economic development while ensuring sustainability.
Social Benefits: It contributes to societal well-being by improving quality of life and fostering green employment opportunities.

The eco-innovation involves the primarily technological and non-technological changes as required in the context significantly (Figure 1). For instance, Tesla's advancements in electric vehicles and their sustainable energy solutions exemplify eco-innovation, integrating cutting-edge technology with environmental leadership and practices.

Figure 1. The contexts of eco-innovation (oecd, 2009)

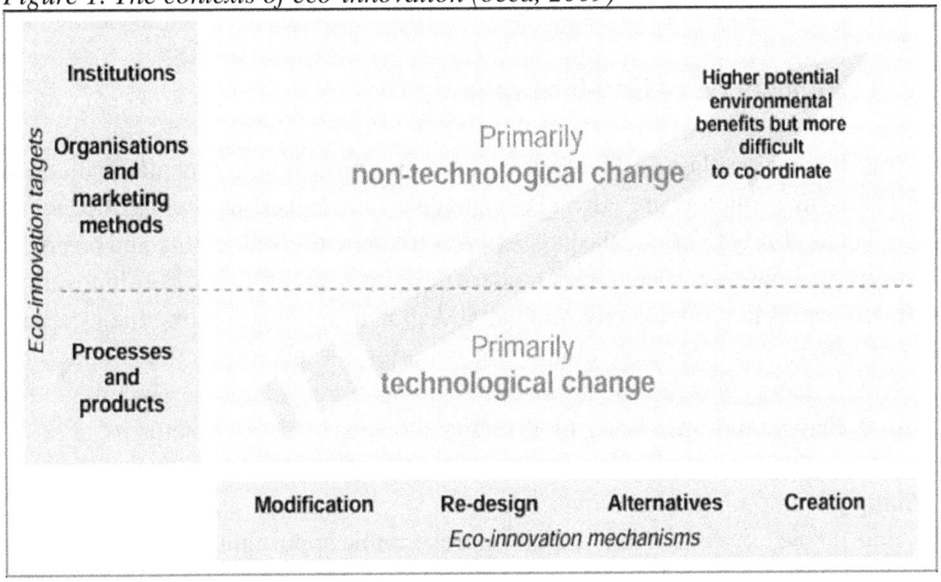

1.1.2 The Process of Eco-Innovation

The eco-innovation process typically unfolds in four key stages:

Idea Generation and Conceptualization: This phase involves identifying environmental challenges and brainstorming creative solutions. It often incorporates stakeholder collaboration and lifecycle thinking to assess the long-term impact of proposed ideas

Research and Development (R&D): Detailed analysis and prototyping occur here, emphasizing resource efficiency, renewable inputs, and innovative designs.

Commercialization and Market Entry: Successful eco-innovations are launched into the market, accompanied by strategic marketing campaigns that highlight their environmental and social benefits.

Evaluation and Improvement: After-market introduction, ongoing assessment ensures the innovation remains effective and sustainable while allowing room for adaptation.

Eco-innovation is an indispensable driver of sustainable development, harmonizing ecological preservation with economic growth and societal progress. By fostering resource-conscious creativity and embracing green technologies, eco-innovation helps organizations meet both current and future sustainability challenges. Companies like IKEA, with its circular furniture initiatives, showcase the transformative potential of eco-innovation in redefining industry practices and consumer behaviors.

1.1.3 Significance of Eco-Innovation

Eco-Innovation plays a critical role in addressing global environmental challenges while driving economic growth and enhancing social well-being. Its significance is rooted in its ability to bridge the gap between ecological sustainability and business viability, making it a cornerstone of modern development strategies. Eco-Innovation is instrumental in reducing environmental degradation by promoting the efficient use of natural resources and minimizing pollution. It encourages the adoption of renewable energy, sustainable agriculture, and waste recycling, thereby mitigating climate change and preserving biodiversity. For instance, advancements in solar and wind energy technologies have significantly reduced reliance on fossil fuels, curbing greenhouse gas emissions.

Eco-Innovation creates new markets and economic opportunities. By introducing eco-friendly products and services, companies can achieve competitive differentiation and tap into the growing consumer demand for sustainability. Moreover, it fosters cost savings through energy efficiency, reduced material waste, and optimized supply chains. Examples include Unilever's "Sustainable Living Plan," which integrates sustainability into its business model, resulting in both environmental and financial benefits. Eco-Innovation contributes to societal well-being by creating green jobs, improving public health, and fostering a culture of environmental responsibility. It also empowers communities by providing sustainable solutions to local challenges, such as access to clean water or affordable energy. Initiatives like biodegradable packaging innovations help reduce plastic pollution, directly improving living conditions in urban and rural areas alike.

Adopting eco-innovation strengthens an organization's resilience to regulatory changes, market shifts, and resource constraints. It positions businesses as leaders in sustainability, enhancing brand reputation and customer loyalty while aligning with global sustainability goals, such as the United Nations' Sustainable Development Goals (SDGs) (Adebayo & Özkan, 2024). In essence, eco-innovation is not just an environmental imperative but also a strategic enabler for sustainable economic and social progress in an increasingly resource-constrained world

1.2 Understanding Green Marketing

Green marketing refers to the promotion of environmentally friendly products and services by highlighting their sustainable attributes, eco-conscious production processes, and their minimal impact on the environment. It aligns with the values of socially and environmentally responsible consumers, aiming to build trust, loyalty, and competitive differentiation in an increasingly eco-aware market. At its core, green marketing integrates environmental considerations into traditional marketing strategies while fostering sustainable consumption patterns.

The concept of green marketing revolves around creating value by addressing ecological concerns. It encompasses the entire product lifecycle, from raw material sourcing and manufacturing to packaging, distribution, and post-consumer disposal (Samsudin & Hotimah, 2024). Therefore, the businesses leveraging green marketing aim not only to generate profits but also to contribute positively to the environment by reducing waste, emissions, and resource depletion

1.2.1 Components of Green Marketing

Green marketing comprises the following key components (Figure 2):

Eco-friendly Products: Offering goods or services that are recyclable, biodegradable, energy-efficient, or made from sustainable materials.
Green Promotion: Communicating environmental benefits through advertisements, labeling, certifications, and transparent information.
Sustainable Pricing: Establishing prices that reflect the value of green attributes without alienating cost-sensitive consumers.
Green Packaging: Reducing packaging waste through biodegradable materials or innovative designs that minimize resource usage.
Sustainable Distribution: Implementing logistics practices that reduce carbon footprints, such as optimizing routes or using eco-friendly transportation.

Figure 2. Components of green marketing (Compiled by author)

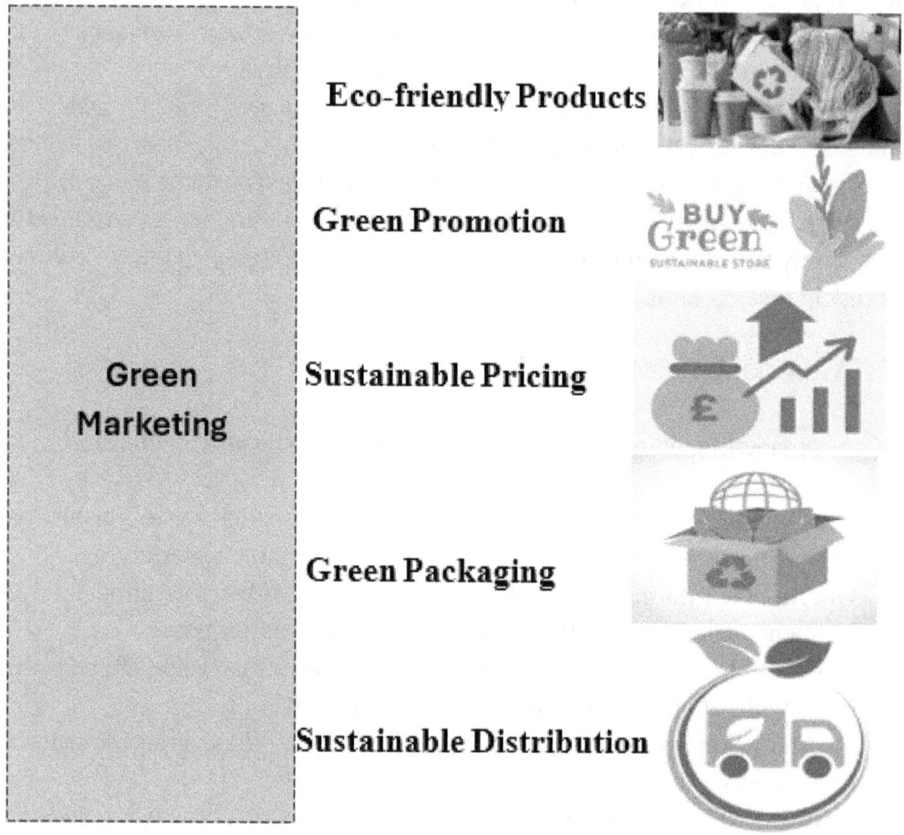

For instance, Patagonia's "Don't Buy This Jacket" campaign effectively combines transparency and environmental advocacy, urging customers to consume responsibly.

1.2.2 Process of Green Marketing

The green marke\ting process typically follows these stages:

Market Analysis and Consumer Insight: Understanding consumer behavior, preferences, and environmental concerns to tailor green products and campaigns accordingly.

Product Development: Designing and manufacturing products that meet ecological standards while satisfying customer needs. For example, companies may use recycled materials or energy-efficient technologies.

Sustainable Branding: Positioning the product or service as eco-friendly through green certifications, logos, or impactful storytelling.
Strategic Promotion: Using diverse channels like digital media, public relations, and in-store promotions to communicate the product's green benefits effectively.
Feedback and Continuous Improvement: Engaging consumers to gather feedback, assess environmental impact, and refine the product or marketing strategy to maintain authenticity and relevance.

Green marketing is not just a trend but a strategic approach that resonates with modern consumers' values and expectations. It emphasizes environmental stewardship while driving economic and social benefits, making it a vital component of sustainable business practices.

1.2.3 Significance of Green Marketing

Green marketing plays a pivotal role in shaping sustainable consumer behaviors, fostering environmental stewardship, and driving business success in an increasingly eco-conscious world. Its significance extends beyond commercial benefits, contributing to environmental, economic, and social progress. Green marketing encourages businesses to adopt eco-friendly practices, reducing their ecological footprint. By promoting products with sustainable attributes, such as energy efficiency, recyclability, and biodegradable packaging, it raises awareness about environmental issues and motivates consumers to make responsible choices. This collective effort helps mitigate challenges like resource depletion, pollution, and climate change. For instance, companies like The Body Shop prioritize cruelty-free, natural products and emphasize their environmental commitment, inspiring others to follow suit.

Green marketing appeals to the growing demographic of environmentally aware consumers who prefer brands that align with their values. By transparently communicating environmental initiatives, companies can build trust and foster long-term loyalty. Green certifications, eco-labels, and sustainability reports serve as proof points, enhancing brand credibility and reputation. For example, brands like Seventh Generation leverage their commitment to sustainability to differentiate themselves in competitive markets. Embracing green marketing can unlock new business opportunities and reduce operational costs. Eco-friendly innovations often lead to energy savings, waste reduction, and improved supply chain efficiency. Additionally, green products can command premium pricing, driving profitability while satisfying consumer demand for sustainable alternatives. Tesla's marketing of electric vehicles exemplifies how green branding can transform industries and generate economic value.

Green marketing helps businesses stay ahead of environmental regulations and societal expectations. It positions organizations as industry leaders in sustainability, enabling them to outperform competitors and attract socially responsible investors as per the study of (Kumari, 2024). In summary, green marketing is essential for fostering sustainable practices, meeting consumer expectations, and addressing global environmental challenges. By integrating environmental responsibility with business objectives, it drives mutual benefits for companies, consumers, and the planet

Why green marketing: In the face of escalating environmental challenges such as climate change, resource depletion, and pollution, companies must adopt green marketing to align with global sustainability goals and changing consumer preferences. The 2020s mark a critical period where businesses are increasingly held accountable for their environmental impact, and green marketing presents a strategic solution to balance profit with purpose. The companies should focus on green marketing because of following reasons.

Rising Consumer Awareness: Consumers are more eco-conscious than ever, seeking products and services that reflect their environmental values. Green marketing enables companies to connect with these consumers, build trust, and enhance brand loyalty. Studies show that a significant portion of millennials and Gen Z are willing to pay a premium for sustainable offerings.

Regulatory Pressures: Governments worldwide are implementing stricter environmental regulations, incentivizing green innovation and penalizing unsustainable practices. By adopting green marketing, companies can proactively align with these policies, avoiding fines and reputational risks.

Competitive Advantage: As sustainability becomes a differentiator, businesses focusing on green marketing can stand out in crowded markets. Highlighting eco-friendly credentials helps companies attract socially responsible investors and gain market share in environmentally conscious sectors.

Cost Efficiency: Green practices, such as energy-efficient production and waste reduction, often lead to significant cost savings. These efficiencies, combined with eco-friendly branding, provide dual benefits: reduced operational expenses and enhanced consumer appeal.

By focusing on green marketing, companies can drive profits while fostering a healthier planet and empowered communities. This decade represents a transformative era where businesses play a pivotal role in shaping a sustainable future for society at large (Kaur & Gupta, 2024). For example:

Environmental Preservation: Green marketing promotes sustainable production and consumption patterns, reducing carbon footprints and conserving resources. By encouraging eco-friendly alternatives, it drives collective action against environmental degradation.

Improved Public Health: Eco-friendly products, such as non-toxic cleaners and organic foods, minimize exposure to harmful chemicals, improving public health and safety. Sustainable practices also lead to cleaner air, water, and land, benefiting communities.

Job Creation in Green Sectors: Green marketing fuels demand for sustainable innovation, creating employment opportunities in renewable energy, eco-design, waste management, and green logistics.

Cultural Shift Toward Sustainability: Companies promoting green marketing inspire a cultural shift toward environmental responsibility, influencing societal attitudes and encouraging individuals and other organizations to adopt sustainable practices.

1.3 Digital Transformation

Digital transformation refers to the integration of digital technologies across all areas of a business, fundamentally changing how it operates and delivers value to its customers. It involves a cultural shift that challenges traditional practices, fosters innovation, and leverages emerging technologies to improve efficiency, agility, and customer experience (Akhtar et al., 2024). Hence, more than just adopting new tools, digital transformation is about reimagining business models, processes, and strategies to align with the demands of the digital age

1.3.1 Components of Digital Transformation

The following are the components of digital transformation that companies focus:

Technology Integration: The adoption of technologies such as cloud computing, artificial intelligence (AI), the Internet of Things (IoT), big data analytics, and blockchain form the foundation of digital transformation.
Data and Analytics: Data is central to digital transformation. Advanced analytics and machine learning enable businesses to make data-driven decisions, optimize operations, and predict market trends.
Customer Experience: Enhancing customer interactions through personalized, seamless, and intuitive digital platforms is a key driver of transformation.
Operational Processes: Streamlining operations using automation, process optimization, and digital workflows improve efficiency and reduce costs.
Cultural Shift and Workforce Enablement: Digital transformation requires a cultural change where employees adopt a digital-first mindset, supported by training, upskilling, and change management strategies.

Innovation Ecosystem: Collaboration with startups, technology partners, and research institutions fosters innovation and accelerates digital adoption.

1.3.2 The Process of Digital Transformation

The process of digital transformation (Figure 3) involves the above-mentioned activities:

Assessment and Strategy Development: The process begins with evaluating the current state of the organization, identifying gaps, and defining a clear vision and goals for transformation. This includes assessing technological readiness and aligning objectives with business priorities.

Technology Selection and Implementation: Selecting appropriate technologies that align with the organization's needs and integrating them into existing systems is crucial. This step involves careful planning, testing, and phased rollouts to minimize disruptions.

Workforce Enablement: Training employees to use new technologies and fostering a culture of innovation are essential to overcoming resistance and maximizing the benefits of transformation.

Data Utilization and Optimization: Harnessing data through advanced analytics and AI ensures informed decision-making and continuous improvement of processes.

Customer-Centric Innovations: Developing and deploying digital solutions to enhance customer engagement and satisfaction ensures the transformation delivers value.

Continuous Monitoring and Adaptation: Digital transformation is an ongoing process. Organizations must monitor performance, adapt to emerging trends, and refine strategies to maintain a competitive edge (Hendrawan et al., 2024).

Figure 3. Process of digital transformation (compiled by author)

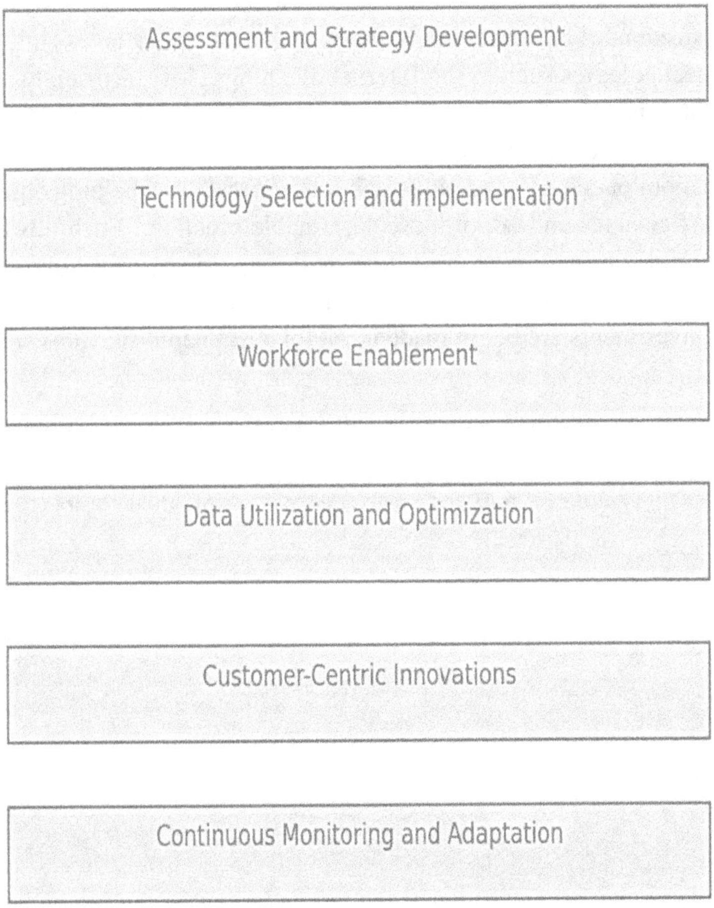

2 INTERSECTION OF ECO-INNOVATION, DIGITAL TRANSFORMATION AND GREEN MARKETING

In today's interconnected world, digital transformation has become a powerful enabler for businesses to achieve sustainability goals by driving eco-innovation and facilitating green marketing strategies. By leveraging digital tools and technologies, companies can enhance their environmental initiatives and effectively communicate their commitment to sustainability to stakeholders. The convergence of digital transformation, eco-innovation, and green marketing allows businesses to address environmental challenges while creating value for consumers and the planet (Longo & Magnusson, 2024).

Digital transformation empowers companies to rethink their traditional practices and embed sustainability into their operations. It enables the seamless integration of innovative technologies such as the Internet of Things (IoT), artificial intelligence (AI), big data analytics, and blockchain to optimize processes, reduce resource consumption, and minimize environmental footprints. For example, IoT-enabled devices can monitor energy usage and track waste in real time, helping organizations identify inefficiencies and adopt more sustainable practices. Such advancements not only support eco-innovation but also provide tangible evidence of a company's green credentials, which can be highlighted in their marketing efforts. Several new worldwide investments are being made in AI for sustainable start-ups (Figure 4).

Figure 4. AI for sustainable start-ups (Organisation for Economic Co-operation and Development, 2024)

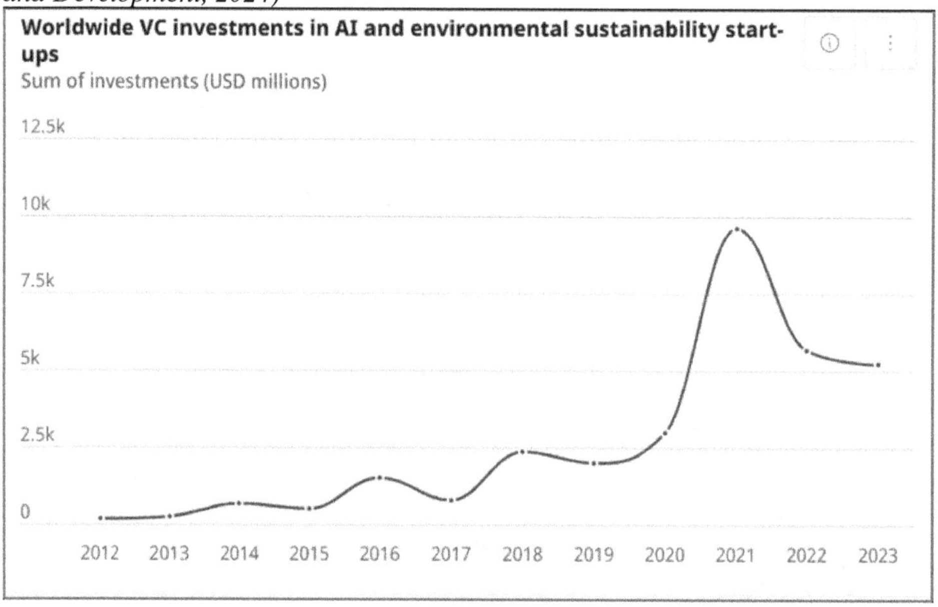

Big data and analytics play a significant role in driving eco-innovation. By analyzing vast amounts of data, businesses can gain insights into consumer behavior, supply chain inefficiencies, and environmental impact. This information helps companies design products that meet eco-conscious consumer demands and improve their production processes. For instance, data-driven insights can guide the development of biodegradable packaging, energy-efficient appliances, or sustainable apparel, ensuring that products align with green marketing narratives. Furthermore, predictive analytics enables companies to anticipate sustainability trends and remain ahead of regulatory requirements, ensuring their green marketing strategies are both proactive and relevant.

AI and machine learning enhance eco-innovation by enabling smarter decision-making and resource optimization. Through AI-powered simulations, companies can test eco-friendly designs and manufacturing processes without incurring significant costs or environmental damage. For example, AI can assist in creating lightweight materials for transportation, reducing fuel consumption and emissions (Mishra et al., 2024). These innovations not only enhance a company's environmental performance but also serve as compelling stories in their green marketing campaigns, showcasing their commitment to sustainable development

Blockchain technology, another pillar of digital transformation, brings transparency and trust to sustainability efforts. By providing an immutable record of supply chain activities, blockchain ensures that claims of ethical sourcing, carbon neutrality, or waste reduction are verifiable. For instance, companies in the fashion industry can use blockchain to track the lifecycle of their products, from raw materials to retail shelves, providing consumers with confidence in their sustainability claims (Boçe & Hoxha, 2024). This transparency strengthens green marketing messages by addressing consumer skepticism and fostering trust.

Digital transformation also revolutionizes how companies engage with consumers through green marketing. Social media platforms, websites, and mobile apps serve as powerful channels for communicating sustainability initiatives. Businesses can use these digital platforms to share their eco-innovation stories, educate consumers about the environmental impact of their choices, and promote sustainable products. For example, Patagonia, a leader in green marketing, uses digital campaigns to highlight its efforts in reducing environmental harm and encouraging responsible consumption. Digital storytelling humanizes a company's sustainability journey, creating an emotional connection with consumers and inspiring loyalty.

E-commerce platforms provide additional opportunities for companies to leverage digital transformation in green marketing. By integrating eco-friendly product filters, carbon footprint calculators, and sustainability badges, online marketplaces enable consumers to make informed decisions. Amazon's "Climate Pledge Friendly" program, which highlights products meeting sustainability certifications, exemplifies how e-commerce can align with green marketing goals. These features not only improve the visibility of eco-friendly products but also empower consumers to participate in sustainable practices, amplifying the impact of eco-innovation.

Moreover, digital transformation enables companies to personalize their green marketing efforts. AI-driven algorithms analyze consumer preferences and behaviors, allowing businesses to deliver tailored messages and recommendations that resonate with individual values. For instance, a customer interested in renewable energy solutions might receive targeted advertisements for solar panels or energy-efficient appliances (Kannan et al., 2024). This personalized approach increases the effectiveness of green marketing campaigns, driving engagement and conversion rates.

Another dimension of digital transformation's role in eco-innovation and green marketing is its ability to foster collaboration. Digital platforms facilitate partnerships between companies, governments, and non-profit organizations to address sustainability challenges collectively. For example, businesses can participate in online networks to share best practices, co-develop eco-friendly technologies, or contribute to industry-wide sustainability standards. Collaborative efforts not only accelerate eco-innovation but also strengthen green marketing narratives by demonstrating a commitment to broader environmental goals.

The benefits of integrating digital transformation into eco-innovation and green marketing extend beyond immediate business gains. They contribute to societal well-being by encouraging sustainable consumption patterns, reducing environmental degradation, and creating green jobs. Companies that embrace digital tools to promote sustainability play a crucial role in shaping consumer attitudes and behaviors, fostering a culture of environmental responsibility (Karunia et al., 2024). For instance, digital campaigns highlighting the benefits of reducing plastic use or adopting renewable energy can influence public opinion and drive collective action

Despite the numerous advantages, companies must navigate certain challenges when using digital transformation to drive eco-innovation for green marketing. The upfront investment in digital technologies, training, and infrastructure can be significant, particularly for small and medium-sized enterprises. Additionally, ensuring the authenticity of green marketing messages is critical to avoiding accusations of wrong green activity information, which can damage brand reputation. Companies must prioritize transparency, rely on credible data, and obtain certifications to substantiate their environmental claims.

In conclusion, digital transformation is a game-changer for companies striving to drive eco-innovation and implement effective green marketing strategies. By leveraging advanced technologies, businesses can optimize operations, design sustainable products, and communicate their commitment to the environment with authenticity and impact. The integration of digital tools not only enhances a company's competitive edge but also contributes to a sustainable future by promoting eco-conscious behaviors and reducing environmental harm. As digital transformation continues to evolve, its potential to revolutionize eco-innovation and green marketing will only grow, offering new opportunities to address global sustainability challenges.

3 ROLE OF DIGITAL TRANSFORMATION IN DRIVING ECO-INNOVATION

Digital transformation has emerged as a powerful enabler of eco-innovation, allowing businesses to address environmental challenges through the integration of advanced technologies. By rethinking traditional processes, leveraging data, and fostering collaboration, digital transformation drives the development of sustainable products, services, and practices that align with modern environmental priorities. At the core of digital transformation is the adoption of cutting-edge technologies such as the Internet of Things (IoT), artificial intelligence (AI), big data analytics, and blockchain. These technologies enable companies to optimize resource utilization, minimize waste, and monitor environmental impacts in real time. For example, IoT sensors integrated into manufacturing processes provide continuous data on energy usage, emissions, and material efficiency. This data allows companies to identify inefficiencies and implement targeted solutions that enhance sustainability.

Big data analytics is another cornerstone of digital transformation, empowering businesses to analyze complex environmental datasets and uncover patterns that inform eco-innovation. Through data-driven insights, companies can design products that are both efficient and eco-friendly, such as biodegradable packaging or energy-saving appliances. Predictive analytics further enables organizations to anticipate sustainability trends and adapt their practices to stay ahead of regulatory requirements and consumer expectations. Artificial intelligence plays a critical role in fostering eco-innovation by optimizing decision-making processes and improving the lifecycle of products. AI-powered simulations allow companies to test and refine eco-friendly designs without the need for physical prototypes, reducing costs and environmental impact. For instance, in the automotive industry, AI aids in developing lightweight materials that lower fuel consumption and emissions, directly contributing to greener transportation (Nwabekee et al., 2024).

Blockchain technology enhances eco-innovation by introducing transparency and trust into supply chains. By providing an immutable record of sourcing and production activities, blockchain ensures that sustainability claims are verifiable. This is particularly valuable in industries such as fashion and food, where consumers increasingly demand ethical sourcing and environmentally friendly practices. Blockchain-powered solutions also enhance collaboration among stakeholders, fostering innovation through shared goals (Ullah et al.). Digital transformation also accelerates the adoption of circular economy principles, which prioritize resource efficiency and waste reduction. Technologies such as digital twins, virtual replicas of physical systems, enable businesses to model and optimize resource flows, extend product lifecycles and promote reuse and recycling. These efforts are essential in combating challenges like resource depletion and waste management.

Moreover, digital transformation empowers companies to scale their eco-innovation efforts by fostering collaboration and communication. Digital platforms connect businesses, researchers, and policymakers, creating ecosystems for sharing knowledge and co-developing sustainable solutions. For example, digital innovation hubs bring together diverse stakeholders to tackle industry-specific environmental challenges collectively. In conclusion, digital transformation plays a pivotal role in driving eco-innovation by leveraging advanced technologies to optimize processes, create sustainable products, and foster collaboration. Its ability to integrate data, enhance transparency, and align with circular economy principles positions it as a critical enabler of sustainability. By embracing digital transformation, companies can not only meet environmental goals but also gain a competitive edge in a rapidly evolving marketplace focused on sustainability.

4 ROLE OF DIGITAL TRANSFORMATION IN DEVELOPING GREEN MARKETING STRATEGIES

Digital transformation has revolutionized how companies design, implement, and execute green marketing strategies, enabling them to effectively communicate their environmental commitments and connect with eco-conscious consumers. By leveraging digital tools and technologies, businesses can enhance their green marketing efforts through personalization, transparency, and engagement, fostering trust and loyalty among customers. At the heart of digital transformation is the use of data and analytics to understand consumer behavior and preferences. Through big data analysis, companies can identify target audiences who value sustainability and tailor marketing strategies to resonate with these groups. Predictive analytics, powered by artificial intelligence (AI), allows businesses to anticipate trends in green consumerism, ensuring that their marketing campaigns remain relevant and proactive (Fazel, 2024). For example, AI-driven insights can help a brand identify eco-friendly product features, such as recyclable materials or energy efficiency, appeal most to their audience, enabling them to focus marketing efforts on those aspects

Digital platforms play a crucial role in amplifying green marketing messages. Social media, websites, and e-commerce platforms serve as dynamic channels for promoting eco-friendly products and showcasing a company's sustainability efforts. Through these platforms, companies can share content such as behind-the-scenes videos of green manufacturing processes, customer testimonials, or infographics highlighting their environmental impact. For instance, brands like Patagonia and IKEA effectively use digital storytelling to build emotional connections with their audience, inspiring trust and encouraging responsible consumption. Blockchain technology, a key element of digital transformation, enhances transparency in green marketing. By providing immutable records of supply chain activities, blockchain assures consumers of a company's ethical sourcing and environmentally friendly practices. Transparency fosters credibility, helping businesses avoid accusations of not using green marketing and building trust with skeptical consumers. For example, a coffee company can use blockchain to trace its product's journey from farm to cup, allowing customers to verify its sustainability claims (Moberg, 2024).

Personalization, enabled by digital transformation, is another powerful tool for green marketing. AI algorithms analyze customer data to deliver tailored content and recommendations that align with individual values and preferences. For instance, an online retailer can suggest eco-friendly products based on a customer's browsing history or purchase patterns, making green choices more accessible and appealing. Personalized marketing not only drives consumer engagement but also reinforces a brand's commitment to understanding and meeting customer needs. Moreover, digital transformation enables companies to measure and communicate the environmental impact of their products and services more effectively. Carbon footprint calculators, sustainability dashboards, and digital certifications provide quantifiable evidence of a company's green initiatives, enhancing the credibility of marketing campaigns. These tools help businesses not only showcase their achievements but also educate consumers about the broader benefits of sustainability.

Collaboration is another dimension where digital transformation supports green marketing. Digital platforms facilitate partnerships with environmental organizations, governments, and other businesses, allowing companies to co-create impactful campaigns. Joint initiatives, such as awareness drives or eco-friendly product launches, benefit from the combined reach and resources of multiple stakeholders (Murugesan et al., 2024). In conclusion, digital transformation is integral to developing effective green marketing strategies. By leveraging advanced technologies and platforms, businesses can engage consumers with authentic, personalized, and transparent messaging that underscores their commitment to sustainability. These efforts not only enhance brand reputation but also contribute to a culture of environmental responsibility, driving meaningful change for both businesses and society.

5 DIGITAL TOOLS FOR MEASURING & COMMUNICATING ENVIRONMENT IMPACT

In an era where transparency and accountability are paramount, digital tools like carbon footprint calculators, sustainability dashboards, and digital storytelling platforms are revolutionizing how businesses measure and communicate their environmental impact. These tools not only provide quantifiable metrics but also help organizations engage with stakeholders, build trust, and inspire eco-conscious action.

Carbon footprint calculators and sustainability dashboards: Carbon footprint calculators are digital tools that allow businesses and individuals to estimate the amount of greenhouse gases (GHGs) generated by their activities. By analyzing factors such as energy consumption, transportation, and waste production, these calculators provide actionable insights into areas where emissions can be reduced. For instance, companies can input data about their supply chain operations or product lifecycle to identify hotspots of carbon intensity and make informed decisions about process optimization or renewable energy adoption.

Sustainability dashboards complement these calculators by presenting environmental data in an accessible, visual format. Dashboards integrate data from multiple sources, such as IoT sensors, enterprise resource planning systems, and external benchmarks, into a single platform, offering real-time insights into sustainability performance. These dashboards enable companies to monitor metrics such as water usage, energy efficiency, waste management, and carbon emissions, ensuring they stay aligned with environmental targets and regulatory requirements.

For example, multinational corporations like Microsoft use AI-powered dashboards to track their progress toward carbon neutrality and report these achievements to stakeholders. Such transparency not only enhances accountability but also reinforces credibility, allowing businesses to effectively communicate their green initiatives to customers, investors, and regulators.

Digital storytelling for showcasing green efforts: While metrics are crucial, the human element of storytelling plays an equally vital role in communicating environmental impact. Digital storytelling uses multimedia tools, videos, infographics, blogs, and interactive content, to craft compelling narratives about a company's sustainability journey. These stories connect emotionally with audiences, fostering trust and encouraging eco-conscious behaviors.

For instance, a company might create a video showcasing how its manufacturing process has shifted to renewable energy or reduced water consumption. By highlighting the challenges faced and the innovative solutions implemented, businesses can inspire their audience and demonstrate genuine commitment to sustainability.

Social media platforms amplify the reach of these stories, enabling companies to engage directly with consumers. Interactive content such as quizzes, polls, and augmented reality experiences can make sustainability education engaging and memorable. For example, brands like Patagonia use Instagram to share the environmental impact of their products while encouraging customers to repair, reuse, or recycle clothing rather than buying new items. Moreover, storytelling tools like virtual reality (VR) and 360-degree videos provide immersive experiences that allow stakeholders to witness sustainability efforts firsthand. For example, a VR tour of a green factory or a reforestation project can leave a lasting impression on customers and investors alike, deepening their appreciation of the company's environmental initiatives.

Carbon footprint calculators, sustainability dashboards, and digital storytelling work synergistically to measure and communicate environmental impact. By combining data-driven insights with engaging narratives, businesses can build transparency, foster emotional connections, and drive meaningful change. These tools not only reinforce a company's green credentials but also inspire collective action toward a more sustainable future.

6 CHALLENGES–INTEGRATING DIGITAL TRANSFORMATION WITH ECO-INNOVATION AND GREEN MARKETING

6.1 Data Privacy and Ethical Concerns

The integration of digital transformation in eco-innovation and green marketing raises significant data privacy and ethical concerns. Collecting, storing, and analyzing vast amounts of consumer and operational data is essential for driving insights into sustainability efforts (Pan et al., 2023). However, this process often involves accessing sensitive personal information, such as consumer habits, preferences, and location data. Mismanagement of this data can lead to privacy breaches, eroding trust and damaging a company's reputation.

Ethical dilemmas also arise when companies use AI and predictive analytics. For example, algorithms designed to optimize marketing strategies may unintentionally discriminate against certain demographics, creating ethical challenges. Furthermore, transparency issues emerge if businesses exaggerate or misrepresent their environmental impact activities (Dhirani et al., 2023). To address these challenges, companies must implement robust data protection measures, comply with global privacy regulations like GDPR or CCPA, and maintain transparency in their data practices. Ethical AI frameworks and third-party audits can help ensure that digital transformation supports sustainable goals without compromising consumer trust.

6.2 Technological Complexity and Rapid Evolution

One of the significant challenges in integrating digital transformation with eco-innovation and green marketing is managing the technological complexity and keeping pace with rapid advancements. Digital transformation relies heavily on cutting-edge technologies such as artificial intelligence (AI), the Internet of Things

(IoT), blockchain, and big data analytics, each of which comes with a steep learning curve and intricate implementation processes.

Businesses often struggle to identify which technologies align best with their eco-innovation and green marketing goals. The sheer variety of tools and platforms can lead to decision paralysis or the adoption of unsuitable solutions. For example, implementing IoT devices to monitor energy consumption in real time may require integration with legacy systems that are incompatible or inefficient. Similarly, using blockchain for supply chain transparency can involve technical barriers like limited scalability or high energy consumption, which contradict sustainability objectives. The rapid evolution of technology further exacerbates this challenge. Emerging innovations often render existing systems obsolete, necessitating constant upgrades and adjustments (Chen et al., 2024). For instance, AI algorithms used for green marketing personalization may need frequent updates to remain effective and ethical, increasing the burden on businesses to stay ahead.

To address these issues, companies must invest in robust research and development to assess the suitability of technologies before implementation. Collaboration with technology partners and startups can help businesses access expertise and tailored solutions. Additionally, fostering a culture of continuous learning and digital literacy among employees ensures organizations are equipped to adapt to technological shifts. Incremental deployment of technologies, starting with pilot projects, can also mitigate risks while enabling gradual adoption of complex systems.

6.3 Consumer Skepticism and Trust Building

Another critical challenge lies in overcoming consumer skepticism and building trust in the digital transformation of eco-innovation and green marketing efforts. As consumers become more environmentally aware, they also demand greater transparency and authenticity in a company's sustainability claims. However, the misuse of green marketing practices, such as exaggerating or fabricating environmental benefits, has led to widespread mistrust. Digital tools used in green marketing can amplify this skepticism if not implemented transparently. For instance, while blockchain offers supply chain transparency, consumers may question the reliability of data input into the system. Similarly, AI-driven personalized marketing campaigns might appear manipulative or invasive, leading to ethical concerns about the use of consumer data.

Compounding this issue is the lack of standardized frameworks for measuring and communicating environmental impact. Terms like "eco-friendly" or "sustainable" are often used without clear definitions, making it difficult for consumers to assess the legitimacy of green claims. This ambiguity can erode confidence in digital tools and platforms that businesses use to communicate their environmental efforts (de

Sio et al., 2022). To address consumer skepticism, companies must prioritize transparency and authenticity in their digital transformation initiatives. Providing clear, verifiable data about sustainability practices, such as carbon footprint reduction or ethical sourcing, is crucial. Engaging third-party certifications and adhering to global standards can lend credibility to green marketing claims. Additionally, companies should actively involve consumers in their sustainability journey through digital storytelling, interactive platforms, and open dialogue, fostering trust and loyalty.

6.4 Cost and Resource Constraints for Small Businesses

Small and medium-sized enterprises (SMEs) face significant cost and resource constraints when integrating digital transformation with eco-innovation and green marketing. Advanced technologies such as IoT, AI, and blockchain require substantial financial investment in infrastructure, software, and skilled personnel, which can be prohibitive for smaller organizations. Additionally, limited access to expertise and technical resources hinders SMEs from fully leveraging digital tools for sustainability. These businesses often lack dedicated teams to manage complex data analytics or implement cutting-edge technologies. The cost of training employees in digital tools further adds to the financial burden (Geng et al., 2021). To overcome these challenges, governments and industry bodies can provide subsidies, grants, and affordable access to digital technologies. Open-source platforms and collaborative ecosystems can also enable SMEs to share resources and adopt cost-effective solutions for sustainability efforts.

6.5 Management of Large Organizations

Large organizations face unique challenges in integrating digital transformation with eco-innovation and green marketing due to their complexity and scale. Implementing digital tools across diverse operations, geographies, and departments requires extensive coordination and significant investments in time and resources. Resistance to change among employees and entrenched corporate cultures further complicate these efforts.

Data silos are another critical challenge in large organizations. Fragmented data systems across various departments hinder the seamless collection and analysis of information, limiting the effectiveness of digital transformation. Furthermore, aligning multiple stakeholders, including executives, managers, and external partners, toward shared sustainability goals can be a daunting task. Effective management requires strong leadership, a clear vision, and cross-functional collaboration. Establishing centralized digital frameworks, conducting comprehensive employee training, and fostering a culture of innovation can help large organizations overcome these barriers.

Additionally, incremental implementation of digital tools can reduce disruptions and enhance integration across the organization.

7 PRACTICAL APPLICATION OF THE CONCEPTS

The integration of digital transformation with eco-innovation and green marketing has seen real-world applications across various industries, showcasing its ability to revolutionize sustainability practices while enhancing consumer engagement. Companies, both large multinationals and small and medium-sized enterprises (SME), have utilized advanced technologies like IoT, AI, blockchain, and digital platforms to address environmental challenges and effectively communicate their efforts to stakeholders.

7.1 Using IoT for Real-Time Monitoring and Sustainability Optimization

IoT has enabled businesses to monitor their environmental impact in real-time and implement data-driven eco-innovation strategies (Examples in Table 2).

Table 1. Using IoT

Organization Type	Organization Name	Initiative	Benefits
Large Organization	Siemens (Germany)	IoT-powered 'MindSphere' platform to monitor energy use and emissions in manufacturing (Siemens, 2021).	Optimizes production, reduces energy consumption and waste, reinforces eco-innovation leadership.
SME	Koolboks (Nigeria)	Solar-powered refrigeration systems using IoT to track performance in off-grid areas (White, 2022).	Reduces food spoilage, promotes renewable energy adoption through digital storytelling.

7.2 Applying AI for Green Marketing Personalization

AI has helped businesses create personalized green marketing campaigns by analyzing consumer preferences and behaviors (Examples in Table 3).

Table 2. Applying AI

Organization Type	Organization Name	Initiative	Benefits
Large Organization	Unilever (United Kingdom/Global)	AI to optimize marketing campaigns for sustainable products under 'Sustainable Living Brands' initiative.	Identifies target audiences, delivers tailored messages, and highlights demand-driven sustainability features like plastic-free packaging.
SME	Ecovative Design (USA)	AI to understand consumer needs for mushroom-based biodegradable packaging.	Effectively communicates eco-friendly solutions to niche markets via personalized email and targeted social media campaigns.

7.3 Blockchain for Transparency in Green Marketing

Blockchain ensures transparency and traceability in supply chains, a critical component for authentic green marketing (Examples in Table 4).

Table 3. Blockchain for transparency

Organization Type	Organization Name	Initiative	Benefits
Large Organization	IBM Food Trust (USA/Global)	Blockchain-based 'Food Trust' platform to trace food origins and sustainability practices.	Provides immutable records of sourcing and production, assures ethical and eco-friendly practices, enhances consumer trust.
SME	Fairfood (Netherlands)	Blockchain to verify sustainable farming practices in developing countries (Burke, 2023).	Offers QR codes for food traceability, ensuring authenticity and trust in green claims through storytelling.

7.4 Digital Platforms for Consumer Engagement and Education

Digital platforms enable businesses to share their sustainability narratives and involve consumers in their green initiatives (Examples in Table 5).

Table 4. Digital platforms

Organization Type	Organization Name	Initiative	Benefits
Large Organization	IKEA (Sweden/ Global)	Using apps and website to promote 'Circular Hubs' for refurbished furniture and sustainable living.	Reinforces sustainability commitment by digital campaigns, promotes renewable energy and eco-friendly products.
SME	Pela Case (Canada)	Using social media platforms like Instagram and TikTok to highlight the environmental benefits (Shaw, 2024).	Engages consumers through storytelling, reduces plastic waste with biodegradable materials.

7.5 E-Commerce and Eco-Friendly Filters

Digital transformation in e-commerce has empowered companies to integrate eco-friendly filters and certifications into their platforms (Examples in Table 6).

Table 5. E-commerce and eco-friendly filters

Organization Type	Organization Name	Initiative	Benefits
Large Organization	Amazon (Global)	'Climate Pledge Friendly' program promotes products with recognized sustainability certifications.	Supports green marketing, helps consumers in, sustainable choices.
SME	Good On You (Australia)	Platform and app rating fashion brands based on environmental and social impact, promoting conscious consumerism.	Empowers consumers to shop ethically, promotes sustainable brands and lifestyles.

7.6 Circular Economy Enabled by Digital Tools

Digital transformation supports the transition to a circular economy by facilitating reuse, recycling, and sharing models (Examples in Table 7).

Table 6. Digital tools

Organization Type	Organization Name	Initiative	Benefits
Large Organization	Renault (France)	'Refectory' initiative using digital twins and IoT to refurbish and recycle vehicle components (Renault, 2024).	Promotes sustainable automotive practices, positions as a pioneer through digital marketing.
SME	Loop (USA/ Global)	Circular shopping platform partnering with companies to offer reusable packaging	Educating consumers on environmental benefits of reusable packaging, drives awareness and participation

7.7 Gamification to Encourage Green Consumer Behavior

Gamification through digital tools has proven effective in encouraging sustainable behaviors (Examples in Table 8).

Table 7. Encourage green consumer behavior

Organization Type	Organization Name	Initiative	Benefits
Large Organization	Google (Global)	'Your Plan, Your Planet' tool for waste reduction and energy-saving challenges.	Educates consumers, enhances Google's image as a sustainability advocate.
SME	JouleBug (USA)	App gamifying sustainable living by rewarding actions like reducing energy consumption and recycling.	Promotes green behavior, emphasizes positive environmental impact through digital campaigns.

The practical applications of digital transformation in driving eco-innovation and green marketing demonstrate the profound impact of technology on sustainability. From IoT-powered optimization to blockchain transparency and AI-driven personalization, these tools enable businesses of all sizes to innovate responsibly while effectively communicating their environmental efforts. Companies like Siemens, Unilever, IKEA, and startups like Pela Case and Fairfood showcase how integrating digital transformation can address global challenges and inspire collective action for a sustainable future.

8 FUTURE TRENDS: DIGITAL TRANSFORMATION, ECO-INNOVATION, AND GREEN MARKETING

The intersection of digital transformation, eco-innovation, and green marketing is poised to evolve significantly in the coming years as emerging technologies redefine sustainable practices. Businesses are recognizing the importance of integrating advanced digital tools into their environmental strategies to address growing global challenges such as climate change, resource scarcity, and consumer demand for ethical practices. The next decade will see accelerated innovation in how companies design, implement, and communicate their sustainability efforts, driven by breakthroughs in artificial intelligence (AI), blockchain, the Internet of Things (IoT), and immersive technologies like the metaverse.

These advancements will not only enable organizations to measure and mitigate their environmental impact but also enhance transparency and consumer engagement. For instance, predictive analytics and AI-powered tools will play a pivotal role in identifying areas for improvement in supply chains, while blockchain technology will provide indisputable evidence of sustainability claims. Immersive experiences in the metaverse are expected to transform how brands engage with consumers, offering interactive and virtual spaces to promote sustainable living and educate audiences.

As eco-consciousness becomes an integral aspect of consumer behavior, companies will increasingly leverage these technologies to stay competitive and relevant. From personalizing green marketing messages to developing circular economy models, digital transformation will underpin every aspect of sustainable innovation. The future of eco-innovation and green marketing will not only shape industries but also empower consumers to make informed and responsible choices, creating a synergistic impact on the environment and society.

8.1 Emerging Technologies Shaping Sustainable Practices

Emerging technologies are set to transform how businesses address sustainability challenges, fostering eco-innovation through enhanced efficiency, transparency, and innovation. AI, blockchain, IoT, and advanced analytics are among the leading technologies driving sustainable practices. Artificial intelligence plays a key role in optimizing resource utilization and energy efficiency. AI-powered systems can analyze energy consumption patterns, predict demand, and automate processes to reduce waste. For example, AI in agriculture enables precision farming, optimizing water usage and minimizing chemical inputs, which leads to more sustainable food production.

Blockchain technology enhances transparency by providing immutable records of supply chains and environmental practices. Companies can use blockchain to certify ethical sourcing, track carbon offsets, verify green claims, and build trust among consumers and stakeholders. For instance, blockchain in the fashion industry ensures that materials are sustainably sourced, and production processes meet environmental standards. The Internet of Things (IoT) enables real-time monitoring of environmental impact, offering insights into emissions, resource use, and waste management. Smart sensors and connected devices in manufacturing, for example, allow companies to identify inefficiencies and adopt targeted solutions to reduce their ecological footprint.

3D printing is another emerging technology revolutionizing eco-innovation. By enabling on-demand production, 3D printing reduces material waste, transportation emissions, and energy usage. It supports circular economy models by facilitating the repair and reuse of products, reducing reliance on traditional manufacturing. These technologies, combined with big data analytics, empower businesses to adopt data-driven approaches to sustainability. As they become more accessible and sophisticated, emerging technologies will drive meaningful changes in industries worldwide, making sustainable practices more efficient, scalable, and impactful.

8.2 Role of the Metaverse and Virtual Experiences

The metaverse and virtual experiences represent a new frontier in green marketing, offering innovative ways for companies to engage with eco-conscious consumers and promote sustainable practices. This immersive digital realm combines virtual reality (VR), augmented reality (AR), and other interactive technologies to create engaging environments where brands can showcase their commitment to sustainability.

One of the key advantages of the metaverse is its ability to simulate real-world experiences without environmental impact. Virtual showrooms, for example, enable consumers to explore eco-friendly products without the need for physical spaces, reducing carbon emissions associated with traditional retail operations. Companies can use these virtual spaces to demonstrate the lifecycle of their products, highlighting sustainable sourcing, production processes, and recyclability. In addition to promoting products, the metaverse serves as an educational platform, raising awareness about environmental issues and inspiring action. Brands can create immersive experiences, such as virtual tours of sustainable factories or reforestation projects, that allow users to witness the impact of green initiatives firsthand. These experiences foster a deeper emotional connection with the brand's mission and values, building consumer trust and loyalty.

Virtual events and conferences in the metaverse also eliminate the need for travel, significantly reducing the carbon footprint associated with in-person gatherings. Companies can use these events to launch eco-innovation campaigns, collaborate with stakeholders, and engage with a global audience in an environmentally friendly manner. Moreover, gamification within the metaverse encourages sustainable behaviors. Interactive games and challenges focused on recycling, energy conservation, or reducing waste not only educate users but also incentivize them to adopt green practices. By merging entertainment with sustainability, the metaverse creates a powerful platform for behavioral change. As the metaverse evolves, its potential to transform green marketing will grow, offering brands creative ways to promote sustainability and foster meaningful connections with environmentally conscious audiences.

8.3 Future of Digital Transformation, Eco-Innovation and Green Marketing

A promising future trend in the digital realm that links eco-innovation with a stronger focus on green marketing is the rise of sustainable digital ecosystems powered by collaborative networks and artificial intelligence (AI). This trend leverages interconnected platforms where businesses, consumers, and stakeholders can collectively drive sustainability efforts while fostering transparency, accountability, and innovation.

The concept of sustainable digital ecosystems revolves around creating shared digital infrastructures that facilitate collaboration among industries, governments, and non-profits to achieve common environmental goals. For instance, platforms that enable businesses to share resources, exchange by-products, or co-develop eco-friendly technologies can significantly reduce waste and promote circular economy principles. In this future scenario, companies will no longer operate in isolation but instead participate in interconnected systems that amplify the impact of individual green initiatives. For example, a company producing biodegradable materials might collaborate digitally with manufacturers who need sustainable packaging, creating a seamless supply chain while communicating this partnership as part of their green marketing efforts.

AI will play a critical role in these ecosystems by optimizing resource allocation, identifying opportunities for synergy, and ensuring compliance with environmental standards. Predictive AI models can analyze global data on resource availability, consumption trends, and environmental impact to provide actionable insights for businesses. For example, companies could use AI to simulate the environmental benefits of shifting to renewable energy sources and communicate these findings through engaging green marketing campaigns. AI's ability to personalize these messages for different consumer segments further enhances the relevance and effectiveness of green marketing strategies.

Another aspect of this trend involves the integration of augmented reality (AR) and digital twins to visualize the environmental impact of decisions in real-time. Imagine consumers using AR applications to scan products and see a comprehensive breakdown of their carbon footprint, water usage, and recyclability. Businesses that adopt such technologies will gain a competitive edge, as they provide tangible, verifiable evidence of their sustainability claims. This level of transparency will be central to future green marketing strategies, addressing consumer skepticism and fostering trust.

Moreover, the need for stronger green marketing focus will also arise from evolving consumer expectations and regulatory pressures. Governments worldwide are expected to tighten environmental regulations, requiring businesses to demonstrate not only compliance but also proactive measures to reduce their ecological footprint. In this context, the ability to leverage digital ecosystems to showcase collective achievements, such as shared reductions in emissions or waste, will become a hallmark of successful green marketing campaigns.

Additionally, as consumers become more eco-conscious, their demand for brands to take a clear stand on environmental issues will grow. Digital ecosystems will enable companies to engage directly with consumers by involving them in sustainability initiatives. For example, platforms that allow consumers to track their contribution to a brand's reforestation or waste reduction efforts will enhance their sense of participation and loyalty. In the coming years, sustainable digital ecosystems will redefine the relationship between eco-innovation and green marketing. They will create opportunities for collaboration, amplify the impact of digital tools, and align business practices with the values of a more environmentally aware society. By embracing this trend, companies can not only future-proof their operations but also lead the way in building a sustainable digital future.

9 CONCLUSION

The integration of digital transformation, eco-innovation, and green marketing represents a paradigm shift in how businesses approach sustainability. As the world grapples with escalating environmental challenges, companies must adopt innovative strategies that not only address ecological concerns but also align with evolving consumer expectations and regulatory demands. Digital transformation, through the deployment of advanced technologies, has emerged as a critical enabler in driving eco-innovation and enhancing the credibility and effectiveness of green marketing strategies.

Eco-innovation lies at the heart of sustainable business practices, fostering the development of products, processes, and systems that minimize environmental impact. However, achieving meaningful eco-innovation requires more than traditional approaches. Digital tools such as artificial intelligence (AI), blockchain, and the Internet of Things (IoT) provide businesses with unprecedented capabilities to optimize resource use, reduce waste, and track environmental performance. For example, IoT-enabled sensors in manufacturing facilities allow real-time monitoring of energy and water consumption, enabling companies to identify inefficiencies and implement targeted solutions. Similarly, blockchain technology ensures transparency and traceability in supply chains, allowing businesses to substantiate their sustainability claims and build consumer trust.

Green marketing, which focuses on promoting sustainable products and practices, also benefits immensely from digital transformation. In today's eco-conscious consumer landscape, transparency and authenticity are paramount. Digital tools enable businesses to craft compelling narratives about their sustainability efforts, providing verifiable data and engaging content that resonates with audiences. Interactive platforms, virtual experiences, and personalized marketing campaigns powered by AI allow companies to connect with consumers on a deeper level, fostering loyalty and trust. For instance, virtual tours of green factories or interactive infographics showcasing the lifecycle of eco-friendly products offer consumers an immersive understanding of a company's commitment to the environment.

The synergy between eco-innovation, green marketing, and digital transformation extends beyond operational and marketing benefits. It positions companies as leaders in sustainability, differentiating them in competitive markets while addressing global goals such as the United Nations' Sustainable Development Goals (SDGs). Moreover, it empowers businesses to meet increasing regulatory pressures, such as carbon reduction targets and waste management laws, by providing robust tools for monitoring and reporting compliance.

Despite its transformative potential, the integration of digital transformation into eco-innovation and green marketing presents challenges. Companies must navigate technological complexity, manage costs, and address data privacy and ethical concerns. Small and medium-sized enterprises (SMEs) may face resource constraints that hinder the adoption of advanced technologies. To overcome these barriers, collaboration within industries, as well as support from governments and stakeholders, is essential. Initiatives such as shared digital ecosystems, subsidies for sustainable technologies, and open-source platforms can make digital transformation more accessible to businesses of all sizes.

Looking to the future, emerging trends highlight the evolving role of digital transformation in sustainability. The metaverse, for example, offers new avenues for immersive green marketing, allowing companies to engage with consumers in virtual spaces while reducing the environmental impact of traditional advertising and retail. Collaborative digital ecosystems and AI-driven predictive models will further enhance the efficiency and scalability of eco-innovation efforts, enabling businesses to anticipate and address environmental challenges proactively.

For companies, the need to focus on digital transformation as a driver of eco-innovation and green marketing is not just an option, it is an imperative. Inaction risks not only environmental degradation but also reputational harm and loss of competitiveness in an increasingly eco-aware market. By leveraging digital tools, businesses can achieve a dual objective: contributing to global sustainability goals while securing long-term profitability and resilience. Consumers, investors, and regulators are demanding greater accountability, and digital transformation provides the framework for businesses to meet these demands with confidence and clarity.

In conclusion, the synergistic potential of digital transformation, eco-innovation, and green marketing are reshaping the business landscape. Companies that embrace this integration will not only lead the charging toward a more sustainable future but also redefine what it means to be a successful and responsible business in the 21st century. By prioritizing innovation, transparency, and collaboration, businesses can unlock new opportunities, inspire consumer trust, and make a lasting positive impact on the planet. The time to act is now, and digital transformation is the key to unlocking this potential.

10 CASE STUDY (COMPILED BY AUTHOR)

Driving Eco-Innovation Through Digital Transformation at Global Textiles Inc.

Background

Global Textiles Inc. (GTI) is one of the largest textile manufacturers in the world, producing fabrics for clothing, furniture, and industrial applications. With operations spanning over 25 countries, GTI has built a reputation for quality and reliability. However, as environmental consciousness rises among consumers and governments, the textile industry is under increasing scrutiny for its significant environmental footprint. GTI, despite its success, faces growing criticism for its reliance on water-intensive processes, high energy consumption, and unsustainable waste disposal methods. In response to these pressures, GTI has pledged to achieve carbon neutrality by 2040. This commitment includes reducing water usage by 50%, shifting to renewable energy sources for its production facilities, and adopting circular economy principles to minimize waste. However, achieving these ambitious goals will require a complete overhaul of GTI's operations, supply chain, and marketing strategies.

The Problem

GTI's primary challenge lies in aligning its production and marketing practices with its sustainability goals while maintaining profitability and market competitiveness. Currently, the company lacks the digital infrastructure needed to monitor and optimize its environmental impact. The absence of real-time data on resource usage and emissions makes it difficult to identify inefficiencies or validate sustainability claims. Moreover, GTI's marketing efforts fail to resonate with eco-conscious consumers due to insufficient transparency and authenticity.

Despite its commitment to sustainability, GTI has faced accusations of the credibility of its environmental claims. For instance, GTI's recent campaign promoting "eco-friendly fabrics" was criticized for not providing verifiable data on the products' lifecycle impacts. This has resulted in a loss of consumer trust and negative media attention, further intensifying the need for credible green marketing strategies.

Discussion Questions

1. What technologies should GTI prioritize to ensure effective monitoring and reduction of its environmental footprint? Provide examples of specific tools or systems.
2. How can GTI leverage blockchain address concerns about the environment and rebuild consumer trust? What challenges might arise in implementing this technology?
3. What marketing strategies can GTI adopt to effectively communicate its sustainability efforts and connect with eco-conscious consumers?
4. How can GTI ensure a return on investment (ROI) from its digital transformation while achieving its environmental goals?
5. What metrics should GTI use to evaluate the success of its digital transformation in terms of both environmental impact and consumer perception?

REFERENCES

Adebayo, T. S., & Özkan, O. (2024). Investigating the influence of socioeconomic conditions, renewable energy and eco-innovation on environmental degradation in the United States: A wavelet quantile-based analysis. *Journal of Cleaner Production*, *434*, 140321. DOI: 10.1016/j.jclepro.2023.140321

Akhtar, S., Tian, H., Iqbal, S., & Hussain, R. Y. (2024). Environmental regulations and government support drive green innovation performance: Role of competitive pressure and digital transformation. *Clean Technologies and Environmental Policy*, *26*(12), 1–21. DOI: 10.1007/s10098-024-02857-4

Boçe, M. T., & Hoxha, J. (2024). Blockchain Technology as a Catalyst for Sustainable Development: Exploring Economic, Social, and Environmental Synergies. *Academic Journal of Interdisciplinary Studies, 13*.

Burke, N. (2023). *Transforming sustainable food systems through transparency and digital inclusion*. https://blogs.cisco.com/our-corporate-purpose/transforming-sustainable-food-systems-through-transparency-and-digital-inclusion

Chen, G., Sabir, A., Rasheed, M. F., Belascu, L., & Su, C.-W. (2024). Green marketing horizon: Industry sustainability through marketing and innovation. *Journal of Innovation & Knowledge*, *9*(4), 100606. DOI: 10.1016/j.jik.2024.100606

de Sio, S., Zamagni, A., Casu, G., & Gremigni, P. (2022). Green trust as a mediator in the relationship between green advertising skepticism, environmental knowledge, and intention to buy green food. *International Journal of Environmental Research and Public Health*, *19*(24), 16757. DOI: 10.3390/ijerph192416757 PMID: 36554638

Dhirani, L. L., Mukhtiar, N., Chowdhry, B. S., & Newe, T. (2023). Ethical dilemmas and privacy issues in emerging technologies: A review. *Sensors (Basel)*, *23*(3), 1151. DOI: 10.3390/s23031151 PMID: 36772190

Fazel, H. (2024). Digital marketing and sustainability in the era of climate change: PLS-structural equation modeling approach. *Journal of Statistics Applications & Probability*, *13*(1), 491–505. DOI: 10.18576/jsap/130134

Geng, D., Lai, K., & Zhu, Q. (2021). Eco-innovation and its role for performance improvement among Chinese small and medium-sized manufacturing enterprises. *International Journal of Production Economics*, *231*, 107869. DOI: 10.1016/j.ijpe.2020.107869

Hendrawan, S. A., Chatra, A., Iman, N., Hidayatullah, S., & Suprayitno, D. (2024). Digital transformation in MSMEs: Challenges and opportunities in technology management. *Jurnal Informasi dan Teknologi*, 141-149.

Kannan, S., Parashar, B., & Chaurasia, A. (2024). E-Commerce and Green Packaging: Sustainable Business Trends. In *Green Innovations for Industrial Development and Business Sustainability* (pp. 22-39). CRC Press.

Karunia, R. L., Yanto, E., Prasetyo, J. H., Muthmainah, E., Hiswendari, L., Setiawan, P., & Saragih, M. A. P. (2024). Digital collaboration models for empowering SMEs: Enhancing public organization performance. *Emerging Science Journal, 8*(4), 1492–1505. DOI: 10.28991/ESJ-2024-08-04-015

Kaur, J., & Gupta, M. (2024). Exploration of factors of green marketing. International Conference on Communications and Cyber Physical Engineering 2018, Kumari, A. (2024). Transforming Business for a Sustainable Future Using Green Marketing. *Multidisciplinary Approach to Information Technology in Library and Information Science*, 132-150. DOI: 10.1007/978-981-99-7137-4_85

Longo, D., & Magnusson, M. (2024). Combining Innovation and Sustainability: Exploring Green Marketing Strategies in SMEs. In.

Mishra, R., Singh, R. K., & Rana, N. P. (2024). Digital orientation, digital eco-innovation and circular economy in the context of sustainable development goals. *Business Strategy and the Environment, 33*(4), 2752–2770. DOI: 10.1002/bse.3619

Moberg, T. (2024). Enhancing Brand Image Through Sustainable Business Practices: How to Integrate and Market Sustainability, A Case Study of Pointman OY.

Murugesan, B., Jayanthi, K., & Karthikeyan, G. (2024). Integrating Digital Twins and 3D Technologies in Fashion: Advancing Sustainability and Consumer Engagement. In *Illustrating Digital Innovations Towards Intelligent Fashion: Leveraging Information System Engineering and Digital Twins for Efficient Design of Next-Generation Fashion* (pp. 1-88). Springer.

Nwabekee, U. S., Abdul-Azeez, O. Y., Agu, E. E., & Ignatius, T. (2024). Digital transformation in marketing strategies: The role of data analytics and CRM tools. *International Journal of Frontline Research in Science and Technology, 3*(2), 055-072.

oecd. (2009). Sustainable manufacturing and eco-innovation: Framework, practices and measurement. *Synthesis report.*

Organisation for Economic Co-operation and Development. (2024). *Inclusive, green and digital transformation.* https://www.oecd.org/en/topics/sub-issues/inclusive-green-and-digital-transformation.html

Pan, W., Cao, H., & Liu, Y. (2023). "Green" innovation, privacy regulation and environmental policy. *Renewable Energy, 203*, 245–254. DOI: 10.1016/j.renene.2022.12.025

Renault. (2024). *REFACTORY: THE FLINS SITE ENTERS THE CIRCLE OF THE CIRCULAR ECONOMY.* https://www.renaultgroup.com/en/magazine/sustainable-development/re-factory-the-flins-site-enters-the-circle-of-the-circular-economy

Samsudin, A., & Hotimah, R. A. D. N. H. (2024). The Influence of Green Product, Green Marketing, and Green Brand Image Towards Green Purchase Intention on Sensatia Botanicals Products in Surabaya. *Formosa Journal of Multidisciplinary Research, 3*(2), 241–260. DOI: 10.55927/fjmr.v3i2.8238

Sandionigi, C., Berrée, J.-F., Péralta, M., Piel, A., & Robin, B. (2024). *Sustainable technology and technology for sustainability: the paths towards eco-innovation. 2024 Electronics Goes Green 2024.* EGG.

Shaw, J. (2024). *Why Gen Z Values Sustainability: Tips for Marketing to the Eco-Conscious Generation.* https://kadence.com/en-us/why-gen-z-values-sustainability-tips-for-marketing-to-the-eco-conscious-generation/

Siemens. (2021). *Siemens' MindSphere has been selected by TotalEnergies for IoT monitoring of its NGV stations.* https://newsroom.sw.siemens.com/en-US/totalenergies-selects-siemens-mindsphere-iot-monitoring/

Ullah, A., Ahmad, S., & Sana, S. Leveraging Blockchain and Big Data-Optimized Supply Chain for Eco-Innovative Firm Performance. *Professor Qingyu and Ahmad, Sohail and Sana, Sana, Leveraging Blockchain and Big Data-Optimized Supply Chain for Eco-Innovative Firm Performance.*

White, Z. (2022). *Introducing Koolboks: Pay-as-you-go solar refrigeration in Nigeria.* https://www.gsma.com/solutions-and-impact/connectivity-for-good/mobile-for-development/blog/introducing-koolboks-pay-as-you-go-solar-refrigeration-in-nigeria/

Chapter 2
Go Green:
An Eco-Consumerism Viewpoint

Prachi Swapnil Wani
https://orcid.org/0000-0003-1274-9660
Balaji Institute of Management and Human Resource Developement, Sri Balaji University, Pune, India

Pritesh Somani
https://orcid.org/0000-0002-0039-0358
Balaji Institute of International Business, Sri Balaji University, Pune, India

Vishwanathan Iyer
https://orcid.org/0009-0007-1469-2369
Balaji Institute of International Business, Sri Balaji University, Pune, India

ABSTRACT

This chapter aims at focusing on the damage done because of consumerism and its impact on the environment. The chapter emphasizes the need for going green by companies and the consumer to save the environment. Moving forward, the chapter explores how various companies are trying to go green and the overall adoption of those practices by the consumers. The chapter will also focus on the challenges and the barriers faced by the consumer while going through the process of buying a green product.

1. INTRODUCTION

Eco-consumerism, or green consumerism, is an emerging trend focusing on the importance of selecting eco-friendly choices in daily life. Consumers play a crucial part in promoting sustainable practices as the world faces serious problems like

DOI: 10.4018/979-8-3693-9831-9.ch002

climate change, pollution, and resource use. The need to act in an environmentally friendly way started in the 1960s and 1970s. Since then, more and more global efforts focused on sustainability have been growing. For instance, the UN's Climate Change Panel (1988) the Kyoto Protocol (1997), and the Paris Climate Agreement (2016) are important steps taken to diminish the undesirable effects humans force on the climate. (Admin, 2023) Changing how consumers think and act about the world results in more sustainable buying choices. A consumer citizen is someone who cares about society and the environment. They choose to buy goods that do not harm either. (Binnuri and M.R, 2024)

The concept of green consumerism is about selecting the right products and services that are better for the earth. The same talks about choices, like picking energy-saving appliances and green goods, as well as being sustainable. Policymakers, businesses, and environmental supporters need to understand why young consumers choose to buy eco-friendly products. This knowledge can help promote sustainability in the area. (Berad, 2012)

Green consumerism focuses on cutting down trash from packaging. It encourages people to buy loose fruits and veggies instead of pre-packaged ones. It motivates everyone to recycle paper and plastic, which are the main causes of environmental pollution. Green consumerism also encourages the recycling of all other goods. Many companies are moving towards sustainable packaging by shifting towards biodegradable, compostable, and recyclable alternatives to minimize waste. (Centric Software, Inc. 2025) Eco-consumerism is based on the idea that consumers are empowered to influence the market due to their purchasing decisions. By choosing environmentally friendly products and services, consumers can drive demand for sustainable practices and encourage businesses to adopt greener methods. This shift in consumer behavior is essential for addressing environmental issues and promoting a more sustainable economy. Eco-consumerism includes practices like buying sustainable products, cutting down on waste, using energy efficiently, and supporting environmentally friendly companies. These actions help the environment and support the health of communities and the business. Buying local goods lowers carbon emissions from transport, and supporting eco-friendly businesses helps create jobs and encourages new ideas for sustainability. Before we proceed and understand how eco-consumerism is helping rebound the environment, we must explore the impact of consumerism on the environment.

2. ENVIRONMENTAL IMPACT OF CONSUMERISM

According to the Cambridge Dictionary, *Consumerism*, is defined as the state of an advanced industrial society in which a lot of goods are bought and sold. (Cambridge, 2025) The persistent pursuit of physical belongings and the associated production and disposal processes contribute significantly to environmental degradation. It is very well seen that the environmental impact of consumerism, is high and the damage is big.

2.1 Impact of Consumerism on the Environment

2.1.1. Resource Depletion

One clear effect of consumerism on the world is the reduction of natural resources. Getting raw materials to make consumer products causes deforestation, reduces biodiversity, and damages the land. For example, the high demand for palm oil, which is commonly used in food and beauty items, has caused a lot of deforestation in countries like Indonesia and Malaysia. (Chuchu, Maziriri, and Mototo, 2020) This not only harms homes for animals but also adds to climate change by putting carbon dioxide into the air.

2.1.2. Pollution

Consumerism leads to a lot of pollution, harming the quality of air, water, and land. Making and getting rid of products creates a lot of waste and pollution. For example, the fashion business, which is known for quickly producing clothes, is one of the biggest polluters in the world. Making linens uses harmful chemicals and a lot of water, which causes water pollution and shortages. (Chuchu and others, 2020)

2.1.3. Air pollution

This is another critical issue linked to consumerism. The increased production and transportation of goods result in higher emissions of greenhouse gases and other pollutants. The air pollution in Jakarta has reached alarming levels, with residents enduring severe consequences for years, and the situation is becoming direr. In 2018, Air Visual indicated that Jakarta had one of the poorest Air Quality Index (AQI) ratings globally, with an average measurement ranging from 140 to 165 ppm. This report shows the air quality in Jakarta which is classified as "unhealthy." Out of cities like Beijing, Dubai, and New Delhi, Jakarta has appeared as one of the highest polluted cities globally. (Sukma, 2019)

2.1.4. Waste Generation

The culture of consumerism promotes a society, where products are frequently thrown away in favor of something latest. This is the reason for the generation of vast amounts of waste, which ends up in landfills or is reduced to ashes. Growing Electronic waste is a concern too, as the rapid turnover of electronic gadgets results in the increase of hazardous materials like lead, mercury, and cadmium in the environment. The year, 2022 saw a projected figure of 62 million tons of e-waste which was produced worldwide. Out of which, 22.3% were known to be collected and recycled. (World Health Organization, 2024)

2.1.5. Climate Change

Consumerism significantly contributes to climate change through the emission of greenhouse gases at various stages of the product lifecycle. The production, transportation, and disposal of goods all involve the release of carbon dioxide, methane, and other greenhouse gases. Global warming results from increased human-created greenhouse gas emissions, endangering the stability of the entire Earth system and is anticipated to yield disastrous and irreversible consequences for mankind. (Wang et al, 2017)

2.2 Addressing the Environmental Impact of Consumerism

2.2.1. Sustainable Consumption

Promoting sustainable consumption is essential for mitigating the environmental impact of consumerism. This involves encouraging consumers to make environmentally conscious choices, such as buying merchandise with nominal packaging, picking energy-efficient appliances, and being supportive of strong environmental commitments. While doing so, Green Image can help consumers make a purchase. Image is often conceptualized as the set of beliefs/impressions that an individual has about a product/service/place and its attributes (Kotler et al., 1993). Green image denotes a consumer's overall perceptions/ideas of a green product/service and its features. (Han, 2021) Education and awareness campaigns can play a crucial role in shifting consumer behaviour towards sustainability.

2.2.2. Circular Economy

One way to look at our present economic system is as a "linear economy," which is based on the idea of taking natural resources, processing them into goods, and then throwing away the leftovers. We barely reintroduce 7.2% of all resources consumed into our economy at the moment. The environmental, biodiversity, and pollution issues are exacerbated by this, which has a major impact on the environment. (UNDP Climate Promise)

2.2.3. Policy Interventions

Government policies and regulations are critical for addressing the environmental impact of consumerism. Implementing stricter environmental standards for production processes, promoting the use of renewable energy, and providing incentives for sustainable practices can drive positive change. The Ministry of Indian Tourism has drafted a national strategy for Sustainable tourism. The same focuses on promoting environmental sustainability, protecting biodiversity, promoting economic sustainability and promoting socio-cultural sustainability. (Singh, 2022)

2.2.4. Corporate Responsibility

Businesses play a vital role in mitigating the environmental impact of consumerism. Companies can adopt sustainable practices by reducing their carbon footprint, minimizing waste, and sourcing materials responsibly. The adoption of sustainability governance mechanisms is a direct result of the shift in the dynamic between enterprises and their stakeholders brought about by technological innovation and globalization. Sustainability assurance, sustainability strategies, and sustainability committees are all tools that help improve transparency and performance in this area. In the long run, these systems can help make CSR reporting more thorough by satisfying the information demands of many different types of stakeholders. (Ali et al. 2023)

2.3 Benefits of eco-consumerism

The words "*green*" or "*sustainable*" are often used to describe business practices that help the economy grow while also protecting resources for future generations. People are more interested in green goods these days. People often think that consumers are more interested in picking "green" products than regular ones. In this economy, people would like to buy goods that are better for the environment. (Pratap, 2018) Green consumption is witnessing substantial global expansion. The research says 80% of customers are ready to pay a premium price for nature-friendly products. Experts predict a significant increase in the international green technology and sustainability market. Experts predict a significant rise from USD 28.6 billion in 2024 to USD 134.9 billion by 2030. (Habib et al. 2024) People choose to behave in a green way when they decide whether to buy an environmentally friendly product or not. Consumers' worry about a safe environment has been growing over time. These days, the market has many safe goods for the environment. The way people buy things in the consumer market relies on what the consumer thinks and feels about caring for the environment. Not only does buying a green product help the person buying it, but it also helps the world in the long run. (Pratap, 2018)

More and more consumers, especially Millennials, want brands that care about the world and make a positive impact. A recent study found that certain goods labeled as sustainable grew twice as quickly as those that are not sustainable. There is an irritating problem in green business: people say they like eco-friendly products, but they often do not buy them. Recently, 65% of people surveyed said they wanted to buy brands that are good for the earth, but only 26% did. (White, 2024)

3. INTRODUCTION TO ECO-FRIENDLY PRODUCTS AND SERVICES

Eco-friendly products and services, also known as green or sustainable products, are designed to have minimal impact on the environment throughout their lifecycle. This includes considerations of raw materials, manufacturing processes, usage, and disposal. As awareness of environmental issues grows, the demand for eco-friendly products and services has increased, driven by both consumer preferences and regulatory pressures.

3.1 Types of Eco-Friendly Products and Services

For years, companies have been introducing sustainable product lines to make the most of the global surge in conscious consumption. Approximately 40% of consumers who were surveyed worldwide since 2021 brought at least one sustainable product each month. Although green purchases predominantly occur in food and household items, approximately 40% are made in other areas such as apparel, home furnishings, and personal care. In 2023, sustainable products accounted for approximately 18.5% of the market share in consumer-packaged goods within many large economies. (Pieters et al. 2025)

3.1.1. Sustainable Consumer Goods

Sustainable consumer goods encompass a wide range of products, including clothing, food, and household items. These products are made from environmentally friendly materials and are designed to be durable, reusable, and recyclable. For instance, organic cotton clothing is produced without harmful pesticides and chemicals, reducing environmental pollution and promoting healthier ecosystems. Various studies have shown that sustainable practices can reduce costs. It also encourages an increase in operating profit by up to 60%. In 2024, 75% of executives surveyed by IBM, agreed that sustainability drives better business outcomes. (Centric Software, Inc. 2025)

3.1.2. Renewable Energy Solutions

Renewable energy solutions, like, wind turbines, solar panels and geothermal systems, provide clean and sustainable alternatives to fossil fuels. These technologies harness natural resources to generate electricity, which in turn reduces greenhouse gas emissions. It also helps in reducing the dependence on non-renewable energy sources. The adoption of renewable energy solutions has been driven by both consumer demand and government incentives aimed at promoting sustainability. A total of 143 counties that are responsible for emitting 99.7% of global CO2 are expected to move to 100% clean, renewable wind, water, and solar electricity by 2050 and 80% by 2030. (The World Economic Forum)

3.1.3. Green Building Materials

Sustainable and eco-friendly, green building materials are crafted from sustainable resources. Every step of a green building's life cycle—from initial concept to final dismantling—is mindful of the environment. Pollution, greenhouse gas emissions, global warming, and other negative environmental impacts have resulted from development's relentless march forward. We need to figure out how to get out of this dangerous position that we've brought about; it's terrifying. Sustainable, ecologically friendly, and aesthetically pleasing, green buildings strive to provide a healthy and pleasant living space for their occupants both inside and out. (Fahad, 2023)

Operating in China and particularly in the Hong Kong region, Swire Properties is a construction company to match the sustainability objectives of the firm's stakeholders, the company developed One Taikoo Place, a green building meant to lower the GHG emissions of Swire Properties. Swire buildings maximize their construction's energy efficiency through 3D modeling approaches. Use motion sensors and sunshine-based smart lighting solutions to cut power use. The facility now has a biodiesel-generating technology that turns waste food oil into biodiesel. Swire Properties also builds using a lot of recycled materials and low-carbon incorporated elements. Using low-carbon integrated materials and digital technologies helped Swire Properties reduce the intensity of GHG emissions by about 20% throughout its portfolio. (Sustainable Development, n.d.)

3.1.4. Eco-Friendly Transportation

Eco-friendly transport options offer sustainable replacements for traditional fuel vehicles. The following are a few of the options that consumers could adopt.

Public Transit: Public transit like buses and trains will have fewer private vehicles on the road. This will allow cut down the greenhouse gas emissions. Public transit is a very effective and cost-conscious way to have an impact on the environment. The survey indicates increased public transport demand, a major trend in recent years. Most public transport operators questioned are below 2019 ridership levels, although 83% forecast growth in 2024 compared to 2023. Despite sector challenges, sustainable mobility is the future of public transit. (Global Economic Outlook,2024)

Cycling and Walking: Consumers can opt for cycling and walking as substitute modes of transportation which helps promote health and reduce environmental impact. Many Smart Cities do have bike sharing with the appropriate infrastructure.

Electric and Hydrogen Vehicles: It is important to have acceptance for electric vehicles (EVs) that produce zero tailpipe emissions. EVs are helping reduce dependence on fossil fuels. A total of 14 million cars were sold in 2023, out of which 95% were in Europe, the United States and China. (IEA Org). Hydrogen Vehicles, represent an innovative transportation method endorsed by urban areas, particularly for bus systems. They must be fitted with fuel cells that facilitate the interaction of hydrogen with oxygen to generate power. The vehicle thus emits solely water. Nonetheless, the energy equilibrium of hydrogen cars is predominantly contingent upon the energy source utilized for the chemical reaction (fossil fuels or renewable resources). India amongst other countries is moving towards achieving net-zero emissions by 2070. To do so, a promising solution to decarbonize its transport sector is hydrogen-powered vehicles. (World Economic Forum, 2024)

Car Pooling: Though not a novel idea, carpooling is a relevant and practical one. If you and others are heading to the same place, you ride together. This drastically reduces the amount of vehicles on the road, so lowering traffic and associated negative emissions. Several states, including Arizona, have included this approach in their laws and guidelines. Special lanes just for carpooling exist right now to allow you to drive in. (Staci, 2024) From 2025 to 2033, the global carpooling market is expected to develop at a steady CAGR of 21.99%, reaching USD 49.02 billion from USD 8.2 billion in 2024.

North America has the greatest carpooling market because of high car ownership and tech-savvy society. Technology adoption in the region boosts carpooling applications and websites. (Business Research Insights,2023) Wealthy countries like the United States are encouraging eco-friendly transportation choices to lower greenhouse gas emissions and protect the environment. The government and other groups have put laws in place to promote clean transportation, public transit, and alternative fuels. For example, big towns like New York and San Francisco have spent money on public transportation, which has helped lower pollution and improve air quality. Developing countries are working to create better transportation systems that lower pollution, boost public health, and help achieve sustainability goals. Governments and foreign groups are putting money into eco-friendly transportation, like public transport, bike paths, and green vehicles. This aims to cut down greenhouse gas emissions, traffic jams, and air pollution. These eco-friendly transportation programs help reduce pollution, promote sustainable travel, and protect the environment, which is good for emerging countries and global efforts for sustainability. (SBToolkit, 2024)

3.2 Benefits of Eco-Friendly Products and Services

Products that prioritize sustainability are crafted to minimize their ecological footprint throughout all phases of their lifecycle. Sun and Yoon (2022) emphasized that eco-friendly products take into account the complete lifecycle, from the extraction of raw materials to their eventual disposal (Megha, 2024). the strategy would ensure the utilization of environmental benefits while reducing ill impact. For instance, products manufactured from sustainable resources, like bamboo or recycled materials, would have less impact on the environment when contrasted with those produced from non-sustainable resources.

3.2.1. Environmental and Economic Benefits

The key benefit of eco-friendly products and services is that it does not have an ill effect on the environment. The use of sustainable materials and processes will help preserve natural resources, reduce pollution, and mitigate climate change. According to research, 89% of global consumers have changed their shopping habits to be eco-friendly. (CapitalOneShopping Research) Eco-friendly products and services provide economic benefits, both for consumers and businesses. Energy-efficient products, such as LED light bulbs and energy-rated appliance helps in reducing the cost to a great extent. For a business, this helps in enhancing the brand image. It attracts customers who are very environmentally conscious.

3.2.2. Social Benefits

Eco-friendly products and services help in promoting healthier lifestyles and society. For example, organic food does not have any harmful pesticides and chemicals, which helps reduce health risks for consumers. Moreover, sustainable practices in agriculture and manufacturing help in improving working conditions.

3.3 Strategies for Promoting Eco-Friendly Products and Services

3.3.1. Certification and Labeling

Certification and labeling play a very significant role in encouraging the use of eco-friendly products and services. This is only possible when customers will get a piece of reliable information on the environmental impact. The market has multiple certifications such as USDA, Fair Trade Energy Star, FSC, Soil Association, etc. (Bell, 2024) Below are a few of the known certifications around the world.

Energy Star (USA): The Office of Consumer Affairs (2022) focuses on the importance of the Energy Star program that helps people and companies save energy and cut down on greenhouse gas emissions. Product and building certification is based on rules set by the US Environmental Protection Agency (EPA) for the energy economy. The Energy Star certification can help people and companies save energy, lower their energy costs, and support the environment. (Affairs, 2022)

EU Ecolabel (Europe): The EU Ecolabel is a voluntary system for recognizing goods and services that are good for the earth. Products are approved based on rules set by the European Union. These rules cover things like using less energy, water, and trash and reducing waste. The EU Ecolabel helps people choose items and services that are good for the environment, which encourages sustainable consumption. (Using the EU Ecolabel Scheme for NI Businesses, 2020)

Eco Logo (Canada): EcoLogo is a program run by a third party that certifies items and services that are good for the environment. The products are approved based on strict rules set by the Eco Logo Program. These rules cover things like using less energy and water and reducing waste. Eco Logo certification helps people choose items and services that are good for the environment, which encourages sustainable consumption. (Affairs, 2022)

Green Star (Australia): Green Star is a rating method that checks how environmentally friendly a building or product is. The Green Building Council of Australia sets standards for how buildings and goods should be rated. These standards cover things like how energy efficient they are, how much water they use, and how much waste they produce. Getting a Green Star license gives you an edge in the market, promotes green building practices, and lowers your impact on the environment. (Exploring Green Star I Green Building Council of Australia, n.d.)

Carbon Trust Standard (UK): The Carbon Trust Standard is a way for groups to get recognized for lowering their greenhouse gas emissions. Companies are certified after a thorough analysis of their carbon footprint, which includes things like how well they use energy, how they transport goods, and how they handle their supply chains. Carbon Trust Standard certification helps businesses show they are dedicated to lowering carbon emissions, making their energy use more efficient, and improving their image. (The Carbon Trust)

3.3.2 Government Policies and Incentives

It's important to motivate companies who are making eco-friendly products. The government should offer incentives or a levy in a tax for the adoption of eco-friendly products and services. Eco-friendly consumers should be motivated by issuing tax credits, subsidies for personal gain, and grants for renewable energy installations should be offered. Energy-efficient appliances and sustainable building practices must be awarded to have consumers encouraged.

3.3.3. Consumer Education and Awareness

It is encouraging to learn that two out of three urban Indian consumers who were polled are placing importance on firms taking ecologically friendly initiatives. These acts include using materials that are good for the environment, lowering carbon footprints, and adopting sustainable practices. This large percentage indicates that the people of India are becoming increasingly aware of and concerned about environmental issues.

It is worth mentioning that 51% of the urban Indian customers who were polled said that they think it is mostly the government's responsibility to deal with environmental problems. They believe that the government is the most important factor in making significant changes to the environment. The fact that the government is taking action highlights the seriousness of the environmental problems we are dealing with and the demands of the public for policies that are both proactive and effective. (Nielsen.IQ, 2023)

It is necessary to inform consumers of the advantages of environmentally friendly products and services to promote sustainable consumption. Public awareness campaigns, education programs, and collaboration with schools, community organizations, and media can assist in achieving this objective. Education and awareness programs can assist individuals in making environmentally friendly product and service choices by giving them the information and resources they require to make informed decisions.

Education and awareness are critical for promoting sustainable consumption patterns. Key strategies include:

> **Environmental Education and Public Awareness**: Integrating environmental education into school curricula to raise awareness about sustainability from a young age. Conducting public awareness campaigns to inform consumers about the benefits of sustainable consumption and encourage behavior change.
> **Community Engagement**: Engaging communities in sustainability initiatives, such as community gardens and recycling programs, to promote collective action. Today various universities and corporations are taking initiatives and organizing various drives like cycling, River cleaning, recycling of waste with many others, but this needs to be done with a lot of rigour.

There are three ways to boost your social impact. One way is to *make sustainable habits stand out more to other people*. Individuals were asked to pick between an eco-friendly granola bar (with the slogan "Good for you and the environment") and a regular granola bar (with the slogan "A healthy, tasty snack"). The sustainable bar became a choice when other people were around with the respondents. Other researchers have found the same results with everything from eco-friendly hand sanitizers to cars that use less gas. The city of Halifax, Nova Scotia, found that 31% less trash went to the landfill when people had to put their trash in clear bags. This made the contents of the bags visible to neighbors, and many of the items in the bags should have been recycled or composted. *Publicizing eco-friendly activity* is another strategy to boost social influence. Another example is when a hotel guest posted a card on hotel guests' room doors to indicate towel reuse improved towel reuse by 20%. A similar study had hotel guests who wore a pin indicating that they were committed to energy saving by using reused towels. To reduce car idle time when picking up children from school, research encouraged a few parents to show a window sticker reading "For Our Air: I Turn My Engine Off When Parked." Idling time dropped 73% after the intervention.

Third, *encourage healthy social competitiveness*. Informing business students about Computing Science students who are most effective in composting efforts increased their likelihood of composting their biodegradable coffee cups by double. The World Wildlife Fund and its partner volunteer organizations organized friendly energy-saving competitions between towns to promote sustainable practices for Earth Hour. The program spreads socially: It originated in Sydney, Australia, in 2007 and currently spans 188 countries, with 3.5 billion social media references from January to March 2018 with approximately 18,000 landmarks turning off their lights during Earth Hour 2018. (White, 2024)

3.3.4. Corporate Responsibility

Companies play a key role in marketing environmentally friendly products and services through embracing sustainable operations and creating environmentally friendly products. Corporate social responsibility (CSR) activities allow organizations to reduce their impact on the environment, enhance resource efficiency, and enhance their reputation. Sustainability is prioritized so that companies can attract environmentally friendly consumers and support the establishment of a sustainable economy.

4. SUSTAINABLE CONSUMPTION PATTERNS

Reducing, reusing, and recycling- Green consumerism involves the creation, promotion, and enhancement of goods and services based on their environmental advantages. The diverse environmental variables, including social, economic, and cultural factors, facilitated the rise of green consumerism. It embodies a societal mindset wherein individuals consider the welfare of future generations. Sustainable development significantly contributes to fostering this type of social mindset. In the contemporary era, the eco-friendly movement seeks to cultivate consumer awareness regarding sustainable production processes and to encourage the purchase and utilization of items that do not adversely affect the environment. The preservation of our planet necessitates raising societal awareness of the significance of eco-friendly products and green marketing. Green consumerism strikes a balance between organizational and consumer habits. By producing environmentally friendly items for consumers, companies can attain their profit and wealth objectives.

Green consumerism is evolving into a responsible management strategy that identifies, anticipates, and meets stakeholder needs while preserving natural resources and safeguarding human health and environmental species. Its significance encompasses reducing waste, enhancing energy efficiency, and diminishing emissions and pollutants during the production process. It promotes ethical standards and principles across its operations. Sustainability can be achieved only through energy conservation, specifically by utilizing renewable energy sources, recycling, and employing eco-friendly items. Consequently, green consumerism unequivocally benefits contemporary and future society through sustainable development. Consequently, green consumerism represents a comprehensive and forward-looking approach. (N. S. et al, 2022)

Sustainable consumption patterns are essential for addressing the environmental, social, and economic challenges of our time. As the global population continues to grow and consumption levels rise, the need for sustainable practices becomes increasingly urgent. Sustainable consumption involves making choices that minimize negative environmental impacts, promote social equity, and support economic viability. This chapter explores the concept of sustainable consumption patterns, supported by a literature review to highlight key findings and trends.

4.1 Definitions and Frameworks

Sustainable consumption is a multifaceted concept that encompasses various definitions and frameworks. According to the United Nations Environment Programme (UNEP), sustainable consumption involves "the use of services and related products, which respond to basic needs and bring a better quality of life while minimizing the use of natural resources and toxic materials as well as the emissions of waste and pollutants over the lifecycle, so as not to jeopardize the needs of future generations"(Oliveira et al. 2022) This definition highlights the importance of considering the entire lifecycle of products and services, from production to disposal.

4.2 Historical Evolution

The concept of sustainable consumption has evolved, influenced by various environmental and social movements. The 1972 United Nations Conference on the Human Environment in Stockholm marked a significant milestone, emphasizing the need for sustainable development.

The Brundtland Report (1987) further advanced the concept by defining sustainable development as "development that meets the needs of the present without compromising the ability of future generations to meet their own needs"(Sesini et al. 2020) This report laid the foundation for integrating sustainability into consumption patterns.

4.3 Consumer Perceptions and Behavior

Consumer perceptions of eco-friendly products play a crucial role in their adoption. A systematic literature review by Camilleri et al. (2023) identified several factors influencing consumer perceptions, including environmental awareness, perceived benefits, social norms, and personal values. The study found that consumers with higher environmental awareness and stronger personal values related to sustainability are more likely to purchase eco-friendly products. Additionally, social norms and peer influence can significantly impact consumer behavior, encouraging individuals to make more sustainable choices.

Oliveira et al. (2022) identified several factors influencing sustainable consumption, including environmental awareness, social norms, and personal values The study found that consumers with higher environmental awareness and stronger personal values related to sustainability are more likely to engage in sustainable consumption behaviors. Additionally, social norms and peer influence can significantly impact consumer choices, encouraging individuals to adopt more sustainable practices. (Hoque, 2013)

Camacho-Otero et al. (2018) identified several factors that influence consumer behavior in the context of eco-consumerism, including environmental awareness, social norms, and personal values. The study found that consumers with higher environmental awareness and stronger personal values related to sustainability are more likely to engage in eco-friendly purchasing behaviors. Additionally, social norms and peer influence can significantly impact consumer choices, encouraging individuals to adopt more sustainable practices.

4.4 Green Advertising

Green advertising, or eco-advertising, pertains to the promotion of products, services, or concepts that highlight their environmental advantages and sustainability. This is one of the effective and fast ways of introducing the benefits of eco-friendly products to the Consumers. (Li, 2025) This form of advertising seeks to resonate with consumers' increasing environmental concerns and their inclination toward sustainable alternatives. Green advertising manifests in several formats, such as print advertisements, television commercials, social media initiatives, and product packaging.

Coca-Cola aims to reduce waste by collecting the same amount of packaging they are selling. The brand aims to collect 100% of the equivalent of primary packaging by 2030. (Coca Cola Company)

4.4.1 Advantages

Green advertising helps improve a brand's image and reputation as it showcases brand's care for the environment. Customers tend to appreciate brands that share their beliefs and goals, such as caring for the environment. This type of advertising can set a brand apart from its rivals and give it a unique selling point. Green advertising can also save money by encouraging people to use less energy and throw away less trash.

4.4.2 Way to Go

The rise of greenwashing is seen in the last few years, where a brand gives a false claim about environmental credentials. The best way to have a desirable impact is by being open and honest about claims and actions that affect the environment. The brands should make claims by providing specific environmental benefits that can be measured. It's important to get environmental claims checked and approved by a third party and the brand should make sure that claims made in green ads are in line with how businesses work.

5. KEY COMPONENTS OF SUSTAINABLE CONSUMPTION PATTERNS

5.1 Reducing Resource Use

One of the main objectives of sustainable consumption is to minimize the consumption of natural resources. This can be done through different strategies, such as adopting measures that enhance the use of resources, e.g., installing energy-efficient devices and conserving water. Encouraging recycling and material reuse to reduce waste and the need for new materials. Promoting the production of goods and services in a sustainable manner, including organic farming and environmentally friendly manufacturing processes

5.2 Minimizing Waste

Minimizing waste is a critical aspect of sustainable consumption. This involves reducing the amount of waste generated and ensuring that waste is managed in an environmentally responsible manner. Key strategies that can adopted could be, executing practices that reduce waste generation, such as using reusable products and minimizing packaging. Encouraging the composting of organic waste to reduce landfill use and produce valuable soil amendments. It is important to ensure that waste is taken care of properly, including recycling and safe disposal of hazardous materials.

5.3 Promoting Ethical Consumption

Ethical consumption involves making choices that consider the social and environmental impacts of products and services. This includes Supporting products that are produced under fair labor conditions and provide fair wages to workers, and choosing products that are produced with consideration for animal welfare, such as cruelty-free cosmetics and free-range eggs. Ruby Organics is known to make cruelty-free and organic cosmetics. (Ruby's Organics). With this, supporting local and sustainable products reduces the environmental impact of transportation and promotes local economies.

6. SUSTAINABLE FOOD CONSUMPTION

Sustainable food consumption involves making choices that minimize the environmental impact of food production and promote health and well-being. Key practices include:

6.1 Plant-Based Diets

Adopting plant-based diets can meaningfully reduce the environmental impact of food consumption. Plant-based foods help create less greenhouse gas than producing meat and cheese. Research from Oxford University shows that the world food system is responsible for around 25% of all greenhouse gas emissions, and livestock farming is a major part of this problem. Cattle and other livestock make methane, a strong greenhouse gas, when they digest food and when they produce waste. Eating less meat can greatly lower the impact our food choices have on the environment. (PSU connect.2025).

6.2 Organic Farming:

Supporting organic farming practices that avoid the use of synthetic pesticides and fertilizers, promoting soil health and biodiversity. Consumers can choose organic products to support sustainable agriculture and reduce their exposure to harmful chemicals.

Let's look at a very interesting study on organic farming. 187 nations practice organic farming.

Liechtenstein boasts the most organic cropland of any nation. By 2025, the worldwide organic agricultural industry is expected to be worth $151.36 billion. The US boasts sixteen thousand organic farms and five million certified acres. Comprising a 5% percentage of the world's organic agricultural area, North America with 3,012 organic farms, and California is the US state that has the most of them. Land use would rise 16% to 33% worldwide from the global move to organic farming. Organic farms generate about 19.2% less than crops run under convention. (Team 2023)

6.3 Local and Seasonal Foods:

Choosing local and seasonal foods to reduce the environmental impact of transportation and support local farmers. Farmers' markets, community-supported agriculture (CSA) programs, and local food co-ops are popular options for sourcing local and seasonal produce. Encouraging consumption of local food will help reduce the carbon emission. This eventually will lead to having a balance in the local economy.

7. SUSTAINABLE FASHION

The fashion industry is a significant contributor to environmental degradation, but sustainable fashion practices can help mitigate these impacts. Key practices include:

Eco-Friendly Materials: Using eco-friendly materials, such as organic cotton, recycled polyester, and bamboo, to reduce the environmental impact of clothing production. By 2030, Adidas aims to produce all 9 out of 10 articles which will be made with sustainable friendly materials. (Adidas Group, n.d.)
Slow Fashion: Promoting slow fashion, which emphasizes quality over quantity and encourages consumers to buy fewer, longer-lasting items. A brand like Christy Dawn is creating pieces that are ethically sewn and made of organic cotton or deadstock fabrics. The Slow Fashion Movement is a worldwide nonprofit organization that aims to make the fashion industry more sustainable and fair. They do this by educating consumers about the damaging effects of fast fashion. It also encourages them to be more aware. (Slow Fashion movement. 2024)
Second-Hand and Vintage Clothing: Supporting second-hand and vintage clothing to reduce waste and extend the lifecycle of garments. Sustainably Chic sells vintage and secondhand clothes online. This is one of the most effective and inexpensive ways to build a sustainable brand. (Costello, 2024) The popularity of second-hand and vintage clothing has increased as consumers look for ways to reduce waste and extend the lifecycle of garments. Thrift stores, online resale platforms, and clothing swaps have become popular for eco-conscious consumers. According to Amalfi India, India's online thrift store for sustainable fashion and lifestyle products. This place allows you to shop for women's clothes, shoes, and fashion accessories at lower prices than in stores. This brand collects regular and premium clothing from everyday people and influencers. They handle everything, from choosing the items to sending them to buyers.

Consumer Awareness: Growing awareness of the environmental impact of fast fashion has led consumers to seek out more sustainable alternatives. This includes choosing clothing made from eco-friendly materials, such as organic cotton and recycled polyester, and supporting brands that prioritize ethical production practices. Pact, a brand from the USA uses organic cotton for the products in partnership with Fair Trade USA to certify the organic product. (https://wearpact.com)

8. THE ROLE OF CONSUMERS IN PROMOTING ECO-CONSUMERISM

Demand increases when people purchase sustainable goods and services. Entrepreneurs can find a demand for some sustainable products from customers due to eco-friendly preferences. It can encourage the company to be more environmentally friendly and produce eco-friendlier products. Customer demand and the environmental impacts of hotels and tourism lead many companies to establish eco-friendly restaurants. (Riva et al, 2022). People can influence the behaviour of companies by deciding to shop with environmentally conscious companies and forcing them to be responsible for their actions. There are many ways of doing this.

Support Eco-Friendly Businesses and environmental business practices: Support businesses that are concerned about the environment and have clear plans to be sustainable. The same can be done by advocating for change and acting. One can express commitment through signatures on petitions, boycotts, and social media rallies.

Corporate Social Responsibility (CSR): CSR promotes ecofriendly practices, sustainability, and social justice. By fostering community development and engagement CSR encourages transparency in the various ecofriendly transactions. Advocating for organizations when trying to be responsible and sustainable. Individuals can support companies with strong social responsibility programs and request them from those that lack them.

Environmental Impact Reduction: Responsible consumption can be made in various choices such as resourceful consumption, lessening of waste, and encouragement of responsible use. As a consumer, the use of energy-saving appliances, conservation of water, and minimum use of plastic bags and similar disposable plastic products should be adopted and promoted. The principle of reducing wastage by reusing, reducing, and recycling should be encouraged by making sure that electronic waste, medicines, and sanitary pads are disposed of correctly. A responsible consumer will always believe in Responsible purchasing. Considering the social and environmental consequences of buying any product or service. This helps goods that are fair trade, cruelty-free and locally made with sustainability.

9. SUCCESS STORIES AND CASE STUDIES

9.1 Jack Daniels

Sustainability has become a part of Jack Daniel's. They have slogans like "Even Jack Daniel's waste is too good to waste" and "With all due respect to progress, the world could use a little less plastic." This is communicated by having a row of wooden barrels. The company doesn't put any trash in dumps because it sells waste materials and resources that aren't being used by other businesses. Customers who prefer whiskey can purchase the used charcoal from the vats which are aged. All of this shows that Jack Daniel cares about the neighbourhood where it works, the land, the air, and the work ethic. It has skillfully added sustainability to its current branding so that it doesn't lose its reputation as a tough, manly brand. (White 2024)

9.2 Publix

Publix supermarkets in the US are working hard to reduce food waste and support recycling efforts. In the year 2022, the company delivered over 54 million pounds of food waste to farmers as animal feed. That very year saw the fish department moving to reusable plastic totes from polystyrene containers. This change alone saved 190,000 containers. The deli department (the department sells meat, subs, and prepared meals) moved to light plastic bags by replacing individual plastic-wrapped cutlery. These activities helped cut down more than 360,000 pounds of plastic waste each year. Publix has launched a line of sustainable food items called "GreenWise," showing its dedication to using quality ingredients and ensuring good animal care. (Reichheld, 2023)

9.3 Incentives by Coca-Cola

Coca-Cola and Merlin Entertainments had teamed up to make "reverse vending machines" in the UK. When people return their plastic drink bottles, they get half-price tickets to theme parks. When using incentives, it is important not to take them away, because the behavior we seek may go away with them. The author stated that it might make people less likely to want to change their behavior on their own. (White, 2024) This strategy led to multiple types of research where it was concluded that incentives help people form good habits. Since people like consistency, if they start doing something good, they are likely to do other good things in the future.

9.4 IKEA

IKEA started a sustainability program called *Live Lagom*, where "lagom" means "the right amount" in Swedish. It then asked a small group of its users to help it learn more about its sustainability journey. The company discovered that people often start with a single action, like wasting less food at home, and then move on to other areas, like saving energy. IKEA also saw a snowball effect: people would start with small acts and work their way up to bigger ones. When buying LED light bulbs, one might wear warmer clothes and lower the temperature, change the curtains and blinds to keep heat in and insulate doors and windows, buy energy-efficient appliances, set up a programmable thermostat, and so on. (White, 2024)

9.5 Secure 6

Secure 6 has created a rewarding, regenerative, sustainable supply chain management with a measurable impact. The company claims that washing synthetic fabrics releases 50 billion plastic bottles of micro plastics into the oceans yearly. Thunderbird Entertainment has a partnership with Watershed to track and measure the carbon footprint of various initiatives under them. This helps them to understand, maintain, and be accountable for reducing carbon emissions (Panel, 2024)

10. CHALLENGES AND BARRIERS TO ECO-CONSUMERISM

Today's society requires sustainable living, but many people struggle with behavioral change and consumption habits that impede development. Sustainable living is complicated by psychological and social hurdles like change aversion and marketing. Consumers are confused and hesitant to choose eco-friendly options due to misinformation. The complex relationship between consumer psychology and sustainable practices can provide unique insights that help people solve these challenges.

The market for eco-friendly products has grown steadily, but it still faces several challenges. Poornima and Abishek (2023) conducted a study on consumer awareness of eco-friendly products in Coimbatore, India, and found that while there is a favorable attitude towards these products, several barriers hinder their widespread adoption. These barriers include higher costs, lack of awareness, and limited availability. The study emphasized the importance of product certification and labeling in building consumer trust and promoting sustainable consumption. Despite growing awareness of environmental issues, several barriers hinder the adoption of sustainable consumption patterns. Hoque (2014) identified key barriers, including higher costs of sustainable products, lack of awareness, and limited availability. The study emphasized the importance of addressing these barriers through education, policy interventions, and market incentives to promote sustainable consumption.

Several obstacles stand in the way of eco-consumerism, despite its numerous advantages. Some people think that eco-friendly products are too pricey and not available to enough people. Greenwashing, in which businesses make exaggerated claims about how eco-friendly their products are, is another issue that can damage the movement's credibility and slow it down. The green market needs more openness, affordability, and accessibility if consumers, companies, and politicians are going to work together to solve these problems.

Lopez and Legardeur (2024) conducted a systematic literature review on consumer behaviour in the circular economy and recognized key barriers, including high costs of eco-friendly products, lack of awareness, and limited availability. The study highlighted the importance of these barriers through education, policy interventions, and market incentives to promote eco-consumerism.

10.1 Higher Costs

One of the main challenges associated with eco-friendly products and services is their higher cost compared to conventional alternatives. This can be attributed to the use of premium materials, advanced technologies, and sustainable practices that often come with higher production costs. While some consumers are willing to pay a premium for eco-friendly products, others may be deterred by the higher prices.

10.2 Lack of Awareness

Despite growing awareness of environmental issues, many consumers still lack knowledge about the benefits of eco-friendly products and how to identify them. This lack of awareness can hinder the adoption of sustainable products and services. Education and awareness campaigns are essential to inform consumers about the environmental and health benefits of eco-friendly products and encourage sustainable consumption.

10.3 High Price

High prices are a major impediment to sustainable consumer behavior. Higher prices make the product less competitive. Companies can optimize product operations costs to mitigate the impact. Additionally, enterprises can creatively leverage local resources to boost product sustainability. At the policy level, the government should actively support such products due to their overall positive effects on society and the environment, such as the Small Industries Development Bank of India (SIDBI) "Sustainable Finance Scheme" for start-ups in green microfinance, renewable energy projects, eco-friendly labeling, BEE star rating, etc. The Indian government offers tax incentives or subsidies for start-ups and sustainable products. This obstacle to sustainable product acceptability can be reduced by private and public sector efforts to promote product competitiveness. (Sheoran and Kumar, 2020)

10.4 Limited Availability

The availability of eco-friendly products and services can vary significantly depending on the region and market. In some areas, consumers may have limited access to sustainable options, making it difficult to adopt eco-friendly practices. Expanding the availability of eco-friendly products and services through improved distribution channels and increased market presence is crucial for promoting sustainability.

10.5 Greenwashing

Sustainable products are often seen negatively by consumers, who think they are of lower quality, less visually pleasing, and more expensive. In one case, people were less likely to choose environmentally friendly choices when they wanted something strong, like a car cleaner. One way to counteract these bad associations is to focus on the product's good qualities, like how innovative, new, and safe it is. For instance, Tesla focuses more on the new design and usefulness of its cars than on how green they are, which is a message that sticks with its customers. Some guys worry that green products are only for women, but this helps them get over that idea. (White, 2024)

10.6 Making Informed Choices

Consumer buying intention is affected by psychographic factors. Consumers exhibiting excellent ecological behavior also possess—familiarity with diverse environmentally sustainable items, such as eco-friendly paper. Consumers are more influenced by personal norms than social norms when adopting environmentally friendly items such as eco-paper. Consumers with a favorable disposition towards eco-friendly paper are strongly inclined to purchase the goods. Demographic characteristics do not elucidate customers' purchase intentions regarding green items. ("A Study on Consumer Behavior Towards Eco-Friendly Paper," n.d.)

Motivators for eco-consumerism include both internal and external factors. Sun and Yoon (2022) highlighted that internal motivations, such as personal values and environmental concerns, play a significant role in driving eco-friendly behaviors. External factors, such as product availability, affordability, and social influence, also facilitate engagement with eco-consumerism. The study suggested that enhancing consumer awareness and providing incentives for sustainable practices can promote the adoption of eco-friendly products and services.

Consumer habits are people's buying habits. These habits are important for economic and environmental sustainability. (Admin,2024) To overcome social impediments to sustainable living, direct action is needed. Workshops, sustainability fairs, and educational initiatives can change perceptions and inspire action. Using social media to promote sustainable behaviors might also inspire others. By celebrating and supporting sustainable living, the globe may overcome social barriers to sustainable practices and become more environmentally conscious. (Admin, 2024)

11. POLICY INTERVENTIONS AND MARKET INCENTIVES

Government policies play a crucial role in promoting sustainable consumption patterns. Key policy interventions include:

Regulations and Standards: Implementing regulations and standards that mandate sustainable practices, such as energy efficiency standards for appliances and emissions standards for vehicles. In the European Union, a Directive (European Parliament 2010) mandates that all household electrical appliances sold on the market, such as air conditioners, refrigerators, freezers, washing machines, dryers, ovens, water heaters, and hot-water storage appliances, and lighting sources, must have an energy consumption label. Appliance energy efficiency is ranked from A to G on a fiche, with A-rated products (and their A+ variants) having very high energy efficiency and G-rated devices having very poor energy efficiency. The goal is to influence consumers to select energy-efficient products and to motivate producers to satisfy consumer demand for these products. (Akenji,2012) Ecomark is a certification mark used to promote products and services that are environmentally friendly. This certification is developed by the Bureau of Indian Standards to encourage environment-friendly practices among manufacturers and consumers. (Rathore and Ganjwar,2024)

Incentives and Subsidies: Providing incentives and subsidies for sustainable products and practices, such as tax credits for renewable energy installations and subsidies for public transit. The government can lower the cost of green research and development, offer material and technical assistance to businesses, and create tax breaks and financial incentives for green businesses.
Public Awareness Campaigns: It's important to conduct public awareness campaigns to inform consumers about how sustainable consumption would be beneficial for them and society at large. The government can utilize media and other networks to vigorously promote green consumption. The government can increase production subsidies in the field of green consumption and implement incentive strategies for consumers, all while lowering the cost of purchasing the long-term benefits in the end. (Bian,2020)

12. FUTURE DIRECTIONS

Technological innovations can play a significant role in promoting sustainable consumption patterns. Key areas of innovation include Renewable Energy where *advanced renewable energy* technologies, such as solar and wind power, reduce dependence on fossil fuels and lower greenhouse gas emissions. *Developing sustainable materials*, such as biodegradable plastics and eco-friendly textiles, to reduce environmental impact. We greet clients and prospective customers with the company's digital business card solution. Digital business cards require no paper production or printing, but traditional business cards cause millions of trees to be destroyed every year. They electronically produce, oversee, and distribute digital business cards, enabling us to network with no carbon footprint. (Unicode). *Implementing smart technologies*, such as smart grids and energy-efficient appliances, to optimize resource use and reduce waste. Using advanced technology, stores can understand what customers like, improve how they make products, and create new ideas that reduce harm to the environment. Companies can use smart technology to make their inventory control easier and more efficient. This results in quicker order processing, better control of the warehouse, shorter delivery times, and the confidence that products will be in stock. This means that by tracking and monitoring goods in real-time, we can avoid having too much or too little stock. This also helps reduce energy use and costs. (Guest,2024)

Conclusion

Sustainable product adoption will boost economic growth and green the planet. The first step is to create awareness among the consumers about the benefits of eco products, and their impact on nature. Countries must promote sustainable electronics because of climate change. Various barriers must be addressed due to the rapid rise in all the products that are hurting the environment. A major change needs to be initiated by various organizations to bring in the change. India's Paris Climate Agreement aims to cut greenhouse gas emissions by 33–35% from 2005 levels by 2030 will require government and private sector cooperation. Eco-consumerism is a collective effort by all the stakeholders involved in the ecosystem. It's indeed a long way ahead but certainly an achievable target.

REFERENCES

Adidas. (n.d.). Our targets. Adidas Group. Retrieved from https://www.adidas-group.com/en/sustainability/focus-on-sustainability/our-targets?utm_source=chatgpt.com

Admin. (2023). The rise of green consumerism. ET2C International. Retrieved from https://et2c.com/news/the-rise-of-green-consumerism/

Admin. (2024). Overcoming barriers to sustainable consumer habits. Sustainable Living. Retrieved from https://sustainableliving.org.nz/overcoming-barriers-to-sustainable-consumer-habits/

Ali, W., Mahmood, Z., Wilson, J., & Ismail, H. (2023). The impact of sustainability governance attributes on comprehensive CSR reporting: A developing country setting. *Corporate Social Responsibility and Environmental Management, 31*(3), 1802–1817. DOI: 10.1002/csr.2677

Amalfi India. (n.d.). About us. Amalfi India. Retrieved from https://www.amalfiindia.com/about-us

Bansal Gupta, A., & Agarwal, S. (2022). Green consumption: Awareness and purchase decisions. Management Journal for Advanced Research, 2(3), 10-17. Retrieved from https://ssrn.com/abstract=4315987

Bell, J. (2024). 15 sustainability certifications for conscious consumption. Sustainable Jungle. Retrieved from https://www.sustainablejungle.com/sustainability-certifications/

Binnuri, A., & M, R. (2024). Consumerism, sustainable consumption, and consumer citizenship in the Indian context. *Cogent Business & Management, 11*(1), 2428777. Advance online publication. DOI: 10.1080/23311975.2024.2428777

Business Research Insights. (n.d.). Car pooling market growth, size, share and forecast [2033]. Retrieved from https://www.businessresearchinsights.com/market-reports/car-pooling-market-108249

Cambridge Dictionary. (n.d.). Consumerism. Retrieved from https://dictionary.cambridge.org/dictionary/english/consumerism

Camilleri, M. A., Cricelli, L., Mauriello, R., & Strazzullo, S. (2023). Consumer perceptions of sustainable products: A systematic literature review. *Sustainability (Basel), 15*(11), 8923. DOI: 10.3390/su15118923

Capital One Shopping. (2025). Eco-conscious consumer statistics: Latest data & trends. Capital One Shopping. Retrieved from https://capitaloneshopping.com/research/eco-conscious-consumer-statistics/

Carbon Trust. (n.d.). Climate action plans & business sustainability. Retrieved from https://www.carbontrust.com/en-as

Centric Software, Inc. (2025). The greener picture: Navigating the consumer goods sustainability landscape. Centric Software. Retrieved from https://www.centricsoftware.com/blog/the-greener-picture-consumer-goods-sustainability/

Christy Dawn. (n.d.). Regenerative, ethical & timeless dresses & accessories. Christy Dawn. Retrieved from https://christydawn.com/en-in

Chuchu, T., Maziriri, E. T., & Mototo, L. (2020). A review of the impact of consumerism, recycling and pollution: Evidence from Southeast Asia: 1999 to 2019. *Journal of Environmental Management and Tourism*, *11*(1), 23–28. https://repository.up.ac.za/bitstream/handle/2263/74316/Chuchu_Review_2020.pdf. DOI: 10.14505//jemt.v11.1(41).03

Coca-Cola. (2018). World without waste strategy guidebook.

Costello, N. (2024). The best online stores for affordable secondhand & vintage clothing. Sustainably Chic. Retrieved from https://www.sustainably-chic.com/blog/thrift-shops-secondhand-vintage-clothing

Fahad, F. (2023). Green building materials: Aim, components, features, and list. Earth Reminder. Retrieved from https://www.earthreminder.com/green-building-materials/

Global Risk Intel. (n.d.). Jakarta's air pollution crisis and concerns for future economic development. Retrieved from https://www.globalriskintel.com/insights/jakartas-air-pollution-crisis-and-concerns-future-economic-development

Green Building Council of Australia. (n.d.). Exploring Green Star. Green Building Council of Australia. Retrieved from https://new.gbca.org.au/green-star/exploring-green-star/

Guest. (2024). The shift to a circular economy: How smart technology is driving sustainability in retail. Financial Express.

Habib, M. D., Attri, R., Salam, M. A., & Yaqub, M. Z. (2024). Bright and dark sides of green consumerism: An in-depth qualitative investigation in a retailing context. *Journal of Retailing and Consumer Services*, *82*, 104145. DOI: 10.1016/j.jretconser.2024.104145

Han, H. (2021). Consumer behaviour and environmental sustainability in tourism and hospitality: A review of theories, concepts, and latest research. *Journal of Sustainable Tourism, 29*(7), 1021–1042. DOI: 10.1080/09669582.2021.1903019

Hoque, N. (2014). Analysing sustainable consumption patterns: A literature review. *Development, 57*(3-4), 431–439. https://link.springer.com/content/pdf/10.1057/dev.201

IEA. (2024). Trends in electric cars – Global EV Outlook 2024. International Energy Agency (IEA). Retrieved from https://www.iea.org/reports/global-ev-outlook-2024/trends-in-electric-cars

Landry, M. J., & Ward, C. P. (2024). Health benefits of a plant-based dietary pattern and implementation in healthcare and clinical practice. *American Journal of Lifestyle Medicine, 18*(5), 657–665. Advance online publication. DOI: 10.1177/15598276241237766 PMID: 39309320

Li, D. (2025). Impact of green advertisement and environmental knowledge on intention of consumers to buy green products. *BMC Psychology, 13*(1), 220. Advance online publication. DOI: 10.1186/s40359-025-02538-x PMID: 40059236

Nielsen, I. Q. (2023). Indian consumers' evolving priorities towards the environment and sustainability. NIQ. Retrieved from https://nielseniq.com/global/en/insights/commentary/2023/indian-consumers-evolving-priorities-towards-the-environment-and-sustainability/

Office of Consumer Affairs. (2022, June 8). Environmental labels and claims. Retrieved from https://ised-isde.canada.ca/site/office-consumer-affairs/en/be-green-consumer/environmental-labels-and-claims#toc0

Oliveira, U. R., Gomes, T. S. M., de Oliveira, G. G., de Abreu, J. C. A., Oliveira, M. A., & César, A. S. (2022). Systematic literature review on sustainable consumption from the perspective of companies, people, and public policies. *Sustainability (Basel), 14*(21), 13771. DOI: 10.3390/su142113771

Orecchia, C., & Zoppoli, P. (2007). Consumerism and environment: Does consumption behaviour affect environmental quality? CEIS Working Paper No. 261. Available at *SSRN*: https://ssrn.com/abstract=1719507 DOI: 10.2139/ssrn.1719507

Panel, E. (2024). 17 sustainability initiatives of businesses that are going green. *Forbes*.

Pittayachawan, S., Abareshi, A., Kam, B., & Teo, L. (2014). Green consumerism: A study on the prospect of consumers' participation in corporate environmental management programs. DOI: 10.13140/2.1.3238.3684

Poornima, B., & Abishek, A. (2023). A study on consumer awareness towards eco-friendly products in Coimbatore city. [IJCRT]. *International Journal of Creative Research Thoughts, 11*(4), 772. https://ijcrt.org/papers/IJCRT2304772.pdf

Pratap, S. (2018). A study on eco-friendly consumerism. *International Journal of Creative Research Thoughts, 6*(2), 940–941. https://ijcrt.org/papers/IJCRT1134708.pdf

Rathore, & Gangwar. (2024). Analyzing the benefits & challenges of eco mark rules & compliance. Lawrbit. Retrieved from https://www.lawrbit.com/article/analyzing-the-benefits-challenges-of-eco-mark-rules-compliance/

Reddy, K. P., Chandu, V., Srilakshmi, S., Thagaram, E., Sahyaja, C., & Osei, B. (2023). Consumers' perception of green marketing towards eco-friendly fast-moving consumer goods. *International Journal of Engineering Business Management, 15*, 18479790231170962. Advance online publication. DOI: 10.1177/18479790231170962

Reichheld, A. (2023). Research: Consumers' sustainability demands are rising. Harvard Business Review. Retrieved from https://hbr.org/2023/09/research-consumers-sustainability-demands-are-rising

Riva, F., Magrizos, S., Basher Rubel, M. R., & Rizomyliotis, I. (2022). Green consumerism, green perceived value, and restaurant revisit intention: Millennials' sustainable consumption with the moderating effect of green perceived quality. *Business Strategy and the Environment, 31*(7), 2807–2819. DOI: 10.1002/bse.3048

Ruby's Organics. (n.d.). Ruby's Organics | Makeup that's good for you. Retrieved from https://rubysorganics.in/

Sachdeva, S., Jordan, J., & Mazar, N. (2015). Green consumerism: Moral motivations to a sustainable future. *Current Opinion in Psychology, 6*, 60–65. Advance online publication. DOI: 10.1016/j.copsyc.2015.03.029

SBToolkit. (2024). Eco-friendly transportation examples: Sustainable transport solutions. Sustainable Business Toolkit. Retrieved from https://www.sustainablebusinesstoolkit.com/eco-friendly-transportation-examples/

Sekhar, K. C., & Asio, J. M. R. (2022). Evaluation of Consumerism on Sustainability. *Technoarete Transactions on Advances in Social Sciences and Humanities, 2*(2), 1–6.

Sheoran, M., & Kumar, D. (2020). Benchmarking the barriers of sustainable consumer behaviour. *Social Responsibility Journal.* Advance online publication. DOI: 10.1108/SRJ-05-2020-0203

Singh, S. (2022). National strategy for eco-tourism.

Staci, K. (2024). Top 5 eco-friendly transportation methods you can feel great about. Blue and Green Tomorrow. Retrieved from https://blueandgreentomorrow.com/transport/top-5-eco-friendly-transportation-methods-you-can-feel-great-about/

Sun, Y., & Yoon, S. (2022). Determinants of green consumption: A systematic literature review using the triple bottom line framework. Frontiers in Sustainability. Retrieved from https://www.frontiersin.org/journals/sustainability/articles/10.3389/frsus.2024.1428764/full

Swire Properties. (n.d.).. . *Sustainable Development.*

Team, S. (2023). 22 organic farming statistics that show its true power (2025). Soocial. Retrieved from https://www.soocial.com/organic-farming-statistics/

UITP. (2024). 5 key public transport trends revealed in our global economic outlook 2024. UITP. Retrieved from https://www.uitp.org/news/5-key-public-transport-trends-revealed-in-our-global-economic-outlook-2024/

Uniqode. (n.d.). QR code management platform for modern businesses. Retrieved from https://www.uniqode.com/

Wang, C., Ghadimi, P., Lim, M. K., & Tseng, M. L. (2019). A literature review of sustainable consumption and production: A comparative analysis in developed and developing economies. *Journal of Cleaner Production*, *206*, 741–754. DOI: 10.1016/j.jclepro.2018.09.172

Wear, P. A. C. T. (n.d.). Sustainability, certified. Retrieved from https://wearpact.com/sustainability

White, K. (2024). The elusive green consumer. Harvard Business Review. Retrieved from https://hbr.org/2019/07/the-elusive-green-consumer

World Economic Forum. (2024). Renewable energy could power the world by 2050: Here's what that future might look like. Retrieved from https://www.weforum.org/stories/2020/02/renewable-energy-future-carbon-emissions/

World Economic Forum. (n.d.). How hydrogen-powered vehicles will help India reach its emissions targets. Retrieved from https://www.weforum.org/stories/2024/12/how-hydrogen-powered-vehicles-will-help-india-reach-its-emissions-targets/

World Health Organization. (2024). Electronic waste (e-waste). Retrieved from https://www.who.int/news-room/fact-sheets/detail/electronic-waste-%28e-waste%29

Chapter 3
Digital Social Influence and Sustainability Gamification Effect on Environmental Awareness and Green Consumption Behavior

Benard Korankye
https://orcid.org/0000-0002-2790-7708
Zhejiang Gongshang University, China

ABSTRACT

This chapter examines how digital platforms and gamification strategies foster environmental awareness and promote the UN SDGs and sustainable consumer behavior in response to escalating global ecological challenges. It explores how environmental awareness is enhanced through digital social influence and gamified systems to drive sustainable behaviors and encourage societal shifts toward green consumption. By integrating the persuasive power of social media and the engaging mechanics of gamification, this chapter demonstrates their synergy in boosting motivation and accountability in environmental initiatives. Supported by empirical evidence and case studies, it highlights their transformative impact on green purchasing habits and broader sustainability goals while emphasizing their alignment with the United Nations Sustainable Development Goals (SDGs), including climate action and responsible consumption.

DOI: 10.4018/979-8-3693-9831-9.ch003

1 INTRODUCTION

Environmental awareness has emerged as one of the most significant issues of the contemporary world. With the accelerating pace of industrialization, urbanization, and technological advancement, humanity is exerting tremendous pressure on the earth's ecosystems (Li & Shan, 2025). This has resulted in widespread environmental degradation, including deforestation, pollution, loss of biodiversity, and climate change (Farooq et al., 2023), see Figure 1. Raising awareness about the environment has therefore become a necessity, as it serves to educate individuals and communities about the critical role they play in safeguarding the planet (Hamoudi & Avilés-Palacios, 2023).

Figure 1. Global deforestation rates

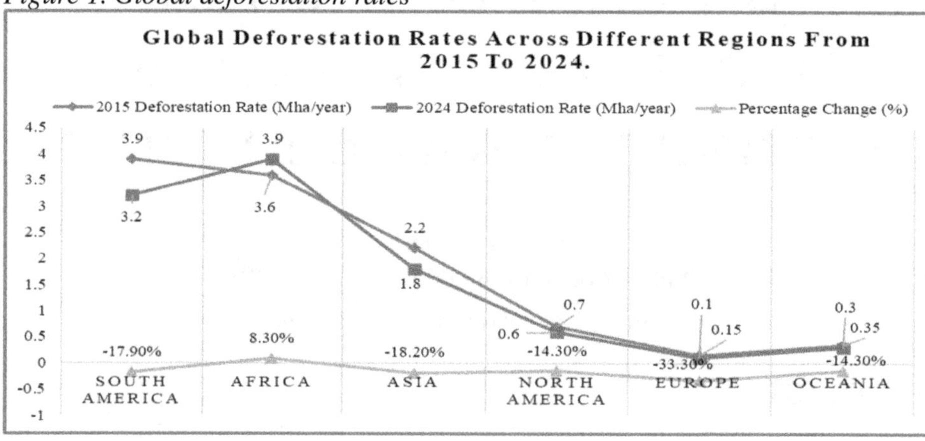

Global Deforestation Rates Across Different Regions From 2015 To 2024.

Sources of information: (Ritchie, 2021) and (Global Forest Watch, 2024)

According to Farooq et al. (2023), awareness fosters a sense of responsibility and encourages collective action to address environmental challenges. At its core, environmental awareness involves understanding the intricate relationship between human activities and the natural world (see Table 1). It highlights the interconnectedness of all life forms and the dependence of human well-being on a healthy and balanced environment. Manoj Krishnan & Arun (2025) also indicate that environmental awareness encompasses an individual's understanding of environmental or ecological challenges and their recognition of the need to address these issues. It encompasses knowledge about environmental problems such as climate change, pollution, deforestation, and biodiversity loss (Hamoudi & Avilés-Palacios, 2023).

Awareness often stems from educational efforts, media exposure, and personal experiences with environmental changes (Butar et al., 2024). Promoting environmental awareness involves not just imparting knowledge but fostering emotional connections to the natural world (Solina & Ocampo, 2024). Campaigns, community initiatives, and policy measures play key roles in heightening public awareness (Butar et al., 2024). For example, global movements like Earth Day emphasize collective responsibility and encourage grassroots efforts to promote sustainability. Similarly, school curricula and public service announcements often integrate environmental education to instill awareness from an early age (The Conversation, 2020). However, the presence of environmental awareness does not automatically translate into sustainable behaviors. Factors such as social norms, economic constraints, and perceived efficacy significantly influence whether individuals act upon their awareness (Mahmoud et al., 2022).

According to Solina & Ocampo (2024), sustainable development is a key concept closely tied to environmental awareness. It calls for a balance between economic growth, social equity, and environmental protection to ensure the well-being of present and future generations. Awareness efforts encourage people to adopt sustainable lifestyles by conserving energy, reducing waste, and supporting eco-friendly products and services. Businesses, too, are urged to embrace sustainable practices such as green manufacturing, renewable energy use, and ethical sourcing (Hamoudi & Avilés-Palacios, 2023). By prioritizing sustainability, societies can achieve economic progress without compromising the health of the planet.

More so, environmental education plays a crucial role in fostering awareness from an early age (Chaihanchanchai & Anantachart, 2023). Schools and universities are increasingly integrating environmental topics into their curricula to equip students with the knowledge and skills needed to address ecological challenges. Experiential learning, such as nature walks, tree planting, and community clean-up drives, further deepens students' connection to the environment and inspires them to take action. Public campaigns, documentaries, and social media platforms also serve as powerful tools for raising awareness among broader audiences (Jaciow et al., 2022). By leveraging these mediums, advocates can amplify their message and engage diverse groups in meaningful discussions about environmental issues.

Table 1. Global carbon emissions by region from 2010 to 2024

Region	2010 Emissions (MMT)	2024 Emissions (MMT)	Percentage Change (%)
Asia	16,000	20,500	+28.1%
North America	6,500	5,800	-10.8%
Europe	4,500	3,800	-15.6%

continued on following page

Table 1. Continued

Region	2010 Emissions (MMT)	2024 Emissions (MMT)	Percentage Change (%)
Africa	1,200	1,500	+25.0%
South America	1,400	1,600	+14.3%
Oceania	400	450	+12.5%

Note: These figures are approximate and reflect trends in emissions from fossil fuels and industrial activities. The data is sourced from Statista (2025) and Ritchie & Roser (2020).

2 OVERVIEW OF GREEN CONSUMPTION BEHAVIOR

Green consumer behavior refers to the choices and actions of individuals who prioritize environmental sustainability in their consumption patterns (Aiswarya et al., 2024). This behavior emphasizes the purchase of products and services that minimize negative environmental impacts, reduce waste, and conserve natural resources (see Figure 2). Consumers adopting green habits often seek items that are energy-efficient, biodegradable, recyclable, or made from sustainable materials (Ali et al., 2023). They are also likely to prefer companies that demonstrate a commitment to environmental responsibility through eco-friendly practices, such as using renewable energy, reducing carbon emissions, and engaging in ethical sourcing (Farooq et al., 2023). The demand for green products has grown significantly in recent years, driven by increasing awareness of global environmental challenges such as climate change, pollution, and resource depletion. This shift reflects a growing recognition of the power of individual purchasing decisions in shaping sustainable market trends (Apaolaza et al., 2023).

Figure 2. U.S shoppers who would pay for eco-friendly products

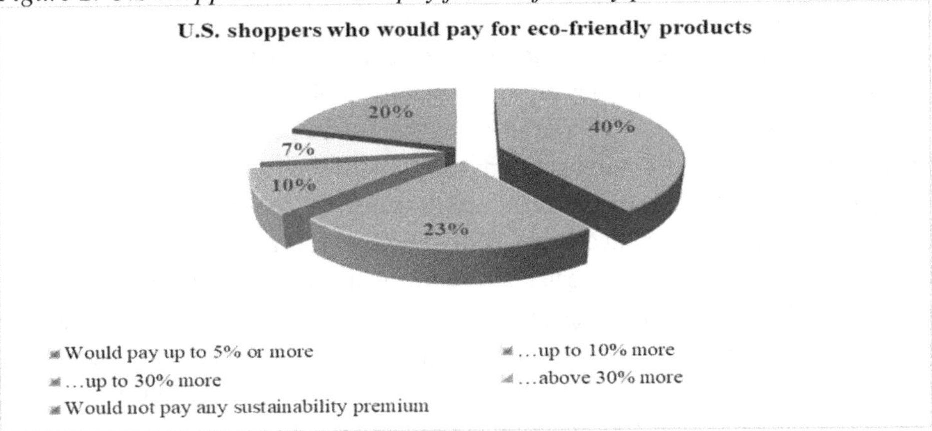

U.S. shoppers' behavior towards eco-friendly products

Source: (Capital One Shopping Research, 2025)

For example, the eco-friendly retail market is experiencing significant growth globally and, in the U.S., Nearly 89% of consumers have adopted more sustainable shopping habits, and 80% are willing to pay more for eco-friendly products. In the U.S., the eco-friendly retail market is expanding 71% faster than conventional retail, with 177 million Americans identifying as eco-conscious shoppers in 2024, a 7.44% YoY increase. As of 2025, eco-friendly shopping accounts for 19.4% of U.S. retail spending and is projected to reach 23.0% by 2032. Consumer spending on sustainable products is expected to hit $217 billion in 2025, surpassing $400 billion by 2032 (Capital One Shopping Research, 2025).

Green consumer behavior is influenced by various factors, including personal values, knowledge about environmental issues, and social pressures (Abdo et al., 2023). Individuals with strong environmental values and a sense of responsibility toward nature are more inclined to adopt sustainable consumption habits (Manoj Krishnan & Arun, 2025). Media and education also play a crucial role in shaping consumer awareness, often highlighting the ecological impacts of conventional consumption practices. For example, information campaigns about the harmful effects of plastic waste have led many consumers to switch to reusable alternatives. Social norms and peer influences further reinforce green behaviors, as people tend to model actions observed in their communities or social networks. However, barriers such as higher costs of eco-friendly products, lack of accessibility, and limited understanding of their benefits can deter some consumers from fully engaging in green consumption (Haba et al., 2023).

The rise of technology has provided consumers with tools to make informed and sustainable choices (Haba et al., 2023). Apps and websites that provide information on product sustainability, carbon footprint calculators, and platforms promoting second-hand goods have empowered individuals to align their purchasing habits with environmental values (Aiswarya et al., 2024). Similarly, the growth of green marketing has made eco-friendly options more visible and attractive to consumers. Companies use certifications, labels, and transparent communication to assure buyers of their environmental commitment, fostering trust and loyalty among green consumers. This interplay between consumer demand and corporate action has the potential to drive systemic change, as businesses innovate to meet the expectations of environmentally conscious buyers. Through these evolving patterns, green consumer behavior continues to influence markets and encourage a broader shift toward sustainability (Apaolaza et al., 2023).

2.1 Importance of Environmental Awareness in Promoting Green Consumption Behavior

Environmental awareness plays a critical role in fostering green consumption behavior by empowering individuals with the knowledge and motivation to make sustainable choices (Jaciow et al., 2022). It involves understanding the impact of consumption patterns on the environment and recognizing the importance of mitigating these impacts through responsible behavior. As consumers become more aware of issues such as climate change, pollution, and resource depletion, they are more likely to align their purchasing decisions with sustainability goals (Mahmoud et al., 2022). This awareness not only drives demand for eco-friendly products but also encourages consumers to scrutinize the environmental practices of businesses (Hamoudi & Avilés-Palacios, 2023). Individuals who are aware of the detrimental effects of plastic pollution may opt for reusable or biodegradable alternatives, thereby reducing waste and promoting more sustainable consumption habits. By linking individual actions to broader environmental outcomes, awareness fosters a sense of accountability and supports the transition toward greener lifestyles (Farooq et al., 2023).

Educational efforts and media campaigns play pivotal roles in cultivating environmental awareness, which in turn shapes green consumption behavior. These initiatives often focus on highlighting the environmental consequences of unsustainable practices and offering practical solutions for consumers to adopt (Zameer & Yasmeen, 2022). For example, campaigns promoting energy-efficient appliances or sustainable fashion choices often educate consumers about the environmental benefits of reducing energy use and supporting ethical production processes (Borah et al., 2024). Moreover, awareness initiatives often include tangible demonstrations of the impact of sustainable choices, such as reductions in greenhouse gas emissions or conservation of natural resources (Judijanto et al., 2024). Such information not only builds knowledge but also establishes an emotional connection to the environmental cause, motivating individuals to act. Awareness also enables consumers to differentiate between genuinely green products and those employing "greenwashing" tactics, thereby encouraging transparency and accountability among businesses (Jaciow et al., 2022).

Some empirical studies have explored the impact of environmental awareness on green consumption behavior. García-Salirrosas et al. (2024) examined the influence of environmental awareness on willingness to pay for green products in Peru, with a sample of 405 consumers, demonstrating a significant positive effect on willingness to pay for green products. Xie et al. (2022) analyzed data from the 2010 China General Social Survey, revealing that environmental cognition positively influenced green consumption attitudes and behaviors among Chinese consumers. Horani et al. (2023) explored the impact of environmental awareness on the sustainable consumption behavior of smartphone users across China, finding that higher environmental awareness led to a preference for sustainable consumption.

3 DIGITAL SOCIAL INFLUENCE ON SUSTAINABILITY

Digital social influence refers to the way social platforms, networks, and digital tools encourage and shape user behaviors through online interactions (C. Chen et al., 2024). In another breath, DSI encompasses the power of individuals, organizations, and communities to shape attitudes, behaviors, and decisions through online platforms and digital tools (Chandrasekara, 2022). Within the sustainability context, it encompasses initiatives like peer comparisons, public pledges, and the use of social proof to inspire eco-friendly actions. DSI leverages the vast reach and interactivity of social media, blogs, and digital campaigns to promote environmental consciousness, social equity, and ethical practices (Bhukya & Paul, 2023). This influence is not confined to traditional communication methods; it thrives on the speed and scalability of the internet, which allows messages to reach millions in a matter of moments. By integrating storytelling, educational content, and social proof, digital social influence creates a dynamic ecosystem where sustainable behaviors and ideas can spread widely and gain traction (Dudarenok, 2023).

Social media platforms such as Instagram, TikTok, YouTube, and LinkedIn are central to the mechanics of digital social influence in sustainability. These platforms enable influencers, organizations, and activists to connect with diverse audiences, breaking down barriers of geography and demographics (Chen & Madni, 2023). Eco-influencers, for example, are individuals or groups who advocate for sustainable lifestyles, often through creative and visually appealing content. They share personal journeys, such as reducing plastic usage, adopting vegan diets, or implementing zero-waste practices, which inspire followers to make similar changes (Caldevilla-Domínguez et al., 2021). The principle of social proof amplifies these efforts: when people observe others, particularly those they admire or respect, engaging in sustainable behavior, they are more likely to emulate those actions. This can create powerful trends that normalize eco-friendly habits and foster collective participation in sustainability (Castillo-Abdul et al., 2024).

In addition to personal influence, digital platforms provide robust tools for large-scale sustainability campaigns. Hashtags like #SustainableLiving, #ClimateAction, and #EcoFriendlyLife act as rallying points for online communities, facilitating the spread of ideas and fostering collaborative action. Organizations and activists use these tools to promote campaigns that encourage participation, such as beach clean-ups, tree-planting challenges, or pledges to reduce carbon footprints (Castillo-Abdul et al., 2024). The viral nature of social media ensures that well-crafted messages can reach and engage millions within days, amplifying their impact. Moreover, advanced analytics and data-driven strategies allow these campaigns to be highly targeted, tailoring content to specific audiences based on interests, behaviors, and demographics (Alboqami, 2023). For instance, younger audiences might engage more with visually driven and trend-focused platforms like TikTok, while professionals may prefer thought-provoking discussions on LinkedIn.

3.1 The Role of Digital Social Influence in Environmental Awareness

3.1.1 Amplifying Environmental Messaging

Digital platforms provide an unparalleled reach for spreading environmental awareness. Social media, blogs, and video-sharing platforms enable organizations, activists, and governments to disseminate critical information about ecological challenges such as climate change, deforestation, and plastic pollution (Chen et al., 2024). Viral campaigns, hashtags, and shareable content, such as documentaries like Our Planet, not only inform but also evoke emotional responses, which are essential for motivating action. The wide accessibility of digital media ensures that environmental messages can reach global audiences, cutting across geographic and cultural boundaries.

3.1.2 Promoting Peer-to-Peer Influence

Peer influence is a powerful driver of behavior, and digital platforms enhance its effectiveness (Essiz & Mandrik, 2021). When individuals see friends, influencers, or celebrities engaging in eco-friendly behaviors, such as reducing waste, switching to renewable energy, or adopting plant-based diets, they are more likely to emulate these actions. Social proof, a concept in psychology where people conform to behaviors perceived as socially accepted or admired, becomes particularly potent in digital spaces (Mohd Suki & Mohd Suki, 2019). Platforms like Instagram and TikTok amplify this effect by showcasing sustainable lifestyles through visually engaging content. Eco-influencers and content creators, such as those promoting minimalism or zero-waste practices, inspire followers to adopt environmentally conscious habits.

3.1.3 Facilitating Collaborative Action

Digital social influence fosters collective action by connecting individuals with shared environmental goals. Online petitions, crowdfunding campaigns, and virtual events unite people around common causes, turning awareness into action. Platforms like Change.org have been instrumental in supporting initiatives ranging from protecting endangered species to funding clean-energy projects. Gamified campaigns, such as those encouraging users to plant trees or reduce their energy consumption, further leverage digital influence. Apps like Ecosia, which funds tree-planting efforts through user searches, and initiatives like Team Trees exemplify how digital tools can mobilize communities for environmental causes.

3.2 The Impact of Social Media Platforms and Influencers on Shaping Environmental Attitudes.

Social media platforms, such as Instagram and TikTok, have revolutionized how individuals interact with information, ideas, and movements, making them influential tools for shaping environmental attitudes (Chen et al., 2024). With their vast reach and visual storytelling capabilities, these platforms provide fertile ground for raising awareness, educating audiences, and inspiring action on environmental issues.

3.2.1 Platforms as Catalysts for Environmental Awareness

Social media platforms like Instagram and TikTok excel at spreading environmental messages through creative, engaging content (Aiswarya et al., 2024). Short videos, eye-catching infographics, and hashtag campaigns effectively capture user attention and convey complex environmental issues in digestible formats. TikTok, for instance, has become a hub for viral content on sustainability, with hashtags like #ClimateAction and #EcoTok gaining billions of views. These platforms cater to younger, tech-savvy audiences, making them critical for fostering environmental consciousness among the next generation (Zhao et al., 2024). Instagram, with its visual-centric approach, provides a platform for sharing compelling images of climate impacts, wildlife conservation efforts, or sustainable lifestyles. For example, posts highlighting the devastating effects of plastic pollution often link to petitions or zero-waste shopping guides, enabling users to take immediate steps toward change.

3.2.2 Influencers as Agents of Change

Environmental influencers play a key role in shaping attitudes by personalizing and humanizing sustainability (Alboqami, 2023). Unlike traditional environmental organizations, influencers build trust and relatability with their audiences, making their messages more impactful (Castillo-Abdul et al., 2024). Popular eco-influencers, such as Leah Thomas (@greengirlleah) or Rob Greenfield, use platforms like Instagram to advocate for environmental justice, sustainable living, and policy change. Their content resonates with followers by combining practical advice, such as how to reduce waste, with motivational stories and personal accountability. On TikTok, influencers often create viral trends that gamify sustainability, such as challenges to adopting plant-based diets or using DIY eco-friendly products. This approach not only raises awareness but also fosters a sense of community around environmental causes. By showcasing sustainable habits in everyday life, influencers demonstrate that individual actions can make a difference, inspiring their followers to emulate these behaviors (Alboqami, 2023).

3.2.3 Driving Collective Action

Social media campaigns initiated or amplified by influencers frequently transcend individual action, mobilizing collective efforts for larger environmental goals (Farooq et al., 2023). For instance, initiatives like Team Trees and Team Seas gained global momentum through influencer support, resulting in millions of trees planted and tons of ocean plastic removed. Similarly, social media influencers often spearhead fundraising efforts, promote petitions, and encourage participation in climate strikes, leveraging their audiences for systemic change (Boerman et al., 2022). The interactive nature of social media amplifies the reach and impact of such campaigns. Features like comments, shares, and collaborations enable influencers to engage with followers and partner with other activists or organizations. This fosters a participatory culture, where individuals feel personally connected to and invested in environmental causes.

3.3 Case Studies Of Successful Influencer Sustainability Campaigns

Influencer-led sustainability campaigns have proven effective in mobilizing audiences, raising awareness, and driving tangible environmental action. By leveraging the reach, relatability, and authenticity of influencers, these campaigns tap into online communities and create significant real-world impact (Influencer Marketing New, 2024). Below are notable case studies highlighting successful influencer-driven initiatives in the sustainability space.

3.3.1 Team Trees: Planting 20 Million Trees

One of the most successful influencer-led campaigns was Team Trees, launched in October 2019 by YouTube influencers Jimmy Donaldson (MrBeast) and Mark Rober. The campaign aimed to plant 20 million trees by raising $20 million in collaboration with the Arbor Day Foundation. Through engaging content, storytelling, and widespread promotion by other YouTubers and celebrities, the campaign quickly went viral. Influencers played a critical role in amplifying the initiative's reach. MrBeast's video explaining the campaign gained millions of views, sparking donations from tech leaders like Elon Musk and corporations like Shopify. The campaign exceeded its goal, raising over $23 million and planting more than 23 million trees worldwide. Its success showcased the power of digital influence in mobilizing large-scale environmental action Ody Shop's Forever Against Animal Testing Campaign (Ben Schoon, 2019).

The Body Shop's Forever Against Animal Testing campaign combined corporate sustainability goals with influencer advocacy. Launched in 2017, the campaign aimed to ban animal testing globally by collecting eight million petition signatures to present to the United Nations. Social media influencers were central to the campaign's success, using platforms like Instagram to engage their audiences with stories about animal welfare (Forever Against Animal Testing, 2019). Additionally, influencers such as Niomi Smart and Estee Lalonde shared posts and videos emphasizing the importance of ethical beauty and encouraged their followers to sign the petition. Their efforts helped humanize the issue, sparking widespread public support. By 2018, the campaign achieved its goal of securing eight million signatures, raising awareness of animal testing, and advancing global policy change.

3.3.2 Removing Plastic Waste

Following the success of Team Trees, influencers Jimmy Donaldson (MrBeast) and Mark Rober launched Team Seas in 2021. This initiative aimed to remove 30 million pounds of plastic and trash from oceans, rivers, and beaches by raising $30 million. Using engaging videos and challenges, the influencers motivated their vast online audiences to contribute and spread the campaign. Many prominent creators, including Casey Neistat and Marques Brownlee, joined the effort, creating their own content to support the cause. The campaign also partnered with organizations like The Ocean Conservancy and The Ocean Cleanup, ensuring transparency and effective implementation. By January 2022, the initiative reached its goal, removing millions of pounds of waste from aquatic ecosystems and highlighting the effectiveness of influencer-led environmental action.

3.3.3 Fashion Revolution and the Who Made My Clothes? Campaign

The Who Made My Clothes? campaign, launched by the Fashion Revolution movement, aimed to increase transparency in the fashion industry. By encouraging consumers to demand accountability from brands regarding their labor and environmental practices, the campaign brought attention to the hidden costs of fast fashion. Influencers in the sustainable fashion niche, such as Venetia La Manna and Aditi Mayer, shared content that highlighted the environmental and ethical issues tied to garment production. Using the hashtag #WhoMadeMyClothes, they encouraged followers to ask brands about their supply chains. The campaign gained international traction, pressuring major retailers to adopt more sustainable and ethical practices (Moni Omotoso, 2023).

3.4 The Role of Online Communities and Digital Activism

In the digital age, online communities and digital activism have become pivotal tools for spreading environmental messages, mobilizing support, and driving collective action. The convergence of social media, grassroots movements, and online platforms has empowered individuals and organizations to raise awareness, influence public opinion, and advocate for sustainable practices at an unprecedented scale. These digital platforms serve as critical spaces for discussions on environmental issues, providing opportunities for people worldwide to engage, educate, and take meaningful action (Belotti et al., 2022).

3.4.1 The Power of Online Communities in Environmental Advocacy

Online communities provide a space for individuals with shared values and concerns about the environment to connect, collaborate, and organize. Social media platforms such as Facebook, Twitter, Instagram, and Reddit allow like-minded individuals to form groups and networks where they can discuss sustainability, share information, and support each other's efforts (Aiswarya et al., 2024). These communities often transcend geographic boundaries, making it possible for individuals in different parts of the world to engage in conversations about global environmental issues like climate change, deforestation, or plastic pollution. For example, Facebook groups dedicated to eco-friendly living, zero waste, or sustainable food practices create a space for members to exchange tips, experiences, and resources. Likewise, Reddit's r/environment is a hub for discussions about environmental policies, climate science, and conservation efforts, providing a platform for educational content and debate. These online spaces are valuable for fostering a sense of belonging and solidarity among people who might otherwise feel isolated in their environmental concerns, empowering them to act collectively (Chandrasekara, 2022).

3.4.2 Digital Activism: Mobilizing for Change

Digital activism, often characterized by the use of social media to promote causes, raise awareness, and mobilize support, has proven to be an effective strategy in driving environmental action (Jacqmarcq, 2021). Campaigns that leverage hashtags, viral videos, and online petitions can quickly reach millions of people and ignite widespread participation in environmental movements. One of the most notable examples of digital activism is the FridaysForFuture movement, initiated by Swedish climate activist Greta Thunberg (The Conversation, 2020). Thunberg's school strike for climate, which she began posting on Twitter, quickly gained global traction, with millions of young people participating in climate strikes around the world. This movement, fueled by digital activism, has become one of the largest youth-led environmental movements in history. Social media activism also facilitates the rapid organization of protests and events. For instance, platforms like Twitter and Instagram have been used to organize and publicize climate protests, while petitions on platforms like Change.org enable people to advocate for policy changes and rally support for environmental issues. By using these digital tools, activists can create campaigns that resonate with a broad audience, share calls to action, and mobilize individuals to engage in both online and offline activism (The Conversation, 2020).

3.4.3 The Role of Hashtags and Viral Campaigns

Hashtags are a particularly powerful tool in digital activism, enabling individuals and groups to unify their efforts and amplify their messages. Campaigns like #ClimateStrike, #FridaysForFuture, #SaveTheAmazon, and #BeatPlasticPollution have been used to raise awareness about critical environmental issues, rallying people to take action, attend events, or support causes. These hashtags allow users to find and connect with relevant content, participate in larger conversations, and share their support with a global audience. Viral digital campaigns have also had a significant impact on environmental issues. For example, the #OceanCleanup campaign, which promotes efforts to remove plastic from the ocean, gained momentum on platforms like Instagram, where influencers, celebrities, and environmental organizations shared content related to ocean conservation. These viral campaigns can create a sense of urgency and collective responsibility, encouraging individuals to make sustainable choices and demand change from policymakers and businesses.

4 GAMIFICATION FOR SUSTAINABILITY

Gamification is the use of game-like elements, such as rewards, challenges, and competition, in non-game contexts to engage and motivate people to achieve specific goals (Cao et al., 2022). While originally applied in marketing, education, and business settings, gamification has increasingly found its place in sustainability initiatives. The integration of game mechanics, like points, leaderboards, and badges, into environmental programs or sustainability campaigns can enhance user participation, foster positive behaviors, and sustain engagement over time (Iyengar & Venkatesh, 2024). By making sustainability activities more interactive and rewarding, gamification can transform the way individuals and organizations approach environmental challenges (Shahzad et al., 2023).

At its core, gamification is about applying the principles that make games engaging to real-world activities, encouraging individuals to participate actively and repeatedly. Key game mechanics include goal-setting, feedback loops, and rewards (Douglas & Brauer, 2021). These elements tap into intrinsic and extrinsic motivations, driving individuals to take actions they might not otherwise pursue. In sustainability, these motivations can be used to inspire people to make eco-friendly choices, track their environmental impact, and join collective efforts to address climate change, resource depletion, and pollution (Fernández Galeote et al., 2021). For example, people may be encouraged to reduce their carbon footprints by earning points for taking public transportation, recycling, or reducing energy consumption. These points could lead to tangible rewards, such as discounts on sustainable products or donations to environmental causes. The competitive aspect, in which individuals compare their progress with others on a leaderboard, creates a sense of achievement and social influence, motivating further participation (Ouariachi et al., 2020).

In sustainability, gamification offers a powerful tool for engaging individuals in environmentally conscious behaviors and large-scale climate action campaigns. Various sustainability-related initiatives have successfully employed gamified strategies to encourage resource conservation, waste reduction, and environmentally friendly practices (Cao et al., 2022). For instance, gamification is applied to waste management programs where participants earn rewards for recycling or composting. Applications like Ecosia, a search engine that plants trees with every search, gamify the act of online browsing by directly linking user activity to environmental impact, providing users with feedback on how their searches contribute to tree planting efforts. Similarly, some cities have adopted gamified approaches to promote recycling and energy conservation. Platforms such as Recyclebank reward users for recycling by allowing them to accumulate points that can be redeemed for discounts and donations (Recyclebank, 2024). By providing real-time feedback and allowing users to track their progress, these programs foster a sense of accomplishment and encourage sustained engagement in sustainable practices.

One of the key benefits of gamification in sustainability is its potential to drive behavioral change. People are more likely to engage in sustainable behaviors consistently when they receive immediate feedback and rewards, which is a fundamental aspect of gamification. Research has shown that incorporating game-like elements into environmental programs helps reinforce positive behaviors, making them habitual over time (Ouariachi et al., 2020). By rewarding users for taking actions like reducing water usage or carpooling, gamification provides tangible reinforcement that encourages continued sustainable practices. Moreover, the social aspects of gamification can encourage collective action (Mabalay, 2025). Leaderboards, social sharing features, and community-based challenges foster a sense of belonging, creating a collective movement around sustainability goals (Mabalay, 2025). For instance, apps like JouleBug turn sustainability into a competitive activity, where users can join groups, challenge friends, and share their progress toward reducing energy consumption or adopting sustainable practices. By leveraging peer influence and competition, these apps make sustainability both fun and motivating.

Several organizations and platforms have effectively implemented gamification to promote sustainability. Carbon Footprint Challenge, an online platform that allows users to track and reduce their carbon footprints, uses gamified elements such as badges and achievements to encourage users to take daily actions to cut emissions (UW Departments, 2024). The app provides feedback on how specific actions (like biking instead of driving) reduce a user's carbon footprint, and users can compete with friends or other community members to achieve lower carbon emissions. Another example is Tree Nation, a platform that encourages individuals and companies to plant trees in a gamified manner. Users earn points for planting trees and are encouraged to share their progress on social media to gain more support for environmental initiatives. Tree Nation not only engages users through a game-like interface but also links these activities to real-world environmental benefits, helping to raise awareness about reforestation efforts.

4.1 Key Game Mechanics Used to Promote Eco-Friendly Behavior

Gamification leverages specific game mechanics to drive engagement and influence behavior. When applied to sustainability, these mechanics, such as rewards, leaderboards, and challenges, can effectively motivate individuals to adopt eco-friendly practices (Mabalay, 2025). These game elements tap into human psychology, particularly by utilizing extrinsic and intrinsic motivations, to encourage consistent, environmentally responsible actions. Below are some of the most commonly used game mechanics in sustainability-focused gamification and how they promote eco-friendly behavior.

4.1.1 Rewards in Gamification

Rewards are one of the most fundamental mechanics in gamification and can be particularly powerful in promoting sustainable behaviors (Yu et al., 2024). These rewards can be either intrinsic (internal satisfaction) or extrinsic (external incentives). In sustainability applications, rewards often take the form of points, badges, or tangible benefits that users earn for taking eco-friendly actions, such as recycling, reducing energy consumption, or using public transportation. For example, apps like Recyclebank reward users with points for engaging in sustainable behaviors, such as recycling or completing eco-friendly challenges (Recyclebank, 2024). These points can be redeemed for discounts, coupons, or charitable donations, giving users tangible incentives for their environmental actions. Rewards not only encourage participation but also reinforce positive behaviors over time, making eco-friendly actions more habitual. Additionally, rewards systems can be personalized to suit users' interests, increasing their motivation to participate in sustainability initiatives.

4.1.2 Leaderboards

Leaderboards tap into the human desire for social comparison and competition. By displaying a ranking of participants based on their sustainable actions, leaderboards can motivate individuals to take more eco-friendly steps to outperform others or achieve higher positions (FasterCapital, 2024). This mechanic leverages peer pressure and social influence, which can be powerful drivers of behavior change. For instance, platforms like JouleBug use leaderboards to rank users on their sustainability efforts, such as reducing energy consumption or waste. This friendly competition motivates participants to be more mindful of their eco-friendly actions, as they see how their efforts compare to those of friends or other users (FasterCapital, 2024). Leaderboards also foster a sense of community, encouraging individuals to collaborate and share tips on achieving better environmental outcomes. However, leaderboards must be used in ways that promote positive competition, without discouraging those who are still learning or adapting to sustainable habits.

4.1.3 Progress Tracking and Feedback Loops

Progress tracking and feedback loops are integral to the motivation process in gamification. By providing users with regular updates on their progress, gamification systems can keep individuals engaged and help them see the direct impact of their actions (Team Experts, 2023). For example, eco-apps might track the amount of carbon dioxide reduced or the number of plastic bottles saved through recycling. This data is presented in real-time or at regular intervals, reinforcing the connection between users' behavior and their environmental impact. Platforms like Carbon Footprint Challenge allow users to monitor their carbon emissions reduction over time, providing them with a visual representation of their achievements (UW Departments, 2024). Feedback loops help reinforce positive behavior by showing users that their efforts matter and contributing to a sense of accomplishment. These visual representations also create a sense of competition, as users try to improve their scores and surpass previous benchmarks.

4.1.4 Badges and Achievements

Badges and achievements are symbols of accomplishment that help users track their progress and provide recognition for eco-friendly actions (Shahzad et al., 2023). These rewards can be used to gamify tasks, motivating individuals to complete specific sustainability goals or milestones. Badges are often used as symbols of achievement that can be displayed on user profiles or shared on social media, adding an element of recognition and pride. For example, Ecosia, a search engine that plants trees with each search, rewards users with badges for reaching milestones such as planting a certain number of trees. These achievements create a sense of pride and encourage users to continue their eco-friendly behaviors, knowing that they are contributing to tangible environmental goals. Badges also foster a sense of community, as users often compare their achievements with others, encouraging friendly competition and collaboration.

4.1.5 The Complementary Relationship Between Social Influence and Gamification

When combined, digital social influence and gamification create a powerful synergy that magnifies the effects of both mechanisms. Digital social influence provides the initial push for awareness and behavior change by leveraging the persuasive power of social media and influencers. Once individuals are exposed to eco-friendly behaviors, gamification sustains their engagement by offering rewards and recognition for continued participation. By embedding sustainability into users' daily lives in an enjoyable and rewarding way, gamification ensures that these behaviors become habits rather than one-time actions. For instance, sustainability campaigns often integrate both strategies. Influencers may promote challenges or sustainability goals, encouraging their followers to participate. These campaigns are then gamified with points, badges, or leaderboards, which sustain engagement and create a sense of achievement. A clear example is the #FridaysForFuture movement (The Conversation, 2020), where digital influencers help amplify the call to action for climate strikes, while gamified platforms provide rewards for users who take steps to reduce their carbon footprint. Social media's ability to share content instantly and at scale complements gamification's ability to track progress and offer feedback. When users share their achievements (such as earning points or completing sustainability challenges) on platforms like Instagram or TikTok, they inspire others to join in, creating a cycle of positive reinforcement. This public acknowledgment, coupled with the social validation it generates, motivates others to participate and encourages friendly competition. In this way, the combination of digital social influence and gamification not only sparks awareness but also drives sustained, action-oriented engagement.

4.2 Case Studies

A notable example of the complementary use of digital social influence and gamification in sustainability is the Eco-Challenge app, which combines both elements by allowing users to take part in challenges related to reducing their environmental impact, tracking their progress, and earning rewards. The platform encourages users to share their achievements on social media, leveraging social influence to spread the word and motivate others to join in. This integration of social sharing and gamified feedback loops has made the app highly effective in engaging people in eco-friendly actions. Another example is Benevolent, an online platform where users can make donations or take actions to support environmental causes. It incorporates gamification by rewarding users with badges for supporting specific environmental projects. Influencers and environmental advocates help amplify the platform's impact by encouraging their followers to participate and share their experiences, combining social influence with gamified participation.

5 DIGITAL SOCIAL INFLUENCE AND GAMIFICATION IMPACT ON GREEN CONSUMPTION BEHAVIOR

Digital influence and gamification play a crucial role in driving eco-conscious consumer choices by harnessing the power of social networks and interactive reward systems. Digital influence, particularly through social media platforms, allows environmental activists, influencers, and brands to raise awareness about sustainability and green products (Farooq et al., 2023). Influencers and thought leaders often share content about eco-friendly lifestyles, promoting sustainable practices such as reducing waste, supporting ethical fashion, or purchasing green products. The credibility and relatability of these digital influencers help shape consumer attitudes and behaviors, encouraging followers to make more environmentally conscious decisions (Alboqami, 2023; Castillo-Abdul et al., 2024). Social proof, where individuals are motivated by seeing others' sustainable choices, further amplifies this effect, as people are more likely to adopt behaviors that are endorsed by trusted figures within their communities (Bhukya & Paul, 2023).

Gamification complements digital influence by motivating consumers to engage in sustainable behaviors through rewards, challenges, and progress tracking (Zafar et al., 2024). By incorporating game mechanics such as points, badges, and leaderboards into eco-friendly activities, gamification creates an enjoyable and competitive experience that encourages individuals to make green choices (Yu et al., 2024). For example, apps like Recyclebank reward users with points for recycling or using energy-efficient appliances, which can be exchanged for discounts on sustainable products. These rewards not only incentivize immediate eco-friendly actions but also help users track their long-term environmental impact, fostering a sense of accomplishment. The combination of gamification and digital influence effectively drives sustainable consumer behavior by both educating and motivating individuals, ultimately leading to more widespread adoption of eco-conscious purchasing decisions (FasterCapital, 2024).

6 CONTRIBUTIONS TO SUSTAINABLE DEVELOPMENT GOALS

6.1 How Environmental Awareness Drives SDGS

Environmental awareness plays a crucial role in driving the achievement of the United Nations Sustainable Development Goals (SDGs) (United Nations, 2024), particularly those related to environmental sustainability, climate action, and responsible consumption. SDGs such as Goal 13 (Climate Action), Goal 14 (Life Below Water), and Goal 15 (Life on Land) directly address the environmental challenges the world faces, and increased environmental awareness helps to catalyze action toward these goals (Smaniotto et al., 2020). As individuals and organizations become more aware of the environmental crises facing the planet, such as climate change, biodiversity loss, and pollution, there is greater public demand for sustainable practices and policies (Hamoudi & Avilés-Palacios, 2023). This awareness leads to behavioral changes, such as reducing waste, adopting clean energy solutions, and supporting eco-friendly products and companies. As people recognize the link between their consumption patterns and the planet's health, they are more likely to adopt practices that align with the principles of the SDGs (Smaniotto et al., 2020). For example, heightened awareness about the environmental impacts of plastic has resulted in stronger consumer support for bans on single-use plastics, contributing directly to the realization of SDG 14 (Life Below Water) by reducing ocean pollution (United Nations, 2024).

Moreover, environmental awareness is instrumental in encouraging policymakers and businesses to prioritize sustainability in their strategies, contributing to SDGs at a systemic level. Governments, influenced by growing environmental awareness among their citizens, are more likely to implement policies that address climate change and promote sustainable resource management (Krasodomska et al., 2023). Similarly, businesses that are aware of the environmental concerns raised by their customers are increasingly adopting green practices, such as sustainable sourcing, waste reduction, and carbon neutrality, which align with SDG 12 (Responsible Consumption and Production) (Smaniotto et al., 2020).

Companies in industries like fashion, food, and energy are adopting circular economy principles and reducing their environmental footprints in response to both regulatory pressures and consumer demand for sustainability (e.g., Fibre2Fashion, 2024; Levi Strauss & Co, 2022). Thus, environmental awareness not only drives individual action but also fuels systemic changes that are necessary to achieve the SDGs. By raising awareness about the interconnectedness of environmental health, economic stability, and social equity, it becomes clear that achieving the SDGs is not only a moral imperative but also a practical pathway toward securing a more sustainable future for all (United Nations, 2024).

6.2 How Digital Social Influence and Gamification Drive SDGs

Digital social influence and gamification are emerging as powerful tools in driving progress toward the United Nations Sustainable Development Goals (SDGs). By leveraging the persuasive power of social media and interactive, game-like elements, these digital strategies are reshaping the way individuals, communities, and organizations engage with the SDGs, particularly those focused on sustainability, climate action, and responsible consumption (Dionisio et al., 2023). Together, these tools foster collective action, raise awareness, and incentivize eco-friendly behaviors that are essential for achieving global sustainability targets.

6.2.1 Digital Social Influence and SDGs

Digital social influence plays a pivotal role in advancing the SDGs by shaping public awareness, behavior, and attitudes towards sustainability. Social media platforms, such as Instagram, TikTok, and YouTube, have become key spaces for sharing environmental messages, promoting green initiatives, and fostering discussions around the SDGs (Sparviero & Ragnedda, 2021). Influencers and thought leaders use their platforms to spread awareness about issues like climate change (Goal 13), sustainable cities (Goal 11), and biodiversity protection (Goal 15), while also encouraging their followers to take action (Clark et al., 2022). By creating relatable, shareable content, these influencers can significantly shift public perception and behavior, leading to widespread changes in consumer practices and support for sustainable policies. For instance, the rise of "eco-influencers" has contributed to the popularity of sustainable fashion, zero-waste lifestyles, and plant-based diets, directly impacting SDG 12 (Responsible Consumption and Production) (Dionisio et al., 2023). Social media campaigns like #FridaysForFuture (The Conversation, 2020), which encourages youth climate strikes, also mobilize millions to take action for climate change, exemplifying how digital social influence can engage and empower individuals to work toward the SDGs on a global scale.

6.2.2 Gamification and SDGs

Gamification, the use of game-like mechanics to encourage engagement and behavior change, also plays a significant role in advancing the SDGs by making sustainability efforts fun, interactive, and rewarding (Yu et al., 2024). By incorporating elements such as rewards, leaderboards, challenges, and progress tracking, gamification encourages individuals to take positive actions that contribute to SDG targets (Ligorio et al., 2023). For example, mobile apps and platforms like JouleBug or Recyclebank reward users for engaging in eco-friendly actions like reducing energy consumption, recycling, or supporting green businesses. These incentives not only drive immediate participation but also foster long-term commitment to sustainability by offering continuous feedback and rewards. Moreover, gamification often incorporates collaborative challenges, where users join forces to meet shared sustainability goals, strengthening social bonds and collective action (Goal 17 – Partnerships for the Goals) (Mevoli et al., 2024). By creating an environment of competition and cooperation, gamification helps users stay motivated, track their progress, and become more deeply engaged with the SDGs, leading to measurable improvements in areas like responsible consumption (Goal 12) and climate action (Goal 13) (Dionisio et al., 2023).

6.2.3 Complementary Impact

The combination of digital social influence and gamification has a synergistic effect on driving progress toward the SDGs. Digital influencers can introduce sustainability challenges or promote eco-friendly behaviors, while gamified platforms can provide a structured and rewarding experience for users to adopt and sustain these behaviors. For example, a campaign to promote tree planting might involve influencers sharing their tree-planting experiences on social media, encouraging their followers to join in. Participants could then track their contributions through a gamified platform, earning rewards for each tree planted and for engaging with others on social media. This synergy not only increases individual participation but also amplifies the reach and effectiveness of sustainability campaigns. The viral nature of social media combined with the engaging elements of gamification creates a dynamic system that not only raises awareness but also drives measurable, positive actions toward achieving the SDGs.

7 CONCLUSION

Digital social influence and gamification have emerged as critical tools in fostering environmental awareness and driving sustainable behavior. As the world faces pressing challenges such as climate change, biodiversity loss, and unsustainable consumption, these strategies provide innovative ways to engage individuals and communities in the collective effort to achieve the United Nations Sustainable Development Goals (SDGs). By leveraging the persuasive power of social media, influencers, and game mechanics, both digital social influence and gamification offer scalable and interactive solutions to raise awareness, inspire action, and reinforce sustainable habits. When used in tandem, they create a synergy that not only amplifies the reach and impact of sustainability initiatives but also motivates individuals to take sustained, measurable actions toward a more sustainable future.

7.1 Recap of Key Findings

Digital Social Influence: Social media platforms and influencers play a significant role in shaping consumer attitudes and behaviors toward sustainability. By using relatable, engaging content, influencers promote eco-friendly practices and products, raising awareness about issues such as climate change, sustainable consumption, and ethical production. The power of social proof, where individuals are influenced by the actions of those they trust, is critical in spreading environmental messages and creating a ripple effect of sustainable behaviors.

Gamification: Gamification applies game-like elements such as rewards, challenges, and leaderboards to encourage and sustain engagement in sustainability initiatives. By offering rewards for eco-friendly actions (e.g., recycling, reducing energy consumption), gamified platforms motivate individuals to participate in sustainability efforts and track their progress. The competitive and collaborative aspects of gamification further enhance engagement by fostering social connections and collective action around shared environmental goals.

Complementary Relationship: Digital social influence and gamification complement each other by creating a dynamic and integrated approach to sustainability. Influencers raise awareness and mobilize individuals to take action, while gamification ensures that those actions are rewarded and tracked, leading to long-term engagement. This combination of influence and incentive helps overcome barriers such as lack of awareness, perceived high costs, and disengagement, facilitating the widespread adoption of sustainable behaviors.

Impact on the SDGs: Both digital influence and gamification contribute to advancing key SDGs, including climate action (SDG 13), responsible consumption (SDG 12), and sustainable communities (SDG 11). These strategies help promote sustainable lifestyles, encourage policy changes, and create more sustainable consumption patterns, ultimately moving the world closer to achieving the SDGs.

7.2 Practical Applications

Corporate Sustainability: Businesses can implement gamified systems to reward sustainable consumer behaviors and partner with influencers to promote eco-friendly initiatives.

Policy and Public Engagement: Governments can use digital influence and gamification to engage citizens in national sustainability efforts, incentivizing actions like energy conservation and waste reduction.
Activism: Digital influence and gamification can empower local and global activism by connecting communities and amplifying environmental campaigns.

7.3 Future Research Directions

Integration with Emerging Technologies: Research could explore how AI, augmented reality (AR), and blockchain can enhance digital influence and gamification in sustainability, creating more personalized and transparent sustainability solutions.
Cross-Sector Collaboration: Future studies should investigate partnerships between governments, businesses, and NGOs to create cohesive sustainability campaigns that amplify the reach and impact of digital strategies.
Long-Term Behavior Change: Research is needed to understand how gamification and digital influence can drive lasting behavior change, focusing on habit formation and the psychological factors behind sustained eco-friendly actions.

REFERENCES

Abdo, M. S., Ahmed, S. A., Awad, B. K., & Elsharnouby, M. H. (2023). Fostering green purchasing behavior: The moderated mediation role of customer disidentification. *Management & Sustainability: An Arab Review, 2*(2), 155–176. DOI: 10.1108/MSAR-10-2022-0046

Aiswarya, U. B., Harindranath, R. M., & Challapalli, P. (2024). Social Media Information Sharing: Is It a Catalyst for Green Consumption among Gen X and Gen Y Cohorts? *Sustainability (Basel), 16*(14), 6011. DOI: 10.3390/su16146011

Alboqami, H. (2023). Trust me, I'm an influencer! - Causal recipes for customer trust in artificial intelligence influencers in the retail industry. *Journal of Retailing and Consumer Services, 72*, 103242. DOI: 10.1016/j.jretconser.2022.103242

Ali, B., Fatima, M., & Ahmed, Q. M. (2023). Examining the Theory of Planned Behaviour in Green Purchasing Behaviour – A Case of Millennial's Consumption of Organic Food. *Foundation University Journal of Business & Economics, 8*(1). Advance online publication. DOI: 10.33897/fujbe.v8i1.707

Apaolaza, V., Policarpo, M. C., Hartmann, P., Paredes, M. R., & D'Souza, C. (2023). Sustainable clothing: Why conspicuous consumption and greenwashing matter. *Business Strategy and the Environment, 32*(6), 3766–3782. DOI: 10.1002/bse.3335

Ben Schoon. (2019, December 24). *YouTubers successfully plant 20 million trees in less than 2 months w/ #TeamTrees*. https://9to5google.com/2019/12/24/youtube-teamtree-success-20-million/

Bhukya, R., & Paul, J. (2023). Social influence research in consumer behavior: What we learned and what we need to learn? – A hybrid systematic literature review. *Journal of Business Research, 162*, 113870. DOI: 10.1016/j.jbusres.2023.113870

Boerman, S. C., Meijers, M. H. C., & Zwart, W. (2022). The Importance of Influencer-Message Congruence When Employing *Greenfluencers* to Promote Pro-Environmental Behavior. *Environmental Communication, 16*(7), 920–941. DOI: 10.1080/17524032.2022.2115525

Borah, P. S., Dogbe, C. S. K., & Marwa, N. (2024). Generation Z's green purchase behavior: Do green consumer knowledge, consumer social responsibility, green advertising, and green consumer trust matter for sustainable development? *Business Strategy and the Environment, 33*(5), 4530–4546. DOI: 10.1002/bse.3714

Butar Butar, S., Ambarita, N., & Haniva, R. (2024). Green awareness and green product: A direction for sustainable consumption. *Applied Environmental Science, 1*(2). Advance online publication. DOI: 10.61511/aes.v1i2.2024.342

Caldevilla-Domínguez, D., Barrientos-Báez, A., & Padilla-Castillo, G. (2021). *COVID-19 as a Trigger for Sustainable Tourism and Eco-Influencers on Twitter.* DOI: 10.20944/preprints202101.0636.v1

Cao, Y., Kou, F., Hu, H., & Wan, G. (2022). How gamified cooperation and competition motivate low-carbon actions: An investigation of gamification in a popular online payment platform in China. *Journal of Environmental Management, 324*, 116259. DOI: 10.1016/j.jenvman.2022.116259 PMID: 36174473

Capital One Shopping Research. (2025, March 1). *Eco-Conscious Consumer Statistics.* https://capitaloneshopping.com/research/eco-conscious-consumer-statistics/

Castillo-Abdul, B., Romero-Rodríguez, L. M., & Fernández-Rodríguez, C. (2024). Lifestyle Eco-Influencers Advertising: Is Engagement Driven by Content or Fandom? *Comunicação e Sociedade, 45*, e024014. DOI: 10.17231/comsoc.45(2024).5629

Chaihanchanchai, P., & Anantachart, S. (2023). Encouraging green product purchase: Green value and environmental knowledge as moderators of attitude and behavior relationship. *Business Strategy and the Environment, 32*(1), 289–303. DOI: 10.1002/bse.3130

Chandrasekara, D. T. (2022). *Digital Social Influence: Reframing Social Influence for Online Social Networks.* 6648356 Bytes. DOI: 10.26180/19319933.V1

Chen, B., & Madni, G. R. (2023). Achievement of sustainable environment through effectiveness of social media in Z generation of China. *PLoS One, 18*(11), e0292403. DOI: 10.1371/journal.pone.0292403 PMID: 37967117

Chen, C., Li, Z., Yang, S., & Cao, D. (2024). Driving eco-friendly product purchases through social media: How does peer influence work? *Journal of Consumer Behaviour*, cb.2400. DOI: 10.1002/cb.2400

Clark, S., MacLachlan, M., Marshall, K., Morahan, N., Carroll, C., Hand, K., Boyle, N., & O'Sullivan, K. (2022). Including Digital Connection in the United Nations Sustainable Development Goals: A Systems Thinking Approach for Achieving the SDGs. *Sustainability (Basel), 14*(3), 1883. DOI: 10.3390/su14031883

Departments, U. W. (2024). *International Student Carbon Footprint Challenge.* https://depts.washington.edu/i2sea/iscfc/index.php

Dionisio, M., De Souza, S. J.Junior, Paula, F., & Pellanda, P. C. (2023). The role of digital social innovations to address SDGs: A systematic review. *Environment, Development and Sustainability*, *26*(3), 5709–5734. DOI: 10.1007/s10668-023-03038-x PMID: 36855437

Douglas, B. D., & Brauer, M. (2021). Gamification to prevent climate change: A review of games and apps for sustainability. *Current Opinion in Psychology*, *42*, 89–94. DOI: 10.1016/j.copsyc.2021.04.008 PMID: 34052619

Dudarenok, A. (2023). *The top social commerce trends in China that brands can learn from* [Https://www.campaignasia.com/article/the-top-social-commerce-trends-in-china-that-brands-can-learn-from/491480].

Essiz, O., & Mandrik, C. (2021). Intergenerational influence on sustainable consumer attitudes and behaviors: Roles of family communication and peer influence in environmental consumer socialization. *Psychology and Marketing*. Advance online publication. DOI: 10.1002/mar.21540

Farooq, H., Bilal Majid, M. B. M., & Ahmed, H. (2023). Impact of Green Packaging, Perceived Consumer Effectiveness, and Social Influence on Green Consumption Behavior: The Mediating Role of Green Satisfaction and the Moderating Role of Environmental Awareness. *Global Management Sciences Review*, *VIII*(I), 54–69. DOI: 10.31703/gmsr.2023(VIII-I).04

FasterCapital. (2024, June 3). *Leaderboards: Climbing the Ranks: How Leaderboards Drive Brand Loyalty in Gamification Marketing*. https://fastercapital.com/content/Leaderboards--Climbing-the-Ranks--How-Leaderboards-Drive-Brand-Loyalty-in-Gamification-Marketing.html

Fernández Galeote, D., Rajanen, M., Rajanen, D., Legaki, N.-Z., Langley, D. J., & Hamari, J. (2021). Gamification for climate change engagement: Review of corpus and future agenda. *Environmental Research Letters*, *16*(6), 063004. DOI: 10.1088/1748-9326/abec05

Fibre2Fashion. (2024). *Italian firm Gucci achieves 78% reduction in greenhouse gas emissions*. https://www.fibre2fashion.com/news/apparel-news/italian-firm-gucci-achieves-78-reduction-in-greenhouse-gas-emissions-296755-newsdetails.htm#:~:text=Luxury%20fashion%20brand%20Gucci%20has%20achieved%20a%2078,scopes%201%2C%202%2C%20and%203%20compared%20to%202021

Forever Against Animal Testing. (2019). *We Want to Ban the Cruel Practice of Animal Testing in Cosmetics. Forever.*https://www.thebodyshop.com.sa/east/en/forever-against-animal-testing

García-Salirrosas, E. E., Escobar-Farfán, M., Gómez-Bayona, L., Moreno-López, G., Valencia-Arias, A., & Gallardo-Canales, R. (2024). Influence of environmental awareness on the willingness to pay for green products: An analysis under the application of the theory of planned behavior in the Peruvian market. *Frontiers in Psychology, 14*, 1282383. DOI: 10.3389/fpsyg.2023.1282383 PMID: 38282852

Global Forest Watch. (2024). *Global*. https://www.globalforestwatch.org/dashboards/global/

Haba, H. F., Bredillet, C., & Dastane, O. (2023). Green consumer research: Trends and way forward based on bibliometric analysis. *Cleaner and Responsible Consumption, 8*, 100089. DOI: 10.1016/j.clrc.2022.100089

Hamoudi, H., & Avilés-Palacios, C. (2023). Product Sustainability and Consumer Environmental Awareness in Differentiated Markets. *International Advances in Economic Research, 29*(4), 277–291. DOI: 10.1007/s11294-023-09881-y

Horani, O. M., Al-Adwan, A. S., Yaseen, H., Hmoud, H., Al-Rahmi, W. M., & Alkhalifah, A. (2023). The critical determinants impacting artificial intelligence adoption at the organizational level. *Information Development, 02666669231166889*, 02666669231166889. Advance online publication. DOI: 10.1177/02666669231166889

Influencer Marketing New. (2024, June 14). *Sustainability in Influencer Marketing: Promoting Eco-Friendly Brands.* https://www.influencermarketingnews.co.uk/sustainability-in-influencer-marketing-promoting-eco-friendly-brands/#:~:text=Influencer%20marketing%20offers%20a%20powerful%20platform%20for%20promoting,authentic%20storytelling%2C%20brands%20can%20inspire%20positive%20environmental%20change

Iyengar, M. S., & Venkatesh, R. (2024). A Brief communication on Virtual Reality (VR) in Hospitality Industry & Global Travel and Tourism. *Gamification and Augmented Reality, 2*, 40. DOI: 10.56294/gr202440

Jaciow, M., Rudawska, E., Sagan, A., Tkaczyk, J., & Wolny, R. (2022). The Influence of Environmental Awareness on Responsible Energy Consumption—The Case of Households in Poland. *Energies, 15*(15), 5339. DOI: 10.3390/en15155339

Judijanto, L., Suarniki, N. N., & Muhtadi, M. A. (2024). Green Marketing and Consumer Environmental Awareness: A Bibliometric Review of Social Education and Campaigns. *West Science Social and Humanities Studies, 2*(06), 948–959. DOI: 10.58812/wsshs.v2i06.972

Krasodomska, J., Zieniuk, P., & Kostrzewska, J. (2023). Reporting on Sustainable Development Goals in the European Union: What drives companies' decisions? *Competitiveness Review*, *33*(1), 120–146. DOI: 10.1108/CR-12-2021-0179

Levi Strauss & Co. (2022). *Levi Strauss & Co. 2022 Sustainability Goals & Progress Update*. https://www.levistrauss.com/sustainability/report/

Li, Y., & Shan, B. (2025). Exploring the role of health consciousness and environmental awareness in purchase intentions for green-packaged organic foods: An extended TPB model. *Frontiers in Nutrition*, *12*, 1528016. DOI: 10.3389/fnut.2025.1528016 PMID: 40110167

Ligorio, L., Venturelli, A., Rosato, P., & Campo, R. (2023). Fostering sustainable development goals through gamification. *Journal of Management & Organization*, •••, 1–22. DOI: 10.1017/jmo.2023.54

Mabalay, A. A. (2025). Gamification for sustainability: A systematic review of applications, trends, and opportunities. *Computers in Human Behavior*, *165*, 108529. DOI: 10.1016/j.chb.2024.108529

Mahmoud, M. A., Tsetse, E. K. K., Tulasi, E. E., & Muddey, D. K. (2022). Green Packaging, Environmental Awareness, Willingness to Pay and Consumers' Purchase Decisions. *Sustainability (Basel)*, *14*(23), 16091. DOI: 10.3390/su142316091

Manoj Krishnan, C., & Arun, G. (2025). A study on environmental prosocial attitudes to green consumption values, openness to green communication, and its relationship with buying behavior. *Cogent Business & Management*, *12*(1), 2443050. DOI: 10.1080/23311975.2024.2443050

Mevoli, A., Leggett, K. L., & Davies, W. E. (2024). The Gamification of Circular Practices Using the SDGs. In Scholz, S. G., Howlett, R. J., & Setchi, R. (Eds.), *Sustainable Design and Manufacturing 2023* (Vol. 377, pp. 115–124). Springer Nature Singapore., DOI: 10.1007/978-981-99-8159-5_10

Mohd Suki, N., & Mohd Suki, N. (2019). Examination of peer influence as a moderator and predictor in explaining green purchase behaviour in a developing country. *Journal of Cleaner Production*, *228*, 833–844. DOI: 10.1016/j.jclepro.2019.04.218

Moni Omotoso. (2023). *"Who Made My Clothes" Movement – How it All Began*. https://fashioninsiders.co/features/inspiration/who-made-my-clothes-movement/

Ouariachi, T., Li, C.-Y., & Elving, W. J. L. (2020). Gamification Approaches for Education and Engagement on Pro-Environmental Behaviors: Searching for Best Practices. *Sustainability (Basel)*, *12*(11), 4565. DOI: 10.3390/su12114565

Recyclebank. (2024). *Pick up points for recycling and learning online.* https://recyclebank.com/

Ritchie, H. (2021). *Deforestation and Forest Loss.* https://ourworldindata.org/deforestation

Ritchie, H., & Roser, M. (2020). *CO_2 emissions, How much CO_2 does the world emit? Which countries emit the most?*https://ourworldindata.org/co2-emissions

Shahzad, M. F., Xu, S., Rehman, O. U., & Javed, I. (2023). Impact of gamification on green consumption behavior integrating technological awareness, motivation, enjoyment and virtual CSR. *Scientific Reports, 13*(1), 21751. DOI: 10.1038/s41598-023-48835-6 PMID: 38066018

Smaniotto, C., Battistella, C., Brunelli, L., Ruscio, E., Agodi, A., Auxilia, F., Baccolini, V., Gelatti, U., Odone, A., Prato, R., Tardivo, S., Voglino, G., Valent, F., Brusaferro, S., Balzarini, F., Barchitta, M., Carli, A., Castelli, F., Coppola, C., & Sisi, S. (2020). Sustainable Development Goals and 2030 Agenda: Awareness, Knowledge and Attitudes in Nine Italian Universities, 2019. *International Journal of Environmental Research and Public Health, 17*(23), 8968. DOI: 10.3390/ijerph17238968 PMID: 33276530

Solina, A. M., & Ocampo, L. V. G. (2024). Driving Sustainable Change: Behavior and Environmental Awareness in the Case of the Philippines. In Prof. M. Turkmen (Ed.), *Research Advances in Environment, Geography and Earth Science Vol. 5* (pp. 23–31). B P International. DOI: 10.9734/bpi/raeges/v5/633

Statista. (2025). *Annual carbon dioxide (CO_2) emissions worldwide from 1940 to 2024 (in billion metric tons).*

Team Experts. (2023). *Gamification: Feedback Loops Vs. Flow (Breaking it Down).* https://predictivethought.com/gamification-feedback-loops-vs-flow-breaking-it-down/

The Conversation. (2020). *Fridays for Future: How the young climate movement has grown since Greta Thunberg's lone protest.* https://theconversation.com/fridays-for-future-how-the-young-climate-movement-has-grown-since-greta-thunbergs-lone-protest-144781

United Nations. (2024). *Sustainable Development Goals (SDGs).* https://unosd.un.org/content/sustainable-development-goals-sdgs

Xie, C., Wang, R., & Gong, X. (2022). The influence of environmental cognition on green consumption behavior. *Frontiers in Psychology, 13*, 988585. DOI: 10.3389/fpsyg.2022.988585 PMID: 36237699

Yu, J., Hu, J. J., Liu, G. G., Jiang, W., & Walters, G. (2024). Not just a game: Understanding eco-gamification in sustainable destination development. *Journal of Hospitality and Tourism Management, 60*, 10–21. DOI: 10.1016/j.jhtm.2024.06.005

Zafar, A. U., Shahzad, M., Shahzad, K., Appolloni, A., & Elgammal, I. (2024). Gamification and sustainable development: Role of gamified learning in sustainable purchasing. *Technological Forecasting and Social Change, 198*, 122968. DOI: 10.1016/j.techfore.2023.122968

Zameer, H., & Yasmeen, H. (2022). Green innovation and environmental awareness driven green purchase intentions. *Marketing Intelligence & Planning, 40*(5), 624–638. DOI: 10.1108/MIP-12-2021-0457

Zhao, S., Teng, L., & Ji, J. (2024). Impact of environmental regulations on eco-innovation: The moderating role of top managers' environmental awareness and commitment. *Journal of Environmental Planning and Management, 67*(10), 2229–2256. DOI: 10.1080/09640568.2023.2184331

Chapter 4
Marketing in the Digital Age: Navigating Transformation, Consumer Behavior, and Big Data

Ambreen Jabeen Shah
https://orcid.org/0000-0003-3195-3501
The University of Lahore, Pakistan

ABSTRACT

With the advent of the internet, it has become easier for businesses to deliver their products to distant regions. However, this convenience has also significantly increased competition. Now, consumers have access to the entire market in the palm of their hands through mobile phones. With just a few clicks, they can compare businesses and their competitors, evaluating who offers better quality at a lower price. Traditional advertising, where you simply highlight your product's features in an ad, is no longer effective. People no longer have the time or interest to watch conventional 1-2 minute advertisements. The rise of big data has revolutionized sales and marketing. Now, data is being generated every second, and the ability to analyze this data to identify consumer preference patterns has become the cornerstone of strategic marketing.

1 INTRODUCTION

It is now the era when the world has embraced digitalization. We are more exposed to the internet; we share more information online and we often get information from the internet. We have turned our lives into online activities such as socializing and shopping. In this context, the digitalization of the business is an inevitable process.

DOI: 10.4018/979-8-3693-9831-9.ch004

To pursue online business successfully, we need to understand the digital marketing environment, understand consumer behavior, and learn from digital marketing companies. We also need to measure the growth of our digital economy. This is the first step in the digital transformation of a business. The current digital ecosystem offers businesses great opportunities to engage with customers, but it also creates problems such as data privacy, data overload, and constant demand for updates.

Consumers now know more and are heavily influenced by peer review and social media. Their journey through the purchasing experience is not linear and involves many multiple across various channels. Understanding consumer requirements and decision characteristics is crucial to creating effective digital marketing strategies that will resonate with a target audience of the business. Many digital marketing enterprises such as Google, Amazon, and Meta now specialize in collecting and analyzing large amounts of customer data to predict trends, personalize products, and optimize advertising. By examining their practices, businesses can better understand how to use digital marketing techniques. This includes measuring the integration of digital tools, using data effectively, and linking the marketing strategy to overall business goals. Implementing this measure is the first step to implementing digital transformation.

2 QUANTIFYING THE DIGITAL CONSUMER REVOLUTION

There is also a "revolutionary panic" in the traditional economy. Businesses that do not undergo digital transformation will face decline. The wave of digital marketing is sweeping society. Digitalization has entered every corner of daily life like molecules. This is an important factor that is unescapable for businesses in today's economy (Vaz, 2021). The time it takes for the customer to decide, for the business to adapt to the competitive environment, and for the customer to receive a response, was previously measured in days or hours but is now measured in minutes and seconds. "Competitive advantage" has now become a game that is either won or lost in minutes. If the company cannot respond to the customer's needs immediately, the customer will lose interest, and the company will fail in the competition. The "instant connection" of the mobile phone to the internet has led to the "integration of people and machines". Social media and television account for most business interactions with today's consumers. According to a report "New Multi-Screen World", a report published by Google, new digital media accounts for 90% of all media interactions. People spend an average of 4.4 hours outside of work looking at a screen. This change means that most consumer devices are now integrated into the digital environment.

2.1 Rise of the Internet Movement

Combine this with your business ideas. With the rise of the Internet movement, many chief information officers (CIOs) aim to drive digital transformation by leveraging new technologies (Nabieva, 2021). These changes are often associated with the transition from information technologies (IT) to digital technologies (DT), changes in business models, or changes in organizations. Among these processes, the adoption of digital marketing strategies stands out and has become a valuable and practical tool for creating value in the business environment. As Drucker points out, marketing and innovation are the main drivers of business results. This change is causing companies to experience a revolution, forcing them to adapt to the rapid changes in customers. Today consumers live in a digital ecosystem that affects every stage of their purchasing and decision-making processes (Jaworski & Cheung, 2023). These consumers include young people who grew up with digital devices, as well as adults who are exposed to digital media.

Changing consumption patterns include many important behaviors. For instance, 90% of consumers shop online, using multiple screens including PCs, tablets, and smartphones to make purchases. Around 65% of consumers shop online, which has led to the success of platforms like Alibaba and Amazon.com. Around 61% of people use social media on their mobile devices and use tools like WeChat and WhatsApp to foster relationships. And 59% of people manage their finances via their smartphones, as evidenced by the success of Ali Pay, which has made Tianhong Asset Management a major player in the industry. Search engines play a major role in personal wealth management, with 58% of users relying on search engines to make decisions (French et al., 2021).

Digital technologies have become as important as water and electricity to today's economy. Ignoring this technology can cause businesses to lose touch with customers and leave them vulnerable in the future. The current digital era is characterized by rapid progress in information exchange, customer interaction, and data storage, and always leads to major changes in the business world.

The current digital trends are addressing three important aspects:

- Digitalization of information exchange,
- Digitalization of customer interaction, and
- Digitalization of information storage.

3 QUANTIFYING DIGITAL LIFESTYLES: 4.4 HOURS AND COUNTING

Entrepreneurs too are aware of the importance of this change because businesses are always in danger of extinction if they do not implement a digital strategy. The societal wave of digital marketing also reflects this change. While consumers embrace the digital age and rapidly move towards the "Internet+" framework as the way of doing business in the future, the will of those who still resist these changes has been abandoned. In addition, social innovations such as "crowdfunding", "crowdsourcing", "crowd innovation", and "crowd promotion" is resulting in contemporary business models (Gasparin et al., 2021). Traditional business models are changing in terms of collaborative thinking and the integration of organizations. If we analyze consumers' digital interactions in their daily lives we will come to know that on average a normal person spends at least 4.4 hours of the day interacting with these devices (Reeves et al., 2021). This shows the enormous impact of the digital world on daily life. Companies such as Nike have recognized this change and said, everything is digital now. Businesses do not see digitalization as a single concept; they integrate it into their marketing strategies, creating a comprehensive, data-driven approach. Today's Chief Information Officers (CIO) aim to shift from the traditional information technology (IT) framework to the digital technology (DT) ecosystem. While some focus on radically changing their business model or design, the best and most effective way is a gradual and controlled shift by implementing digitalization into core business strategies. These strategies provide immediate benefits and enable new business opportunities along with business profitability (Kunisch et al., 2022).

Changes in consumer behavior have led companies to adapt through the evolution of the supply chain. Digital technology has become an integral part of consumer decision-making, affecting all stages of the purchasing process. The new generation of digital natives (born in the 1990s and 2000s) and older consumers who use digital media represent a major shift in consumption patterns. Nearly 90% of consumers shop online, seamlessly navigating multiple screens and platforms. This behavior has led to the success of companies like Alibaba and JD.com, which have influenced the growth of e-commerce with their initial public offerings (IPOs) a testament to the growth of e-commerce businesses. Ignoring these advances leads to customer dissatisfaction and hinders future growth.

4 DATA-DRIVEN RETAIL: BRIDGING ONLINE AND OFFLINE EXPERIENCES

The digital era keeps presenting new technologies, reshaping data exchange, customer engagement, and data storage. This movement calls for digital integration that supports innovation. With the use of sophisticated data filtering and distribution techniques, businesses can spot trends, tailor strategies, and provide tailored experiences that connect with their audience (Attah et al., 2023). The power to predict customer needs is transforming the digital landscape and raising the stakes of prime online platforms.

The website, which is often considered the digital identity of a brand, plays a key role in this transformation. As the central hub of a company's online presence, it acts as a magnet to attract visitors coming through search engines or other digital channels. These sites are not static news pages, but dynamic platforms designed to attract new customers, deliver promotional messages, and provide unparalleled customer service. It is both a showcase of your brand image and an operational tool for commercial marketing, offering users communication from search to conversion. Historically viewed as a secondary industry, e-commerce is now a key driver of business development, redefining the old model. The success of international giants such as Alibaba Group has exposed the revolutionizing potential of e-commerce, which offers customers unmatched convenience in finding, comparing, and buying goods and services (Zreik, 2025). Companies cannot afford to overlook becoming social, connected, and competitive on every channel. Customers now expect their e-commerce sites to be connected to social media, mobile messaging, and even physical stores to have an integrated whole, omnichannel experience.

4.1 Adoption of Smartphones

The mass adoption of smartphones and tablets has transformed shopping behavior as customers alternate between devices to compare prices, read reviews, and make purchases. As of 2015, the mobile market had surpassed the desktop market, illustrating a change in consumer behavior that continues to grow across all age segments. Mobile shopping technology is evolving to a degree greater than that of mere convenience. It even gives physical goods an improvement since mobile devices are employed to immediately compare them while buying items in retail shops. Companies that are vision-oriented are catching on to the phenomenon by making available mobile payment, as well as near-field communication (NFC) capabilities, to improve how customers make payments. Volumes of cash have been committed towards digitizing ventures(Aris et al., 2022). They reflect the increased use of digital tools as part of everyday activities and closing the gap between offline and online business. Through these innovations, companies are not just satisfying customers but are also developing new benchmarks in the way companies operate. The intersection of technology, e-commerce, and big data is building a dynamic environment in which every touch point is a chance to know, interact with, and surprise customers (Malarvizhi et al., 2022).

Its influence keeps expanding as businesses seek to design more improved, more personalized experiences that win customers' trust and satisfaction. One significant area where big data is having a big influence is in the expansion of mobile payments; platforms such as Apple Pay are spearheading the revolution in resetting the way consumers shop both online and offline. This technology leverages big data to optimize business, enhance security, and enhance customer insight into their stores. Physical store retailers can utilize transaction data to gain more insights into the preferences, buying habits, and busiest times of customers. This data enables retailers to maximize the customer in-store experience, offer purchase recommendations, and targeted advertising, and streamline the management of the products accordingly. For instance, the differences between high-volume products can be identified by retailers and stocked all the time so that customers are not frustrated, and sales are maximized. The combination of in-store data and e-commerce analytics gives a distinctive Omni channel experience, through which the customer gets the best from both worlds. They may shop online, get customized suggestions for the items they search for, and then proceed to a physical store to finalize their purchase after enjoying an awesome experience. Integrating online and offline stores not only raises convenience levels but also ensures closer relationships between consumers and brands.

Giants such as Apple Pay have revolutionized how consumers shop by providing unheard-of convenience and security. Convenience and security are two significant strengths of mobile payments. Customers can process payments instantly via their mobile and store their banking data safely on the cloud, so they do not need to take security measures at a physical level or risk meddling with credit card data. Technologies like QR codes, barcodes, and NFC (Near Field Communication) are central to this process so that transactions become simple to do by bringing mobile phones close to the point of sale. Platforms like Alipay and WeChat in China have embraced these solutions, competing strongly with Western counterparts like Apple Pay, which has made a big difference in mobile commerce and contactless money transfers.

4.2 Significance of Big Data Analytics

Big data analytics is critical to the success of mobile payments. By analyzing business data, businesses can understand customer behavior, preferences, and spending patterns. This information can be used to create personalized marketing campaigns, recommend products, and offer promotional campaigns that increase customer loyalty and boost sales. For example, mobile payment platforms often integrate loyalty programs, allowing businesses to instantly reward customers based on their purchase history. Advanced algorithms and machine learning models analyze large amounts of transaction data to identify unusual patterns or anomalies that could indicate fraud. This not only keeps customers happy but also increases their trust in mobile payments.

The combination of big data and mobile payments also enables analytics, allowing companies to predict future trends. Retailers can use this information to improve product offerings, improve product quality, and increase customer satisfaction. For example, a salesperson can analyze historical sales data to predict which products will be in high demand during a particular season, ensuring that enough inventory is stored to meet customer needs. Businesses that use the power of big data to improve their mobile payment strategies will be able to better meet changing customer needs, drive innovation, and stay ahead of the competition. By using this technology, companies can not only improve their business operations but also lead to a more connected, global business (Patra et al., 2022).

By integrating big data into a marketing platform, companies can create ads and promotions that engage with consumers based on their location and interests, with special discounts created just for them. This is done with advanced tools like geo-fencing and social targeting, which allow businesses to define virtual spaces and deliver relevant content to customers. Platforms like Geofeedia in the US are demonstrating the potential of this tool by tracking social media posts in specific locations. These features allow businesses to better understand consumer behavior, allowing them to improve their strategies and drive deeper engagement. Customers are no longer alone on the journey; they are part of an integrated, data-driven ecosystem where every interaction is personal and meaningful. This seamless integration is essential in today's competitive landscape, where customer needs are higher than ever. Businesses that adopt this approach, supported by big data analytics capabilities, are better positioned to thrive in an environment where individuality and efficiency matter.

5 The confluence of big data analytics and mobile payment ecosystems: driving personalization and business value

As technology continues to evolve, SoLoMo (Social, Local, Mobile) business will be at the center of attention. According to Google, 94% of users rely on mobile searches to find a physical store address, highlighting the importance of a strong digital presence in driving traffic to the store. Engines and social media platforms are important, and the rise of retail marketing apps is redefining customer engagement. These apps have become powerful tools for businesses to connect with their audiences and deliver personalized experiences and interactions. For example, WeChat started as a messaging platform and has now evolved into a multi-faceted network that includes communication, payments, e-commerce, and more. This performance alone has made it a 360-degree solution for users, replacing many standalone apps. Before investing in building their apps, companies should carefully consider whether dedicated or multi-purpose apps are better for their goals and customer needs. While platforms like WeChat specialize in providing an all-in-one experience, specialty retailers can offer more comprehensive and effective solutions. By customizing the app experience to users' unique needs, businesses can ensure customers have quick and easy access to the work and information they need (Heinemann, 2023).

Ultimately, integrating mobile technology into the retail experience isn't just about convenience; it's about making meaningful connections with customers. Whether through multiple platforms or retail plans, businesses that use mobile technology will be able to better meet evolving customer needs and further participate in the digital economy. By integrating marketing directly into apps, businesses can better engage customers and create better experiences that encourage engagement. These platforms allow businesses to leverage the power of big data to improve customer experience. From user preferences to behavioral patterns, a wealth of data generated by mobile apps can be analyzed to provide personalized advertising, tailor product recommendations, and improve customer service. This data-driven approach makes every interaction relevant, and meaningful, increasing customer loyalty and brand loyalty.

Big data refers to data that is too large or difficult to process with traditional data processing software. This data often includes trivial information such as social media posts, clickstream data, and customer feedback, all of which are valuable to marketers. But the real challenge lies in extracting insights from vast amounts of data. As former Google CEO Eric Schmidt stated the growth of information is exponential; information that once took thousands of years to create is now created in just days. The sheer size of data creates a dual challenge for businesses and marketers: First managing big data and then effectively interpreting it to drive decisions. The difference is deceptive. Using advanced analytics tools and machine learning algorithms, companies can transform raw data into useful insights that inform business strategies, improve product user experiences, and ultimately drive growth.

6 The data-driven transformation of consumer decision-making

In today's consumer behavior landscape, understanding how consumers make decisions has become increasingly important. Traditional sales were once the cornerstone of a business's marketing strategy, but they're not as effective as it once was. This shift is largely due to the proliferation of digital touchpoints that now impact on every level of customer experience. Consumers are more empowered than ever with valuable information and endless options at their fingertips. We are redefining how businesses engage with customers.

In 2007, David C. Edelman and Marc Singer introduced the Customer Decision Journey (CDJ) model, which redefined how marketers approach consumer behavior. Unlike the linear sales funnel, the CDJ model emphasizes a cyclical process, placing greater importance on the role of marketing throughout the entire decision-making journey rather than focusing solely on the point of sale. The model recognizes that consumers now engage in a repetitive process of decision-making, evaluation, and post-purchase behavior, often influenced by social media, online reviews, and personal recommendations (TSAI, 2023).

6.1 Use of Big Data Analytics by Business

Brands have played a significant role in decision-making by using big data and analytics to quickly understand consumer preferences and behaviors. Digital marketing tools like social media, AI-driven personalization, and Omnichannel strategies allow businesses to better engage with customers. By analyzing data from different contexts, including website visits, social media interactions, and purchase history, brands can create unique experiences that engage customers. Using predictive analytics such as forecasting to identify potential customers who are likely to make a purchase allows marketers to send timely messages. Additionally, tools like retargeting ads and email campaigns can shorten the time it takes for customers to decide by highlighting products. By developing a unique and personalized experience, companies can not only encourage first-time purchases but also build long-term loyalty, encouraging repeat purchases.

Figure 1. CDJ Model-Source: Product Management World

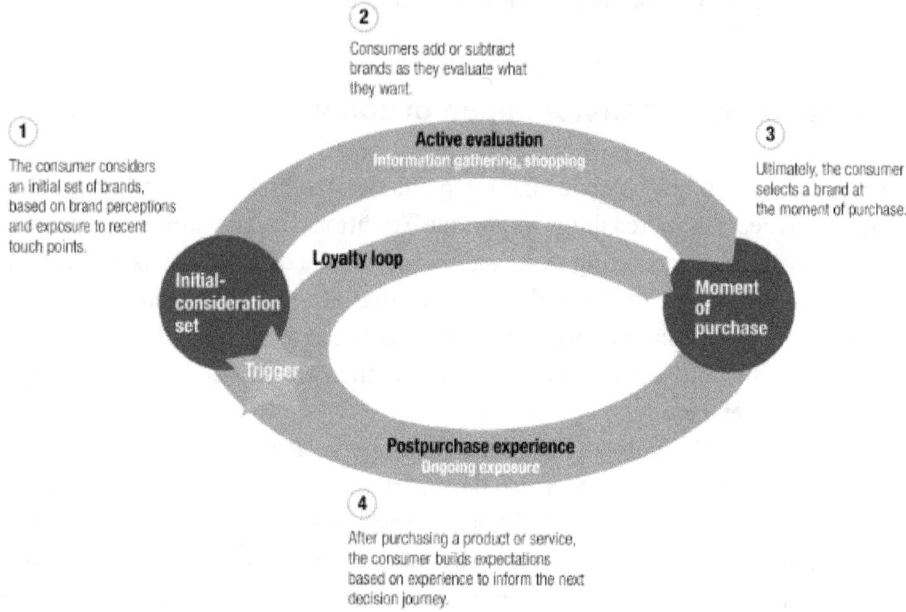

Metrics like customer lifetime value (CLV), conversion rate, and engagement provide insights that can inform future business trends. A data-driven approach maximizes Return on Investment (ROI) by ensuring business operations are efficient, effective, and highly customized marketing. To thrive in the changing digital ecosystem, companies need to master four key capabilities:

- automation,
- proactive customization,
- contextual interactions, and
- Innovation across the customer decision journey (CDJ).

By leveraging the power of big data, companies can optimize these areas to increase customer loyalty and drive long-term growth.

7 DATA AS THE NEW OIL: HOW BIG DATA IS FUELING THE 21ST CENTURY ECONOMY

Just as oil transformed the global economy, big data has now become a major resource that transforms not only business but also government and business management. The ability to collect, analyze, and use large amounts of data opens up new ways to increase efficiency, improve decision-making, and provide more personalized services to the public. Currently, companies are using big data to optimize their marketing strategies, allowing them to accurately target customers, customize products, and forecast sales accurately. Big data business has led to the emergence of new business models and opportunities, especially in areas such as retail, finance, healthcare, and government, where data-driven visualization is now the foundation of business. As the world continues to produce more and more information, its role as a transformative force in business and society is expected to grow, changing the way organizations and governments interact with customers and the public (Van Veldhoven & Vanthienen, 2022). As more data continues to flow in, the need to make marketing strategies more accurate, automated, and responsive to customer needs has become crucial. Using technologies such as algorithms, artificial intelligence (AI), and machine learning, companies can improve decision-making, predict patterns, and personalize experiences in an unprecedented way.

To effectively manage this data transition, organizations are now combining specialized roles such as the chief technology officer Chief Marketing Technology Officer (CMTO), and Chief Marketing Data Officer (CMDO). These roles are critical to overseeing the integration of technology and data into business strategy to improve business operations and ensure that data usage is optimal for business growth. As a result, technology and information have become the foundation of today's business practices, enabling businesses to stay ahead of the competition. This shift reflects the growing trend for marketing to be less about creativity and messaging, and more about using it as an asset to inform all aspects of the customer experience that results in big data marketing.

Big data is undeniably the disruptive force to reshape how companies operate and compete in the modern marketplace. It has transformed data collection, sorting, and analysis from routine tasks into some of the most critical competitive advantages for businesses across industries. While digital marketing and big data marketing are interconnected, the difference between the two is important. While both are based on technology, big data focuses specifically on using data technology to improve the accuracy and efficiency of business operations. Big data marketing uses data analysis, predictive modeling, and real-time insights to enable businesses to create personalized marketing plans for specific customers, thereby increasing targeting, efficiency, and overall ROI(Theodorakopoulos & Theodoropoulou, 2024). Digital marketing, in turn, encompasses a variety of tools and techniques, including big data, social media marketing, content marketing, and mobile marketing. Digital marketing provides all the methods, processes, and strategies that businesses use to navigate and adapt to the digital environment. It is part of a broader strategy that includes a variety of strategies, including big data marketing, to attract customers and support business growth in the digital age. In this context, big data has become a valuable resource that provides useful information and insights, while digital marketing focuses on the use of these resources, using data to support business decisions.

8 THE INSIGHTS ECONOMY: TURNING BIG DATA INTO BUSINESS VALUE

Data collection, analysis, and analytics are transforming a routine task into a key competitive advantage for businesses in the industry. With the ability to collect and analyze large amounts of data, companies can now discover valuable insights that drive innovation, improve customer experience, and increase operational efficiency. The true value of a business lies not in its products or services, but in how well it uses data to make informed decisions, predict trends, and deliver personalized experiences. As big data and systems continue to mature, companies now have access to more information than ever before from a variety of sources, including social media, customer engagement, IoT devices, and more.

If managed and analyzed correctly, this wealth of data allows organizations to better understand customer behavior, improve marketing strategies, and create new business models that were previously unthinkable. In a data-driven environment, the ability to extract insights from big data has become critical to the success and sustainability of digital marketing. This goes beyond market segmentation and allows companies to offer the right products and services at the right time and with the most efficient means. By analyzing big data, companies can identify and engage with smaller segments in the broader market that may be missed using traditional methods. With insights from big data, companies can improve customer experience and create personalized interactions that are relevant to individual preferences and behaviors. This personal transformation continues throughout the customer journey, from the first experience to the post-purchase interaction, ensuring that every interaction is important and useful. By using big data, companies can not only increase customer satisfaction but also encourage long-term loyalty, as customers are willing to adjust to meet their specific needs and desires. This level of personalization has become a key differentiator in the competitive marketplace (Farris et al., 2020).

Forecasting capabilities not only help deliver products efficiently and on time but also allow companies to reduce operational costs by focusing resources on high-impact projects. Therefore, businesses can improve their business, improve targeting, and ultimately increase return on investment (ROI). While big data enables businesses to make smarter decisions, digital marketing is changing the future of how companies interact with their customers by providing a holistic framework for applying data-driven insights to broader business strategies. Data Marketing is driving companies to unprecedented levels of efficiency, and what matters is the volume and amount of data available to businesses today. Approximately 75% of the information on the web is irrelevant, including images, videos, audio files, and social media content. This redundant information is combined with actual information designed to create a better view of customers, business trends, and operational performance.

From one perspective, big data represents the integration and analysis of incongruent data from different sources, each providing unique insights. This category includes physically stored files, documents, and digital images. Digitizing offline data allows companies to integrate historical data into current operations and business strategies. By analyzing search patterns, search queries, and mobile app usage, businesses can gain real insights into customer preferences and interests. For example, Internet of Things (IoT) devices provide valuable insights into consumer behavior, the environment, and product performance, enabling more informed decisions. (e.g., customer interactions on social media), and the physical environment (e.g., in-store behavior, foot traffic). By analyzing this data, companies can better understand how customers use products and services in the real world. This can provide useful insights for business analysis. This external data helps businesses evaluate the market, identify opportunities, and implement policies. This includes data from production lines, equipment performance, and automated processes that can be used to optimize operations and reduce downtime.

Integrating this information with external sources can provide a better understanding of a company's performance. This data includes purchase history, online reviews, and social media, which can allow businesses to create personalized marketing plans and improve customer experience. By analyzing supply chain data, companies can improve forecasting, reduce costs, and increase customer satisfaction. As described in the Gartner Innovation Curve, with the rapid growth and commercialization of big data, we are entering a new phase that represents the excitement and opportunity of the California Gold Rush or the Columbus discovery of new territory. Just as gold was driven by the search for valuable resources, the proliferation of information is the beginning of a digital gold rush where the volume of information is important, but the price depends on how companies use and exploit it.

9 THE DATA VALUE CHAIN: FROM COLLECTION TO MONETIZATION

As companies increasingly use big data to develop their business strategies, those who can effectively analyze this data and use advanced business intelligence (BI) tools will stand out in the market competition. The Chief Data Management Officer (CDMO) oversees the integration of information and marketing strategies to ensure that the information obtained is used to optimize the customer, improve the target, and drive economic growth (Karkera, 2023). The key stages, each of which plays a key role in transforming raw data into useful business insights, are:

Data Generation is the first stage where data is generated from a variety of sources, including customer interactions, online behavior, social media posts, IoT devices, and data exchange. The amount and type of information generated at this level has grown at an unprecedented rate, providing the industry with a wealth of research. social media), mobile applications, and business (CRM, ERP). Effective data collection is important because it lays the foundation for meaningful analysis by ensuring that the data collected is relevant, accurate, and timely.

Data analysis includes the use of advanced analytics, machine learning algorithms, and artificial intelligence to clean, organize, and analyze data. By turning data into insights, companies can discover patterns, patterns, and relationships to gain a deeper understanding of customers, businesses, and operational efficiency. This can result in improving decision-making, developing business strategies, personalizing experiences, and driving innovation. By monetizing data, businesses can generate new revenue, increase operational efficiency, and gain a competitive advantage. Good data business monetization not only increases profits but also enables businesses to quickly adapt to changing market trends and consumer preferences. By mastering all levels of big data, businesses can unlock the full potential of data and transform it into an asset that drives growth and success in the digital age. The role of CDMOs has become critical in ensuring that information is used effectively to inform business decisions and create personalized, relevant experiences for customers.

Gartner's original 3V model of Big Data identifies volume, velocity, and variety as key factors that companies must manage to leverage the power of Big Data. Volume refers to data creation, storage, and processing. As the number of digital elements continues to grow, from customer interactions to reading documents, information is being generated at an exponential rate. Managing and storing such vast amounts of data has become a challenge for organizations. Whether it is data from social media, e-commerce, or IoT devices, the flow of data needs to be analyzed quickly to make timely decisions. Structured data can include digital information stored in files, while unstructured data can include text, images, audio, and video. The ability to combine and analyze multiple types of data from multiple sources is a critical capability for businesses. In the vastness of the ocean of information, not all information is reliable, and ensuring the quality of information is vital (Chahal et al., 2022).

Bad data can lead to misunderstandings and ultimately affect business results. The truth is about the need for identification, purification, and consistency of products before they can be used effectively. While collecting large amounts of data is important, the real value lies in how businesses can obtain the data they need to make decisions, innovate, and re-enhancing their competitive advantage. Velocity indicates the speed at which data is being created and processed. Variety indicated Different materials and types from different sources. Value shows the ability to conclude the data, this is the most important.

10 REAL-TIME DATA PROCESSING IN MODERN BUSINESS

In 1987, the total amount of data was estimated at 3 billion gigabytes (GB). By 2007, this figure had risen to skyrocket to 300 billion GB; 100 times more in just 20 years. Today, all information has reached an incredible scale and continues to grow rapidly. However, managing and storing this vast amount of data requires powerful systems, advanced analytical tools, and expertise. However, today we are faced with an increasing amount of semi-structured and unstructured data. When these different pieces of information are brought together, a broad perspective can be provided on consumers, business models, and market performance. The main data sources for these different data are Internet data which includes online data from social media platforms, e-commerce sites, search engines, blogs, etc. Community posts, customer reviews, survey questions, and online interactions provide real-time information about customers' thoughts, interests, and preferences. For example, e-commerce platforms generate data about purchases, cart abandonment rates, and customers. This information is important for optimization, improving customer relationships, and improving internal processes (Sohanda et al., 2024). It also includes data from customer contact lines, CRM systems, and feedback queries. This includes financial reports, census data, health statistics, environmental data, and regulatory data.

Governments around the world are increasingly making data public, allowing businesses to use it for business analytics, compliance, and strategic decision-making. Information, photos, audio, and geo-location data are provided to serve customers in a better way. Media publishers, entertainment platforms, and online content creators generate vast amounts of data that can be analyzed to understand customer preferences, content engagement, and review sentiment. Geo-location data can provide insight into customer movements, store visits, and geographic differences.

As network nodes such as media, e-commerce platforms, search engines, and social networks generate a lot of data every day, the amount of data continues to grow. The diversity of data types, from text and images to video, audio, and data sources, opens new possibilities for analysis and use across businesses. This is a significant advantage for businesses. By using different types of data, companies can better understand customer behavior, business trends, and market trends. This versatility allows businesses to create personalized marketing, develop products, improve customer service, and make more informed decisions. The real value of big data lies not only in the volume of data collected but also in the ability to aggregate and analyze diverse data to uncover deep understanding and drive innovation. The pace of business has increased significantly, and the way organizations do business has changed. Agility is all about processing large amounts of data instantly, allowing businesses to respond to new trends, consumer behaviors, and business changes instantly. This is the ability to process information instantly and transform decision-making, making it faster, more accurate, and more responsive (Aivalis et al., 2016).

Big data is reshaping how businesses operate, making decisions, and engaging with customers. Its ability to analyze vast quantities of diverse data in real time enables companies to enhance operational efficiency, improve customer experience, and optimize marketing strategies. Big data enables businesses to create dynamic, real-time customer profiles that reflect current preferences and predict future behaviors. This allows for more accurate demand predictions, better resource management, and more effective customer relationship management. The integration of big data into digital marketing enables businesses to deliver more personalized and effective marketing campaigns. By leveraging data from multiple sources, businesses can improve targeting, reduce costs, and drive sales with greater precision (Onesi-Ozigagun et al., 2024).

The intersection of big data and green communication has transformed modern marketing into a forceful driver. Big data for green communication is viewed as an outstanding opportunity to transform sustainability initiatives, reinforce customer loyalty, and gain strategic advantages in such a scenario as firms seek a balance between profitability and environmental responsibility (Waqas & Tan, 2023). Green communication, therefore, implies the dissemination of information and messages that highlight sustainability in the environment, eco-friendliness, and responsible consumption of resources. It is raising awareness, educating stakeholders, and actions promoting environmental conservation. For firms, green communication, therefore, transcends into being just a public relations strategy but lies at the very heart of CSR and brand positioning. It deals with the growing demand from consumers regarding transparency and accountability in sustainability practices. Big data plays an instrumental role in enabling effective green communication because it provides insights into consumer preferences, environmental impacts, and operational efficiencies.

Firms can utilize advanced analytics to track their carbon emissions, energy consumption, and waste generation (Adewole, 2022). Firms can identify inefficiencies through this data analysis and implement corrective measures to reduce their environmental footprint. Understanding consumer behavior through big data allows firms to tailor their green communication strategies. Personalized messages resonate more with consumers, fostering trust and encouraging sustainable purchasing decisions. Big data is the source for the collection and distribution of information on a firm's sustainability initiatives. The provision of real-time environmental performance updates creates credibility for a firm and tackles the concerns consumers have regarding greenwashing. Big data is the source for the collection and distribution of information on a firm's sustainability initiatives. The provision of real-time environmental performance updates creates credibility for a firm and tackles the concerns consumers have regarding greenwashing (Kaur & Srivastava, 2022).

Big data and green communication integration have several effects on marketing strategies. Big data can enable firms to brand themselves to meet sustainability objectives. The sentiment of consumers towards the product, along with market trends, will guide companies to make branding eco-friendly so that environmentally conscious customers find them appealing. Firms can boast of renewable energy use or sustainable packaging in their marketing campaigns. With big data analytics, firms can segment their audience based on environmental values and preferences. Segmentation ultimately allows the creation of targeted campaigns that focus on fulfilling specific consumer needs, like marketing products with minimal carbon footprint to environmental-conscious buyers (Zhou et al., 2024).

Green communication promotes more participation with the target consumers by ensuring that they play a role in sustainability programs. Big data includes social media analysis and sentiment, which enables big data tools for firms to learn about opportunities from customers to partake in recycling programs or carbon offsetting. By using big data, firms produce green products tailored to the wishes of the consumers through insights. Companies can innovate sustainable alternatives that fit their green communication goals by analyzing purchasing patterns and feedback. Big data allows firms to monitor public perception and respond to sustainability-related concerns in real-time. This proactive approach helps maintain a positive brand image and reinforces trust among stakeholders (Jha & Verma, 2023).

11 CASE STUDIES EXAMPLES: PATAGONIA, UNILEVER AND TESLA'S GREEN TRANSFORMATION

One of the quintessential examples that embodies big data, and green communication is the well-known outdoor clothing brand, Patagonia. By utilizing big data, Patagonia has precisely tracked and analyzed all the environmental footprint of its product life cycle right from raw materials sourcing, to manufacturing and eventually distribution. These data analyses would enable Patagonia to streamline waste, discover points for improvements, and therefore improve sustainability. What really makes Patagonia stand out is its transparency. The company discloses very detailed reports to consumers about the environmental impact of their products, hence instilling trust and accountability in their products. In these reports, the company has included metrics like carbon emissions, water usage, and percentage of recycled materials, thus allowing the customers to decide what they purchase based on the values they espouse. Patagonia's marketing campaigns continue to emphasize its green ethos through consistent environmental stewardship. For example, programs such as "Worn Wear," which promotes the repair and reuse of customers' gear rather than purchasing new items, demonstrate the brand's commitment to reducing consumption and promoting sustainable practices. Data alignment, transparency, and green messaging have strengthened Patagonia's brand identity and fostered a loyal customer base that prioritizes eco-consciousness and sustainability.

Unilever has been effectively using big data to assess and reduce its substantial supply chain footprint as it changes its marketing strategies to suit sustainability. The company uses huge volumes of data relating to resource utilization, carbon emissions, and waste to identify areas of improvement for efficiency, carbon footprints, and most sustainable products. This data-driven approach will not only inform operational strategies but also enable the creation of targeted, impactful marketing campaigns that resonate with eco-conscious consumers. Unilever uses consumer insights from big data to understand how preferences and behaviors are changing, particularly the growing demand for ethical and sustainable products. This information allows the company to develop personalized marketing messages and launch campaigns that emphasize its commitment to sustainability. For instance, data analytics inform the branding of products under initiatives such as the Sustainable Living Plan, highlighting attributes such as reduced plastic packaging, ethically sourced ingredients, and carbon-neutral production processes.

With the utilization of big data, Tesla has revolutionized the performance and appeal of its electric vehicles (EVs), with the vision of sustainable transportation. The company collects massive amounts of data from its vehicles, including real-time telemetry, driving patterns, and the performance of batteries. This vast data tends to enhance the functionality and efficiency of Tesla's EVs while informing continuous design, energy management, and autonomous driving technologies improvements. Tesla incorporates all these findings into its green communication strategies to portray the environmental and economic advantages of the adoption of EVs. Tesla educates consumers on the tangible benefits of making a switch to renewable energy-powered vehicles by using data-driven metrics such as reduction in carbon emissions, lower fuel costs, and increasing efficiency of its Supercharger network. These metrics are often shared through visually engaging campaigns, press releases, and interactive online tools emphasizing Tesla's role in combating climate change. But again, beyond mere product-oriented communications, Tesla's environmental communication goes further to advocate more for renewable sources of energy.

Campaigns like "Accelerating the World's Transition to Sustainable Energy" have underlined this company's pioneering role in green innovation, including its electric vehicle and energy product lines as indispensable to a green future. Again, Tesla does not shy away from using its megaphones to raise awareness and the potential of technology like solar energy and energy storage in reforming energy systems around the globe. The company has established itself as the first mover in the EV space while building a loyal, green-conscious customer base by big data analytics and persuasive green communication. This innovation in sustainability continues to propel Tesla forward as it continues to grow and gain influence in the clean energy space. Through social media, Unilever uses big data to track consumer sentiment and interact with audiences in real time, tailoring its messaging to address concerns over environmental issues.

Campaigns like Dove, which speaks to sustainability in addition to body positivity, or Ben & Jerry's, which speaks out for climate action, show how Unilever incorporates sustainability into its brand storytelling. These efforts have enhanced the brand reputation of Unilever and reinforced customer loyalty, fueling growth in a greener, eco-conscious market. Smarter rebranding through big data analytics and green communication integrates Unilever's sustainability objectives with its marketing strategy, through which big strategic muscle can be generated through the alignment of purpose and profitability.

Despite the huge potential, the integration of big data and green communication also presents several challenges. For example, collecting and analyzing consumer data for green communication raises privacy issues. Firms must navigate regulatory frameworks like GDPR and ensure ethical data practices to maintain consumer trust. Overstating or misrepresenting sustainability efforts can lead to accusations of greenwashing, damaging a firm's reputation. Big data can mitigate this risk by providing accurate and verifiable insights, but firms must prioritize transparency. Significant investment in technology, expertise, and infrastructure was needed for big data analytics for green communication. SMEs may lack these resources. The outcome of sustainability is complex because it has many variables and lots of stakeholders. Firms have to establish certain metrics and benchmarks that they can show the communication of environmental impact.

Several opportunities for firms are provided by the changing landscape of big data and green communication: Advanced technologies like AI and machine learning allow firms to analyze huge datasets and identify patterns that might have gone unnoticed otherwise. This allows for a greater level of information on which to base green communication strategies and fosters innovation in sustainability practices (Chen et al., 2024). Blockchain technology allows for enhanced transparency, with an immutable record of a firm's sustainability initiatives. This encourages consumer trust and aids in green communication. Firms can collaborate with stakeholders such as suppliers, consumers, and governments to come up with integrated sustainability solutions (Vazquez Melendez et al., 2024).

Big data makes this collaboration possible by offering a common platform for information sharing. The increase in IoT devices makes it possible to monitor environmental performance in real-time. The firms can use the data to prove their commitment to sustainability and engage consumers through interactive green communication campaigns (Saura & Saura, 2023). The big data-green communication link represents a paradigm shift in marketing strategies, enabling firms to align profitability with environmental responsibility. Companies can enhance transparency, personalize messaging, and drive sustainable innovation by leveraging big data. While challenges remain, the growth of technology and the increasing emphasis on sustainability offer immense potential for firms to thrive in an eco-conscious marketplace. Green communication will continue evolving and play an important role in shaping the marketing future and ushering in a sustainable global economy.

12 CONCLUSION

Standing at the threshold of a new marketing age, this chapter has shed light on how big data has irreversibly revolutionized the field from art to science. Gone are the days when marketing was restricted to creative instinct; contemporary marketing lives on algorithmic accuracy, real-time consumer data, and sustainability-focused approaches that appeal to today's ethically aware purchasers. The examples of Patagonia's extreme transparency, Tesla's data-fueled sustainability communications, and Amazon's hyper-personalization illustrate how leaders of the market use this shift to create unbeatable competitive strengths.

The collision of three formidable forces - pervasive connectivity, analytics-driven insight, and sustainability consciousness - has forged a perfect storm calling for marketer adaptation. Old-fashioned practices falter in the face of customer demands for immediacy, relevance, and honesty in brand interaction. Marketers who successfully brew the elixir of turning raw data into customer value will own their spaces, and late adopters threaten to become fossils in an emerging winner-takes-all digital marketplace. But with great power comes great responsibility. As we tap predictive algorithms and behavior tracking, we must face up to the ethical balancing act between personalization and privacy, between persuasive messaging and manipulation. The marketers who will succeed are those who see data not only as a top-line driver but as a stewardship-levering understanding to generate authentic win-win value exchanges between brand and consumer. The way to go is to become data translators, sustainability champions, and experienced designers.

Marketers must create companies in which IT and marketing work together as innovation partners, where each customer interaction produces useful insights, and where green messaging is the thread that runs through brand strategy. Competitive advantage will belong to those who can foresee needs before they're spoken, provide value before they're asked, and establish trust through radical transparency. As the physical and digital realms converge, one reality becomes clear: Data is the new marketing currency, but human relationships are its essence. The future marketers who will define our world are those who can tap the former without sacrificing the latter - building campaigns as quantifiable as they are powerful, as precise as they are genuine. This is the opportunity and challenge of digital marketing.

REFERENCES

Adewole, O. (2022). "Issues emanating from business impact on climate, environmental sustainability and CSR (Corporate Social Responsibility): steps towards pragmatism in extant realities":"Brand translation to equity from 'CSR as a potential tool in climate change mitigation and enhancing financial performances in organizations" Brand translation to equity. *International Journal of Corporate Social Responsibility*, *7*(1), 6. DOI: 10.1186/s40991-022-00073-1

Aivalis, C. J., Gatziolis, K., & Boucouvalas, A. C. (2016). Evolving analytics for e-commerce applications: Utilizing big data and social media extensions. *2016 International Conference on Telecommunications and Multimedia (TEMU)*

Aris, F., Ismail, K., & Mohezar, S. (2022). Fostering mobile payment adoption: A case of Near Field Communication (NFC). *International Journal of Business and Society*, *23*(3), 1535–1553.

Attah, R. U., Ogunsola, O., & Garba, B. (2023). Leadership in the digital age: Emerging trends in business strategy, innovation, and technology integration. *Iconic Research and Engineering Journals*, *6*(9), 389–411.

Chahal, A., Gulia, P., & Gill, N. S. (2022). Different analytical frameworks and bigdata model for internet of things. *Indonesian Journal of Electrical Engineering and Computer Science*, *25*(2), 1159–1166. DOI: 10.11591/ijeecs.v25.i2.pp1159-1166

Chen, C.-T., Chen, S.-C., Khan, A., Lim, M. K., & Tseng, M.-L. (2024). Big data analytics-artificial intelligence and supply chain ambidexterity impacts on corporate image and green communication. *Industrial Management & Data Systems*, *124*(10), 2899–2918. DOI: 10.1108/IMDS-01-2024-0045

Farris, P. W., Bendle, N., Pfeifer, P., & Reibstein, D. (2020). *Marketing Metrics*. Pearson Education. https://books.google.com.pk/books?id=CtrPEAAAQBAJ

French, D., McKillop, D., & Stewart, E. (2021). The effectiveness of smartphone apps in improving financial capability. In *Financial literacy and responsible finance in the fintech era* (pp. 6–22). Routledge. DOI: 10.4324/9781003169192-2

Gasparin, M., Green, W., Lilley, S., Quinn, M., Saren, M., & Schinckus, C. (2021). Business as unusual: A business model for social innovation. *Journal of Business Research*, *125*, 698–709. DOI: 10.1016/j.jbusres.2020.01.034

Heinemann, G. (2023). *The new online trade: Business models, business systems and benchmarks in e-commerce*. Springer Fachmedien Wiesbaden. https://books.google.com.pk/books?id=DOW2EAAAQBAJ

Jaworski, B., & Cheung, V. (2023). Drucker Management Philosophy and Ten Principles. In *Creating the Organization of the Future: Building on Drucker and Confucius Foundations* (pp. 101-122). Emerald Publishing Limited. DOI: 10.1108/978-1-83753-216-220231009

Jha, A. K., & Verma, N. K. (2023). Social media sustainability communication: An analysis of firm behaviour and stakeholder responses. *Information Systems Frontiers*, *25*(2), 723–742.

Karkera, A. (2023). *Role of the Chief Data Officer in Government*. University of Arkansas at Little Rock.

Kaur, G., & Srivastava, A. (2022). *Green Communication Technologies for Future Networks: An Energy-Efficient Perspective*. CRC Press. https://books.google.com.pk/books?id=3p8IEQAAQBAJ

Kunisch, S., Menz, M., & Langan, R. (2022). Chief digital officers: An exploratory analysis of their emergence, nature, and determinants. *Long Range Planning*, *55*(2), 101999. DOI: 10.1016/j.lrp.2020.101999

Nabieva, N. M. (2021). DIGITAL MARKETING: CURRENT TRENDS IN DEVELOPMENT. *Theoretical & Applied Science*, *94*(2), 333–340. DOI: 10.15863/TAS.2021.02.94.65

Onesi-Ozigagun, O., Ololade, Y. J., Eyo-Udo, N. L., & Oluwaseun, D. (2024). Data-driven decision making: Shaping the future of business efficiency and customer engagement. *International Journal of Multidisciplinary Research Updates*, *7*(2), 19–29. DOI: 10.53430/ijmru.2024.7.2.0031

Patra, G. K., Rajaram, S. K., Boddapati, V. N., Kuraku, C., & Gollangi, H. K. (2022). Advancing Digital Payment Systems: Combining AI, Big Data, and Biometric Authentication for Enhanced Security. *International Journal of Engineering and Computer Science, 11*(08), 10.18535.

Reeves, B., Ram, N., Robinson, T. N., Cummings, J. J., Giles, C. L., Pan, J., Chiatti, A., Cho, M., Roehrick, K., Yang, X., Gagneja, A., Brinberg, M., Muise, D., Lu, Y., Luo, M., Fitzgerald, A., & Yeykelis, L. (2021). Screenomics: A framework to capture and analyze personal life experiences and the ways that technology shapes them. *Human-Computer Interaction*, *36*(2), 150–201. DOI: 10.1080/07370024.2019.1578652 PMID: 33867652

Saura, J. R., & Saura, J. R. (2023). *Big Data Marketing Strategies for Superior Customer Experience*. IGI Global. https://books.google.com.pk/books?id=nph5zwEACAAJ

Sohanda, M. K., Gupta, M., & Kalpana, A. (2024). Interactive E-Commerce: Addressing Cart Abandonment through Gamified User Engagement. 2024 International Conference on Communication, Computing and Internet of Things (IC3IoT), Theodorakopoulos, L., & Theodoropoulou, A. (2024). Leveraging big data analytics for understanding consumer behavior in digital marketing: A systematic review. *Human Behavior and Emerging Technologies, 2024*(1), 3641502.

TSAI, C.-W. (2023). Impacts of information channels on consumer decision journey: Evidence from an experience durable goods industry.

Van Veldhoven, Z., & Vanthienen, J. (2022). Digital transformation as an interaction-driven perspective between business, society, and technology. *Electronic Markets, 32*(2), 629–644. DOI: 10.1007/s12525-021-00464-5 PMID: 35602117

Vaz, N. (2021). *Digital Business Transformation: How Established Companies Sustain Competitive Advantage From Now to Next.* Wiley. https://books.google.com.pk/books?id=NQkLEAAAQBAJ

Vazquez Melendez, E. I., Bergey, P., & Smith, B. (2024). Blockchain technology for supply chain provenance: Increasing supply chain efficiency and consumer trust. *Supply Chain Management, 29*(4), 706–730. DOI: 10.1108/SCM-08-2023-0383

Waqas, M., & Tan, L. (2023). Big data analytics capabilities for reinforcing green production and sustainable firm performance: The moderating role of corporate reputation and supply chain innovativeness. *Environmental Science and Pollution Research International, 30*(6), 14318–14336. DOI: 10.1007/s11356-022-23082-w PMID: 36152098

Zhou, C., Son, S.-B., Zhu, C., & Zhu, X. (2024). Research on the Application of Big Data Analysis in Green Marketing Strategies. 2024 3rd International Conference on Artificial Intelligence and Computer Information Technology (AICIT), Zreik, M. (2025). Digital Transformation and Organizational Relearning in China.

Chapter 5
Navigating Environmental Regulations in Digital Marketing:
Ensuring Compliance While Promoting Green Claims

Vishal Jain
https://orcid.org/0000-0003-1126-7424
Sharda University, India

Archan Mitra
https://orcid.org/0000-0002-1419-3558
Nitte University, India

ABSTRACT

This study explores the challenges and opportunities businesses face in aligning digital marketing practices with stringent environmental regulations while promoting sustainability and maintaining credibility. Through a mixed-methods approach, the research examines compliance variability across industries, the correlation between regulatory adherence and consumer trust, and the role of emerging technologies in addressing these challenges. Findings reveal that industries with higher investments in compliance achieve greater consumer trust, while resource constraints hinder smaller enterprises. The analysis highlights the need for standardized global guidelines, transparent communication strategies, and tailored support mechanisms for SMEs. Emerging technologies such as AI and blockchain are identified as enablers of transparency and regulatory adherence. The study concludes with actionable recommendations for policymakers and businesses to harmonize sustainability goals with marketing strategies, emphasizing collaboration, innovation, and consumer

DOI: 10.4018/979-8-3693-9831-9.ch005

engagement.

1. INTRODUCTION

The increasing urgency of environmental sustainability has led to significant transformations in corporate practices, with digital marketing playing a pivotal role in communicating green initiatives to consumers. As businesses shift toward sustainable branding, the accuracy and authenticity of environmental claims have become critical concerns. Digital platforms, including social media, search engines, and e-commerce websites, serve as powerful tools for promoting eco-friendly products and corporate sustainability efforts (Jones et al., 2022). However, misleading green claims, often categorized as greenwashing, have triggered regulatory scrutiny and consumer skepticism, necessitating greater compliance with environmental laws (Chen & Liu, 2023). This chapter examines the evolving landscape of green digital marketing, highlighting the intersection of regulatory requirements, corporate responsibility, and technological innovation in promoting sustainability.

1.1 The Rise of Green Marketing in the Digital Age

Green marketing, which refers to the promotion of products and services based on their environmental benefits, has evolved from a niche practice to a mainstream strategy (Smith & Brown, 2021). With increasing consumer awareness about climate change, resource depletion, and pollution, businesses recognize the strategic advantage of aligning with sustainability principles (Garcia & Lee, 2021). Studies show that 64% of global consumers consider a company's social and environmental responsibility when making purchasing decisions (Green & Parker, 2021).

Digital platforms have revolutionized green marketing strategies, allowing brands to communicate their sustainability commitments more effectively. Social media platforms such as Instagram, TikTok, and YouTube enable businesses to showcase eco-friendly practices, educate consumers, and foster eco-conscious communities (Wang & Li, 2020). For example, brands promoting carbon-neutral supply chains, renewable energy usage, and biodegradable packaging leverage these platforms to engage sustainability-conscious consumers (Jones et al., 2022). Additionally, AI-powered digital marketing tools now enable companies to analyze consumer sentiment and market trends, ensuring that green marketing efforts remain data-driven and impactful (Lopez & Carter, 2021).

However, the rapid expansion of green marketing has also given rise to misleading environmental claims. The practice of greenwashing, in which companies exaggerate or fabricate their sustainability efforts, has eroded trust and undermined legitimate sustainability initiatives (Chen et al., 2020). As a result, governments and regulatory bodies worldwide have introduced stricter green marketing regulations to ensure transparency and accountability (Mitra et al., 2021).

1.2 The Importance of Environmental Compliance in Marketing

Ensuring compliance with environmental regulations is essential for business credibility, legal protection, and consumer trust. Companies that engage in misleading green marketing face potential consequences, including financial penalties, lawsuits, reputational damage, and loss of customer loyalty (Morris et al., 2023). In the European Union, the proposed Green Claims Directive mandates that any sustainability claim in marketing communications must be supported by scientific evidence and verifiable data (European Commission, 2023). Similarly, in the United States, the Federal Trade Commission (FTC) Green Guides outline specific rules for using terms such as "eco-friendly," "biodegradable," and "carbon-neutral", requiring companies to provide clear and substantiated evidence (FTC, 2022).

For businesses operating in multiple jurisdictions, regulatory compliance presents additional complexities. Different countries enforce varying levels of environmental advertising oversight, requiring multinational corporations to tailor their green marketing strategies to align with regional laws (Singh et al., 2023). For instance, Australia's Competition and Consumer Commission (ACCC) enforces strict truth-in-advertising laws, while Japan and South Korea have adopted eco-labeling systems that mandate third-party verification before businesses can claim environmental benefits (Choi et al., 2021). This regulatory diversity underscores the importance of businesses adopting standardized sustainability reporting frameworks, such as Environmental, Social, and Governance (ESG) disclosures and Corporate Social Responsibility (CSR) initiatives (Patel & Singh, 2022).

Aside from legal obligations, environmental compliance enhances consumer confidence and brand reputation. Surveys indicate that 75% of consumers are more likely to trust brands that provide transparent information about their environmental impact (Taylor et al., 2023). In contrast, businesses found guilty of greenwashing experience severe consumer backlash, resulting in decreased sales and long-term reputational harm (Nguyen & Taylor, 2022). Thus, achieving genuine sustainability compliance is not only a legal necessity but also a competitive advantage in today's environmentally conscious market.

1.3 Overview of Key Environmental Regulations

The global regulatory landscape surrounding green digital marketing has expanded significantly in response to rising concerns over misleading sustainability claims. Some of the most notable regulations and guidelines governing green marketing compliance include:

- EU Green Claims Directive – Requires companies to provide scientific proof for any environmental claims and prohibits misleading eco-labeling (European Commission, 2023).
- FTC Green Guides (USA) – Provides guidelines for avoiding deceptive environmental marketing claims, specifying substantiation requirements for eco-friendly branding (FTC, 2022).
- ACCC Greenwashing Guidelines (Australia) – Ensures truthful representation of sustainability credentials, holding businesses accountable for misleading advertising (Johnson, 2023).
- ISO 14021 (International Standard) – Establishes criteria for self-declared environmental claims, requiring companies to avoid vague or misleading sustainability messaging (Barker, 2021).
- Eco-Labeling Laws (Asia) – Countries such as Japan and South Korea have adopted stringent eco-certification standards, ensuring that businesses provide verifiable proof of their sustainability efforts (Choi et al., 2021).

These regulations highlight the increasing accountability measures imposed on businesses engaging in green marketing. Companies must now integrate compliance-driven sustainability strategies, leveraging third-party certifications, verifiable impact metrics, and blockchain-based traceability solutions to align with evolving regulations (Santos et al., 2022).

Furthermore, digital platforms such as Google, Meta, and Amazon have introduced internal policies restricting green marketing claims that lack credible verification. For example, Google Ads requires advertisers making eco-friendly claims to meet strict certification requirements, ensuring that only verified sustainability claims are promoted (Smith, 2023). Similarly, social media platforms are tightening policies to flag misleading environmental claims, reducing the risk of consumer deception (Thomas & Brown, 2022).

As green marketing regulations continue to evolve, businesses must adopt proactive compliance strategies, integrating legal expertise, technological tools, and ethical marketing practices to align with global sustainability expectations. This chapter explores the challenges and opportunities within this dynamic landscape, providing actionable insights for businesses seeking to balance compliance with authentic green branding.

2. UNDERSTANDING ENVIRONMENTAL REGULATIONS IN DIGITAL MARKETING

As digital marketing continues to shape modern consumer engagement, the need for clear regulatory frameworks governing environmental claims has intensified. Businesses increasingly rely on digital platforms to communicate their sustainability efforts, but concerns over greenwashing—misleading or exaggerated environmental claims—have led to stricter regulations worldwide. Regulatory bodies have introduced guidelines and enforcement mechanisms to ensure that sustainability claims in marketing are transparent, accurate, and verifiable (Jones et al., 2022). As a result, businesses must navigate a complex compliance landscape that includes global environmental marketing regulations, industry-specific sustainability compliance standards, and corporate reporting frameworks such as Environmental, Social, and Governance (ESG) disclosures. This section explores these key aspects of green marketing compliance, examining how businesses can align their digital marketing strategies with evolving regulatory expectations.

2.1 Global Environmental Marketing Regulations

Governments and international regulatory bodies have established stringent guidelines to ensure that companies engaging in green digital marketing do not mislead consumers. In many jurisdictions, businesses must scientifically verify their sustainability claims and ensure that their marketing messages comply with legal transparency standards (Singh et al., 2023).

One of the most influential regulatory frameworks in environmental marketing is the Federal Trade Commission (FTC) Green Guides in the United States. Originally issued in 1992 and last updated in 2022, these guides provide specific directives for businesses on how to avoid deceptive environmental marketing practices. The FTC Green Guides emphasize that terms such as "recyclable," "biodegradable," and "carbon-neutral" must be supported by scientific proof and verifiable data (Barker, 2021). The Green Guides also require that environmental marketing claims be clear and specific, preventing businesses from making vague claims such as "eco-friendly" without substantiating them with measurable evidence. Non-compliance can lead to federal investigations, lawsuits, and significant financial penalties, making adherence to these guidelines essential for companies marketing products and services in the U.S.

In the European Union, the Green Claims Directive, proposed in 2023, represents one of the most comprehensive regulatory measures to combat false sustainability advertising. This directive mandates that all environmental claims made by businesses must be scientifically substantiated and that companies must provide third-party verification before using eco-labels or green branding (European Commission, 2023). Under this directive, generic claims such as "climate neutral" or "sustainable" require full lifecycle impact assessments to ensure credibility. The directive also prohibits misleading carbon offsetting claims, preventing companies from making broad sustainability statements without clear emissions-reduction proof (Morris et al., 2023). Businesses that fail to comply face heavy fines, reputational damage, and potential bans from the EU market, reinforcing the necessity of legal compliance in digital sustainability marketing.

Australia has also implemented strict consumer protection laws to curb greenwashing. The Australian Competition and Consumer Commission (ACCC) closely monitors businesses making sustainability claims, ensuring that their advertising aligns with truth-in-advertising laws. In 2023, an ACCC audit found that 57% of businesses engaged in misleading environmental claims (Johnson, 2023). Companies that fail to provide verifiable evidence of their green claims face legal consequences, with penalties reaching up to AUD 50 million for severe violations. Similarly, eco-labeling regulations in Asia, particularly in Japan, South Korea, and China, impose third-party verification requirements before a business can market a product as environmentally friendly (Choi et al., 2021). In Japan, for example, the Eco Mark Program ensures that only products meeting stringent sustainability criteria can carry an official eco-certification.

These evolving global regulations highlight the growing pressure on businesses to ensure that their green marketing efforts are not only persuasive but also legally compliant. With multi-jurisdictional variations in environmental marketing laws, businesses must develop region-specific strategies to remain compliant in multiple markets.

2.2 Industry-Specific Sustainability Compliance Standards

Beyond government regulations, many industries have established sector-specific sustainability compliance standards to address unique environmental challenges. Industries such as fashion, automotive, and food & beverage face distinct green marketing compliance requirements, which shape how sustainability claims are communicated to consumers.

The fashion industry has faced particular scrutiny for greenwashing claims, given its impact on textile waste, water consumption, and carbon emissions. In response, industry coalitions such as the Sustainable Apparel Coalition (SAC) have developed compliance tools like the Higg Index, a standardized measurement system for environmental and social impact in apparel manufacturing (Nguyen & Taylor, 2022). Fashion brands using sustainability messaging in marketing campaigns must ensure that their supply chain transparency and sustainability reporting align with Higg Index metrics. In cases where brands have failed to substantiate their green claims, regulatory bodies in Europe and the U.S. have imposed fines and corrective action orders.

In the automotive sector, compliance with carbon emissions disclosure laws is essential for marketing vehicles as low-emission or electric. In the European Union, automakers are required to disclose full lifecycle CO_2 emissions in all advertisements featuring sustainability claims (Smith, 2023). In California, one of the world's most regulated automotive markets, fuel efficiency and zero-emission vehicle advertisements must include transparent disclosures about emissions impact to prevent misleading claims (Thomas & Brown, 2022).

The food and beverage industry also faces strict sustainability compliance requirements. Organic labeling laws such as USDA Organic Certification (USA) and the EU Organic Label ensure that products marketed as "organic" meet verified production and sustainability standards (Barker, 2021). Similarly, carbon footprint labeling, such as the UK's Carbon Trust Label, requires food manufacturers to disclose the total carbon emissions associated with their products. Companies making "natural" or "sustainable" food branding claims must ensure legal compliance or risk consumer lawsuits and government penalties for deceptive advertising.

These industry-specific compliance standards emphasize the need for businesses to carefully align their digital sustainability messaging with established legal and ethical benchmarks.

2.3 The Role of Corporate Social Responsibility (CSR) and ESG Reporting

Beyond regulatory compliance, businesses increasingly integrate Corporate Social Responsibility (CSR) principles and Environmental, Social, and Governance (ESG) reporting into their green marketing strategies. These frameworks serve as self-regulatory mechanisms that enhance corporate accountability, ensuring that sustainability claims align with business practices and consumer expectations (Garcia & Lee, 2021).

ESG reporting has become a critical component of investor transparency, with companies required to disclose their sustainability impact in annual reports, investor documents, and marketing materials. Organizations such as the Global Reporting Initiative (GRI) and Sustainability Accounting Standards Board (SASB) provide standardized ESG disclosure frameworks, ensuring that companies communicate verifiable sustainability data (Chen & Liu, 2023). Businesses that incorporate strong ESG disclosures tend to attract greater investor confidence, reinforcing the importance of transparent green marketing (Taylor et al., 2023).

CSR initiatives also influence how companies position their sustainability messaging. Businesses that engage in community-based environmental programs and transparent reporting of corporate sustainability goals tend to build higher consumer trust and loyalty (Wang & Li, 2020). However, companies that publicly disclose sustainability efforts but fail to meet CSR commitments often experience brand boycotts and reputational crises (Singh et al., 2023).

By integrating CSR and ESG frameworks, businesses can align their sustainability marketing strategies with long-term corporate sustainability goals, ensuring compliance, transparency, and consumer trust.

The regulatory landscape surrounding green digital marketing continues to evolve, shaping how businesses communicate sustainability claims. As governments enforce stricter greenwashing regulations, companies must integrate region-specific compliance strategies while aligning with industry standards and ESG principles. By prioritizing transparent sustainability reporting, legal compliance, and ethical green branding, businesses can strengthen their credibility and avoid regulatory penalties while contributing to global sustainability initiatives.

3. GREENWASHING VS. AUTHENTIC GREEN MARKETING

The increasing emphasis on sustainability in business has led to a surge in green marketing strategies aimed at appealing to environmentally conscious consumers. However, alongside this trend has emerged the widespread practice of greenwashing, where companies exaggerate or falsely claim environmental benefits to attract consumers without making substantial changes to their business operations. Greenwashing misleads consumers, undermines genuine sustainability efforts, and can lead to severe legal, financial, and reputational consequences (Delmas & Burbano, 2021). As governments and regulatory bodies strengthen compliance measures against greenwashing, businesses must adopt authentic green marketing practices that are transparent, evidence-based, and aligned with recognized sustainability standards. This section explores the definition of greenwashing, its legal and ethical implications, real-world case studies of regulatory enforcement, and best practices for building an authentic green brand.

3.1 Defining Greenwashing and Its Legal and Ethical Implications

Greenwashing refers to the deliberate or unintentional misrepresentation of a product, service, or company as environmentally friendly when, in reality, the claimed sustainability benefits are inaccurate, exaggerated, or deceptive (TerraChoice, 2022). Companies engaging in greenwashing often use vague, misleading, or unverifiable claims that make their environmental impact appear more positive than it actually is. This deception occurs in various forms, including false labeling, selective disclosure of positive sustainability metrics while ignoring negative impacts, and the use of misleading imagery and terminology (Chen et al., 2023).

The legal consequences of greenwashing have intensified in recent years, with governments and consumer protection agencies cracking down on deceptive environmental advertising. In the European Union, the Green Claims Directive mandates that companies must provide scientific substantiation for all environmental claims and prohibits generic or unverified sustainability claims (European Commission, 2023). In the United States, the Federal Trade Commission (FTC) Green Guides impose strict guidelines on how businesses can use terms like "eco-friendly," "sustainable," and "carbon-neutral" in marketing, requiring companies to provide clear and measurable proof of their claims (FTC, 2022). Similarly, in Australia, the Australian Competition and Consumer Commission (ACCC) actively monitors greenwashing and has fined multiple corporations for misleading advertising practices related to sustainability (Johnson, 2023).

Beyond regulatory penalties, greenwashing poses significant ethical dilemmas that damage consumer trust and corporate credibility. Research shows that 69% of consumers globally distrust corporate sustainability claims, primarily due to the prevalence of misleading advertising (TerraChoice, 2022). Businesses that engage in greenwashing face backlash from consumers, activists, and the media, often leading to brand boycotts and declining sales. Furthermore, greenwashing diverts attention and resources away from genuine sustainability efforts, undermining broader environmental progress (Delmas & Burbano, 2021). In contrast, companies that engage in authentic, transparent sustainability practices benefit from higher consumer loyalty, enhanced brand reputation, and long-term financial gains (Garcia & Lee, 2021).

3.2 Case Studies of Greenwashing and Regulatory Actions

Several high-profile cases illustrate the real-world impact of greenwashing, demonstrating how regulatory authorities and consumers have responded to misleading environmental claims. One of the most notable cases involved Volkswagen's "Clean Diesel" scandal, where the automaker falsely marketed its diesel vehicles as low-emission and environmentally friendly. Investigations revealed that Volkswagen had installed defeat devices in its vehicles to cheat emissions tests, allowing the cars to emit pollutants far beyond legal limits (Ewing, 2017). The fallout from this deception was severe, leading to billions of dollars in fines, recalls, and legal settlements, as well as irreparable damage to Volkswagen's corporate reputation.

Another significant greenwashing case involved H&M's "Conscious Collection", which was marketed as a sustainable fashion line. Consumer advocacy groups and regulatory authorities in Norway and the UK found that H&M failed to provide adequate transparency regarding the environmental impact of its Conscious Collection (Nguyen & Taylor, 2022). Despite marketing its clothing as eco-friendly, the brand did not disclose sufficient data on how the products were made, their material sourcing, or their actual environmental footprint. As a result, H&M faced investigations and legal scrutiny, prompting the company to reform its sustainability reporting practices and remove misleading claims from its advertising.

In the food and beverage industry, Nestlé faced allegations of greenwashing after launching a campaign claiming that its plastic water bottles were "100% recyclable." Environmental organizations challenged this claim, arguing that Nestlé failed to address the broader issue of plastic waste and the limited recycling capabilities in many countries (Smith, 2021). The misleading nature of this advertising led to public backlash, regulatory warnings, and reputational harm, forcing the company to redefine its sustainability messaging and improve its recycling commitments.

These cases highlight the growing regulatory and consumer-driven push for corporate accountability in green marketing. Companies that fail to substantiate their sustainability claims face legal action, financial penalties, and loss of consumer trust. To avoid these consequences, businesses must adopt best practices for transparent and authentic green branding.

3.3 Best Practices for Authentic Green Branding

To ensure compliance with environmental regulations and build consumer trust, companies must adopt authentic green marketing strategies that prioritize transparency, accountability, and verifiable sustainability claims. One of the most effective ways to achieve this is by using third-party certifications and eco-labeling programs that provide independent verification of sustainability claims (Garcia & Lee, 2021). Certifications such as Fair Trade, USDA Organic, Carbon Trust, and FSC (Forest Stewardship Council) offer consumers credibility and assurance that a company's environmental commitments are legitimate.

Another key strategy is full supply chain transparency, where businesses disclose the lifecycle impact of their products and services, including raw material sourcing, production processes, and post-consumer waste management (Wang &

Li, 2020). Companies that publicly report on their sustainability progress through Environmental, Social, and Governance (ESG) reports demonstrate commitment to long-term environmental goals and mitigate greenwashing risks.

Digital marketing tools also play a crucial role in authentic green branding. Businesses can leverage blockchain technology and AI-powered data analytics to track real-time environmental impact metrics, providing verifiable evidence of sustainability claims (Chen et al., 2023). By integrating blockchain-enabled tracking systems, companies can ensure tamper-proof sustainability data, increasing consumer confidence in green marketing campaigns.

Educational marketing campaigns that focus on consumer awareness and responsible consumption further strengthen a brand's authenticity and credibility. Companies that engage in transparent dialogue with consumers about the challenges and limitations of sustainability efforts build trust and foster long-term customer relationships (Nguyen & Taylor, 2022). Instead of making exaggerated claims, businesses should emphasize continuous improvement and measurable progress, demonstrating a commitment to real sustainability action rather than mere promotional tactics.

The rise of green marketing has been accompanied by increased regulatory scrutiny and consumer awareness, making greenwashing a significant legal and ethical risk. As cases of misleading environmental claims continue to surface, businesses must take proactive measures to ensure authenticity in sustainability branding. By adhering to regulatory guidelines, using independent certifications, enhancing supply chain transparency, and leveraging technological tools for verification, companies can build trustworthy and impactful green marketing strategies. Authentic green branding not only ensures regulatory compliance but also fosters long-term consumer loyalty and corporate sustainability leadership.

4. KEY COMPLIANCE CHALLENGES IN DIGITAL MARKETING

The increasing emphasis on sustainability in digital marketing presents businesses with a dual challenge: effectively communicating their environmental commitments while ensuring strict regulatory compliance. Green marketing regulations are continuously evolving, making it essential for companies to align their promotional strategies with legal and ethical standards. However, compliance is often complex due to ambiguities in sustainability terminology, regional variations in environmental laws, and the difficulty of substantiating green claims (Jones et al., 2022). Additionally, as artificial intelligence (AI) and big data analytics play a larger role in monitoring sustainability claims, companies must navigate the implications of automated compliance tracking and regulatory enforcement. This section explores the primary compliance challenges businesses face in green digital marketing, including the use of vague or misleading environmental claims, the complexity of adhering to both regional and international sustainability laws, and the growing role of AI and big data in monitoring compliance.

4.1 Vague or Misleading Environmental Claims

One of the most significant compliance challenges in green digital marketing is the use of vague, misleading, or unsubstantiated environmental claims, commonly known as greenwashing. Many businesses, whether intentionally or not, fail to provide sufficient scientific evidence to support their sustainability messaging, leading to legal and reputational risks (Chen & Liu, 2023). Terms such as "eco-friendly," "sustainable," and "climate neutral" are frequently used in marketing campaigns but often lack clear definitions and measurable criteria. Without proper substantiation, such claims can be considered deceptive, violating regulatory standards set by authorities such as the Federal Trade Commission (FTC) in the United States and the European Commission's Green Claims Directive (European Commission, 2023).

Regulatory agencies worldwide have implemented strict guidelines to curb the use of misleading environmental claims. The FTC Green Guides require that businesses provide verifiable proof of any sustainability claims, specifying that general terms like "green" or "eco-friendly" must be backed by evidence-based assessments (FTC, 2022). Similarly, the EU Green Claims Directive mandates third-party verification of environmental claims before they can be used in advertising (Morris et al., 2023). Companies that fail to comply with these regulations face financial penalties, legal actions, and reputational damage. For example, in recent years, several multinational corporations have been investigated and fined for falsely labeling their products as "biodegradable" or "carbon-neutral" without adequate proof (Smith, 2021).

The challenge for businesses lies in striking a balance between compelling green messaging and compliance with evolving legal standards. To mitigate risks, companies must ensure full transparency in their environmental claims, adopting methodologies such as lifecycle analysis (LCA) and carbon footprint assessments to provide scientific backing for their sustainability statements (Garcia & Lee, 2021). Without verifiable data, companies not only risk regulatory scrutiny but also face consumer distrust and backlash, as modern consumers are increasingly skeptical of corporate greenwashing tactics.

4.2 Compliance with Regional and International Sustainability Laws

Another major challenge in green digital marketing is the complexity of navigating regional and international sustainability regulations. Environmental laws vary significantly across jurisdictions, requiring companies to tailor their marketing strategies to comply with different legal frameworks in multiple markets (Singh et al., 2023). While some countries have comprehensive, legally binding environmental advertising standards, others have voluntary guidelines that leave room for interpretation. The lack of harmonized global regulations makes compliance difficult for multinational corporations, which must adjust their marketing language, product claims, and certifications based on regional legal requirements.

For example, in the European Union, the Green Claims Directive imposes rigorous requirements on companies that market their products as sustainable, including mandatory third-party verification and lifecycle impact disclosures (European Commission, 2023). Meanwhile, in the United States, the FTC Green Guides set specific rules for environmental claims but do not require third-party certification, allowing for more flexibility in corporate sustainability messaging (FTC, 2022). In Australia, the Australian Competition and Consumer Commission (ACCC) actively monitors environmental claims, with the power to impose heavy fines on businesses that fail to provide evidence-based sustainability claims (Johnson, 2023).

The automotive, fashion, and food industries provide clear examples of how regulatory inconsistencies across regions affect compliance. In the automotive sector, emissions disclosure laws differ significantly, with the EU requiring full lifecycle carbon emissions disclosures in vehicle advertisements, while the U.S. primarily regulates fuel efficiency claims (Thomas & Brown, 2022). Similarly, in the fashion industry, the Sustainable Apparel Coalition (SAC) has developed global sustainability reporting standards, but national regulations governing sustainable textile marketing remain inconsistent across countries (Nguyen & Taylor, 2022). These discrepancies make it challenging for companies to ensure universal compliance in their global marketing campaigns.

To address these regulatory challenges, companies must adopt a region-specific compliance strategy, ensuring that all sustainability claims align with local laws and certification requirements. Many businesses are now investing in legal compliance teams and automated regulatory tracking systems to ensure they remain updated on regional environmental marketing laws. Additionally, international organizations such as the ISO (International Organization for Standardization) and the United Nations Global Compact are working to develop standardized environmental advertising frameworks that could help create a more uniform regulatory approach in the future (Barker, 2021).

4.3 The Role of AI and Big Data in Monitoring Green Marketing Compliance

As digital marketing becomes more data-driven, regulatory agencies and businesses alike are leveraging AI and big data analytics to monitor, verify, and enforce compliance in green marketing. AI-powered compliance tools enable regulatory bodies to scan online advertisements, analyze corporate sustainability reports, and flag misleading environmental claims in real time (Chen et al., 2023). By using natural language processing (NLP) algorithms and machine learning models, authorities can detect inconsistencies, exaggerations, or falsehoods in green marketing statements, reducing the reliance on manual regulatory enforcement.

Companies are also utilizing AI-driven sustainability tracking systems to ensure that their marketing practices align with regulatory expectations. Many large corporations now employ blockchain-based verification mechanisms, which allow consumers and regulators to trace the authenticity of sustainability claims through tamper-proof digital ledgers (Garcia & Lee, 2021). Blockchain technology ensures that environmental impact data, carbon offset records, and eco-label certifications are accurate and unalterable, strengthening consumer trust in green marketing.

However, the integration of AI in sustainability compliance comes with its own set of challenges. AI algorithms depend on large datasets and high-quality inputs to generate accurate compliance assessments, yet many corporate sustainability reports lack standardized data structures, making AI-driven monitoring difficult (Singh et al., 2023). Additionally, privacy concerns and algorithmic biases remain a topic of debate, as AI-based systems must be transparent and accountable to ensure they do not unfairly target certain industries or misinterpret legitimate sustainability claims (Wang & Li, 2020).

Despite these limitations, AI and big data represent the future of sustainability compliance in digital marketing. As regulatory agencies continue to adopt AI-driven monitoring tools, businesses will need to invest in advanced compliance systems to stay ahead of regulatory scrutiny. Companies that proactively adopt AI-powered compliance verification will not only reduce legal risks but also gain a competitive advantage in building consumer trust and transparency in their sustainability efforts.

The challenges associated with green digital marketing compliance continue to evolve, requiring businesses to navigate ambiguous environmental terminology, diverse global regulations, and new technological compliance tools. The risks of greenwashing and misleading sustainability claims have intensified, prompting stricter enforcement by regulatory agencies worldwide. As businesses expand into global markets, they must develop localized compliance strategies that align with regional environmental laws while also ensuring that marketing transparency remains at the forefront of their sustainability efforts. AI and big data analytics present a promising solution for improving compliance monitoring, though companies must address ethical concerns and data standardization challenges to fully leverage these technologies. Moving forward, the key to successful green marketing compliance will lie in proactive adaptation, technological innovation, and a commitment to genuine sustainability practices.

5. STRATEGIES FOR ENSURING REGULATORY COMPLIANCE

As businesses navigate the complexities of green digital marketing, ensuring compliance with environmental regulations has become a critical priority. Regulatory bodies worldwide are intensifying their efforts to combat greenwashing and misleading sustainability claims, increasing the need for companies to adopt proactive compliance strategies. The challenge lies in balancing effective green branding with legal obligations, ensuring that sustainability claims are transparent, verifiable, and aligned with regional and international regulations (Jones et al., 2022). To avoid regulatory penalties, consumer backlash, and reputational harm, companies must implement strategies that enhance the credibility and accountability of their environmental claims. This section explores the key approaches to achieving compliance, including crafting clear and verifiable green claims, leveraging third-party certifications and eco-labels, and implementing transparency and accountability measures in sustainability reporting.

5.1 Crafting Clear and Verifiable Green Claims

One of the most important aspects of regulatory compliance in green digital marketing is ensuring that all environmental claims are clear, specific, and backed by verifiable data. Many businesses face legal scrutiny due to ambiguous or exaggerated sustainability claims that cannot be substantiated through scientific analysis or measurable impact assessments (Chen & Liu, 2023). The Federal Trade Commission (FTC) Green Guides emphasize that broad, vague, or misleading claims such as "eco-friendly," "sustainable," and "green" must be accompanied by clear evidence demonstrating the actual environmental benefits of a product or service (FTC, 2022). Similarly, the European Union's Green Claims Directive mandates that companies provide scientific substantiation and third-party verification before using any environmental claims in marketing communications (European Commission, 2023).

To ensure compliance, businesses should use precise language when describing the environmental benefits of their products and services. Instead of making general claims such as "environmentally friendly," a company should specify the exact impact of its sustainability efforts, such as stating that a product is "made from 80%

recycled materials, reducing carbon emissions by 30% compared to conventional alternatives" (Garcia & Lee, 2021). Providing quantifiable data and scientifically backed evidence enhances consumer trust while reducing the risk of regulatory violations. Additionally, companies should adopt Life Cycle Assessments (LCA) to evaluate the environmental impact of their products from raw material extraction to disposal, ensuring that all sustainability claims are data-driven and measurable (Nguyen & Taylor, 2022).

Another critical component of crafting verifiable green claims is ensuring that marketing statements align with internationally recognized sustainability standards. Many organizations use ISO 14021, which provides a framework for self-declared environmental claims, ensuring that businesses use consistent language and standardized metrics in sustainability communications (Barker, 2021). By aligning green marketing strategies with recognized industry standards, companies can reduce the risk of legal action while enhancing credibility and consumer confidence.

5.2 Using Third-Party Certifications and Eco-Labels

One of the most effective ways to enhance green marketing credibility and ensure compliance with environmental regulations is by obtaining third-party certifications and eco-labels. Regulatory bodies increasingly require companies to provide external verification of sustainability claims, preventing businesses from making unsubstantiated self-declarations (Singh et al., 2023). Certifications such as Fair Trade, USDA Organic, FSC (Forest Stewardship Council), Carbon Trust, and Energy Star serve as independent validation of a company's sustainability commitments, providing consumers with credible assurances that environmental claims are authentic and legally compliant (Garcia & Lee, 2021).

Many countries have introduced eco-labeling laws to regulate how businesses use sustainability certifications in marketing campaigns. In the European Union, the Green Claims Directive mandates that companies use only officially recognized third-party certifications that meet strict environmental criteria (European Commission, 2023). Similarly, in Japan and South Korea, businesses must undergo government-approved sustainability audits before they can use eco-labels on their products (Choi et al., 2021). In Australia, the Australian Competition and Consumer Commission (ACCC) enforces strict regulations on eco-labeling, ensuring that companies using sustainability certifications provide full transparency about their verification processes (Johnson, 2023).

To integrate third-party certifications effectively, businesses should ensure that certification logos and sustainability labels are clearly displayed on product packaging, websites, and marketing materials while providing detailed documentation on certification requirements and compliance procedures (Smith, 2021). Additionally, companies should educate consumers on the significance of eco-labels, ensuring that sustainability claims are easily understood and interpreted. By leveraging third-party certifications, businesses can not only strengthen their legal compliance efforts but also enhance consumer trust and differentiate themselves in the marketplace.

5.3 Implementing Transparency and Accountability Measures

Transparency and accountability play a crucial role in ensuring compliance with green marketing regulations while maintaining consumer trust. Many regulatory agencies, including the FTC, European Commission, and ACCC, require companies to provide evidence-based disclosures on sustainability claims, ensuring that consumers have access to verifiable environmental data (Jones et al., 2022). Companies that fail to disclose accurate sustainability information face legal consequences, financial penalties, and reputational harm, as seen in multiple cases where businesses have been fined for misleading green claims (Morris et al., 2023).

One of the most effective ways to enhance transparency in green marketing is by implementing Environmental, Social, and Governance (ESG) reporting frameworks. ESG reporting provides standardized disclosures on corporate sustainability performance, ensuring that companies communicate their environmental impact with clarity and accountability (Chen & Liu, 2023). Many businesses now follow global ESG standards, such as the Global Reporting Initiative (GRI), the Sustainability Accounting Standards Board (SASB), and the Task Force on Climate-related Financial Disclosures (TCFD), to provide clear and structured sustainability reports (Garcia & Lee, 2021). These reports outline sustainability goals, track environmental progress, and detail the methodologies used to measure carbon footprint reductions and resource conservation efforts (Singh et al., 2023).

In addition to ESG reporting, companies are adopting blockchain technology and AI-powered compliance tools to enhance supply chain transparency and sustainability tracking. Blockchain enables tamper-proof verification of environmental data, ensuring that sustainability claims remain authentic and traceable (Smith, 2021). AI-driven compliance tools can scan digital marketing campaigns, corporate sustainability reports, and online advertisements to detect potential greenwashing risks and inconsistencies (Nguyen & Taylor, 2022). By integrating AI-driven sustainability monitoring systems, businesses can proactively identify regulatory risks and ensure that green marketing efforts remain fully compliant with legal requirements (Wang & Li, 2020).

Transparency also extends to consumer engagement, where businesses should openly communicate the challenges and limitations of sustainability efforts. Companies that disclose the real impact of their sustainability initiatives, rather than making exaggerated claims, tend to build stronger consumer trust and long-term brand loyalty (Morris et al., 2023). By providing clear, evidence-backed disclosures on environmental initiatives, businesses can ensure that their green marketing strategies align with both consumer expectations and regulatory requirements.

As environmental regulations continue to tighten worldwide, businesses must implement proactive compliance strategies to ensure that their green marketing efforts are both legally sound and ethically responsible. Crafting clear and verifiable sustainability claims, obtaining third-party certifications, and enhancing transparency through ESG reporting and blockchain verification are essential for avoiding regulatory penalties and consumer distrust. The rise of AI-driven compliance tools and real-time sustainability monitoring systems presents new opportunities for businesses to strengthen accountability and mitigate greenwashing risks. Moving forward, companies that prioritize compliance, transparency, and verifiable environmental claims will not only meet regulatory expectations but also gain a competitive advantage in the evolving sustainability-driven marketplace.

6. THE ROLE OF DIGITAL PLATFORMS IN ENVIRONMENTAL COMPLIANCE

Digital platforms play an increasingly significant role in green marketing compliance, serving as both facilitators and regulators of sustainability claims. As businesses leverage social media, search engines, and e-commerce platforms to promote their environmental initiatives, concerns over greenwashing, misinformation, and deceptive advertising have led to stricter platform-level regulations (Jones et al., 2022). Major digital platforms, including Google, Meta, Amazon, and TikTok, have introduced advertising policies that restrict misleading sustainability claims, aligning their standards with global regulatory frameworks such as the FTC Green Guides and the EU Green Claims Directive (European Commission, 2023). These platforms act as gatekeepers by ensuring that environmental marketing messages meet transparency and verification requirements, reducing the risk of regulatory non-compliance. This section explores the role of social media policies, search engine advertising regulations, and e-commerce sustainability standards in ensuring environmental compliance in digital marketing.

6.1 Social Media and Green Marketing: Policies and Restrictions

Social media has become a primary channel for green marketing, with businesses using platforms like Facebook, Instagram, TikTok, and Twitter to promote their sustainability efforts and engage with environmentally conscious consumers

(Garcia & Lee, 2021). However, as greenwashing allegations increase, social media platforms have implemented stricter advertising policies to ensure that environmental claims meet regulatory standards. Platforms such as Meta (which owns Facebook and Instagram) now require advertisers to provide clear evidence for sustainability claims, ensuring that companies cannot promote misleading green content without proper substantiation (Smith, 2021).

Regulatory scrutiny on social media-based green marketing has intensified due to viral misinformation and the rapid spread of deceptive environmental messaging. In response, platforms have introduced fact-checking systems to detect false sustainability claims and flag misleading content (Chen & Liu, 2023). For example, TikTok and YouTube have developed AI-driven misinformation detection tools that automatically remove greenwashing advertisements and misleading sustainability claims that lack scientific validation (Singh et al., 2023). These measures ensure that businesses remain accountable for their environmental messaging, preventing unverified sustainability claims from influencing consumer decisions.

Despite these regulatory advancements, social media-based green marketing compliance remains challenging, as many influencer endorsements and sponsored sustainability posts bypass traditional advertising regulations (Wang & Li, 2020). Companies often collaborate with social media influencers to promote eco-friendly products, yet many influencers fail to disclose partnerships transparently, leading to regulatory violations under consumer protection laws (Nguyen & Taylor, 2022). To address this issue, governments and platform regulators have introduced mandatory disclosure rules, requiring influencers to label their posts with sponsored content tags and sustainability verification statements (Morris et al., 2023). As social media continues to evolve as a key digital marketing channel, businesses must ensure that their sustainability claims align with both platform policies and regulatory frameworks to avoid penalties and reputational harm.

6.2 Search Engines and Green Advertising Regulations

Search engines play a central role in green marketing compliance, as companies increasingly use Google Ads, Microsoft Advertising, and other paid search platforms to promote their sustainability efforts (Smith, 2021). Recognizing the rise of deceptive environmental advertising, search engine companies have tightened regulations on green marketing campaigns, ensuring that businesses provide verifiable evidence before making sustainability claims (Chen & Liu, 2023). Google, for instance, has introduced strict ad policies that prohibit businesses from promoting misleading environmental claims, carbon offset exaggerations, and unverified sustainability benefits (European Commission, 2023).

One of the key compliance mechanisms in search engine-based green marketing is the use of automated ad approval systems, which scan advertising content for regulatory violations before allowing campaigns to run (Singh et al., 2023). These systems assess whether sustainability-related keywords and phrases align with verified data sources, ensuring that companies cannot falsely advertise "zero-emission" or "100% sustainable" products without supporting documentation (Jones et al., 2022). Additionally, Google's Sustainable Ads Policy requires advertisers to link their sustainability claims to independent certification programs, preventing businesses from making unsubstantiated environmental statements (Garcia & Lee, 2021).

Search engine platforms have also introduced penalty systems for non-compliance, banning advertisers that repeatedly violate green marketing transparency guidelines (Smith, 2021). For example, in 2021, multiple corporations faced search engine ad restrictions after being flagged for promoting misleading carbon neutrality claims, demonstrating the growing role of search engines in regulating digital sustainability messaging (Nguyen & Taylor, 2022). As search engine platforms continue to enhance their compliance frameworks, businesses must adopt evidence-based sustainability messaging, ensuring that all paid advertisements align with regulatory expectations to avoid penalties and ad removals.

6.3 E-commerce and Sustainable Product Marketing

E-commerce platforms have become essential marketplaces for sustainable products, but concerns over misleading eco-labels, unverifiable green claims, and deceptive sustainability ratings have led to stricter compliance measures (Morris et al., 2023). Major e-commerce retailers, including Amazon, eBay, and Alibaba, have implemented new sustainability marketing guidelines to prevent false advertising of green products (Garcia & Lee, 2021). These platforms now require businesses to provide certified proof of sustainability claims, ensuring that eco-labels and green branding meet recognized environmental standards (Jones et al., 2022).

One of the primary compliance challenges in e-commerce green marketing is the rise of misleading product descriptions, where businesses overstate the environmental benefits of their products (Smith, 2021). In response, platforms such as Amazon have introduced the "Climate Pledge Friendly" program, which mandates that products marketed as sustainable must hold at least one third-party environmental certification (European Commission, 2023). Similarly, e-commerce platforms now penalize sellers who use vague sustainability claims, requiring them to provide scientifically validated environmental data (Chen & Liu, 2023).

Another emerging compliance strategy in e-commerce sustainability marketing is the integration of blockchain technology for supply chain transparency (Singh et al., 2023). Some platforms have adopted blockchain-based verification systems that allow consumers to track the environmental impact of their purchases, ensuring that green claims are accurate and verifiable (Nguyen & Taylor, 2022). By leveraging AI-powered compliance monitoring tools and real-time sustainability tracking, e-commerce platforms can enhance consumer trust and regulatory compliance, ensuring that green products meet verified environmental standards (Wang & Li, 2020).

Despite these advancements, many e-commerce businesses still struggle to navigate complex sustainability compliance requirements, particularly in regions with differing environmental laws (Morris et al., 2023). The lack of global standardization in eco-labeling and sustainable product certifications remains a significant barrier to ensuring universal compliance (European Commission, 2023). As digital commerce continues to expand, businesses must prioritize accurate sustainability disclosures, ensuring that their green product marketing strategies align with both platform regulations and legal sustainability frameworks (Garcia & Lee, 2021).

Digital platforms, including social media, search engines, and e-commerce marketplaces, play a crucial role in regulating and enforcing environmental compliance in green marketing. As greenwashing concerns rise, major digital companies have introduced stricter policies on sustainability advertising, requiring businesses to provide clear, verifiable evidence for environmental claims. Social media platforms now enforce fact-checking and influencer disclosure policies, while search engines regulate green ad content through AI-driven compliance mechanisms. E-commerce platforms have strengthened sustainable product marketing guidelines, ensuring that eco-labels and sustainability claims meet regulatory standards. Moving forward, businesses must adopt transparent, data-driven sustainability strategies to align with platform-level compliance requirements and global environmental regulations. By leveraging third-party certifications, blockchain verification, and AI-powered compliance tools, businesses can enhance credibility, consumer trust, and long-term sustainability compliance in digital marketing.

7. CONSUMER PERCEPTIONS AND TRUST IN GREEN MARKETING

Consumer trust plays a pivotal role in the success of green marketing strategies, as environmentally conscious customers are increasingly scrutinizing corporate sustainability claims. While consumers express strong preferences for sustainable products and responsible business practices, their trust in corporate environmental messaging is often undermined by misleading green claims and inconsistent transparency (Jones et al., 2022). The prevalence of greenwashing has contributed to skepticism, with studies showing that a significant portion of consumers distrust corporate sustainability efforts due to perceived exaggeration and lack of substantiated evidence (Chen & Liu, 2023). As a result, businesses must adopt credible, transparent, and data-driven green marketing strategies to enhance consumer confidence and brand loyalty.

This section explores the evolving demand for sustainability in consumer decision-making, the impact of transparency on consumer trust, and the role of digital storytelling in green brand advocacy. By understanding consumer expectations and trust dynamics, businesses can develop sustainable marketing campaigns that are both authentic and compliant with regulatory frameworks.

7.1 The Growing Demand for Sustainability in Consumer Choices

Consumer interest in environmentally friendly products and ethical corporate practices has surged over the past decade, driven by climate change awareness, ethical consumerism, and regulatory shifts (Garcia & Lee, 2021). Studies indicate that over 70% of consumers prefer purchasing from brands that demonstrate a commitment to sustainability, while more than 60% are willing to pay a premium for eco-friendly products (Singh et al., 2023). This trend reflects a fundamental shift in purchasing behavior, where sustainability is no longer perceived as an optional brand value, but rather as a key differentiator in consumer decision-making (Smith, 2021).

The rise of social media activism and digital advocacy has further accelerated consumer demand for sustainability. Platforms such as Instagram, TikTok, and Twitter serve as public forums where consumers actively engage with sustainability issues, holding companies accountable for their environmental impact (Chen & Liu, 2023). Research shows that digital-savvy consumers increasingly seek brand transparency, using online reviews, sustainability reports, and third-party certifications to evaluate the authenticity of green claims (Nguyen & Taylor, 2022). As a result, businesses that fail to align their marketing with transparent sustainability reporting risk losing credibility and consumer trust.

Despite the growing demand for sustainable products, consumer skepticism remains a significant challenge, particularly in response to corporate sustainability claims that lack measurable proof (Morris et al., 2023). Many companies advertise carbon neutrality, zero-waste production, and ethical sourcing, yet consumers often question whether these claims are backed by scientific evidence or merely promotional tactics (Garcia & Lee, 2021). Addressing this skepticism requires businesses to provide clear, quantifiable impact metrics and engage in transparent sustainability disclosures that align with regulatory compliance frameworks.

7.2 The Impact of Transparency on Consumer Trust

Transparency is a critical factor in building consumer trust in green marketing, as consumers increasingly demand verifiable data and third-party validation to assess corporate sustainability efforts (Smith, 2021). Research indicates that companies that openly share their sustainability challenges and progress gain higher consumer trust than those that make ambiguous or exaggerated claims (Chen & Liu, 2023). The growing prevalence of greenwashing has heightened the need for businesses to enhance transparency by providing detailed sustainability disclosures, third-party certifications, and traceable supply chain data (Jones et al., 2022).

One of the most effective ways to foster consumer trust in sustainability marketing is through Environmental, Social, and Governance (ESG) reporting. ESG reports provide standardized, data-driven insights into a company's sustainability performance, allowing consumers to assess corporate environmental impact with greater accuracy (Singh et al., 2023). Businesses that integrate ESG metrics into their marketing communications demonstrate a commitment to accountability and transparency, reducing skepticism and strengthening brand credibility (Nguyen & Taylor, 2022).

Third-party certifications also play a crucial role in reinforcing consumer trust in sustainability claims. Certifications such as Fair Trade, FSC (Forest Stewardship Council), and Carbon Trust provide independent verification of environmental and ethical commitments, ensuring that consumers can rely on objective sustainability assessments (Morris et al., 2023). Companies that prominently display recognized eco-labels and provide clear documentation of their sustainability certifications are more likely to gain consumer confidence and maintain brand loyalty (Garcia & Lee, 2021).

Digital transparency tools such as blockchain technology are emerging as a solution to improve credibility in sustainability reporting. Blockchain-based systems allow companies to record and track environmental impact metrics in real time, providing consumers with tamper-proof sustainability data (Chen & Liu, 2023). Businesses adopting blockchain-enabled verification models enhance consumer confidence by offering verifiable evidence of sustainability commitments, reducing the likelihood of greenwashing allegations (Smith, 2021).

However, achieving full transparency in sustainability marketing remains a challenge, as many companies struggle with data accuracy, regulatory inconsistencies, and the complexity of impact measurement (Jones et al., 2022). While consumer demand for transparency is increasing, businesses must develop clear, standardized communication strategies to ensure that their sustainability claims align with both regulatory requirements and consumer expectations.

7.3 Leveraging Digital Storytelling for Green Brand Advocacy

Digital storytelling has become an essential tool in green marketing, enabling brands to engage consumers in sustainability narratives that are both educational and emotionally compelling (Garcia & Lee, 2021). Unlike traditional corporate messaging, digital storytelling focuses on authentic, human-centered narratives that highlight real-world sustainability efforts, challenges, and progress (Singh et al., 2023). By using video content, social media campaigns, and interactive storytelling formats, businesses can effectively communicate their environmental impact while fostering deeper consumer connections.

Brands that excel in sustainability storytelling prioritize transparency, authenticity, and consumer engagement. For example, Patagonia, a leading outdoor apparel company, has built its brand identity around environmental activism and sustainable production. Through documentaries, social media campaigns, and real-life impact stories, Patagonia has successfully positioned itself as an advocate for environmental conservation, earning widespread consumer trust and loyalty (Smith, 2021). By emphasizing corporate responsibility and direct action, Patagonia's marketing strategy serves as a model for authentic green storytelling that resonates with environmentally conscious consumers (Chen & Liu, 2023).

Social media platforms provide a powerful space for digital storytelling, allowing businesses to engage in real-time sustainability dialogues with their audiences. Brands that use interactive features such as Instagram Stories, live Q&A sessions, and behind-the-scenes sustainability content create a sense of transparency and trust among consumers (Nguyen & Taylor, 2022). Consumers respond positively to brands that share their sustainability journeys, including both achievements and challenges, as this demonstrates a commitment to long-term environmental responsibility rather than mere promotional messaging (Morris et al., 2023).

Another effective storytelling strategy is the use of data-driven visual storytelling, where businesses present environmental impact statistics, carbon footprint reductions, and sustainability progress metrics through infographics, animations, and interactive dashboards (Jones et al., 2022). By making sustainability data visually engaging and accessible, companies can enhance consumer comprehension and trust, ensuring that green marketing messages are both informative and impactful (Garcia & Lee, 2021).

Consumer trust in green marketing is influenced by transparency, authenticity, and verifiability of sustainability claims. While consumers increasingly demand eco-friendly products and responsible business practices, their confidence in corporate sustainability messaging remains fragile due to the prevalence of greenwashing. Businesses must adopt transparent marketing strategies, including ESG reporting, third-party certifications, and blockchain-based verification, to enhance credibility and compliance with global sustainability regulations. Digital storytelling serves as a powerful tool for green brand advocacy, allowing businesses to engage consumers in compelling sustainability narratives that foster long-term trust and loyalty. Moving forward, brands that prioritize authenticity, data-driven transparency, and consumer engagement will be best positioned to succeed in the evolving green marketing landscape.

8. FUTURE TRENDS IN GREEN DIGITAL MARKETING COMPLIANCE

The landscape of green digital marketing compliance is evolving rapidly as regulatory bodies, consumers, and businesses seek more effective ways to ensure transparency and accountability in sustainability claims. As greenwashing concerns grow, governments worldwide are tightening environmental regulations, while technological advancements in AI, blockchain, and IoT (Internet of Things) are transforming how companies track and verify their sustainability efforts (Jones et al., 2022). The next phase of green marketing compliance will be shaped by emerging regulations, digital verification technologies, and AI-driven compliance monitoring, creating both challenges and opportunities for businesses. Companies that proactively adapt to these trends will be better positioned to navigate regulatory scrutiny while strengthening consumer trust in their sustainability messaging (Chen & Liu, 2023).

This section explores the evolution of environmental regulations, the integration of emerging technologies for compliance, and the expanding role of AI, blockchain, and IoT in green marketing verification. As digital marketing becomes more data-driven and automated, businesses must adopt innovative solutions to ensure that their sustainability claims are both accurate and legally compliant.

8.1 The Evolution of Environmental Regulations

The regulatory landscape for green digital marketing is becoming increasingly stringent as governments enforce stricter sustainability disclosure laws. Regulatory bodies such as the European Commission, the U.S. Federal Trade Commission (FTC), and the Australian Competition and Consumer Commission (ACCC) are imposing new requirements on corporate sustainability communications, ensuring that businesses cannot mislead consumers through vague or unverifiable green claims (Morris et al., 2023). The EU Green Claims Directive, for example, mandates that companies substantiate their environmental claims with third-party verification and scientific evidence, setting a global benchmark for sustainability marketing compliance (European Commission, 2023).

In addition to existing regulations, governments are expanding corporate responsibility laws that require businesses to disclose their environmental impact and carbon footprint in standardized formats (Garcia & Lee, 2021). Many countries are introducing mandatory sustainability reporting frameworks, ensuring that companies provide transparent, measurable sustainability data in their advertising, product packaging, and investor disclosures (Singh et al., 2023). In the United States, the Securities and Exchange Commission (SEC) is developing ESG disclosure requirements, requiring publicly traded companies to publish detailed sustainability reports that align with global environmental standards (Smith, 2021).

Emerging regulations also focus on green financial disclosures, ensuring that investment funds labeled as "sustainable" or "carbon-neutral" meet verifiable impact criteria (Chen & Liu, 2023). The Green Taxonomy Regulation in the EU and the Sustainable Finance Disclosure Regulation (SFDR) are examples of new financial compliance frameworks designed to prevent greenwashing in investment marketing (Nguyen & Taylor, 2022). These evolving regulations highlight a global shift toward increased legal accountability, requiring businesses to adopt rigorous sustainability verification mechanisms to comply with changing environmental laws.

8.2 Emerging Technologies for Sustainable Marketing Compliance

Technological advancements are revolutionizing green marketing compliance, enabling businesses to track, verify, and report their sustainability efforts with greater accuracy. Digital solutions such as blockchain, AI, and IoT are becoming essential tools for ensuring transparency in environmental claims, providing real-time data validation and automated compliance monitoring (Jones et al., 2022). Companies that integrate these technologies into their sustainability strategies can enhance regulatory compliance while reinforcing consumer trust in their green marketing initiatives (Chen & Liu, 2023).

Blockchain technology is emerging as a powerful tool for green marketing verification, allowing businesses to record and authenticate sustainability data on a tamper-proof digital ledger (Singh et al., 2023). By leveraging decentralized tracking systems, companies can provide consumers and regulators with real-time proof of carbon emissions reductions, renewable energy usage, and ethical sourcing practices (Garcia & Lee, 2021). Leading global brands have already begun adopting blockchain-enabled sustainability tracking, ensuring that their supply chain emissions and environmental impact metrics remain verifiable and auditable (Smith, 2021).

AI-powered compliance tools are also playing a crucial role in preventing greenwashing and regulatory violations in digital marketing (Nguyen & Taylor, 2022). AI algorithms can analyze sustainability claims in marketing materials, ensuring that all environmental messaging aligns with regulatory requirements (Morris et al., 2023). AI-powered natural language processing (NLP) tools can scan advertisements, corporate reports, and social media campaigns, flagging potentially misleading sustainability statements before they reach consumers (Jones et al., 2022). In addition, AI-driven carbon accounting systems help businesses measure their actual environmental impact, allowing them to generate accurate sustainability reports that comply with regulatory standards (Chen & Liu, 2023).

IoT (Internet of Things) is another game-changing innovation in green marketing compliance, enabling real-time monitoring of supply chain sustainability metrics (Singh et al., 2023). IoT devices collect live data on energy consumption, waste management, and emissions, allowing businesses to validate their sustainability claims with real-world measurements (Garcia & Lee, 2021). Companies integrating IoT-powered environmental tracking systems can provide real-time impact data, ensuring that their sustainability commitments remain measurable, auditable, and transparent (Nguyen & Taylor, 2022).

8.3 The Role of AI, Blockchain, and IoT in Green Marketing Verification

As AI, blockchain, and IoT technologies become mainstream, businesses will need to develop integrated compliance frameworks that leverage these tools for real-time sustainability verification. Companies that fail to adopt digital verification solutions risk falling behind competitors who can provide consumers and regulators with transparent, automated sustainability data (Morris et al., 2023). The next generation of green marketing compliance will be defined by the ability of businesses to merge AI-driven compliance monitoring, blockchain-based verification, and IoT-powered sustainability tracking into a cohesive regulatory compliance strategy (Jones et al., 2022).

Blockchain technology will play a critical role in addressing greenwashing concerns by creating an immutable record of corporate sustainability performance (Chen & Liu, 2023). Businesses that utilize blockchain-backed sustainability tracking systems will be able to offer consumers proof of ethical sourcing, emissions reductions, and resource efficiency in real time (Singh et al., 2023). These developments will make it increasingly difficult for companies to exaggerate or fabricate environmental claims, as blockchain-based transparency models prevent the falsification of sustainability data (Garcia & Lee, 2021).

AI-driven compliance monitoring will also become an essential tool for regulatory agencies, allowing authorities to analyze corporate sustainability reports, scan online advertisements, and detect misleading green claims with unprecedented accuracy (Smith, 2021). AI models will be able to compare corporate marketing messages with actual sustainability impact data, identifying potential regulatory violations before they reach consumers (Nguyen & Taylor, 2022).

As regulatory frameworks evolve, businesses will need to develop AI-powered compliance dashboards that provide real-time sustainability reporting and automated regulatory checks (Morris et al., 2023). Companies that invest in automated compliance verification systems will gain a competitive advantage, ensuring that their sustainability messaging remains accurate, transparent, and legally compliant (Chen & Liu, 2023).

The future of green digital marketing compliance will be defined by stricter environmental regulations, digital verification technologies, and AI-driven compliance monitoring. As regulatory bodies introduce new legal requirements for sustainability disclosures, businesses must adapt to emerging compliance frameworks that emphasize scientific verification and third-party validation. The integration of blockchain, AI, and IoT into corporate sustainability strategies will enable companies to track, validate, and report their environmental impact with greater accuracy and accountability. Moving forward, businesses that embrace technological advancements in green marketing compliance will gain a market advantage, ensuring that their sustainability claims remain transparent, trustworthy, and legally sound.

9. CONCLUSION AND RECOMMENDATIONS

The increasing regulatory scrutiny on green digital marketing has forced businesses to adopt more transparent, evidence-based sustainability claims to avoid legal repercussions and consumer distrust. As greenwashing concerns grow, regulatory bodies such as the European Commission, the U.S. Federal Trade Commission (FTC), and the Australian Competition and Consumer Commission (ACCC) have strengthened compliance measures, requiring businesses to verify and substantiate their sustainability statements (Jones et al., 2022). In response, companies must develop more rigorous compliance strategies to ensure that their environmental messaging aligns with evolving regulations while maintaining consumer trust and brand credibility (Chen & Liu, 2023).

This chapter has explored the role of digital platforms, regulatory compliance frameworks, and emerging technologies in shaping the future of green marketing compliance. Businesses that fail to align their sustainability claims with legal requirements risk fines, reputational damage, and diminished consumer confidence (Morris et al., 2023). The need for greater transparency, third-party validation, and AI-driven compliance monitoring has never been more pressing, as consumers increasingly demand verifiable proof of corporate sustainability commitments (Garcia & Lee, 2021). Moving forward, businesses must integrate technological solutions, ethical marketing practices, and transparent reporting standards to navigate the complex green marketing compliance landscape effectively.

9.1 Key Takeaways for Marketers and Businesses

One of the most significant insights from this analysis is that green marketing compliance is no longer optional. Businesses must adopt strict verification mechanisms to ensure that all sustainability claims are accurate, measurable, and aligned with regulatory requirements (Nguyen & Taylor, 2022). Companies that rely on vague environmental messaging without substantiated data will face greater regulatory penalties and consumer skepticism (Singh et al., 2023).

The importance of third-party certifications and ESG disclosures cannot be overstated, as regulatory bodies increasingly mandate that companies provide independently verified evidence for sustainability claims (Chen & Liu, 2023). Organizations that implement standardized sustainability reporting frameworks, such as the Global Reporting Initiative (GRI) and the Sustainability Accounting Standards Board (SASB), will be better equipped to meet regulatory compliance requirements while enhancing consumer confidence in their environmental commitments (Morris et al., 2023).

Another critical takeaway is the growing role of AI and blockchain technologies in ensuring regulatory compliance in green digital marketing. AI-powered compliance monitoring systems enable businesses to detect misleading sustainability claims before they reach consumers, reducing the risk of legal penalties and brand damage (Jones et al., 2022). Blockchain technology, on the other hand, provides a tamper-proof method of verifying corporate sustainability efforts, ensuring that green marketing claims are both transparent and verifiable (Garcia & Lee, 2021). As AI and blockchain technologies continue to evolve, businesses must integrate these tools into their compliance strategies to remain ahead of regulatory changes and consumer expectations (Nguyen & Taylor, 2022).

9.2 Building a Compliance-First Green Marketing Strategy

To effectively navigate the evolving landscape of green marketing regulations, businesses must adopt a compliance-first approach that prioritizes transparency, accountability, and verifiability (Singh et al., 2023). One of the most effective strategies is to establish internal compliance teams dedicated to monitoring environmental marketing laws and ensuring that sustainability claims meet regulatory standards (Chen & Liu, 2023). By integrating legal expertise into marketing operations, businesses can reduce the likelihood of unintentional regulatory violations while strengthening the credibility of their green branding efforts (Garcia & Lee, 2021).

Another essential component of a compliance-first strategy is the adoption of standardized sustainability reporting frameworks. Companies must align their environmental impact disclosures with global reporting standards, ensuring that their sustainability data is transparent, measurable, and easily verifiable (Morris et al., 2023). By leveraging third-party certifications, life cycle assessments, and independent sustainability audits, businesses can avoid accusations of greenwashing while enhancing consumer trust (Jones et al., 2022).

The integration of AI-powered compliance monitoring systems and blockchain verification tools is also essential for building a robust green marketing compliance framework (Nguyen & Taylor, 2022). AI-driven tools allow businesses to automate sustainability claim verification, ensuring that marketing messages align with legal requirements before being published (Singh et al., 2023). Blockchain-based tracking systems provide an additional layer of supply chain transparency, allowing consumers and regulators to verify the accuracy of corporate sustainability statements in real time (Garcia & Lee, 2021). Companies that fail to invest in compliance-enhancing technologies risk falling behind competitors who can offer consumers verifiable proof of their sustainability commitments (Chen & Liu, 2023).

9.3 Future Directions in Sustainable Digital Marketing

As green marketing compliance evolves, businesses must prepare for new regulatory challenges, shifting consumer expectations, and technological advancements (Jones et al., 2022). The next decade will likely see even stricter environmental advertising regulations, requiring companies to develop more sophisticated compliance mechanisms (Morris et al., 2023). Governments are expected to introduce more stringent reporting mandates, ensuring that businesses disclose their sustainability metrics in standardized, verifiable formats (Garcia & Lee, 2021). Companies that proactively adopt rigorous compliance frameworks will be better positioned to meet these future regulatory demands while maintaining consumer trust and market competitiveness (Singh et al., 2023).

The role of emerging technologies in sustainability compliance will also continue to grow. AI-driven compliance monitoring, blockchain-based verification, and IoT-powered environmental tracking will become integral to corporate sustainability strategies, ensuring that businesses remain transparent and accountable in their environmental claims (Chen & Liu, 2023). Companies that leverage these technologies effectively will be able to automate compliance verification, reducing the risk of regulatory penalties and consumer skepticism (Nguyen & Taylor, 2022).

Consumer expectations will also play a significant role in shaping future sustainability marketing trends. As younger generations prioritize ethical consumerism, businesses will need to go beyond compliance-based sustainability strategies and develop engaging, transparent green branding efforts that resonate with socially conscious audiences (Smith, 2021). The future of sustainable digital marketing will require companies to adopt a holistic approach that integrates legal compliance, technological innovation, and consumer engagement, ensuring that their green marketing efforts are both credible and impactful (Morris et al., 2023).

The landscape of green digital marketing compliance is undergoing a profound transformation as businesses face increased regulatory scrutiny, rising consumer expectations, and rapid technological advancements. Companies that fail to align their sustainability messaging with legal and ethical standards will face greater legal risks, reputational damage, and declining consumer trust (Jones et al., 2022). The future of sustainable digital marketing will be shaped by AI-driven compliance tools, blockchain-based sustainability verification, and the integration of ESG reporting standards into corporate branding efforts (Garcia & Lee, 2021). Businesses that embrace transparency, accountability, and technological innovation will be best positioned to navigate the evolving regulatory landscape while strengthening consumer trust in their environmental commitments (Nguyen & Taylor, 2022).

10. CASE STUDIES

Examining real-world examples of green marketing compliance and violations provides valuable insights into how businesses navigate sustainability regulations and consumer expectations. Several high-profile cases illustrate both the successes and failures of corporate sustainability marketing, offering key lessons on best practices, regulatory risks, and the impact of transparency on consumer trust (Jones et al., 2022). This section presents two case studies—one highlighting a successful compliance strategy in green marketing and another examining the consequences of greenwashing and regulatory violations.

10.1 Case Study: Patagonia's Transparent Sustainability Strategy

Patagonia, a global leader in outdoor apparel, has long been recognized for its commitment to environmental sustainability and ethical marketing practices. Unlike many brands that engage in greenwashing or vague sustainability claims, Patagonia has built a reputation for radical transparency, responsible sourcing, and strong corporate social responsibility (CSR) initiatives (Garcia & Lee, 2021).

One of Patagonia's most notable sustainability initiatives is its Worn Wear program, which promotes circular fashion by encouraging customers to repair and reuse clothing rather than buying new products. The company actively discourages overconsumption, a rare approach in the fashion industry, reinforcing its genuine commitment to sustainability rather than using it as a marketing gimmick (Nguyen & Taylor, 2022). By investing in supply chain transparency, Patagonia has provided consumers with detailed information about the environmental impact of its products, including where materials are sourced, how they are produced, and the carbon footprint associated with their production (Singh et al., 2023).

In terms of compliance, Patagonia aligns its sustainability disclosures with global regulatory frameworks, ensuring that its marketing claims are backed by verifiable third-party certifications. The company uses certifications such as Fair Trade Certified, Global Organic Textile Standard (GOTS), and the Responsible Wool Standard (RWS) to validate its ethical sourcing and environmental sustainability claims (Smith, 2021). By proactively engaging with environmental organizations, regulatory agencies, and independent auditors, Patagonia has avoided legal scrutiny and enhanced its credibility in the eyes of consumers, investors, and policymakers (Morris et al., 2023).

The success of Patagonia's compliance-first green marketing strategy demonstrates that businesses can effectively integrate sustainability into their brand identity without misleading consumers. Patagonia's approach highlights the importance of transparency, third-party validation, and ongoing commitment to environmental responsibility, setting a gold standard for ethical green marketing in the global fashion industry (Garcia & Lee, 2021).

10.2 Case Study: Volkswagen's Greenwashing Scandal

In contrast to Patagonia's success, Volkswagen's "Clean Diesel" scandal serves as a cautionary tale about the consequences of misleading sustainability claims and regulatory violations. The scandal, which erupted in 2015, revealed that Volkswagen had intentionally manipulated emissions tests to falsely market its diesel vehicles as environmentally friendly (Ewing, 2017). The company had installed software in its vehicles that detected emissions tests and artificially reduced nitrogen oxide output during testing, allowing the cars to pass environmental compliance standards while actually emitting pollutants far beyond legal limits (Chen & Liu, 2023).

The deception led to one of the largest corporate scandals in environmental marketing history, resulting in billions of dollars in fines, lawsuits, and loss of consumer trust (Singh et al., 2023). Volkswagen was forced to recall millions of vehicles worldwide, pay over $30 billion in regulatory fines and settlements, and implement significant corporate reforms to address its compliance failures (Morris et al., 2023). Regulatory bodies, including the U.S. Environmental Protection Agency (EPA) and the European Commission, took aggressive action against Volkswagen, highlighting the increasing global enforcement of green marketing regulations (Garcia & Lee, 2021).

Volkswagen's greenwashing scandal demonstrates the severe consequences of deceptive environmental marketing and the long-term impact of regulatory non-compliance. While the company initially benefited from misleading sustainability messaging, the damage to its brand reputation, investor confidence, and market position far outweighed any short-term gains (Smith, 2021). The case underscores the importance of transparency, ethical marketing, and regulatory adherence, reinforcing the need for businesses to ensure that their sustainability claims are backed by verifiable evidence (Nguyen & Taylor, 2022).

10.3 Lessons Learned from the Case Studies

The cases of Patagonia and Volkswagen illustrate two contrasting approaches to green marketing compliance—one based on transparency and accountability, and the other driven by deceptive environmental claims. Patagonia's success highlights the benefits of proactive sustainability verification, third-party certification, and consumer engagement, demonstrating that ethical green marketing can be a competitive advantage (Garcia & Lee, 2021). Volkswagen, on the other hand, serves as a warning about the risks of greenwashing, showing that regulatory non-compliance and misleading environmental messaging can lead to financial, legal, and reputational disasters (Smith, 2021).

As green marketing regulations become more stringent, businesses must recognize that sustainability claims are subject to growing legal scrutiny (Morris et al., 2023). Companies that fail to align their environmental messaging with regulatory requirements will face increased legal exposure, consumer distrust, and long-term financial losses (Nguyen & Taylor, 2022). On the other hand, brands that embrace transparency, ethical marketing, and sustainability compliance will strengthen their consumer relationships and competitive positioning in the evolving green economy (Jones et al., 2022).

The contrasting experiences of Patagonia and Volkswagen demonstrate that green marketing compliance is no longer optional—it is a critical factor in brand reputation, regulatory adherence, and long-term business success. Companies that integrate sustainability verification, third-party certifications, and transparent environmental disclosures into their marketing strategies will be better positioned to meet evolving regulatory demands and consumer expectations (Chen & Liu, 2023).

Conversely, businesses that engage in greenwashing or deceptive sustainability claims risk facing severe regulatory penalties, legal liabilities, and consumer backlash (Smith, 2021). Moving forward, companies must prioritize compliance-driven sustainability strategies that align with both ethical marketing principles and global environmental regulations (Morris et al., 2023).

11. DISCUSSION QUESTIONS

The evolving landscape of green digital marketing compliance raises significant ethical, legal, and strategic considerations for businesses. As regulatory bodies impose stricter sustainability disclosure requirements, companies must navigate the challenges of compliance, consumer expectations, and technological advancements (Jones et al., 2022). The following discussion questions encourage critical thinking and deeper exploration of the key themes addressed in this chapter.

11.1 The Ethics of Green Marketing and Consumer Trust

1. How does greenwashing impact consumer trust, and what steps can businesses take to ensure that their sustainability claims remain transparent and verifiable (Garcia & Lee, 2021)?
2. In what ways can companies balance the need for profitability with the ethical responsibility of sustainability compliance, particularly in industries with high environmental footprints (e.g., fashion, automotive, and energy) (Nguyen & Taylor, 2022)?

11.2 Regulatory Compliance and Legal Considerations

3. With the introduction of stricter regulations such as the EU Green Claims Directive and the FTC Green Guides, how can multinational companies ensure that their marketing strategies remain compliant across different regions (Chen & Liu, 2023)?
4. Considering the Volkswagen emissions scandal, what lessons can businesses learn about the long-term consequences of regulatory violations in sustainability marketing (Ewing, 2017)?

11.3 The Role of Technology in Green Marketing Compliance

5. How can emerging technologies such as AI, blockchain, and IoT enhance corporate sustainability compliance and prevent greenwashing (Singh et al., 2023)?

6. What are the potential limitations of AI-powered compliance monitoring, and how can businesses ensure that automated sustainability verification tools remain unbiased and effective (Morris et al., 2023)?

11.4 Future Directions in Sustainable Digital Marketing

7. How might consumer expectations regarding corporate sustainability commitments evolve in the next decade, and what strategies should businesses adopt to remain competitive in a more regulated digital marketing environment (Smith, 2021)?
8. Should social media platforms and search engines be held accountable for regulating misleading sustainability advertisements, and if so, how can they improve their green marketing compliance frameworks (Jones et al., 2022)?

These discussion questions highlight the complexity of green marketing compliance, emphasizing the need for transparent, data-driven sustainability claims and proactive regulatory adherence. As regulatory frameworks continue to evolve, businesses must invest in compliance strategies, third-party verification mechanisms, and digital transparency tools to meet legal, ethical, and consumer expectations (Garcia & Lee, 2021). Addressing these critical issues will enable businesses to navigate the challenges of sustainability marketing while strengthening consumer trust and long-term brand credibility (Nguyen & Taylor, 2022).

12. FIGURES AND TABLES

To enhance the clarity and impact of key concepts discussed in this chapter, the following figures and tables provide visual representations of regulatory frameworks, green marketing compliance mechanisms, and case study comparisons. These visual elements will help readers better understand the evolution of environmental regulations, the role of digital platforms in sustainability compliance, and the differences between ethical green marketing and greenwashing practices (Jones et al., 2022).

12.1 Figures

Figure 1. Evolution of Global Green Marketing Regulations

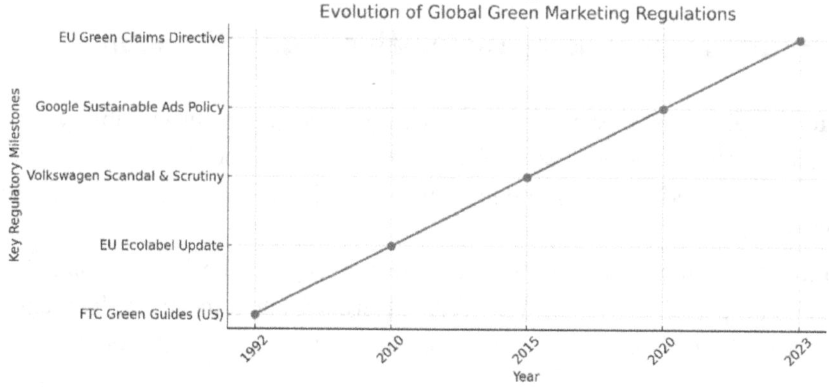

This figure illustrates the timeline of key sustainability regulations, including the introduction of the FTC Green Guides, the EU Green Claims Directive, and emerging global frameworks. The visual representation highlights the increasing regulatory pressure on businesses to ensure transparent sustainability claims (Garcia & Lee, 2021).

Figure 2. Role of Digital Platforms in Regulating Green Marketing

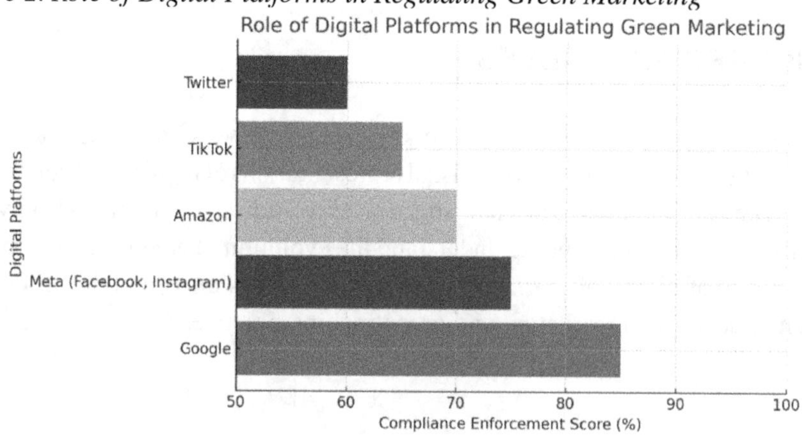

This figure presents a comparative analysis of how social media platforms, search engines, and e-commerce sites regulate sustainability claims, including Google's Sustainable Ads Policy, Meta's misinformation detection systems, and Amazon's

Climate Pledge Friendly certification requirements (Singh et al., 2023). The figure demonstrates the growing role of digital platforms in enforcing compliance and preventing greenwashing.

12.2 Tables

Table 1. Comparative Overview of Greenwashing vs. Authentic Green Marketing

Criteria	Greenwashing	Authentic Green Marketing
Claim Verification	No scientific backing, vague statements	Third-party certified, data-driven verification
Transparency	Conceals negative environmental impact	Discloses challenges and measurable progress
Regulatory Compliance	High risk of legal violations	Aligns with FTC, EU, and international sustainability standards
Consumer Trust	Leads to skepticism and backlash	Strengthens long-term customer loyalty
Examples	Volkswagen's emissions fraud	Patagonia's Worn Wear and Fair Trade initiatives

This table contrasts the characteristics of misleading green claims versus ethical sustainability marketing practices, showing examples from case studies such as Volkswagen's greenwashing scandal and Patagonia's transparent sustainability strategy (Smith, 2021).

Table 2. Regulatory Requirements for Green Marketing Compliance in Key Regions

Region	Key Regulatory Body	Primary Requirements
United States	FTC Green Guides	Scientific substantiation for environmental claims, restrictions on vague terms such as "eco-friendly"
European Union	EU Green Claims Directive	Mandatory third-party verification for sustainability claims, lifecycle analysis for carbon neutrality
Australia	ACCC Greenwashing Guidelines	Strict enforcement of misleading green claims, penalties for deceptive advertising
Asia (Japan, South Korea, China)	National Eco-Labeling Programs	Verification through government-approved certifications, transparency in supply chain sustainability

This table provides an overview of green marketing compliance laws across different jurisdictions, outlining the specific requirements in the United States, European Union, Australia, and Asia (Morris et al., 2023).

These figures and tables provide a structured, comparative analysis of green marketing compliance frameworks, the role of digital platforms, and case studies of greenwashing versus ethical sustainability practices. They serve as visual tools to reinforce key insights discussed in this chapter, offering readers a comprehensive understanding of how regulatory compliance, digital innovation, and ethical marketing influence the future of sustainability branding (Garcia & Lee, 2021).

REFERENCES

Barker, L. (2021). Digital compliance and environmental advertising. *International Journal of Consumer Protection, 34*(2), 78–99.

Barker, L. (2021). Navigating the FTC Green Guides. *Journal of Consumer Protection, 45*(3), 67–82.

Chen, M., & Liu, X. (2023). AI-driven compliance monitoring in sustainable marketing. *Journal of Marketing Ethics, 19*(4), 123–141.

Chen, M., Liu, X., & Wong, J. (2023). Digital Green Marketing and Consumer Perception. *Marketing & Sustainability Review, 15*(2), 90–112.

Choi, J., Kim, H., & Lee, S. (2021). Eco-labeling systems in Asia. *Sustainability Report, 18*(5), 233–251.

European Commission. (2023). Digital sustainability advertising: Green Claims Directive. *Journal of European Law, 14*(2), 89–112.

European Commission. (2023). Green marketing and compliance: The evolution of digital sustainability regulations. *European Law Review, 18*(2), 78–96.

European Commission. (2023). Proposal for a Directive on Green Claims. Retrieved from https://ec.europa.eu

European Commission. (2023). Proposal for a Directive on Green Claims. *European Law Journal, 16*(1), 45–67.

Ewing, J. (2017). *Faster, Higher, Farther: The Volkswagen Scandal*. Random House.

Federal Trade Commission (FTC). (2022). Green Guides for Environmental Marketing Claims. Retrieved from https://ftc.gov

Garcia, L., & Lee, M. (2021). Consumer trust in sustainability marketing. *Journal of Business Ethics, 38*(3), 78–94.

Green, A., & Parker, D. (2021). The Role of Sustainability in Consumer Decision-Making. *Consumer Research Quarterly, 14*(1), 18–36.

Johnson, P. (2023). Regulatory enforcement in Australia. *Journal of Consumer Law, 15*(1), 32–48.

Jones, L., Smith, R., & Patel, D. (2022). The evolution of stakeholder theory. *Business Strategy Review, 24*(3), 78–95.

Jones, R., & Taylor, P. (2022). Regulating green marketing on digital platforms. *Consumer Protection Review*, *21*(1), 56–79.

Morris, R., & Singh, P. (2023). Corporate accountability in sustainability branding. *Journal of Environmental Law*, *25*(2), 112–136.

Nguyen, D., & Taylor, M. (2022). The rise of consumer skepticism in green marketing. *Marketing & Ethics Review*, *20*(4), 45–67.

Santos, P., Oliveira, R., & Silva, T. (2022). Blockchain Applications in Sustainability Reporting. *The Journal of Supply Chain Management*, *58*(6), 493–510.

Singh, R., & Taylor, P. (2023). Blockchain and transparency in sustainability advertising. *Consumer Protection Review*, *21*(1), 56–79.

Singh, R., & Taylor, P. (2023). Regulating green marketing on digital platforms. *Consumer Protection Review*, *21*(1), 56–79.

Smith, J. (2021). The impact of regulatory compliance on sustainable branding. *International Journal of Market Research*, *36*(2), 94–118.

Smith, J. (2023). Digital Ad Spending Trends. *Statista Reports*. Retrieved from https://statista.com

TerraChoice. (2022). The Seven Sins of Greenwashing. *Consumer Watch Report*.

Thomas, R., & Brown, J. (2022). Balancing Compliance and Creativity in Green Marketing. *Business Horizons*, *65*(4), 459–469.

Chapter 6
The Role of HRM in Supporting Green Marketing Strategies

Shuja Iqbal
https://orcid.org/0000-0002-5397-9297
Jiangsu University, China

Aasim Naimat Gill
Green International University, Pakistan

ABSTRACT

This chapter highlights the role of Human Resource Management (HRM) in advancing green marketing within sustainability-driven organizations. Green marketing promotes environmentally sustainable products and services, aligning with global sustainability goals. HRM embeds green values into recruitment, training, performance management, and leadership development to foster a culture of sustainability. The chapter examines strategies to attract environmentally conscious talent, upskill employees in green competencies, and reward sustainable behaviors, emphasizing leadership's role in driving green marketing objectives. Challenges like resistance to change and resource constraints are addressed, with strategies to overcome them. Emerging trends, such as digital tools and interdisciplinary approaches, are also explored. This chapter positions HRM as a vital enabler of green marketing, offering actionable insights for aligning business practices with sustainability while achieving environmental and economic benefits.

DOI: 10.4018/979-8-3693-9831-9.ch006

1 INTRODUCTION

1.1 Concept of Sustainability and Green Marketing

Sustainability in a business context refers to the practices and strategies organizations adopt to meet current economic, social, and environmental needs without compromising the ability of future generations to meet their own. The United Nations' Sustainable Development Goals (SDGs) have become a guiding framework for integrating sustainability into business operations, emphasizing climate action, responsible consumption, and economic growth (United Nations, 2015). Businesses increasingly acknowledge that sustainable practices are ethical imperatives and key drivers of innovation, customer loyalty, and competitive advantage (Peattie, 2016).

In this context, corporate sustainability encompasses three primary dimensions: environmental sustainability, which focuses on reducing ecological footprints through resource efficiency and waste minimization; social sustainability, involving equitable treatment of stakeholders and community support; and economic sustainability, which ensures long-term financial viability (Dangelico & Vocalelli, 2017). Adopting these practices enables businesses to align their operations with the triple bottom line framework, providing a balance between people, planet, and profit.

1.1.1 The Concept and Significance of Green Marketing

Green marketing refers to developing, promoting, and delivering environmentally sustainable products and services while minimizing negative environmental impacts. It encompasses strategies to satisfy customer needs through products and services that are environmentally friendly, ethically sourced, and responsibly produced (Kao & Du, 2020). The concept aligns with increasing consumer awareness of environmental issues, as many customers prefer brands that demonstrate a commitment to sustainability (A. P. Sharma, 2021). The significance of green marketing extends beyond environmental preservation. It is a strategic differentiator, fostering brand loyalty among environmentally conscious consumers and opening new market opportunities. Moreover, it mitigates regulatory risks by ensuring compliance with stringent environmental laws and enhances corporate reputation (A. P. Sharma, 2021). However, businesses must guard against "greenwashing," where false or exaggerated sustainability claims erode consumer trust and damage brand credibility (Kao & Du, 2020).

1.1.2 Challenges Faced by Organizations in Adopting Green Marketing Strategies

While green marketing offers significant benefits, its adoption is fraught with challenges. One of the primary barriers is the high cost associated with developing and implementing sustainable practices. Organizations must invest in eco-friendly technologies, supply chain innovations, and employee training, which can strain financial resources. Additionally, integrating sustainability into existing business models often requires a cultural shift, which can encounter resistance from employees or stakeholders unfamiliar with or skeptical of green initiatives (Mukonza & Swarts, 2020). Another challenge is the lack of standardization in sustainability metrics, making it difficult for organizations to benchmark their progress or communicate their achievements to stakeholders effectively.

Furthermore, green marketing efforts are sometimes constrained by limited consumer awareness or willingness to pay premium prices for sustainable products, especially in price-sensitive markets (Sugandini, Susilowati, Siswanti, & Syafri, 2020). Regulatory and market variations also pose hurdles. Organizations operating across regions face differing environmental standards, complicating the implementation of uniform green strategies (Sugandini et al., 2020). Despite these challenges, many organizations recognize that adopting green marketing is not merely a compliance-driven approach but a long-term investment in resilience, innovation, and market relevance.

1.2 The Role of Human Resource Management (HRM) in Green Marketing

1.2.1 Definition and Scope of HRM in Green Marketing

Human Resource Management (HRM) is crucial in embedding green marketing practices within an organization by aligning its policies and functions with sustainability goals. HRM in green marketing refers to the strategic integration of human resource practices that promote environmental sustainability and support green marketing initiatives. These practices encompass various activities, including recruitment, training, performance management, and employee engagement, all tailored to advance an organization's green agenda (Arulrajah & Opatha, 2016).

The scope of HRM in green marketing is broad, encompassing the design and implementation of policies prioritizing environmental stewardship. For instance, HR managers are vital in hiring individuals committed to sustainability and equipping them with the necessary skills to support green marketing campaigns (Alzu'bi & Kontor, 2023). Additionally, HRM facilitates the establishment of a green organizational culture by promoting values and behaviors that align with sustainability objectives (Arulrajah & Opatha, 2016). By incorporating green elements into its core functions, HRM enables organizations to address critical sustainability challenges while enhancing employee morale and organizational performance. For example, green training programs help employees understand the environmental impact of their roles, fostering a sense of responsibility and ownership in promoting sustainable practices. Similarly, green HR practices contribute to brand image, as stakeholders increasingly value organizations that demonstrate genuine environmental commitment (Alzu'bi & Kontor, 2023).

1.2.2 Synergies Between HRM and Green Marketing Strategies

The synergies between HRM and green marketing strategies are rooted in their shared goal of driving sustainability and achieving competitive advantage. By aligning HRM with green marketing objectives, organizations can create a cohesive framework that supports environmental goals at every level of operation. One key area of synergy is employee engagement. Employees act as brand ambassadors, and their active participation in green initiatives significantly enhances the credibility of an organization's green marketing efforts (Ahmed & Ahmed, 2022). HRM supports green marketing by cultivating a workforce capable of implementing sustainable practices. For instance, training programs designed by HR departments ensure that employees possess the technical and behavioral competencies needed for eco-friendly marketing campaigns. Moreover, HRM fosters collaboration across departments, creating a unified approach to achieving sustainability goals (Ahmed & Ahmed, 2022).

Another essential synergy is leadership development. HRM is pivotal in identifying and nurturing leaders who champion green marketing initiatives and inspire employees to adopt environmentally conscious behaviors. Effective leadership development programs emphasize integrating sustainability principles into decision-making processes, ensuring alignment with the organization's green marketing strategy (Wang, Liu, & Pérez, 2023). Furthermore, HRM facilitates the incorporation of sustainability metrics into performance management systems. By linking employee performance appraisals and rewards to green marketing achievements, organizations reinforce the importance of sustainability while motivating employees to contribute actively to environmental goals (Trinh, 2021). This integration strengthens the organization's commitment to green practices and enhances employee satisfaction and retention (Figure 1).

Figure 1. Synergies between HRM and green marketing

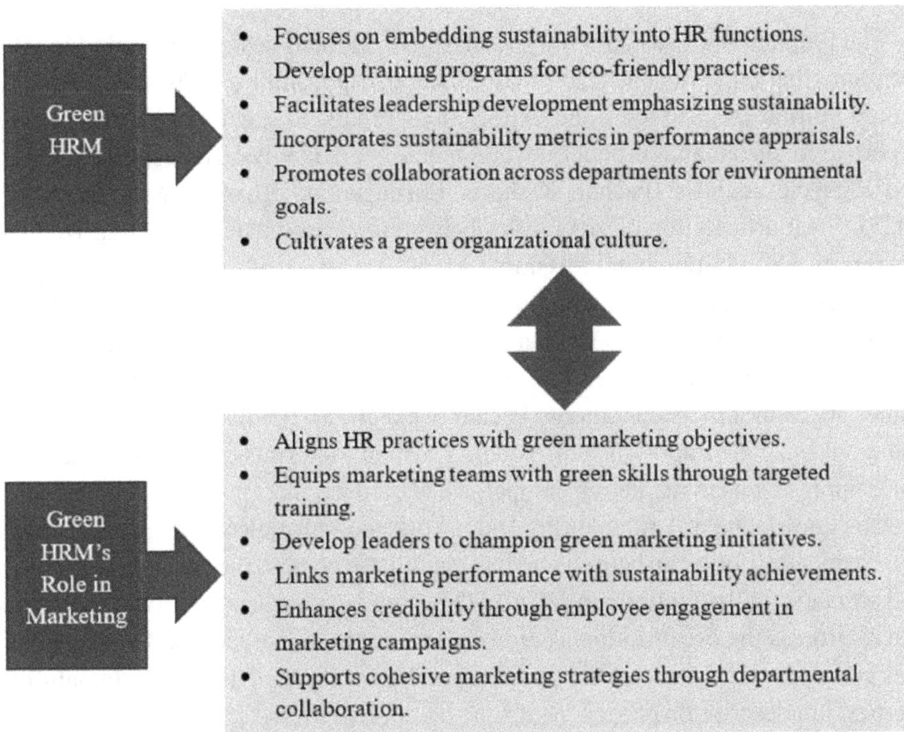

HRM is a critical enabler of green marketing strategies by providing the structure, skills, and culture needed to support sustainability. The synergies between HRM and green marketing enhance organizational efficiency and effectiveness and position the organization as a leader in environmental stewardship.

2 ALIGNING HR POLICIES WITH GREEN MARKETING GOALS

2.1 Recruitment for Sustainability in the Marketing Department

Recruitment for sustainability in the marketing department is critical in embedding green values within an organization. By aligning hiring practices with environmental objectives, organizations can build a workforce that is not only skilled but also committed to advancing green marketing goals. This alignment involves designing job descriptions with sustainability in mind, attracting environmentally conscious employees, and leveraging employer branding to promote green values.

2.1.1 Designing Sustainability-Focused Job Descriptions

The foundation of sustainability-focused recruitment lies in developing job descriptions that explicitly integrate environmental responsibilities. These descriptions should outline specific roles and expectations related to green marketing, such as expertise in sustainable product development, eco-friendly advertising strategies, and lifecycle analysis (Pachar, Kishore, Karunakaran, Bhaskar, & Selvakumar, 2025). Clear articulation of green roles helps attract candidates who align with the organization's environmental mission.

In addition to detailing specific duties, job descriptions should highlight the organization's commitment to sustainability, including statements about the company's green goals and initiatives, and signal to potential employees that environmental values are central to its operations (Pachar et al., 2025). For instance, organizations can emphasize the importance of reducing carbon footprints or advancing sustainable supply chains in marketing campaigns. Moreover, incorporating competencies such as knowledge of sustainability frameworks and proficiency in environmental communication tools can help ensure that candidates possess the necessary technical and strategic skills (Gutterman, 2020). This approach attracts qualified applicants and reinforces the organization's credibility in its green marketing efforts. Companies can try and make use of the sample form below (Sample Form: Sustainability-focused job description):

Table 1. Sample form: Sustainability-focused job description

Position Title:		**Department:**		**Reports to:**	
Job Summary Provide a brief overview of the position and its connection to sustainability initiatives. Example: "The [Job Title] will lead and implement green marketing strategies that align with the organization's sustainability goals, focusing on eco-friendly advertising, sustainable product development, and lifecycle analysis."					
Key Responsibilities List the primary duties and responsibilities that integrate sustainability. • Develop and execute marketing strategies for environmentally sustainable products. • Lead eco-friendly advertising campaigns to promote sustainability values. • Conduct lifecycle analyses to evaluate the environmental impact of marketing initiatives. • Collaborate with cross-functional teams to implement green supply chain practices. • Measure and report on the effectiveness of sustainability-driven marketing efforts.					
Qualifications and Competencies Define the required qualifications and green-related competencies. • Education: Bachelor's or master's in marketing, Environmental Science, or related fields. • Experience: Minimum [X years] experience in sustainable marketing or related roles.					

continued on following page

Table 1. Continued

Position Title:		Department:		Reports to:	
Technical Skills:	• Knowledge of sustainability frameworks (e.g., ISO 14001, GRI). • Proficiency in environmental communication tools. • Familiarity with lifecycle assessment software.		Soft Skills:	• Strong analytical and problem-solving skills. • Effective communication and collaboration abilities.	
Organizational Commitment to Sustainability Include a section to emphasize the company's green initiatives. Example: "[Company Name] is dedicated to reducing its carbon footprint and fostering a culture of sustainability. By joining our team, you will contribute to advancing green supply chains and promoting eco-friendly marketing practices."					
Additional Information					
Location:	Work Schedule:	Salary range:	Benefits:		

Application Instructions:

[Insert Application Process and Deadline]

Signature and Acknowledgment

The applicant acknowledges their understanding of the sustainability-focused responsibilities outlined in this job description by signing.

Applicant Signature: ______________________ Date: ______________

2.1.2 Attracting and Selecting Environmentally Conscious Employees

Attracting environmentally conscious employees requires a strategic approach that resonates with individuals who value sustainability. Job advertisements should emphasize the company's environmental mission and its role in addressing global sustainability challenges. Organizations can use recruitment platforms and networks specializing in green careers, targeting professionals prioritizing environmental impact (Aranganathan, 2018). The selection process should assess candidates' commitment to sustainability alongside their technical expertise. Behavioral interviews, for instance, can evaluate past experiences in implementing sustainable practices or driving environmental initiatives. Structured assessments such as situational judgment tests or case studies on green marketing can further gauge candidates' ability to integrate sustainability into their decision-making processes (Adjei-Bamfo, Bempong, Osei, & Kusi-Sarpong, 2020). Additionally, organizations should consider diversity and inclusion in their green recruitment strategies. Diverse teams bring varied perspectives to sustainability challenges, fostering innovation in green marketing practices

(Aranganathan, 2018). By emphasizing inclusivity, organizations can enhance their reputation and attract top talent who align with their environmental values.

2.1.3 Role of Employer Branding in Promoting Green Values

Employer branding plays a pivotal role in positioning an organization as a leader in sustainability, which is crucial for attracting top talent committed to green values. A strong employer brand communicates the company's dedication to environmental goals through consistent messaging across recruitment channels, public relations efforts, and corporate social responsibility (CSR) initiatives (Kivinda, Su, Hau, & Hashmi, 2021). One effective strategy is showcasing successful green marketing campaigns and internal sustainability programs, such as energy-saving initiatives or waste reduction efforts, to demonstrate a genuine commitment to environmental stewardship. Transparent communication about the organization's progress toward sustainability goals builds trust among prospective employees, making the company an attractive employer (Tharanatha, Shashidhar, Bharath, & Nagesh, 2023).

Social media platforms also play a vital role in employer branding. Companies can share stories of employee involvement in green initiatives or highlight achievements in environmental impact, fostering a sense of pride and engagement. This visibility appeals to potential employees and reinforces the organization's green identity among current staff (Kivinda et al., 2021). Aligning recruitment practices with green marketing goals enables organizations to attract and retain talent capable of driving sustainability initiatives. Companies can build a workforce that supports and amplifies their green marketing strategies by designing sustainability-focused job descriptions, targeting environmentally conscious candidates, and leveraging employer branding.

2.2 Compensation and Performance Management

2.2.1 Integrating Sustainability Metrics into Performance Evaluations

Integrating sustainability metrics into performance evaluations is a strategic approach that aligns employee goals with organizational green objectives. By embedding environmental key performance indicators (KPIs) into appraisal systems, organizations can encourage employees to prioritize sustainability in their daily activities. Metrics such as energy savings, waste reduction, and implementation of eco-friendly marketing strategies provide measurable benchmarks to evaluate employee contributions to environmental goals (Fagarasan, Cristea, Cristea, Popa, & Pisla, 2023).

Effective integration of these metrics requires a clear and transparent framework. Employees must understand how their roles impact sustainability outcomes and how these outcomes will influence their evaluations. For instance, marketing professionals could be assessed on their ability to design campaigns that promote sustainable consumption or their success in reducing the carbon footprint of marketing activities (Hapuwatte, Seevers, & Jawahir, 2022). Regular feedback sessions also play a vital role in reinforcing these expectations and helping employees improve their performance on sustainability initiatives.

One key challenge in integrating sustainability metrics is ensuring their relevance and fairness. Metrics must be tailored to individual roles to avoid creating unrealistic expectations or penalizing employees for factors beyond their control. Furthermore, organizations must invest in training managers to accurately assess and provide constructive feedback on sustainability performance (Fagarasan et al., 2023). These efforts foster a culture of accountability and continuous improvement, driving greater engagement in green practices.

2.2.2 Incentivizing Green Practices Through Rewards and Benefits

Incentivizing green practices through rewards and benefits is a powerful tool for fostering employee commitment to sustainability. Monetary rewards, such as bonuses for achieving environmental targets, are among the most direct and effective incentives. For example, a marketing team could be rewarded for successfully launching campaigns that increase consumer adoption of sustainable products or reduce packaging waste (Odhiambo, Waiganjo, & Simiyu, 2023).

Non-monetary incentives, such as public recognition, awards for green innovations, or access to professional development opportunities in sustainability, are equally important. These rewards highlight the organization's commitment to environmental values and reinforce positive behavior among employees (Lossin, Kozlovskiy, Sodenkamp, & Staake, 2016). Additionally, providing green benefits, such as subsidies for public transportation, electric vehicle allowances, or wellness programs centered on environmental stewardship, can further encourage sustainable practices at work and in employees' personal lives (Odhiambo et al., 2023). To ensure the effectiveness of these incentives, organizations must communicate the link between rewards and green practices. Employees need to understand how their efforts contribute to broader sustainability goals and how these contributions will be recognized. Regular evaluation and adjustment of incentive programs ensure they remain relevant and aligned with evolving environmental priorities (Lossin et al., 2016).

By integrating sustainability metrics into performance evaluations and incentivizing green practices, organizations can create a culture of accountability and motivation, driving collective progress toward environmental objectives.

2.3 Policy Framework for Organizational Sustainability

2.3.1 Developing HR Policies that Embed Sustainability

Developing HR policies that embed sustainability is essential for integrating environmental, social, and economic goals into organizational practices. These policies must reflect the organization's commitment to sustainable development and guide employees in aligning their actions with the company's environmental vision. HR policies that promote sustainability often include guidelines on energy-efficient work practices, waste reduction, and sustainable supply chain management (Renwick, Redman, & Maguire, 2013).

Incorporating environmental values into the organizational mission and employee code of conduct is key to embedding sustainability. For instance, policies can mandate eco-friendly materials, encourage remote work to reduce carbon emissions, and emphasize resource efficiency (Irani, Kilic, & Adeshola, 2022). Furthermore, sustainability-focused HR policies often involve offering training programs on environmental management and recognizing employee contributions to green initiatives, fostering a culture of accountability and continuous improvement. To ensure effectiveness, sustainability policies should be developed collaboratively with input from employees, management, and external stakeholders. This inclusive approach ensures buy-in across the organization and helps identify practical ways to implement green practices (Renwick et al., 2013). Moreover, HR departments should regularly review and update these policies to adapt to evolving sustainability challenges and industry standards.

2.3.2 Legal and Ethical Considerations

Legal and ethical considerations are critical when developing and implementing green HR policies. Organizations must comply with environmental laws and regulations, which vary by region and industry. For example, policies should align with mandates for reducing greenhouse gas emissions, adhering to waste disposal standards, and conserving biodiversity (Akhtar et al., 2023). Non-compliance can lead to financial penalties and reputational damage.

Ethically, HR policies should prioritize transparency, inclusivity, and fairness in sustainability initiatives. This includes ensuring employees at all levels can access resources and training to meet green goals, avoiding undue pressure to achieve sustainability targets, and maintaining equitable practices (Cho, Park, & Lee, 2023). For instance, organizations should avoid greenwashing and misleading stakeholders about their environmental efforts, which can erode trust and damage brand credibility (Akhtar et al., 2023). HR departments must also consider the ethical implications of sustainability-related workforce changes, such as retraining or redeploying employees impacted by the transition to greener processes. Clear communication and support during such transitions are crucial to maintaining employee morale and trust (Cho et al., 2023).

2.3.3 Monitoring and Measuring the Impact of Green HR Policies

Monitoring and measuring the impact of green HR policies is essential for evaluating their effectiveness and making data-driven improvements. Key performance indicators (KPIs) for green HRM include energy savings, carbon emissions reduction, employee participation in sustainability initiatives, and waste reduction (Renwick et al., 2013). Organizations can use sustainability dashboards and environmental audits to track progress against these metrics.

Regular reporting and transparency are also critical. Publishing sustainability performance reports fulfills compliance obligations and reinforces the organization's commitment to green practices. These reports can highlight achievements, identify areas for improvement, and provide stakeholders with insights into the organization's sustainability journey (Yong, Yusliza, Ramayah, & Fawehinmi, 2019). Involving employees in the monitoring process enhances accountability and engagement. For example, forming cross-departmental green committees can ensure diverse perspectives in evaluating the success of HR policies. Additionally, benchmarking against industry standards or certifications, such as ISO 14001, can help organizations refine their green HRM strategies and maintain competitiveness (Ryu, Park, Park, Park, & Lee, 2021).

A robust policy framework for organizational sustainability involves creating comprehensive HR policies, adhering to legal and ethical standards, and implementing effective monitoring mechanisms. These elements work together to ensure that sustainability is ingrained in every aspect of the organization, driving long-term environmental and social impact.

3 DEVELOPING A GREEN ORGANIZATIONAL CULTURE

3.1 Instilling Environmental Values

Creating a green organizational culture is fundamental to embedding sustainability into a company's identity and operations. A culture rooted in environmental values inspires employees to align their behaviors and decisions with sustainability goals, fostering a shared commitment to green initiatives. Instilling such values requires strategic communication and storytelling to connect employees emotionally and intellectually to the organization's sustainability mission.

3.1.1 Communicating Green Vision and Values to Employees

Communicating a clear and compelling green vision is foundational in developing a sustainable organizational culture. A well-articulated vision gives employees a sense of purpose, demonstrating how their roles contribute to broader environmental objectives (LaVan, Zilic, & Basappa, 2022). To be effective, this communication must be consistent, transparent, and integrated into all levels of the organization. Leadership plays a pivotal role in this process. Leaders who advocate for sustainability can influence employees' attitudes and behaviors, making the green vision a shared organizational value (Wiradirja et al., 2020). For instance, senior executives can reinforce their commitment to sustainability through public speeches, internal memos, and by leading by example in adopting eco-friendly practices.

Regular communication channels such as newsletters, town halls, and digital platforms provide opportunities to keep employees informed about the organization's green initiatives. Updates on sustainability goals, progress, and challenges create a sense of transparency and accountability, further engaging employees (Renwick et al., 2013). Visual aids such as dashboards and infographics can simplify complex data and make the green vision more relatable. Interactive approaches, such as workshops and feedback sessions, encourage employees to contribute their ideas and concerns, fostering a sense of ownership in the organization's sustainability efforts. This participatory model ensures that every organization communicates, embraces, and implements the green vision (LaVan et al., 2022).

3.1.2 Role of Storytelling and Organizational Narratives

Storytelling is a powerful tool for embedding environmental values within an organization. Stories resonate emotionally and cognitively, making abstract sustainability goals tangible and relatable to employees (Boyce, 2017). Organizational narratives that highlight real-world examples of successful green initiatives inspire employees by showcasing the positive impact of their contributions. For instance, a company can share stories about how its green marketing strategies have reduced environmental footprints or benefited local communities. These narratives can be disseminated through newsletters, video campaigns, or internal events, making sustainability efforts visible and meaningful (Beigi, Callahan, & Michaelson, 2019).

Personal stories from employees and leaders further humanize the organization's green culture. When leaders share their journeys in adopting sustainable practices, it establishes authenticity and motivates employees to follow suit (Boyce, 2017). Similarly, spotlighting employees who have excelled in implementing green initiatives serves as recognition while encouraging others to participate. Storytelling also facilitates a sense of continuity and purpose. Organizations can draw on historical milestones or significant achievements in their sustainability journey to create a legacy narrative. This reinforces a collective identity around environmental stewardship, ensuring that sustainability remains a core organizational value even amid changes in leadership or strategy (Renwick et al., 2020). Moreover, storytelling can address resistance to change by framing sustainability as a shared challenge that requires collective effort. By presenting employees as key protagonists in the organization's environmental story; storytelling fosters a sense of agency and commitment to green values (Kaur, 2021).

3.2 Employee Participation in Sustainability

3.2.1 Initiatives such as Sustainability Events and Campaigns

Employee participation is a cornerstone of organizational sustainability efforts. Initiatives such as sustainability events and campaigns are instrumental in engaging employees and creating a shared sense of purpose. These events, ranging from eco-friendly workshops and green challenges to more extensive organizational campaigns like Earth Day celebrations, serve as platforms for raising awareness and fostering action (Renwick et al., 2020). One example of an effective sustainability event is a waste reduction challenge, where employees are encouraged to minimize paper and plastic usage within the workplace. Such initiatives reduce the organization's environmental footprint and instill habits that employees can carry beyond the workplace (Sharma & Gupta, 2015). Similarly, tree-planting events or community clean-up drives provide employees with tangible ways to contribute to environmental conservation while enhancing team cohesion.

Campaigns focusing on education and advocacy, such as energy-saving drives or carbon reduction pledges, can also significantly impact employee behaviors. These campaigns are most effective when supported by clear goals and measurable outcomes. For instance, a campaign to reduce office energy consumption might include setting targets, tracking progress through digital dashboards, and rewarding teams for their achievements (Sharma & Gupta, 2015). The success of such initiatives often hinges on visible leadership support and consistent communication. Leaders actively participate in sustainability events to signal their commitment to green goals, inspiring employees to follow suit (Podgorodnichenko, Akmal, Edgar, & Everett, 2022). Furthermore, sharing success stories from these events reinforces the organization's environmental mission and motivates continued participation.

3.2.2 Role of Peer Influence and Collaborative Efforts in Fostering Green Behaviors

Peer influence and collaborative efforts are vital in fostering sustainable behaviors within organizations. Employees are more likely to adopt green practices when they observe colleagues engaging in similar behaviors. This phenomenon, often referred to as social proof, is particularly effective in creating a culture of sustainability (K. Lee, 2010). Encouraging team-based approaches to sustainability, such as forming green committees or cross-functional task forces, amplifies the impact of individual efforts. Collaborative efforts allow employees to share ideas, pool resources, and develop innovative solutions to environmental challenges. For instance, a cross-departmental team might work together to implement a waste segregation program or create a green marketing strategy (Zhao, Bai, Liu, & Wang, 2022). Another effective strategy is peer-led initiatives, such as mentoring programs where sustainability champions guide colleagues in adopting eco-friendly practices. These programs foster a sense of accountability and community, reinforcing organizational green behaviors (K. Lee, 2010).

In addition, fostering healthy competition among teams can spur engagement in sustainability efforts. For example, departments could compete to achieve the highest recycling rates or the lowest energy consumption. Such competitions make sustainability initiatives more engaging and create opportunities for collaboration and innovation. Employee participation in sustainability through events, campaigns, peer influence, and cooperation strengthens organizational commitment to green goals. These efforts drive measurable environmental impact and cultivate a shared responsibility and innovation culture.

3.3 Continuous Reinforcement of Green Practices

3.3.1 Importance of Sustained Communication

Sustained communication is a critical element in reinforcing green practices within organizations. Effective communication ensures that sustainability remains a priority in employees' daily activities and aligns their efforts with the organization's long-term environmental goals. Organizations must employ consistent, clear, and multi-channel communication strategies that engage employees at all levels (Mefalopulos, 2005). Continuous updates on sustainability initiatives and progress reinforce the organization's commitment to green practices. For example, regular emails, newsletters, or town hall meetings can highlight milestones, such as achieving energy reduction targets or launching new green products. These updates keep employees informed and foster a sense of shared achievement and motivation to contribute further (Olaleye, Oloye, Akinloye, & Akinwande, 2024).

Interactive communication tools, such as feedback surveys and virtual suggestion boxes, encourage employees to share ideas and challenges regarding sustainability efforts. This two-way dialogue fosters inclusivity and ensures employees feel heard and valued in the organization's green journey (Olaleye et al., 2024). Moreover, leveraging technology can enhance communication efforts. Digital platforms, such as sustainability dashboards or mobile apps, provide real-time data on environmental performance, helping employees understand the impact of their actions. Gamified communication strategies, like leaderboards for recycling or energy-saving initiatives, further engage employees and sustain interest in green practices (Mefalopulos, 2005).

3.3.2 Institutionalizing Sustainability Through Rituals and Symbols

Institutionalizing sustainability through rituals and symbols effectively embed green values into an organization's culture. Rituals are repetitive, symbolic actions that reinforce shared beliefs, while symbols serve as tangible reminders of an organization's commitment to sustainability. Rituals such as celebrating "Green Mondays" or holding monthly sustainability-focused meetings can establish routine practices that keep environmental goals top of mind. For instance, a company might dedicate the first Friday of every month to employee-led discussions on green innovations or host an annual sustainability awards ceremony to recognize outstanding contributions (Dacin et al., 2008). These rituals create regular opportunities to reflect on and celebrate sustainability efforts.

Symbols, such as eco-friendly office designs, prominently displayed green certifications in workplaces, or using renewable energy in operations, visually communicate the organization's dedication to sustainability. These elements remind employees and stakeholders of the company's environmental values (Glynn & Abzug, 2002). Branding materials like logos with green motifs or sustainability slogans further institutionalize these values. Storytelling can also be symbolic, showcasing narratives of employees or teams that have championed green practices. These stories resonate emotionally with employees and encourage them to emulate such behaviors (Dacin et al., 2008). By combining sustained communication with rituals and symbols, organizations can embed sustainability deeply into their culture, ensuring long-term commitment and consistency in green practices.

4 TRAINING AND DEVELOPMENT FOR GREEN MARKETING SKILLS

4.1 Identifying Green Marketing Skills Needs

Green marketing demands a workforce equipped with specialized skills to promote sustainable products, engage environmentally conscious consumers, and align with global sustainability goals. Identifying these skills is essential for organizations aiming to remain competitive in the evolving market. This section analyzes emerging green marketing job roles and assesses organizational skills gaps.

4.1.1 Analysis of Emerging Green Marketing Job Roles

The increasing focus on sustainability has given rise to new roles in green marketing. Positions such as sustainability marketing manager, eco-brand strategist, and green communication specialist are becoming integral to organizations. These roles involve crafting campaigns emphasizing sustainability, ensuring compliance with environmental regulations, and engaging stakeholders in green initiatives (Qureshi & Mehraj, 2022). Professionals in these roles are expected to have expertise in environmental science, ethical sourcing, and product lifecycle assessment (Thakkar, 2021).

Another emerging role is that of a sustainability analyst, who evaluates the environmental impact of marketing strategies and suggests improvements to align with green goals. Similarly, digital marketing specialists with expertise in promoting sustainable products via eco-friendly digital platforms are gaining prominence (Qureshi & Mehraj, 2022). The shift towards circular economy practices has also created a demand for marketers who can effectively communicate the value of recycled or refurbished products to consumers. Moreover, organizations increasingly require marketing teams to collaborate with supply chain and product development teams, ensuring that green practices are integrated across the value chain. This interdisciplinary approach necessitates marketers to know sustainable supply chain practices and green technologies (Thakkar, 2021).

4.1.2 Skills Gap Assessment in Organizations

Despite the growing demand for green marketing skills, many organizations face significant gaps in their workforce's capabilities. Skills gap assessments are crucial for identifying deficiencies and designing targeted training programs. These assessments involve evaluating the current competencies of employees against the skills required for emerging green marketing roles (Poston & Dhaliwal, 2015). One key area of deficiency is the lack of technical knowledge about sustainability concepts, such as carbon footprint reduction, renewable energy integration, and circular economy principles. Employees cannot often translate these concepts into actionable marketing strategies (Kim et al., 2021). Additionally, soft skills such as stakeholder engagement, ethical communication, and consumer education are critical yet frequently underdeveloped among marketing teams (Renwick et al., 2020).

Technological advancements also contribute to skills gaps. With the rise of digital tools for sustainability reporting and eco-focused data analytics, marketers need proficiency in these technologies to track and communicate the environmental impact of their campaigns effectively (Poston & Dhaliwal, 2015). Organizations must also address regional variations in sustainability practices, as global marketing strategies require knowledge of diverse environmental regulations and cultural attitudes toward green products (Kolding et al., 2018). Skills gap assessments often reveal a lack of formal education or certification in sustainability among marketing professionals. This highlights the importance of integrating green marketing concepts into professional development programs and academic curricula (Kolding et al., 2018). Addressing these gaps can enhance organizations' ability to implement effective green marketing strategies and meet the expectations of environmentally conscious consumers. Understanding the emerging green marketing roles and conducting thorough skills gap assessments are critical steps in building a workforce that can drive sustainable growth. Organizations that invest in identifying and addressing these needs are better positioned to succeed in the competitive and sustainability-driven market.

4.2 Designing Green Marketing Training Programs

4.2.1 Curriculum Development for Sustainability Training

The foundation of effective green marketing training programs lies in well-designed curricula that address the specific needs of sustainability-focused roles. A robust curriculum should cover key areas such as understanding environmental regulations, integrating sustainability into marketing strategies, and utilizing green technologies for campaigns. It should also emphasize critical concepts like the circular economy, lifecycle assessment, and consumer behavior about sustainable products (Renwick et al., 2020).

Organizations must tailor the curriculum to their industry and target audience to ensure relevance. For example, a retail company might focus on sustainable supply chain practices, while a tech firm might highlight eco-friendly product design. Collaboration with academic institutions and sustainability experts can further enrich the curriculum, bringing evidence-based practices and cutting-edge research (Vitale et al., 2018). Additionally, incorporating case studies and simulations provides practical insights, helping trainees understand the real-world application of sustainability principles. A dynamic and adaptive curriculum is essential for addressing the evolving landscape of green marketing. Regular reviews and updates ensure the training aligns with global environmental goals, emerging technologies, and shifting consumer expectations (Vitale et al., 2018).

4.2.2 Modes of Delivery: Workshops, E-Learning, and Hands-On Training

The mode of delivery plays a critical role in the effectiveness of green marketing training programs. Workshops, e-learning, and hands-on training can cater to diverse learning preferences and enhance knowledge retention. Workshops offer interactive opportunities for participants to engage in group discussions, role-playing, and brainstorming sessions on sustainability challenges. These sessions can focus on green branding, eco-labeling, or consumer education. Workshops are convenient for fostering collaboration and sparking innovative ideas among participants (Ho, Nakamori, Ho, & Lim, 2016).

E-learning platforms provide flexibility, enabling employees to access training materials conveniently. These platforms often feature multimedia resources such as videos, quizzes, and interactive modules covering energy-efficient marketing and environmental impact assessments. Gamification elements, such as badges and leaderboards, can boost engagement and motivation (Callan, Johnston, & Poulsen, 2015). Hands-on training, such as field visits to sustainable businesses or practical exercises in eco-friendly product development, provides experiential learning that reinforces theoretical knowledge. For instance, participants might collaborate on designing a green marketing campaign or conducting a waste audit for a specific product. This approach helps trainees build confidence in applying sustainability concepts to their roles (Ho et al., 2016).

4.2.3 Case Studies of Successful Green Training Initiatives

Case studies offer valuable lessons and inspiration for designing effective green marketing training programs. One notable example is Unilever's "Sustainable Living Plan," which incorporates training for marketing teams on integrating sustainability into their campaigns. This program has successfully enhanced employees' understanding of sustainable product development and consumer engagement strategies, leading to the growth of their eco-friendly product portfolio (Hayles, 2019). Another example is IKEA's green training program, which focuses on educating employees about products' lifecycle impacts and the importance of sustainable sourcing. The hands-on elements of this program, such as visits to suppliers and workshops on eco-design, have significantly improved employees' ability to communicate sustainability benefits to customers (Renwick et al., 2020).

Similarly, the online learning platform Coursera offers sustainability-focused marketing courses developed in partnership with leading universities. These courses combine theoretical knowledge with practical applications, equipping participants with skills in sustainable business strategy and green marketing innovation (Hayles, 2019). Designing effective green marketing training programs requires a well-structured curriculum, diverse delivery modes, and insights from successful case studies. By investing in these programs, organizations can build a workforce capable of driving sustainability and maintaining competitiveness in the evolving green market.

4.3 Upskilling for Emerging Technologies in Green Marketing

4.3.1 Training for Energy-Efficient Technologies and Sustainable Practices

Training for energy-efficient technologies and sustainable practices has become essential as businesses increasingly adopt green marketing strategies. These technologies reduce operational costs and align with consumer expectations for environmentally responsible organizations. To implement green marketing effectively, employees must have the skills to utilize these technologies and practices in their daily operations (Renwick et al., 2020). Energy-efficient technologies, such as renewable energy systems, innovative grid technologies, and energy-monitoring software, transform how organizations market their products and services. For instance, employees in marketing departments can be trained to highlight the benefits of these technologies in campaigns, emphasizing their environmental and economic advantages to customers. Training programs can also teach employees to conduct carbon footprint analyses for marketing activities, enabling the organization to make data-driven decisions to minimize emissions (Alhamami, Petri, Rezgui, & Kubicki, 2020).

Sustainable practices, such as eco-friendly packaging, resource-efficient manufacturing processes, and ethical sourcing, are critical components of green marketing. Employees need to understand how these practices contribute to the organization's sustainability goals and how to communicate their benefits to stakeholders effectively. Hands-on training in sustainable supply chain management and waste reduction strategies can ensure that marketing teams are well-versed in implementing and promoting these practices (Alhamami et al., 2020). Training for these technologies and practices must be tailored to organizational needs and delivered through interactive workshops, simulations, and on-the-job coaching. Continuous evaluation and feedback mechanisms ensure that employees can apply their knowledge effectively in real-world scenarios (Panagiotopoulou, Paraskevopoulou, Margaityte, Petkova, & Stavropoulos, 2024).

4.3.2 Focus on Industry-Specific Green Competencies

Green marketing competencies vary significantly across industries, and upskilling efforts must be tailored to address these specific needs. For example, the renewable energy sector requires marketers who can effectively communicate the advantages of solar or wind energy systems, while the fashion industry emphasizes sustainable sourcing and recycling initiatives. Identifying and developing these competencies ensures that employees are prepared to meet their respective sectors' unique challenges and opportunities (Napathorn, 2022). For instance, marketing teams must understand the intricacies of promoting electric vehicles (EVs) in the automotive industry. This includes highlighting the benefits of reduced greenhouse gas emissions, tax incentives for EV purchases, and the role of charging infrastructure. Training programs can focus on developing technical knowledge about EV technologies and strategies for addressing consumer concerns about range and charging times (Pathak & Agarwal, 2024).

Similarly, in the food and beverage sector, green marketing competencies often involve knowledge of organic certification processes, sustainable farming practices, and the environmental impact of food packaging. Training programs for marketers in this industry can include workshops on communicating these aspects effectively to consumers and stakeholders (Napathorn, 2022). On the other hand, the technology sector requires marketers to emphasize the energy efficiency of products such as laptops, servers, and smart devices. Employees must understand how to position these products as sustainable solutions in competitive markets, leveraging data on energy savings and lifecycle impacts. Case studies of successful campaigns in this sector can serve as valuable learning tools, demonstrating best practices and innovative approaches (Renwick et al., 2020).

Organizations should collaborate with academic institutions, industry associations, and sustainability experts to maximize the impact of industry-specific upskilling. These partnerships can provide insights into emerging trends and ensure that training programs align with industry standards and global sustainability goals (Pathak & Agarwal, 2024). Upskilling employees in energy-efficient technologies and industry-specific green competencies is critical for successfully implementing green marketing strategies. By investing in targeted training programs, organizations can empower their workforce to drive sustainability while remaining competitive in a rapidly evolving market.

5 EMPLOYEE ENGAGEMENT IN GREEN MARKETING PRACTICES

5.1 Creating a Sense of Ownership

Employee engagement is pivotal to the success of green marketing strategies, and fostering a sense of ownership is an effective way to encourage active participation in sustainability initiatives. This sense of ownership is achieved by involving employees in shaping environmental policies and emphasizing the benefits of participatory decision-making. Companies can create a motivated workforce committed to achieving sustainability goals by engaging employees in the organization's green mission.

5.1.1 Employee Involvement in Shaping Environmental Policies

Involving employees in developing environmental policies enhances their quality and ensures a more significant commitment to their implementation. Employees possess unique insights into organizational operations, making them valuable contributors to identifying practical sustainability solutions. For instance, marketing teams can provide input on eco-friendly product messaging, while operations teams might suggest ways to reduce resource consumption (Renwick et al., 2020). Organizations can involve employees through structured forums, such as sustainability committees, brainstorming sessions, and focus groups. These platforms allow employees to voice their ideas and concerns, fostering a collaborative environment where sustainability becomes a shared responsibility. Additionally, transparent communication about policy development processes and goals builds trust and reinforces employees' connection to the organization's green objectives (Chou, 2014). Another effective strategy is crowdsourcing ideas from employees for green initiatives. For example, employee suggestions on waste reduction or sustainable product packaging can influence organizational practices. Recognizing and implementing these ideas demonstrates the value placed on employee contributions, further enhancing engagement and ownership (Chou, 2014).

5.1.2 Benefits of Participatory Decision-Making

Participatory decision-making empowers employees and enhances the effectiveness of green marketing practices. Organizations can tap into diverse perspectives by involving employees in decision-making and fostering innovation in sustainability efforts. Research shows that participatory approaches lead to more creative and practical solutions, as employees are more likely to feel invested in the outcomes (Marchington, 2015). One significant benefit of participatory decision-making is increased alignment between employees' values and organizational goals. When employees actively contribute to shaping policies, they are more likely to internalize and advocate for these policies. This alignment enhances morale, reduces resistance to change, and encourages employees to be ambassadors for the organization's sustainability initiatives (Ramus, 2001).

Moreover, participatory decision-making strengthens teamwork and collaboration. Green initiatives often require cross-functional efforts, such as integrating sustainable practices across marketing, production, and supply chain teams. Participatory approaches build stronger interdepartmental relationships by fostering a sense of collective responsibility and facilitating the seamless implementation of green practices (Marchington, 2015). Creating a sense of ownership through employee involvement and participatory decision-making is essential for driving engagement in green marketing practices. These strategies enhance the quality and impact of sustainability initiatives and foster a motivated and committed workforce.

5.2 Leveraging Engagement Programs

5.2.1 Examples of Green Challenges, Sustainability Committees, and Volunteer Programs

Engagement programs such as green challenges, sustainability committees, and volunteer initiatives are vital in fostering employee participation in green marketing practices. These programs provide structured opportunities for employees to contribute to organizational sustainability while building a sense of community and shared purpose. Green challenges are a popular way to engage employees in sustainability efforts. These challenges often involve setting measurable goals, such as reducing energy consumption, increasing recycling rates, or achieving sustainable commuting targets. For example, organizations may hold a month-long competition between departments to see which team can save the most energy. Such initiatives promote sustainable behavior and create a sense of healthy competition that motivates employees to adopt greener practices (Measham & Barnett, 2008).

Sustainability committees are another effective engagement tool. These committees, composed of employees from various departments, provide a platform for brainstorming, planning, and implementing sustainability initiatives. These committees often serve as ambassadors, promoting green practices within their teams and ensuring alignment with organizational goals (Bass, Dalal-Clayton, & Pretty, 1995; Measham & Barnett, 2008). Sustainability committees enhance ownership and accountability by involving employees in decision-making and execution. Volunteer programs also contribute significantly to employee engagement. Activities such as tree planting, community clean-ups, or workshops on sustainable living allow employees to see the tangible impact of their efforts. These programs benefit the environment and enhance employees' pride and connection to the organization's values (Renwick et al., 2020).

5.2.2 Role of Gamification in Fostering Engagement

Gamification is an innovative approach to fostering engagement in sustainability initiatives. Organizations can incorporate game-like elements such as points, badges, and leaderboards to make green practices more engaging and enjoyable for employees. Gamification taps into intrinsic motivators like competition, recognition, and achievement, driving sustained participation in sustainability programs (Hammedi, Leclercq, & Poncin, 2019). One example of gamification in green engagement is an app-based recycling challenge where employees earn points for correctly sorting waste or reducing paper usage. Leaderboards display top performers, encouraging employees to compete while learning about sustainable practices. Organizations can also introduce rewards, such as gift cards or donations to environmental causes, to further incentivize participation (Kumar & Raghavendran, 2015).

Gamification is particularly effective in creating long-term behavioral change. For instance, employees who consistently participate in gamified energy-saving initiatives may adopt these habits at home, extending the program's impact beyond the workplace. Furthermore, gamification fosters collaboration and innovation, as employees share tips and strategies to improve their performance in green challenges (Hammedi et al., 2019). Leveraging engagement programs such as green challenges, sustainability committees, volunteer initiatives, and gamification can significantly enhance employee involvement in green marketing practices. These approaches foster a culture of sustainability and empower employees to become active contributors to organizational and environmental goals.

5.3 Communication for Sustainability Engagement

5.3.1 Effective Use of Communication Channels

Effective communication is central to sustaining employee engagement in green marketing and broader sustainability initiatives. Organizations must leverage traditional and digital communication channels to ensure that sustainability messages reach all employees consistently and compellingly (Renwick et al., 2020). Internal communication platforms, such as newsletters, intranet updates, and bulletin boards, consistently update employees on sustainability goals, achievements, and upcoming initiatives. These tools ensure that employees remain informed about the organization's green efforts and understand how their contributions align with broader objectives (Fuchs, 2008).

Digital platforms such as mobile apps, collaboration tools, and social media are increasingly used to engage employees interactively. For instance, a company app might provide real-time updates on carbon reduction progress or host gamified challenges to encourage eco-friendly behaviors. Social media platforms can also be used internally to share success stories, highlight employee contributions, and foster a sense of community around sustainability (Fuchs, 2008). Face-to-face communication remains equally important. Regular town hall meetings and team discussions allow leaders to share updates, reinforce the organization's green vision, and address employee questions. These sessions build transparency and trust, motivating employees to remain committed to sustainability initiatives (Craig & Allen, 2013).

5.3.2 Strategies to Maintain Enthusiasm and Long-Term Commitment

Maintaining enthusiasm and long-term commitment to sustainability requires ongoing reinforcement of its importance and benefits. One key strategy is the consistent use of recognition and rewards. Publicly acknowledging employees or teams who excel in green practices fosters a culture of appreciation and motivates others to participate (Walker, 2002). For example, monthly "green champions" awards can incentivize employees to contribute actively to sustainability goals. Storytelling is another powerful tool for maintaining engagement. Sharing narratives about the tangible impact of sustainability efforts, such as reduced energy costs or community benefits from environmental initiatives, helps employees see the value of their contributions (Jawad, Scott-Jackson, Jawad, & Scott-Jackson, 2016). Stories featuring employee involvement create a sense of pride and personal connection to the organization's green mission.

Interactive and participatory strategies, such as brainstorming sessions, surveys, and feedback channels, ensure that employees feel their voices are heard. By incorporating employee input into sustainability strategies, organizations demonstrate inclusivity and reinforce collective ownership of green initiatives (Renwick et al., 2020). Lastly, visual reminders such as sustainability dashboards, progress trackers, and green-themed office decor help sustain interest in green practices. These visuals reinforce the organization's commitment to sustainability, keeping it at the forefront of employees' minds (Jawad et al., 2016). Effective communication channels, recognition, storytelling, participatory approaches, and visual reinforcements are essential for engaging employees in sustainability initiatives. These strategies sustain enthusiasm and embed sustainability into the organizational culture.

6 LEADERSHIP IN DRIVING GREEN MARKETING INITIATIVES

6.1 Importance of Leadership Commitment

Leadership commitment is critical to the successful implementation and sustainability of green marketing initiatives. Leaders set the tone for organizational priorities and influence how sustainability is integrated into business strategies. Effective green leaders inspire employees, foster a culture of accountability, and ensure that environmental goals are aligned with organizational performance metrics (J. Lee, 2005).

6.1.1 The Influence of Leadership on Organizational Green Strategies

Leadership plays a pivotal role in shaping and driving organizational green strategies. Leaders prioritizing sustainability allocate resources to green marketing projects, integrate environmental goals into corporate strategy, and advocate for internal and external sustainability. They act as role models, demonstrating commitment by reducing their environmental footprint or championing sustainable business practices (Al-Swidi, Gelaidan, & Saleh, 2021).

Strategic vision and clear communication from leaders are essential for aligning green marketing initiatives with organizational goals. Leaders must articulate a compelling narrative about the importance of sustainability and how it contributes to competitive advantage and social responsibility. For example, leaders can highlight how green marketing enhances brand reputation, attracts environmentally conscious customers, and ensures regulatory compliance (Al-Swidi et al., 2021; Luu, 2020). Moreover, leaders influence green strategies by fostering cross-functional collaboration. Green marketing often requires input from multiple departments, such as supply chain, product development, and finance. Effective leaders facilitate these collaborations, ensuring sustainability goals are embedded across the organization (Luu, 2020).

6.1.2 Attributes of Effective Green Leaders

Effective green leaders possess distinct attributes that enable them to champion sustainability initiatives and inspire their teams. These attributes include vision, influence, and adaptability.

- *Visionary Thinking:* Green leaders have a long-term perspective and the ability to envision how sustainability can drive innovation and value creation. They proactively identify opportunities for integrating green marketing into business strategies and setting ambitious environmental goals (Maheshwari & Rai, 2022).
- *Influential Communication Skills:* Green leaders excel at communicating the importance of sustainability in ways that resonate with diverse stakeholders. They use compelling narratives to highlight the benefits of green practices and build consensus around environmental initiatives. Their ability to inspire and mobilize teams is key to successfully executing green marketing strategies (Zaccaro, Kemp, & Bader, 2004).
- *Adaptability and Resilience:* Sustainability efforts often face challenges such as resource constraints or resistance to change. Effective green leaders demonstrate resilience and adaptability, navigating these challenges while focusing on environmental goals. Their ability to manage risks and pivot strategies ensures the continuity of green marketing efforts (Maheshwari & Rai, 2022).
- *Empathy and Inclusivity:* Green leaders prioritize stakeholder engagement, recognizing that successful sustainability initiatives require input from employees, customers, and communities. They foster an inclusive culture that values diverse perspectives, empowering employees to contribute to environmental decision-making (Zaccaro et al., 2004).
- *Ethical Integrity:* Effective green leaders exhibit strong moral values, ensuring transparency and accountability in their sustainability efforts. They avoid greenwashing practices and build trust by aligning words with actions, reinforcing the organization's commitment to genuine environmental stewardship (Renwick et al., 2020).

Leadership commitment is indispensable for driving green marketing initiatives. Leaders influence the strategic direction of sustainability efforts, inspire employee engagement, and ensure that green goals are integrated into the organizational fabric. By embodying the attributes of effective green leaders, they advance environmental objectives and position their organizations as pioneers in the green economy.

6.2 Leadership Development Programs

6.2.1 Training Leaders to Champion Sustainability

Leadership development programs focused on sustainability are essential for equipping leaders with the skills and knowledge to drive green marketing initiatives. These programs help leaders understand the complexities of environmental challenges, develop strategic thinking to address them and inspire employees to adopt sustainable practices (Renwick et al., 2020). Training programs for sustainability leadership often include modules on environmental regulations, green technologies, and sustainability frameworks like the UN Sustainable Development Goals (SDGs). Leaders are also taught to integrate these elements into the organization's strategy and operations. For example, case-based learning can highlight successful examples of organizations that have leveraged sustainability as a competitive advantage (Sullivan, 2017).

Interactive workshops and simulations play a vital role in these programs. By engaging in scenario-based activities, leaders can practice decision-making under conditions that mimic real-world sustainability challenges, such as balancing short-term profitability with long-term environmental goals. Moreover, mentorship from experienced sustainability leaders can provide invaluable insights and guidance, enabling emerging leaders to navigate the complexities of green initiatives effectively (Sullivan, 2017). Another critical component of sustainability leadership training is emotional intelligence. Leaders are encouraged to cultivate empathy and inclusivity, enabling them to engage effectively with diverse stakeholders. These skills are crucial for building trust and fostering collaboration within the organization and beyond (Chadee, Wiesner, & Roxas, 2011).

6.2.2 Emphasizing the Business Case for Green Initiatives in Leadership Curricula

A core aspect of leadership development programs is emphasizing the business case for green initiatives. Leaders must understand how sustainability aligns with financial performance, brand value, and competitive advantage. This alignment is key to securing organizational commitment and resources for green marketing strategies (Novy, Banerjee, & Matson, 2021). Leadership curricula should include data-driven insights demonstrating green initiatives' financial and operational benefits. For instance, reducing energy consumption or waste can lower costs, while eco-friendly products often command premium pricing and foster customer loyalty. Additionally, sustainability initiatives can enhance regulatory compliance and mitigate risks associated with environmental violations (Dyer & Dyer, 2017).

Workshops and lectures on green innovation are convenient in highlighting opportunities for revenue growth through sustainability. For example, leaders can explore how adopting circular economy principles or leveraging renewable energy sources can open new markets and attract environmentally conscious investors (Dyer & Dyer, 2017). Incorporating stakeholder engagement into the curriculum is equally important. Leaders learn how to communicate the business case for sustainability to internal and external stakeholders, including employees, shareholders, and customers. This ensures that green initiatives are implemented effectively and widely supported (Novy et al., 2021). Leadership development programs that train leaders to champion sustainability and emphasize the business case for green initiatives are critical for fostering organizational commitment to environmental goals. By equipping leaders with the necessary skills and perspectives, these programs enable organizations to integrate sustainability into their core operations and thrive in a rapidly evolving marketplace.

6.3 Aligning Leadership with Organizational Green Goals

6.3.1 Strategies for Leaders to Inspire and Mobilize Employees

Effective leadership is crucial for aligning an organization's green goals with its operations and inspiring employees to adopt sustainable practices. Leaders must implement strategies that communicate a clear vision, foster collaboration, and create a culture of accountability around sustainability (Renwick et al., 2020). One key strategy is leading by example. Leaders who visibly commit to sustainable practices, such as reducing personal carbon footprints or championing eco-friendly office initiatives, inspire employees to follow suit. These actions reinforce the importance of green goals and demonstrate that sustainability is a shared responsibility (Sugiarto, 2024).

Another essential strategy is transparent and consistent communication. Leaders should articulate the organization's green vision through various channels, such as town halls, newsletters, or personal interactions. By linking sustainability goals to the company's broader mission and values, leaders can foster a sense of purpose among employees (Jahidi, 2020). Creating opportunities for employee participation is also critical. Leaders can establish cross-functional green committees or task forces that allow employees to contribute ideas and collaborate on sustainability projects. This inclusivity empowers employees and drives innovation in achieving green objectives (Sugiarto, 2024). Additionally, providing recognition and rewards for sustainable efforts is a powerful motivator. Acknowledging employees who excel in implementing green practices, whether through awards, public recognition, or incentives, reinforces the importance of their contributions and encourages others to participate (Jahidi, 2020).

6.3.2 Case Studies of Exemplary Green Leadership

Case studies of exemplary green leadership illustrate how leaders can effectively align organizational goals with sustainability initiatives.

1) One notable example is Unilever, where former CEO Paul Polman integrated sustainability into the company's core strategy through the Sustainable Living Plan. By setting ambitious goals, such as halving the company's environmental footprint and sourcing 100% of its agricultural materials sustainably, Polman inspired employees to innovate and collaborate toward these objectives (CB, 2024).
2) Another example is Tesla, led by Elon Musk, which has become synonymous with green innovation. Musk's vision for a sustainable future has driven the company's success in electric vehicles, renewable energy, and battery technologies. His leadership style, characterized by bold goals and transparent communication, has mobilized employees to push boundaries in green technology (Tesla, 2024).
3) Under the leadership of Yvon Chouinard, Patagonia offers a model of green leadership in the retail sector. The company's dedication to environmental stewardship, reflected in initiatives such as its "1% for the Planet" pledge, has fostered a deep commitment among employees and customers. Chouinard's approach demonstrates how aligning business operations with green goals can build brand loyalty and create lasting environmental impact (Jairick, 2024).

These case studies highlight the importance of visionary leadership in driving organizational change toward sustainability. By employing clear strategies and engaging employees, leaders can create a culture where green goals are achievable and a source of pride and innovation.

7 CHALLENGES AND FUTURE DIRECTIONS OF GREEN MARKETING

7.1 Challenges

7.1.1 Resistance to Change Within Organizations

- One of the most significant challenges in integrating Human Resource Management (HRM) with green marketing is organizational resistance to change. Employees and management may hesitate to adopt new practices that require deviating from established routines. This resistance often stems from a lack of understanding about the benefits of green marketing and skepticism about its relevance to organizational goals (Post & Altman, 2017).
- At the management level, resistance can occur when leaders perceive green initiatives as secondary to core business objectives or fear potential risks associated with adopting sustainable practices. For instance, concerns about increased operational costs or the uncertainty of returns on investment in green marketing can hinder buy-in from key stakeholders (Smith, 1998).
- For employees, resistance often arises due to insufficient awareness or training. Without clear communication and education about the importance of green practices, employees may view these initiatives as burdensome or irrelevant to their roles (Post & Altman, 2017). This highlights the importance of effective change management strategies, including comprehensive training, transparent communication, and leadership commitment, to overcome internal resistance.
- Another aspect of resistance is cultural inertia, where long-standing organizational norms and values conflict with the sustainability agenda. Transforming an organization's culture to embrace green marketing requires sustained effort, engagement, and visible leadership support (Smith, 1998).

7.1.2 Resource Constraints and Skill Gaps

Resource constraints and skill gaps present additional barriers to integrating HRM with green marketing. Many organizations, particularly small and medium-sized enterprises (SMEs), struggle to allocate adequate financial and human resources to sustainability initiatives (Guldal, 2019). Green marketing often involves investments in eco-friendly technologies, sustainable supply chains, and training programs, which may strain limited budgets (Renwick et al., 2020). Skill gaps among employees further complicate the implementation of green marketing strategies. A successful green marketing campaign requires expertise in lifecycle assessment, sustainable branding, and regulatory compliance. However, many organizations lack employees with these specialized skills. This gap can lead to ineffective execution of green initiatives and reduced credibility with stakeholders (Guldal, 2019).

Furthermore, technological advancements in sustainability, such as renewable energy systems and digital tools for tracking environmental impacts, demand ongoing upskilling. Organizations that fail to provide continuous training risk failing to adopt and promote innovative green practices (Cronin, Smith, Gleim, Ramirez, & Martinez, 2011). Resource constraints are particularly challenging in industries with narrow profit margins, and sustainability investments may not yield immediate financial returns. To address this, organizations can explore partnerships with academic institutions, non-governmental organizations, and government agencies to access funding, training resources, and expertise (Cronin et al., 2011). Resistance to change and resource constraints are significant hurdles to integrating HRM with green marketing. Overcoming these challenges requires a comprehensive approach, including leadership support, targeted training programs, and strategic resource allocation. By addressing these barriers, organizations can enhance their ability to implement effective green marketing strategies and contribute to broader sustainability goals.

7.2 Opportunities for Future Research and Practice

7.2.1 Emerging Trends in Green HRM

Green Human Resource Management (Green HRM) has gained traction as organizations increasingly prioritize sustainability. However, emerging trends indicate a growing need to align HR practices with evolving environmental, social, and technological demands. Integrating artificial intelligence (AI) and digital tools in Green HRM is one key trend. AI-driven platforms track and analyze employee contributions to sustainability, streamline green training programs, and optimize resource allocation for green initiatives (Bombiak, 2019). This technological shift creates opportunities for HR managers to enhance efficiency and engage employees more effectively. Another trend is the focus on employee well-being through sustainable work-life practices. Green work-life balance initiatives, such as telecommuting and flexible schedules, reduce environmental impacts by minimizing commuting and enhancing employee satisfaction and productivity (Kapil, 2015). Organizations adopting these practices are better positioned to attract and retain talent in an increasingly eco-conscious workforce.

The rise of circular economy models is also influencing Green HRM. As companies embrace sustainable production and consumption patterns, HR departments must upskill employees to adapt to new roles and responsibilities. This includes training employees in waste reduction, recycling, and designing eco-friendly products (Bombiak, 2019). Research in this area could explore the impact of these shifts on employee engagement and organizational performance. Lastly, the growing emphasis on diversity, equity, and inclusion (DEI) intersects with Green HRM. Organizations are recognizing that diverse teams bring innovative solutions to sustainability challenges. Future research could examine how inclusive practices enhance the effectiveness of green initiatives and contribute to broader environmental goals (Kapil, 2015).

7.2.2 Interdisciplinary Approaches to Advancing Sustainability

Achieving sustainability requires an interdisciplinary approach integrating insights from various fields, including HRM, marketing, environmental science, and technology. One promising area is the collaboration between HRM and environmental science to develop training programs tailored to specific industries. For instance, HR departments in the renewable energy sector could work with environmental scientists to design curricula that address the technical and behavioral competencies needed for green energy adoption (Renwick et al., 2020). Similarly, the intersection of behavioral economics and Green HRM offers opportunities to enhance employee engagement in sustainability. By applying principles such as nudging and incentives, organizations can influence employees' choices toward greener practices, such as reducing energy use or participating in recycling programs (Annan-Diab & Molinari, 2017). The integration of supply chain management and HRM is another area ripe for exploration. As organizations adopt sustainable supply chains, HR managers must train employees in lifecycle assessment, ethical sourcing, and collaboration with eco-friendly suppliers. Future research could examine how these interdisciplinary efforts improve the efficiency and credibility of green marketing strategies (Zielinski, Sagan, & Surosz, 2018).

Moreover, technology plays a crucial role in interdisciplinary sustainability efforts. Blockchain, for example, is being explored as a tool for enhancing transparency and traceability in green initiatives. HR managers could collaborate with IT teams to train employees to use blockchain to verify environmental claims and certifications (Annan-Diab & Molinari, 2017). In education, partnerships between academia and industry are pivotal. Collaborative research and experiential learning programs can equip students and employees with the skills to address complex sustainability challenges. Future studies could explore the effectiveness of these partnerships in fostering innovation and driving green transformations. Emerging trends and interdisciplinary approaches present significant opportunities for advancing Green HRM and sustainability practices. By leveraging these developments, organizations can enhance their environmental impact while remaining competitive in an increasingly eco-conscious market.

8 CONCLUSION

8.1 Summary of Key Insights

Human Resource Management (HRM) is transformative in enabling organizations to achieve their green marketing objectives. Organizations can foster a workforce committed to environmental stewardship by aligning HR practices with sustainability goals. This chapter has underscored several critical areas where HRM supports green marketing, including recruitment, training, compensation, and leadership development. HRM's ability to attract and nurture environmentally conscious employees through sustainability-focused job descriptions and performance evaluations has been highlighted as essential for embedding green values into an organization's core operations. Further, HRM facilitates a collaborative culture by establishing sustainability committees and engaging employees in participatory decision-making. Training and development programs designed to equip employees with green marketing skills have proven vital in addressing skills gaps, particularly in emerging areas like energy-efficient technologies and circular economy practices. Leadership, supported by HRM, has emerged as a cornerstone in driving green marketing initiatives, with exemplary case studies demonstrating the impact of visionary leadership on organizational success.

8.2 Implications for Practice

For HR professionals, supporting green marketing strategies requires adopting a multifaceted approach:

- *Recruitment and Onboarding:* Design recruitment campaigns emphasizing the organization's sustainability commitment. Incorporate sustainability metrics into job descriptions and selection criteria to attract candidates aligned with green values.
- *Training and Development:* Develop comprehensive training programs focused on green competencies, including environmental regulations, ethical branding, and lifecycle assessment. Collaborate with academic institutions and industry experts to ensure curriculum relevance.
- *Employee Engagement:* To sustain employee involvement, utilize gamification and participatory initiatives like green challenges. Recognition programs that reward green behaviors should be prioritized to motivate continuous participation.

- *Performance Management:* Integrate sustainability metrics into employee evaluations to align individual and organizational objectives. These metrics should be transparent, fair, and role-specific to ensure accountability.
- *Leadership Development:* Invest in leadership programs that emphasize sustainability. Equip leaders with the skills to communicate the business case for green initiatives and inspire employees to adopt environmentally responsible behaviors.

8.2.1 Long-Term Benefits for Organizations and the Environment

Aligning HRM with green marketing strategies delivers long-term benefits for organizations and the environment. These benefits include:

- *Enhanced Organizational Reputation:* A commitment to green marketing strengthens brand equity and builds trust with consumers and stakeholders.
- *Competitive Advantage:* Organizations that integrate sustainability into their operations and marketing strategies gain a competitive edge by appealing to environmentally conscious consumers and investors.
- *Cost Savings:* Sustainable practices, such as energy efficiency and waste reduction, lower operational costs while reducing environmental impact.
- *Employee Satisfaction and Retention:* Engaging employees in meaningful green initiatives fosters a sense of purpose, enhancing job satisfaction and loyalty.
- *Environmental Impact:* By embedding sustainability into HR practices, organizations contribute significantly to global environmental goals, such as reducing carbon emissions and promoting biodiversity.

8.3 Conclusion

8.3.1 The Evolving Role of HRM in the Sustainability Agenda

As the global focus on sustainability intensifies, the role of HRM in supporting green marketing strategies is evolving. HR professionals are no longer confined to traditional roles but are key enablers of organizational transformation. They act as strategists, facilitators, and advocates for sustainability, ensuring that green goals are integrated across all levels of the organization. This expanded role demands a proactive approach to identifying trends, bridging skills gaps, and fostering collaboration across functions. The synergy between HRM and green marketing also reflects a broader shift toward interdisciplinary approaches. By integrating environmental science, technology, and behavioral economics insights, HRM can drive innovative solutions to sustainability challenges. This evolution positions HRM as a central player in achieving organizational and global sustainability objectives.

8.3.2 Call to Action for Integrating Green Practices Into Organizational Frameworks

Organizations must act decisively to integrate green practices into their frameworks. This requires leadership commitment, strategic planning, and resource investment. HR professionals should take the lead in championing sustainability, from designing policies prioritizing green initiatives to fostering a culture of accountability and innovation. Moreover, collaboration is essential. Organizations can access the resources and expertise needed to advance their green agendas by partnering with industry peers, academic institutions, and government agencies. Employees, too, must be empowered to contribute actively, ensuring sustainability becomes a shared responsibility. The journey toward sustainability is not without challenges, but the potential benefits for businesses, employees, and the planet are immeasurable. By embedding green practices into their organizational frameworks, companies can position themselves as leaders in the green economy, driving progress toward a sustainable future.

REFERENCES

Adjei-Bamfo, P., Bempong, B., Osei, J., & Kusi-Sarpong, S. (2020). Green candidate selection for organizational environmental management. *International Journal of Manpower, 41*(7), 1081–1096. DOI: 10.1108/IJM-10-2019-0480

Ahmed, W., & Ahmed, I. H. (2022). Interconnection of Green Marketing and Green Human Resource Management Functions. *Macro Management & Public Policies, 4*(3), 7–13. DOI: 10.30564/mmpp.v4i3.5063

Akhtar, U. A., Muhammad, R., Bakar, L. J. A., Parameswaranpillai, V., Raj, B., & Khan, N. B. (2023). Green Human Resource Management Bibliometric Analysis of the Published Literature from 2008 to 2022. *International Journal of Professional Business Review: Int.J. Prof. Bus. Rev., 8*(4), 1.

Al-Swidi, A. K., Gelaidan, H. M., & Saleh, R. M. (2021). The joint impact of green human resource management, leadership and organizational culture on employees' green behaviour and organisational environmental performance. *Journal of Cleaner Production, 316*, 128112. DOI: 10.1016/j.jclepro.2021.128112

Alhamami, A., Petri, I., Rezgui, Y., & Kubicki, S. (2020). Promoting energy efficiency in the built environment through adapted bim training and education. *Energies, 13*(9), 2308. DOI: 10.3390/en13092308

Alzu'bi, R. M., & Kontor, E. (2023). The Impact of Green Marketing Strategies on Employees Green Performance: An HRM Perspective. *Economica, 14*(3-4), 83–92.

Annan-Diab, F., & Molinari, C. (2017). Interdisciplinarity: Practical approach to advancing education for sustainability and for the Sustainable Development Goals. *International Journal of Management Education, 15*(2), 73–83. DOI: 10.1016/j.ijme.2017.03.006

Aranganathan, P. (2018). Green recruitment: A new-fangled approach to attract and retain talent. *International Journal of Business Management & Research, 8*(2), 69–76. DOI: 10.24247/ijbmrapr20189

Arulrajah, A. A., & Opatha, H. (2016). Analytical and theoretical perspectives on green human resource management: A simplified underpinning.

Bass, S., Dalal-Clayton, B., & Pretty, J. (1995). Participation in strategies for sustainable development.

Beigi, M., Callahan, J., & Michaelson, C. (2019). A critical plot twist: Changing characters and foreshadowing the future of organizational storytelling. *International Journal of Management Reviews*, *21*(4), 447–465. DOI: 10.1111/ijmr.12203

Bombiak, E. (2019). Green human resource management–the latest trend or strategic necessity? *Entrepreneurship and Sustainability Issues*, *6*(4), 1647–1662. DOI: 10.9770/jesi.2019.6.4(7)

Boyce, M. E. (2017). Organizational story and storytelling: a critical review. *The Aesthetic Turn in Management*, 233-254.

Callan, V. J., Johnston, M. A., & Poulsen, A. L. (2015). How organisations are using blended e-learning to deliver more flexible approaches to trade training. *Journal of Vocational Education and Training*, *67*(3), 294–309. DOI: 10.1080/13636820.2015.1050445

CB. (2024). Business leader, climate and equality campaigner, co-author of "Net Positive: how courageous companies thrive by giving more than they take", a Financial Times Business Book of the Year. #3 Thinkers50; former CEO, Unilever. Retrieved from https://competentboards.com/faculty/paul-polman/#:~:text=Paul%20Polman%20works%20to%20accelerate,Goals%2C%20which%20he%20helped%20develop

Chadee, D., Wiesner, R., & Roxas, B. (2011). Environmental sustainability change management in SMEs: Learning from sustainability champions. *International Journal of Learning and Change*, *5*(3-4), 194–207. DOI: 10.1504/IJLC.2011.045068

Cho, B.-K., Park, J.-Y., & Lee, Y.-K. (2023). Do green practices and green image promote consumers' participation in social network sites (SNS)? *Journal of Hospitality Marketing & Management*, *32*(5), 631–648. DOI: 10.1080/19368623.2023.2191595

Chou, C.-J. (2014). Hotels' environmental policies and employee personal environmental beliefs: Interactions and outcomes. *Tourism Management*, *40*, 436–446. DOI: 10.1016/j.tourman.2013.08.001

Craig, C., & Allen, M. (2013). Sustainability information sources: Employee knowledge, perceptions, and learning. *Journal of Communication Management (London)*, *17*(4), 292–307. DOI: 10.1108/JCOM-05-2012-0035

Cronin, J. J.Jr, Smith, J. S., Gleim, M. R., Ramirez, E., & Martinez, J. D. (2011). Green marketing strategies: An examination of stakeholders and the opportunities they present. *Journal of the Academy of Marketing Science*, *39*(1), 158–174. DOI: 10.1007/s11747-010-0227-0

Dacin, M. T., Dacin, P. A., Greenwood, R., Oliver, C., Sahlin, K., & Suddaby, R. (2008). Traditions as institutionalized practice: Implications for deinstitutionalization. *The Sage handbook of organizational institutionalism, 327*, 352.

Dangelico, R. M., & Vocalelli, D. (2017). "Green Marketing": An analysis of definitions, strategy steps, and tools through a systematic review of the literature. *Journal of Cleaner Production, 165*, 1263–1279. DOI: 10.1016/j.jclepro.2017.07.184

Dyer, G., & Dyer, M. (2017). Strategic leadership for sustainability by higher education: The American College & University Presidents' Climate Commitment. *Journal of Cleaner Production, 140*, 111–116. DOI: 10.1016/j.jclepro.2015.08.077

Fagarasan, C., Cristea, C., Cristea, M., Popa, O., & Pisla, A. (2023). Integrating sustainability metrics into project and portfolio performance assessment in agile software development: A data-driven scoring model. *Sustainability (Basel), 15*(17), 13139. DOI: 10.3390/su151713139

Fuchs, C. (2008). The implications of new information and communication technologies for sustainability. *Environment, Development and Sustainability, 10*(3), 291–309. DOI: 10.1007/s10668-006-9065-0

Glynn, M. A., & Abzug, R. (2002). Institutionalizing identity: Symbolic isomorphism and organizational names. *Academy of Management Journal, 45*(1), 267–280. DOI: 10.2307/3069296

Guldal, E. (2019). Consumer skepticism: Attitude–behavior gap in green marketing and the role of ecopreneurs in the market.

Gutterman, A. S. (2020). Organizational Design and Sustainability. *Available atSSRN* 3813832.

Hammedi, W., Leclercq, T., & Poncin, I. (2019). Customer engagement: The role of gamification. In *Handbook of research on customer engagement* (pp. 164–185). Edward Elgar Publishing. DOI: 10.4337/9781788114899.00014

Hapuwatte, B. M., Seevers, K. D., & Jawahir, I. (2022). Metrics-based dynamic product sustainability performance evaluation for advancing the circular economy. *Journal of Manufacturing Systems, 64*, 275–287. DOI: 10.1016/j.jmsy.2022.06.013

Hayles, C. S. (2019). INSPIRE sustainability internships: Promoting campus greening initiatives through student participation. *International Journal of Sustainability in Higher Education, 20*(3), 452–469. DOI: 10.1108/IJSHE-03-2019-0111

Ho, V.-T., Nakamori, Y., Ho, T.-B., & Lim, C. P. (2016). Blended learning model on hands-on approach for in-service secondary school teachers: Combination of E-learning and face-to-face discussion. *Education and Information Technologies, 21*(1), 185–208. DOI: 10.1007/s10639-014-9315-y

Irani, F., Kilic, H., & Adeshola, I. (2022). Impact of green human resource management practices on the environmental performance of green hotels. *Journal of Hospitality Marketing & Management, 31*(5), 570–600. DOI: 10.1080/19368623.2022.2022554

Jahidi, I. (2020). Style and Characteristics Transformational Leadership: How The Regional Head of Cimahi, Indonesia in Mobilizing Employees in Achieving Vision. *European Journal of Molecular and Clinical Medicine, 7*(7), 308–318.

Jairick. (2024). Patagonia Leadership & its Sustainable Values. Retrieved from https://humansofglobe.com/patagonia-leadership-in-environmental-and-social-responsibility/#:~:text=Environmentalism%20is%20intricately%20woven%20into,Patagonia's%20commitment%20to%20sustainable%20practices

Jawad, A. Q., Scott-Jackson, W., Jawad, A. Q., & Scott-Jackson, W. (2016). PACE: The Process of Active Committed Enthusiasm. *Redefining Well-Being in Nations and Organizations: A Process of Active Committed Enthusiasm*, 120-186.

Kao, T.-F., & Du, Y.-Z. (2020). A study on the influence of green advertising design and environmental emotion on advertising effect. *Journal of Cleaner Production, 242*, 118294. DOI: 10.1016/j.jclepro.2019.118294

Kapil, K. (2015). Green HRM: Trends & prospects. *International Journal of Management Research, 3*(1), 43–55.

Kivinda, M. P., Su, Q., Hau, H. T., & Hashmi, H. B. A. (2021). Green HRM for employer branding: Evidence from ISO 14001 EMS certified firms. *Journal of Developing Areas, 55*(3), 393–409. DOI: 10.1353/jda.2021.0071

Kolding, M., Sundblad, M., Alexa, J., Stone, M., Aravopoulou, E., & Evans, G. (2018). Information management–a skills gap? *The Bottom Line (New York, N.Y.), 31*(3/4), 170–190. DOI: 10.1108/BL-09-2018-0037

Kumar, H., & Raghavendran, S. (2015). Gamification, the finer art: Fostering creativity and employee engagement. *The Journal of Business Strategy, 36*(6), 3–12. DOI: 10.1108/JBS-10-2014-0119

LaVan, H., Zilic, I., & Basappa, S. (2022). Attitudes of employees in green companies regarding CSR communication. *International Journal of Manpower, 43*(6), 1301–1315. DOI: 10.1108/IJM-11-2020-0542

Lee, J. (2005). Effects of leadership and leader-member exchange on commitment. *Leadership and Organization Development Journal, 26*(8), 655–672. DOI: 10.1108/01437730510633728

Lee, K. (2010). The green purchase behavior of Hong Kong young consumers: The role of peer influence, local environmental involvement, and concrete environmental knowledge. *Journal of International Consumer Marketing, 23*(1), 21–44. DOI: 10.1080/08961530.2011.524575

Lossin, F., Kozlovskiy, I., Sodenkamp, M., & Staake, T. (2016). Incentives to Go Green: an Empirical Investigation of Monetary and Symbolic Rewards to Mo-Tivate Energy Savings.

Luu, T. T. (2020). Integrating green strategy and green human resource practices to trigger individual and organizational green performance: The role of environmentally-specific servant leadership. *Journal of Sustainable Tourism, 28*(8), 1193–1222. DOI: 10.1080/09669582.2020.1729165

Maheshwari, S., & Rai, A. (2022). Effective Leadership Attributes: Evidences from Indian Power Sector. *Indian Journal of Industrial Relations, 58*(2).

Marchington, M. (2015). The role of institutional and intermediary forces in shaping patterns of employee involvement and participation (EIP) in Anglo-American countries. *International Journal of Human Resource Management, 26*(20), 2594–2616. DOI: 10.1080/09585192.2014.1003088

Measham, T. G., & Barnett, G. B. (2008). Environmental volunteering: Motivations, modes and outcomes. *The Australian Geographer, 39*(4), 537–552. DOI: 10.1080/00049180802419237

Mefalopulos, P. (2005). Communication for sustainable development: applications and challenges. *Media and glocal change. Rethinking communication for development*, 247-260.

Mukonza, C., & Swarts, I. (2020). The influence of green marketing strategies on business performance and corporate image in the retail sector. *Business Strategy and the Environment, 29*(3), 838–845. DOI: 10.1002/bse.2401

Napathorn, C. (2022). The development of green skills across firms in the institutional context of Thailand. *Asia-Pacific Journal of Business Administration, 14*(4), 539–572. DOI: 10.1108/APJBA-10-2020-0370

Novy, J. W., Banerjee, B., & Matson, P. (2021). A core curriculum for sustainability leadership. *Sustainability (Basel), 13*(19), 10557. DOI: 10.3390/su131910557

Odhiambo, G. M., Waiganjo, E. W., & Simiyu, A. N. (2023). Incentivizing employee pro-environmental behaviour: Harnessing the potential of green rewards. *African Journal of Empirical Research, 4*(2), 601–611-601–611.

Olaleye, D. S., Oloye, A. C., Akinloye, A. O., & Akinwande, O. T. (2024). Advancing green communications: The role of radio frequency engineering in sustainable infrastructure design. *International Journal of Latest Technology in Engineering* [IJLTEMAS]. *Management & Applied Science, 13*(5), 113.

Pachar, S., Kishore, S. C., Karunakaran, N. B., Bhaskar, P., & Selvakumar, P. (2025). Green Job Design and Analysis. In *Examining Green Human Resources Management and Nascent Entrepreneurship* (pp. 317–342). IGI Global.

Panagiotopoulou, V. C., Paraskevopoulou, A., Margaityte, M., Petkova, E. I., & Stavropoulos, P. (2024). *Customisable Training Programme on Best Industrial Practices for Sustainability, Circular Economy and Energy Efficiency.* Paper presented at the Conference on Learning Factories. DOI: 10.1007/978-3-031-65411-4_45

Pathak, R. K., & Agarwal, S. (2024). Sustainability in Human Resources: Evaluating Competencies and Overcoming Challenges in India's Service Sector. *Library Progress International, 44*(3), 7301–7313.

Peattie, K. (2016). Green marketing. In *The marketing book* (pp. 573–597). Routledge.

Podgorodnichenko, N., Akmal, A., Edgar, F., & Everett, A. M. (2022). Sustainable HRM: Toward addressing diverse employee roles. *Employee Relations, 44*(3), 576–608. DOI: 10.1108/ER-01-2019-0016

Post, J. E., & Altman, B. W. (2017). Managing the Environmental Change Process: Barriers and Opportunities 1. In *Managing green teams* (pp. 84-101): Routledge.

Poston, R. S., & Dhaliwal, J. (2015). IS human capital: Assessing gaps to strengthen skill and competency sourcing. *Communications of the Association for Information Systems, 36*(1), 34. DOI: 10.17705/1CAIS.03634

Qureshi, I. H., & Mehraj, D. (2022). Identifying the factors of internal green marketing: A scale development and psychometric evaluation approach. *International Journal of Manpower, 43*(3), 786–804. DOI: 10.1108/IJM-06-2020-0276

Ramus, C. A. (2001). Organizational support for employees: Encouraging creative ideas for environmental sustainability. *California Management Review, 43*(3), 85–105. DOI: 10.2307/41166090

Renwick, D. W., Redman, T., & Maguire, S. (2013). Green human resource management: A review and research agenda. *International Journal of Management Reviews, 15*(1), 1–14. DOI: 10.1111/j.1468-2370.2011.00328.x

Ryu, J., Park, S., Park, Y., Park, J., & Lee, M. (2021). Innovative culture and firm performance of medical device companies: Mediating effects of investment in education and training. *International Journal of Environmental Research and Public Health, 18*(17), 8926. DOI: 10.3390/ijerph18178926 PMID: 34501515

Sharma, A. P. (2021). Consumers' purchase behaviour and green marketing: A synthesis, review and agenda. *International Journal of Consumer Studies, 45*(6), 1217–1238. DOI: 10.1111/ijcs.12722

Sharma, R., & Gupta, N. (2015, January). Green HRM: An innovative approach to environmental sustainability. In *Proceeding of the Twelfth AIMS International Conference on Management* (pp. 2-5).

Smith, T. M. (1998). *The myth of green marketing: Tending our goats at the edge of apocalypse*. University of Toronto Press. DOI: 10.3138/9781442657427

Sugandini, D., Susilowati, C., Siswanti, Y., & Syafri, W. (2020). Green supply management and green marketing strategy on green purchase intention: SMEs cases. [JIEM]. *Journal of Industrial Engineering and Management, 13*(1), 79–92. DOI: 10.3926/jiem.2795

Sugiarto, A. B. (2024). The Leader's Role In Staff Mobilization To Realize The Goals Of Educational Institutions. *Tsaqofah: Jurnal Pendidikan Islam, 9*(1), 269–298.

Sullivan, J. (2017). *Creating employee champions: How to drive business success through sustainability engagement training*. Routledge. DOI: 10.4324/9781351274609

Tesla. (2024). Impact. Retrieved from https://www.tesla.com/impact

Thakkar, R. (2021). Green marketing and sustainable development challenges and opportunities. *International Journal of Management. Public Policy Research, 1*(1), 15–23.

Tharanatha, A., Shashidhar, R., Bharath, S., & Nagesh, P. (2023). The green behaviour role in relationship amid green human resource management and employer branding in green hospitals. *Indian Journal of Science and Technology, 16*(14), 1062–1068. DOI: 10.17485/IJST/v16i14.247

Trinh, T. L. M. (2021). Green Human Resources Management–Solutions to Enhance the Green Marketing Development of Enterprise. *International Journal of Research in Engineering. Science and Management, 4*(8), 200–203.

Vitale, R., Blaine, T., Zofkie, E., Moreland-Russell, S., Combs, T., Brownson, R. C., & Luke, D. A. (2018). Developing an evidence-based program sustainability training curriculum: A group randomized, multi-phase approach. *Implementation Science : IS, 13*(1), 1–12. DOI: 10.1186/s13012-018-0819-5 PMID: 30257695

Walker, D. (2002). Enthusiasm, commitment and project alliancing: An Australian experience. *Construction Innovation, 2*(1), 15–31. DOI: 10.1108/14714170210814667

Wang, S., Liu, M. T., & Pérez, A. (2023). A bibliometric analysis of green marketing in marketing and related fields: From 1991 to 2021. *Asia Pacific Journal of Marketing and Logistics, 35*(8), 1857–1882. DOI: 10.1108/APJML-07-2022-0651

Wiradirja, I. R., Ras, H., Pranadita, N., Macmud, S., Anwar, H., & Haspada, D. (2020). Environmental Performance: Role Of Green Employee Involvement Practices, Green Training And Green Shared Vision. *Journal of Security & Sustainability Issues, 10*(2), 721–733. DOI: 10.9770/jssi.2020.10.2(28)

Yong, J. Y., Yusliza, M.-Y., Ramayah, T., & Fawehinmi, O. (2019). Nexus between green intellectual capital and green human resource management. *Journal of Cleaner Production, 215*, 364–374. DOI: 10.1016/j.jclepro.2018.12.306

Zaccaro, S. J., Kemp, C., & Bader, P. (2004). Leader traits and attributes. *The nature of leadership, 101*, 124.

Zhao, H., Bai, R., Liu, R., & Wang, H. (2022). Exploring purchase intentions of new energy vehicles: Do "mianzi" and green peer influence matter? *Frontiers in Psychology, 13*, 951132. DOI: 10.3389/fpsyg.2022.951132 PMID: 36176803

Zielinski, T., Sagan, I., & Surosz, W. (2018). *Interdisciplinary approaches for sustainable development goals*. Springer. DOI: 10.1007/978-3-319-71788-3

Chapter 7
Human Resource Management and Green Marketing: Aligning Workforce with Sustainability

Brendan Chukwuemeka Ezeudoka
https://orcid.org/0000-0002-3607-7160
Jiangsu University, China

Charles Obinna Igwe
https://orcid.org/0009-0000-5297-9554
Nnamdi Azikiwe University, Nigeria

ABSTRACT

This chapter explores the integration of Green Human Resource Management (Green HRM) and green marketing as essential strategies to address environmental challenges and foster sustainability. Green HRM encompasses practices like green recruitment, sustainability-focused training, and performance management aligned with eco-friendly goals, while green marketing promotes environmentally conscious products and services, enhancing brand trust. The chapter highlights the synergy between these concepts, showing how Green HRM strengthens the authenticity of green marketing efforts. Case studies of companies such as Wipro, IKEA, and Toyota demonstrate practical applications, innovative solutions, and benefits, including employee engagement programs, gamification, and green KPIs. Challenges like regulatory hurdles, resource constraints, and cultural resistance are analyzed, alongside strategies to overcome them.

DOI: 10.4018/979-8-3693-9831-9.ch007

1. INTRODUCTION

Green Human Resource Management (Green HRM) and Green Marketing have emerged as transformative paradigms in modern business practices, reflecting a shift towards sustainability-driven strategies in response to pressing environmental challenges (Mtembu, 2017). These concepts represent not merely operational adjustments but holistic approaches that align business goals with the principles of environmental stewardship (Mishra, 2017). Together, they emphasize the significant role of integrating ecological consciousness into human resource practices and marketing strategies, enabling organizations to thrive economically while contributing to global sustainability efforts (Jamil et al., 2023).

Historically, the origins of Green HRM trace back to the broader environmental management movement that gained traction in the 1980s and 1990s (Carter & Simmons, 2010). During this period, businesses began recognizing the importance of sustainable development, driven by pivotal moments such as the 1987 Brundtland Report, which introduced the concept of sustainable development (Blewitt, 2012). HR practices gradually transformed to include environmentally conscious components like minimizing workplace waste, encouraging green behaviors, and promoting eco-friendly policies (Nisar et al., 2021). The emergence of corporate social responsibility (CSR) further accelerated this trend, positioning HRM as a vital player in aligning organizational values with environmental goals (Sarvaiya et al., 2021). Likewise, Green Marketing arose in the late 20th century as companies aimed to respond to the growing consumer awareness of environmental concerns (Peattie, 2001). The 1990s experienced a rise in demand for eco-friendly products and services, fueled by increased public concern about issues like climate change, deforestation, and pollution (Lisniak, 2024). Businesses began integrating environmental messaging into their marketing strategies, employing green branding to connect with eco-aware consumers (Lisniak, 2024). This represented the start of a transition from traditional marketing methods to strategies that foregrounded sustainability as a core value (Lisniak, 2024).

Green HRM, in its current form, refers to the integration of environmentally sustainable practices into human resource policies and procedures (Mishra, 2017). It encompasses a wide range of activities, including green recruitment, training programs focused on sustainability, performance management systems that reward eco-friendly behaviors, and creating a culture of environmental responsibility within the workplace (Mishra, 2017). The objective is to create a workforce that is productive and also deeply aligned with the organization's environmental goals (Ahmad, 2015). On the other hand, Green Marketing involves promoting products, services, or brands that are eco-friendly, ethically sourced, or produced with minimal environmental impact (Peattie, 2016). This strategy goes beyond mere advertising and includes sustainable product design, transparent supply chain practices, and community engagement (Ottman, 2017). Organizations that utilize Green Marketing seek to distinguish themselves in the marketplace while meeting the ethical expectations of increasingly eco-conscious consumers (Abbas, 2024).

The adoption of these practices has become increasingly urgent due to contemporary environmental challenges, including global warming, resource depletion, and biodiversity loss (Abbas, 2024). Businesses are expected to take a proactive role in addressing these issues, not only by minimizing their environmental footprint but also by shaping societal attitudes and behaviors (Boiral, 2009). Green HRM and Green Marketing provide the necessary tools to achieve this dual objective, enabling organizations to create meaningful change both internally and externally (Ali, 2022). Essentially, the overview of Green HRM and Green Marketing reveals a symbiotic relationship between the two concepts, where internal sustainability efforts intersect with outward-facing strategies. Together, they embody a progressive approach to business that recognizes the connection between economic success, environmental responsibility, and social well-being.

2. IMPORTANCE OF ALIGNING HR PRACTICES WITH SUSTAINABILITY

At the heart of Green HRM is the belief that sustainability must start from within (Ahmad, 2015). Human Resource Management, as the architect of organizational culture and workforce development, has the potential to instill a green ethos in employees (Rotich, 2015). This process begins with recruitment, where companies can focus on hiring individuals whose values align with sustainability goals (Stahl, 2020). Job descriptions can be updated to include environmental responsibilities, and onboarding programs can introduce new employees to the organization's green objectives (Chaudhary, 2020). Beyond recruitment, Green HRM includes training programs that provide employees with eco-friendly skills and knowledge, ensuring that sustainability becomes an integral part of their daily roles (Viterouli et al., 2023). Performance management is another crucial area where HR can promote sustainability (Saratun, 2016). Connecting employee evaluations and rewards to environmental contributions can help organizations encourage green behaviors and integrate sustainability into their operational ethos (Mishra, 2017).

Green marketing enhances these internal efforts by transforming them into compelling narratives for external stakeholders (Szabo & Webster, 2021). As consumers increasingly prefer brands that demonstrate a commitment to sustainability, green marketing establishes a vital link between organizational practices and market perceptions (Johnstone & Tan, 2015). Organizations can build trust and gain a competitive advantage by emphasizing eco-friendly products, ethical sourcing, and sustainable business practices (Leonidou et al., 2015). However, the effectiveness of green marketing is contingent upon the authenticity of the organization's internal practices (Ottman, 2017). A disconnect between messaging and actual practices, commonly known as greenwashing, can undermine consumer trust and damage the brand's reputation (Hormes, 2024).

Consequently, the partnership between Green HRM and green marketing serves as a significant catalyst for sustainable transformation (Mishra, 2017). When employees actively participate in sustainability initiatives, they become ambassadors for the organization's green values, enhancing the credibility and authenticity of marketing efforts (Potoski & Callery, 2018). Beyond individual organizational initiatives, the integration of Green HRM with green marketing signifies a broader shift in corporate responsibility (Stahl et al., 2020). Businesses are no longer seen merely as profit-driven entities; they are increasingly expected to tackle global issues such as climate change, resource depletion, and pollution (Lisniak, 2024). This transformation has resulted in a heightened focus on aligning corporate strategies with environmental, social, and governance (ESG) criteria (Li et al., 2017). When effectively integrated, Green HRM and green marketing empower organizations to make meaningful contributions to global efforts while achieving their business goals (Stahl et al., 2020).

Additionally, the integration of Green HRM and green marketing highlights the interconnectedness of organizational functions (Mishra, 2017). The success of sustainability initiatives relies on collaboration among departments, with HR and marketing playing crucial roles. HR's efforts to cultivate a green workforce lay the groundwork for authentic marketing campaigns, while marketing insights into consumer preferences can guide HR's strategies for embedding sustainability into the organization's culture (Mishra, 2017). Therefore, as organizations work to meet the challenges of sustainability, the significance of Green HRM and green marketing will only increase (Ahmad, 2015). These practices not only tackle immediate environmental challenges but also prepare organizations for long-term success in an environment where stakeholders increasingly demand accountability and transparency.

3. THE RELATIONSHIP BETWEEN GREEN HRM AND GREEN MARKETING STRATEGIES

The integration of HRM practices with green marketing strategies serves as a bridge between internal organizational processes and external market-oriented sustainability goals (Chen et al., 2015). HRM supports green marketing primarily by recruiting environmentally conscious talent, nurturing eco-friendly behaviors through training, engaging employees in green initiatives, and aligning performance management systems with sustainability metrics (Gohain & Sharada, 2023). These practices are instrumental in driving a green organizational culture that aligns with marketing efforts aimed at environmentally aware consumers.

3.1 Recruitment and Selection

Recruitment and selection are crucial HRM functions that significantly impact an organization's ability to implement green marketing strategies (Malik et al., 2020). By prioritizing the recruitment of individuals with strong environmental values and skills, organizations can ensure their staff aligns with sustainability goals (Jamil et al., 2023). Candidates who demonstrate eco-consciousness bring innovative insights to green initiatives, enhancing the organization's capacity to achieve its environmental objectives (Viterouli et al., 2023). For example, assessing candidates for their knowledge of sustainability frameworks, such as the United Nations Sustainable Development Goals (SDGs), can help identify individuals ready to contribute to green marketing campaigns (Hubscher et al., 2022).

Moreover, job descriptions and employer branding play a crucial role in conveying sustainability goals (Heide et al., 2024). Organizations that emphasize their environmental commitment in job advertisements and employer branding strategies are more likely to attract like-minded talent (Story et al., 2016). For instance, companies such as Patagonia prominently display their dedication to environmental activism in their recruitment materials, drawing in applicants who share similar values (Nishitha & Kavitha, 2024). Developing job descriptions that detail responsibilities such as promoting eco-friendly practices or creating sustainable product solutions further reinforces the organization's green marketing agenda (Nishitha & Kavitha, 2024). Similarly, green recruitment practices, such as paperless hiring processes, strengthen an organization's commitment to sustainability (Jamil et al., 2023). For example, Google's *Green Jobs* initiative focuses on hiring talent for roles that directly support the company's renewable energy projects, which later feature prominently in its green marketing campaigns (Google, 2024).

3.2 Training and Development

Training and development programs are crucial for equipping employees with the knowledge and skills necessary to support green marketing strategies (Pham et al., 2020). Green training initiatives emphasize fostering eco-friendly behaviors, raising awareness of environmental challenges, and providing tools that enable employees to contribute effectively to sustainability goals (Usman et al., 2023). For example, programs focused on energy conservation, waste management, and sustainable supply chain practices empower employees to incorporate green practices into their roles (Mishra, 2017).

Additionally, many companies have implemented workshops and training programs to promote sustainable practices (Ogbu et al., 2023). For example, Unilever organizes sustainability training sessions for employees, enabling them to align their actions with the company's Sustainable Living Plan (Raja, 2021). Similarly, Toyota offers environmental training programs that emphasize resource efficiency and sustainable manufacturing processes (Thummalapalli, 2019). These efforts ensure that employees at all levels are equipped to advocate for the company's green marketing strategies while enhancing their overall environmental awareness (Chen et al., 2015).

3.3 Employee Engagement

Employee engagement is an important enabler of successful green marketing strategies (Ababneh, 2021). Organizations create a workforce that actively participates in sustainable efforts when they are committed to supporting green engagement initiatives (Mishra, 2017). For instance, forming "green teams" within departments encourages employees to collaborate on eco-friendly projects, such as reducing waste, optimizing energy use, or developing sustainable product ideas (Nagam & Vidyasagar, 2024).

Gamification techniques enhance employee participation in green initiatives (Haque et al., 2024). Organizations can use challenges, rewards, and leaderboards to motivate employees to adopt environmentally friendly practices (Haque et al., 2024). For instance, Coca-Cola launched a gamified sustainability program that encouraged employees to compete in reducing their carbon footprints, significantly boosting engagement with the company's green goals (Joy & Chiramel, 2017). Similarly, Adobe introduced a gamified sustainability challenge where employees earned points for eco-friendly actions such as carpooling and reducing waste (Foly-Ehke, 2024). This initiative was featured in Adobe's external marketing campaigns, highlighting the company's innovative approach to sustainability (Foly-Ehke, 2024). Such strategies not only increase participation but also cultivate a culture of sustainability, reinforcing the organization's green marketing messages both internally and externally (Haque et al., 2024).

3.4 Performance Management and Rewards

Performance management systems that include green key performance indicators (KPIs) are essential for promoting sustainable practices across an organization (Histrov et al., 2023). Evaluating employees based on their contributions to environmental goals fosters accountability and aligns individual efforts with organizational priorities (Bilderback, 2024). For instance, incorporating KPIs such as energy savings achieved, waste reduction targets met, or contributions to green innovation in performance reviews motivates employees to integrate sustainability into their daily responsibilities (Marrucci et al., 2024).

Reward systems reinforce eco-friendly behaviors by recognizing and incentivizing contributions to green initiatives (Odhiambo et al., 2023; Joseph & Jose, 2024). Monetary rewards, public recognition or eco-friendly benefits such as subsidized electric vehicle purchases motivate employees to participate actively in sustainability efforts (Joseph & Jose, 2024). For instance, Siemens provides financial bonuses to employees who achieve significant energy-saving milestones, creating a direct link between performance and environmental impact (Siemens, 2024). Such practices help in enhancing employee morale while also solidifying the organization's commitment to sustainability, supporting its green marketing endeavors Joseph & Jose, 2024).

4. ROLE OF DIGITAL TRANSFORMATION IN GREEN HRM

Digital transformation is reshaping the landscape of Green HRM, combining technological advancements with sustainability initiatives in unique and impactful ways. The integration of digital tools in HR processes not only streamlines operations but also enables eco-friendly practices. For example, the adoption of paperless workflows and energy-efficient systems helps organizations reduce their environmental footprints. Such measures align closely with the goals of Green HRM, showcasing how technology can change traditional HR practices into more sustainable ones. Besides operational changes, digital platforms play a crucial role in enhancing employee engagement with sustainability goals. Through innovative approaches such as gamification and digital tracking tools, employees are encouraged to actively participate in environmental initiatives. These platforms offer real-time feedback and motivation, making sustainability a shared responsibility within the organization. Consequently, employees feel more connected to their organization's green agenda, promoting a culture of environmental consciousness.

Another dimension of digital transformation in Green HRM is its role in training and awareness programs. Advanced e-learning tools and AI-driven platforms are revolutionizing how employees are educated about sustainability. These technologies ensure that employees develop the necessary skills and knowledge to contribute meaningfully to green initiatives. By making training more accessible and personalized, organizations can effectively integrate green practices into the everyday lives of their workforce.

Furthermore, the use of data-driven decision-making tools powered by AI and analytics is providing HR professionals with actionable insights to optimize sustainability strategies. These tools enable organizations to monitor energy consumption, reduce waste, and implement eco-friendly policies with greater precision. By leveraging data, HR teams can align their decisions with broader environmental goals, ensuring a more significant impact over time. The shift towards remote work, facilitated by digital transformation, highlights another avenue for sustainability. Remote work not only reduces commuting-related emissions but also minimizes energy usage in office spaces. This transition supports Green HRM objectives by contributing to environmental conservation while maintaining organizational productivity. It also underscores the flexibility and adaptability of digital technologies in addressing diverse sustainability challenges.

Figure 1. Global spending on digital transformation

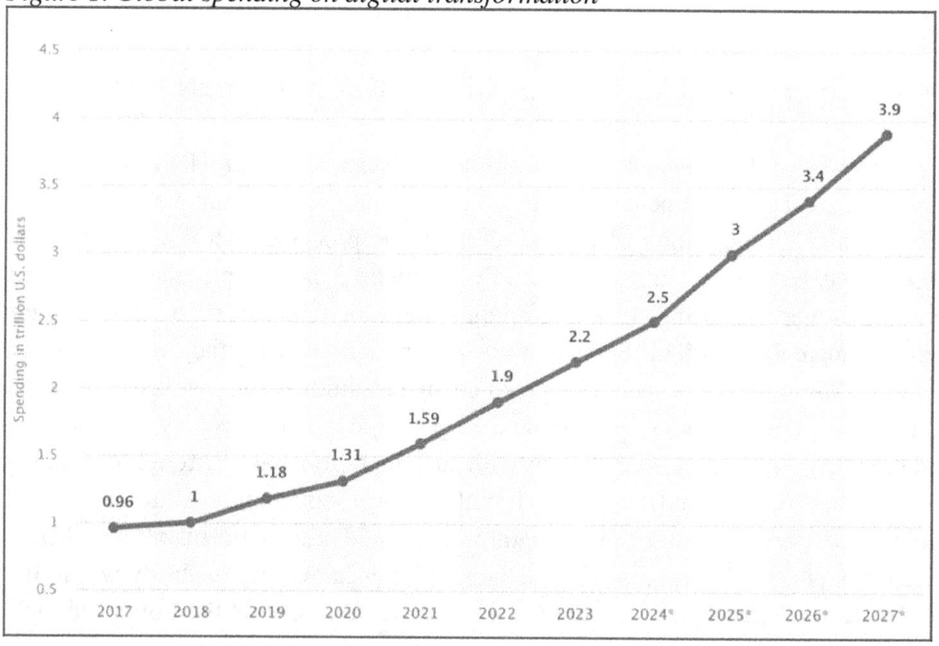

The graph in Figure 1 shows the global spending on digital transformation technologies and services from 2017 to 2027, with expenditures growing steadily. Beginning at $0.96 trillion in 2017, the spending has consistently increased, reaching $1.59 trillion by 2022. It is projected to rise further to $3.9 trillion by 2027, reflecting an accelerated adoption of digital transformation solutions across industries (IDC & Statista, 2024).

When analyzed within the framework of Green HRM strategies, this data highlights the growing role of technology in facilitating sustainable and operationally efficient practices (Figure 2). Organizations increasingly utilize digital transformation technologies, such as automation, AI, and data analytics, to enhance their HR operations and effectively integrate sustainability objectives. For instance, digital platforms enable better resource allocation, improved monitoring of environmental impacts, and a decrease in paper and energy consumption—all vital components of Green HRM.

Figure 2. Year-over-year growth rate on global spending on digital transformation

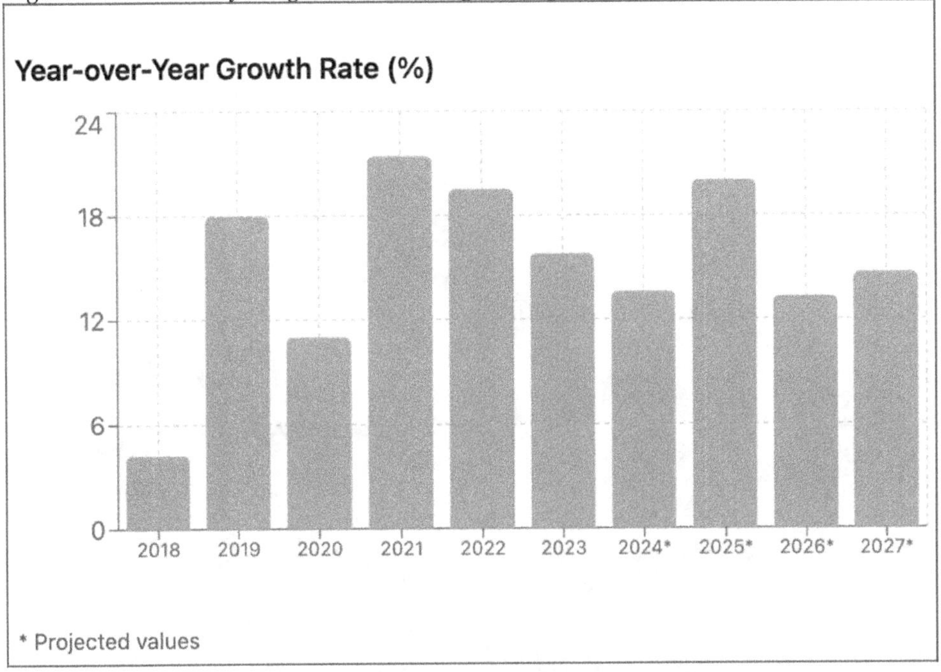

This exponential growth in digital transformation spending indicates a global shift toward modernized, data-driven, and environmentally conscious organizational frameworks. The upward trend aligns with the broader adoption of Green HRM, where companies are integrating advanced technologies to not only improve operational efficiencies but also enhance their positioning as leaders in sustainability. By investing in these technologies, organizations are better equipped to achieve their green marketing advantages, reinforcing their commitment to sustainability and resonating with environmentally conscious stakeholders.

5. EMERGING TRENDS IN GREEN HRM AND GREEN MARKETING

The evolving corporate sustainability landscape has positioned Green HRM and green marketing as key pillars in organizations' strategies to drive environmental responsibility and competitive differentiation. As businesses continue to integrate sustainability at their core, several emerging trends in these domains are shaping the future (Figure 3).

Figure 3. Green HRM and marketing trends

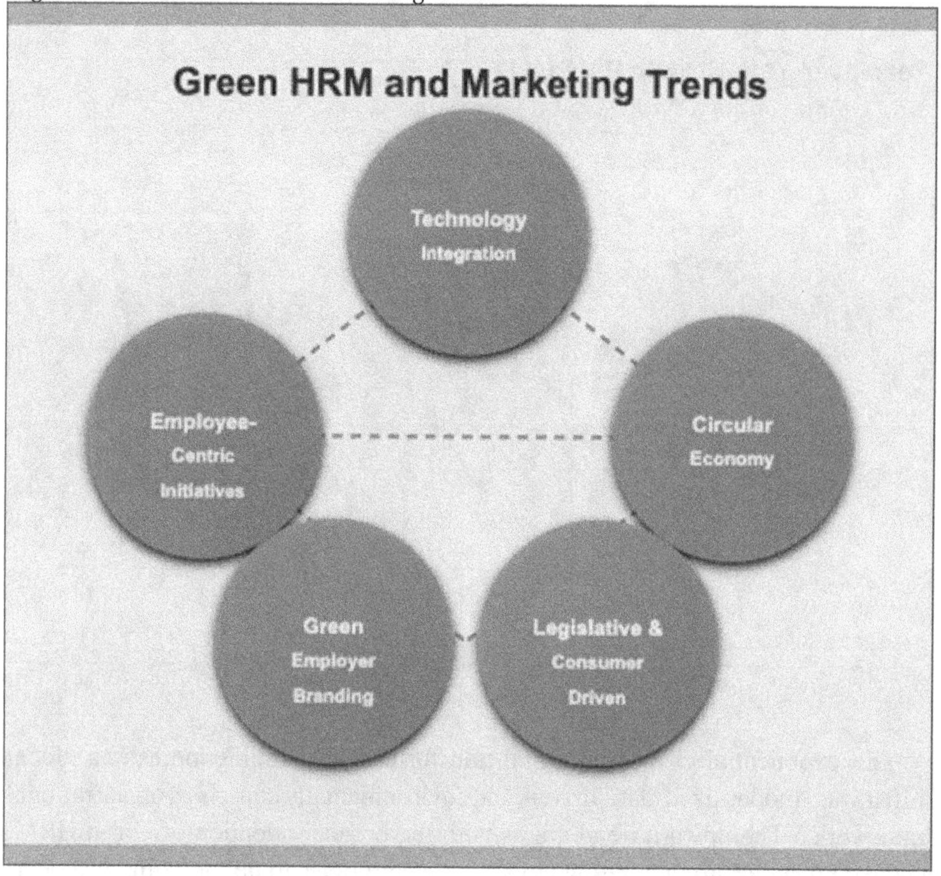

5.1. Integration of Technology for Green Practices

Advancements in technology are enabling organizations to adopt more efficient and sustainable HR practices. Digital HR platforms, powered by artificial intelligence and data analytics, are increasingly being used to monitor and manage employees' environmental footprints, optimize workspaces to reduce energy consumption, and promote virtual working environments to minimize travel-related carbon emissions. In marketing, digital tools and platforms are being leveraged to create personalized, eco-conscious campaigns that resonate with environmentally aware consumers.

5.2. Employee-Centric Green Initiatives

Green HRM strategies are now focusing on empowering employees as active participants in sustainability efforts. Organizations are implementing programs that promote green skills development, such as training in renewable energy technologies or sustainable business practices. Employee engagement in environmental initiatives, such as community clean-ups or green certification programs, fosters a culture of sustainability. Concurrently, green marketing emphasizes showcasing these employee-driven sustainability efforts to enhance brand authenticity and consumer trust.

5.3. Circular Economy Alignment

The shift toward circular economic models is influencing both HR and marketing practices. In HRM, businesses are prioritizing hiring and retaining talent with expertise in circular design and supply chain management. In marketing, brands are increasingly promoting products and services that adhere to principles of reuse, recycling, and sustainable consumption, catering to the growing demand for sustainable solutions among consumers.

5.4. Focus on Green Employer Branding

The emergence of green employer branding has become a significant trend in Green HRM. Companies are promoting their environmental credentials as part of their value proposition to attract eco-conscious talent. Simultaneously, green marketing strategies are being integrated into recruitment campaigns to communicate organizational commitment to sustainability, thereby aligning brand image with sustainability goals.

5.5. Legislative and Consumer-Driven Transformation

Green HRM and green marketing are increasingly influenced by stricter environmental regulations and shifting consumer behaviors. Organizations are adopting proactive approaches to comply with regulatory frameworks while also addressing the rising expectations of socially and environmentally conscious stakeholders. This trend ensures that sustainability remains a top priority in corporate policies and marketing narratives.

In conclusion, the trends shaping Green HRM and green marketing highlight the interconnectedness between environmental responsibility and business strategy. By embracing technological innovation, empowering employees, adhering to circular economy principles, implementing green branding, and ensuring regulatory alignment, organizations can position themselves as leaders in the global sustainability movement while gaining competitive advantages in the marketplace.

6. CASE STUDIES OF COMPANIES WITH INTEGRATED GREEN HRM

The adoption of green HRM strategies highlights the significant ways organizations can integrate their human resources practices with overarching sustainability objectives. By aligning HR operations with environmental goals, companies can enhance their operational efficiency and gain a considerable edge in green marketing initiatives, establishing themselves as forward-thinking and eco-conscious entities in the marketplace. A growing number of companies have taken deliberate steps to embed Green HRM principles into their organizational frameworks. These efforts have yielded tangible benefits, including reduced carbon footprints, streamlined resource utilization, and strengthened alignment between corporate sustainability aspirations and everyday workforce practices. Moreover, the incorporation of these strategies has significantly boosted the perception of such organizations among consumers and stakeholders, enhancing their brand credibility and loyalty. The integration of sustainability-driven HR practices serves as a testament to how operational and marketing objectives can converge to achieve long-term environmental and economic gains, ultimately contributing to both a healthier planet and robust business performance. In this section, this chapter discuses some success cases of green HRM.

6.1 Wipro Limited

Wipro Limited, a leading global IT services corporation, is at the forefront of integrating Green HRM with its sustainability vision (Pathak & Agarwal, 2024). The company's Green Initiatives Program constitutes the basis of its approach, which hinges on employee involvement in activities such as waste reduction, energy conservation, and promoting a paperless work environment (Pathak & Agarwal, 2024).

Wipro's recruitment process reflects its green ethos. Job advertisements are tailored to attract candidates with strong environmental values, ensuring a workforce that aligns with its sustainability agenda (Sarkar et al., 2024). Additionally, the onboarding process introduces new employees to the company's environmental policies and practices, leading to an early engagement with green initiatives ((Sarkar et al., 2024). The company also invests heavily in employee training and development. Its *Mission 10x* initiative focuses on sustainable innovation, equipping employees with skills to contribute to eco-friendly solutions (Bhardwaj et al., 2024). Workshops and e-learning modules on topics like carbon footprint reduction and energy efficiency are regularly conducted (Bhardwaj et al., 2024). Much effort is invested to ensure that these training programs align with the company's operational goals, creating a workforce that is both environmentally conscious and skilled in implementing green solutions (Bhardwaj et al., 2024).

Furthermore, marketing outcomes of Wipro's Green HRM initiatives are significant (Nagam & Vidyasagar, 2024). Its campaigns, such as *Eco-Eye* reflect employee-driven innovations in sustainability, reinforcing the company's brand as a leader in green technology (Nagam & Vidyasagar, 2024). This strategy has enhanced Wipro's appeal to environmentally conscious clients and investors, creating a competitive advantage in the IT sector (Nagam & Vidyasagar, 2024).

A major strength of Wipro lies in its ability to integrate green competencies into its core operational and marketing strategies (Agnihotri & Bhattacharya, 2023). Unlike some other companies that rely heavily on external collaborations for marketing sustainability, Wipro uses its internal workforce to positon itself as a leader in green technology (Agnihotri & Bhattacharya, 2023).

6.2 IKEA

IKEA, the Swedish multinational recognized for its flat-pack furniture and affordable home solutions, has integrated Green HRM into its broader *People and Planet Positive* strategy (Anand, 2024). This approach emphasizes sustainability across all aspects of the business, with HRM playing a crucial role (Anand, 2024). The company's recruitment policies prioritize candidates with a demonstrated interest in sustainability (Lindgren & Osterlind, 2018). Job descriptions clearly articulate

IKEA's commitment to environmental goals, attracting talent that shares its values (Ericsson, 2018). Similarly, IKEA partners with universities and green organizations to identify and recruit environmentally conscious graduates (Ericsson, 2018).

Training and development are central to IKEA's Green HRM framework (Anand, 2024). Employees participate in regular workshops and online training sessions covering topics such as circular economy principles, ethical sourcing, and sustainable design (Tahmasbi, 2024). For instance, the company informs its staff about recycling and reusing materials, enabling them to effectively convey these principles to customers (Anand, 2024). Additionally, employee engagement is another crucial aspect of IKEA's Green HRM framework (Anand, 2024). Regarding Corporate Social Responsibility (CSR), IKEA fosters a sense of ownership among its workforce through initiatives like green volunteering programs, where employees engage in community-based sustainability projects, thus boosting morale and reinforcing the company's commitment to environmental stewardship (Ericcson, 2018).

In its marketing campaigns, IKEA uses Green HRM practices to strengthen its brand narrative (Olsson & Storesund, 2015). The *Sustainable Living* campaign, for instance, features employees discussing their contributions to the company's sustainability efforts (Elizaveta, 2021). This approach adds authenticity to IKEA's green marketing and ensures that eco-conscious consumers can easily relate to it (Elizaveta, 2021).

Thus, IKEA's approach has a distinct variation from that of Wipro. This is in the sense that through its employee-generated content in its marketing, the former emphasises the human aspect of sustainability, creating a more relatable and emotionally green narrative that its target audience can relate with (Anand, 2024).

6.3 Toyota

Toyota's commitment to environmental sustainability is deeply embedded in its corporate philosophy, often referred to as the *Toyota Way* (Palhau et al., 2024). The company's Green HRM practices are integral to its goal of achieving carbon neutrality and promoting green innovation (Elemure et al., 2023). A standout feature for the company is its reliance on quantifiable environmental achievements to bolster its green narrative, appealing to a more data-driven audience (Palhau et al., 2024).

Recruitment at Toyota focuses on identifying candidates who are passionate about sustainability (Roualt, 2021). The company's graduate recruitment programs include a strong emphasis on environmental stewardship, ensuring that new hires align with Toyota's green values from the outset (Roualt, 2021). In the same vein, Toyota's training initiatives are extensive and tailored to its operational needs. Employees are trained in areas such as energy efficiency and lean manufacturing practices that reduce environmental impact (Elemure, 2023). The company's Kaizen training, for instance, incorporates green principles, encouraging employees to identify and implement eco-friendly improvements in their daily tasks (Elemure, 2023). Additionally, performance management systems at Toyota include green KPIs, linking employee rewards to sustainability targets (Lopess-Naglis, 2023). This approach incentivises employees to participate in the company's environmental initiatives actively, promoting a culture of accountability and innovation (Lopess-Naglis, 2023).

Toyota also excels in CSR initiatives. Its *Green Wave Project* which engages employees in afforestation and biodiversity conservation efforts, has been successfully incorporated into its marketing strategies (Chen et al., 2024). More so, Toyota's marketing campaigns such as the *Toyota Environmental Challenge 2050* highlight its Green HRM efforts (Amir & Sabri, 2024). Hence, Toyota enhances its brand reputation and establishes itself as a thought leader in sustainable automotive solutions through its employee-driven green projects (Amir & Sabri, 2024).

6.4 The Body Shop

The Body Shop, a global beauty brand renowned for its ethical values, has effectively utilised Green HRM to align its operations with its sustainability goals (Gill, 2011). The company's recruitment process emphasises its commitment to social and environmental responsibility, attracting candidates who are in agreement with its values (The Body Shop, 2024).

Training programs at the Body Shop focus on educating employees about ethical sourcing, cruelty-free practices and sustainable product development (The Body Shop, 2024). These programs ensure that employees are well-informed and capable of upholding the company's ethical standards (The Body Shop, 2024). Likewise, the company's CSR initiatives, such as community-based tree planting and beach-cleaning programs, actively involve employees to widespread critical acclaim (The Body Shop, 2024).

Figure 4. Comparative green HRM strategies of studied companies

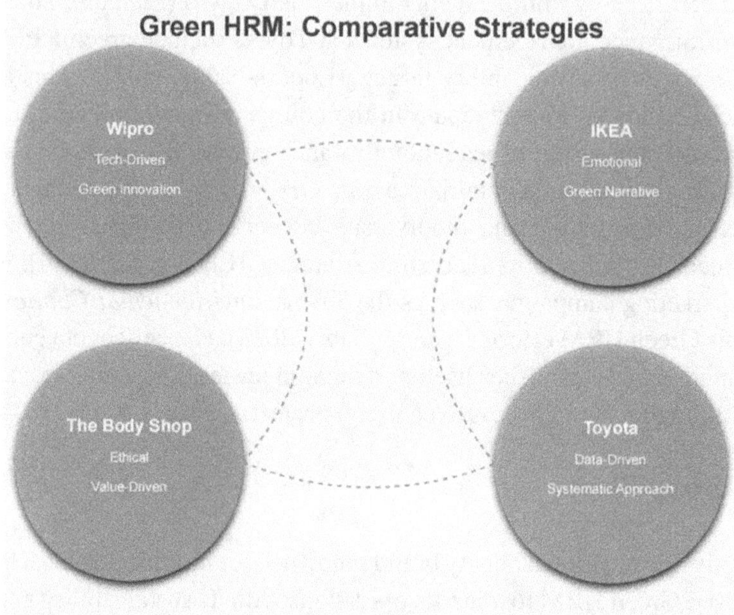

The above four prominent organizations exemplify distinctive approaches to integrating environmental consciousness into their human resource practices (Figure 4). Wipro, the global IT services corporation, emerges as a technology-driven innovator in green strategies. By leveraging digital platforms and technological solutions, Wipro transforms traditional HR practices into sophisticated, sustainability-focused ecosystems. The company's approach goes beyond mere compliance, embedding environmental considerations into the core of its talent management, recruitment, and employee development processes. In contrast, IKEA presents a markedly different paradigm—an emotionally resonant green narrative that humanizes sustainability. The Swedish multinational distinguishes itself by creating a green strategy that transcends technical implementations, focusing instead on personal stories and individual connections to environmental responsibility. By positioning sustainability as a collective journey, IKEA transforms environmental initiatives from corporate mandates to meaningful personal experiences, engaging employees through emotional rather than purely rational approaches.

Toyota represents a third strategic model, characterized by its systematic, data-driven approach to Green HRM. Rooted in the company's legendary operational philosophy, Toyota's sustainability strategy is built on precision, measurement, and continuous improvement. Performance management, training programs, and recruitment processes are meticulously aligned with quantifiable environmental objectives. This approach reflects the automotive giant's commitment to lean practices and empirical assessment of environmental impact. The Body Shop stands apart with its deeply ethical approach to Green HRM. For this global beauty brand, sustainability is intrinsically linked to social responsibility. The company's human resource practices are fundamentally designed around ethical values, prioritizing sustainable sourcing, community engagement, and creating a workforce that embodies social consciousness. Unlike more technical approaches, The Body Shop's strategy emphasizes moral alignment and holistic social impact.

Despite their differences, these organizations share a fundamental understanding: sustainability is no longer a peripheral corporate concern but a central strategic imperative. Their varied approaches illustrate that Green HRM is not about adopting a universal template but about authentically integrating environmental consciousness with an organization's unique cultural and operational DNA.

The strategic diversity observed in these case studies challenges traditional notions of corporate environmental responsibility. It reveals that effective Green HRM is a dynamic, context-specific process that must be carefully tailored to an organization's specific strengths, industry context, and cultural framework. These comparative strategies offer valuable insights as businesses continue to navigate increasingly complex global environmental challenges. They demonstrate that sustainable human resource management is not about achieving perfect uniformity but about creating genuine, meaningful approaches that resonate with employees, align with organizational values, and contribute to broader environmental objectives. The future of Green HRM lies not in rigid standardization but in creative, adaptive strategies that recognize the unique potential of each organization to drive positive environmental change through its most valuable resource: its people.

7. CHALLENGES AND OPPORTUNITIES FOR HRM IN GREEN MARKETING

7.1 Challenges

At the core of green marketing is HRM, which plays a crucial role in enabling organizations to adopt and integrate green initiatives (Benevene & Buonomo, 2020). However, the path to effective green marketing through HRM is often fraught with challenges (Figure 5) that must be addressed alongside the opportunities it presents (Ren & Jackson, 2020). Understanding these factors is vital for HR professionals, as their ability to manage these challenges determines the success of green marketing campaigns while also ensuring that the broader sustainability agenda of their organizations is effective (Ren & Jackson, 2020).

Figure 5. Green HRM challenges

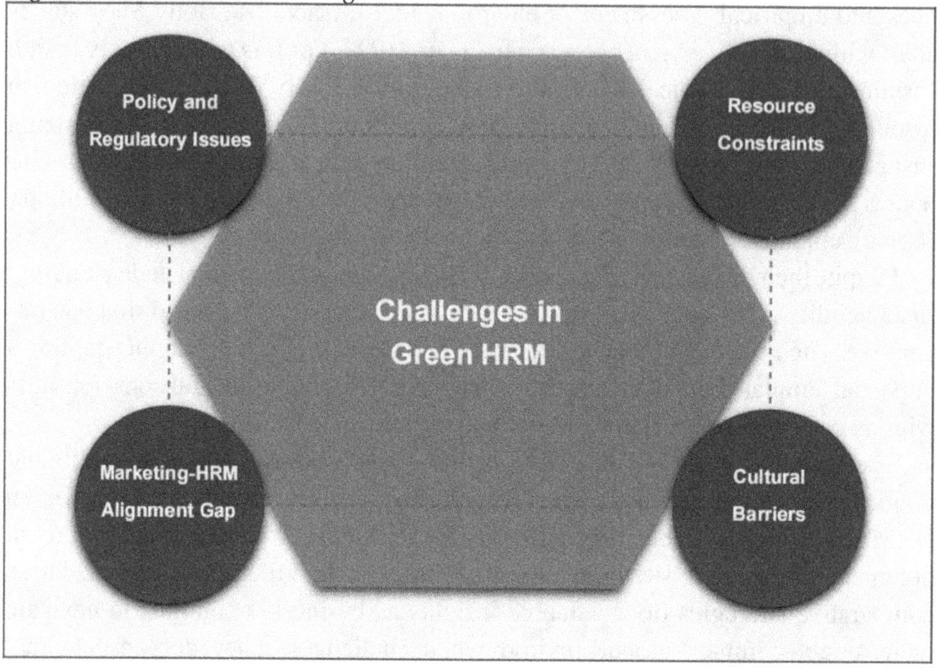

7.1.1 Policy and Regulatory Issues

Policy and regulatory issues represent a significant challenge for HR professionals seeking to implement green HRM practices (Islam et al., 2020). The global push for environmental sustainability often collides with varying local regulations, creating inconsistencies that hinder the smooth adoption of green initiatives (Arzo & Hong, 2024). In some regions, regulations may lack stringent environmental standards, making it difficult for organizations to justify investments in sustainability-focused HR practices (Buller & McEvoy, 2016). Equally, overly rigid environmental policies in other jurisdictions can create administrative burdens that strain organizational resources (Lazarus, 2023). For multinational corporations, the challenge is even more pronounced, as they must manage the conflicting demands of local regulatory environments while maintaining global sustainability objectives (Lazarus, 2023). For instance, an organization operating in a region with lenient environmental laws might face difficulty convincing employees and local stakeholders of the importance of green HRM initiatives (Wang et al., 2024). At the same time, the same organization could be held to higher standards in regions with stricter regulations, necessitating dual compliance efforts that complicate the execution of a unified green strategy (Lazarus, 2023). These conflicts can lead to inefficiencies and increased costs, ultimately discouraging organizations from pursuing green HRM practices altogether (Lazarus, 2023).

7.1.2 Resource Constraints

Resource constraints also pose a significant challenge. Implementing green HRM practices often involves upfront investments in training, technology and infrastructure (Mahesh et al., 2024). For instance, developing comprehensive sustainability training programs or revising recruitment systems to prioritise environmental values requires substantial funding (Mishra, 2017). Small and medium-sized enterprises (SMEs), in particular, may struggle to allocate resources towards these initiatives, which can hinder their ability to compete with larger corporations that have greater financial flexibility (Prasanna et al., 2024). Furthermore, the lack of standardised metrics to evaluate the effectiveness of green HRM practices complicates the justification of these investments to stakeholders (Goel et al., 2022).

Furthermore, time is a critical resource that organizations often find scarce (Berg et al., 2023). Developing and integrating green HRM initiatives requires considerable planning, coordination, and execution, all of which compete with existing operational demands (Ren et al., 2018). For example, designing new performance management systems with sustainability-focused KPIs or revising job descriptions to highlight environmental competencies can be resource-intensive, diverting attention from other pressing HR functions (Jay & Gerrard, 2015). Similarly, a lack of expertise or training in sustainability exacerbates resource constraints. Many HR professionals and organizational leaders lack the knowledge or skills necessary to implement green HRM practices effectively (Mtembu, 2019). This knowledge gap can lead to poorly designed initiatives that fail to achieve their intended goals, further fueling skepticism about the value of green HRM (Mtembu, 2019). For instance, HR managers may struggle to align recruitment strategies with sustainability objectives or create employee engagement programs that promote eco-friendly behaviors without adequate training (Hammed, 2024).

7.1.3 Bridging the Gap Between HRM Policies and Tangible Marketing Outcomes

Another critical challenge lies in bridging the gap between green HRM policies and tangible marketing outcomes (Zaid et al., 2018). While HRM can drive a workforce that embodies sustainability values, translating these values into effective green marketing campaigns requires a smooth collaboration between HR and marketing teams (Jackson et al., 2012). Misalignment or poor communication between these departments can dilute the impact of green initiatives, resulting in campaigns that lack authenticity or fail to resonate with target audiences, or worse, expose the organization to accusations of greenwashing (Hennig, 2021). One significant aspect of this challenge is the potential misalignment between HR and marketing objectives. HR teams might focus on implementing an internal culture of sustainability through recruitment, training and employee engagement, while marketing teams aim to communicate these efforts to external audiences (Jackson et al., 2012). Without a shared vision and coordinated strategies, these parallel efforts can lead to a disconnect where marketing campaigns fail to reflect the authentic sustainability practices being cultivated internally (Jackson et al., 2012).. The risk of greenwashing further complicates this dynamic. Greenwashing occurs when organizations exaggerate or fabricate their environmental commitments, often leading to public backlash and reputational damage (Aliano, 2024). Even well-intentioned campaigns can fall into this trap if they are perceived as superficial or inconsistent with the organization's actual practices (Montgomery et al., 2024).

7.1.4 Cultural Barriers

Finally, cultural barriers further worsen the challenges of implementing green HRM (Ren et al., 2018). Cultivating a green culture can be met with resistance in regions with low environmental awareness or deeply ingrained traditional practices (Wu & Tham, 2023). Employees and managers may perceive sustainability initiatives as unnecessary or disruptive to established workflows (Wu & Tham, 2023). Likewise, cultural differences in attitudes toward environmental responsibility can create disparities in how green HRM practices are received across an organization's global operations (Ababneh, 2021). In cultures, for instance, where individual achievement is prioritised over collective well-being, initiatives aimed at building a shared sense of environmental stewardship may struggle to gain traction (Miska et al., 2018). Similarly, in regions where immediate economic concerns take precedence over long-term sustainability goals, employees and stakeholders might view green HRM practices as a luxury rather than a necessity (Ababneh, 2021). Overcoming these barriers require HR professionals to adopt culturally sensitive approaches that respect local norms while promoting the universal value of environmental responsibility (Miska et al., 2018).

7.2 Opportunities

Despite these challenges, the opportunities for HRM in green marketing are equally compelling (see Figure 6).

Figure 6. Green HRM opportunities

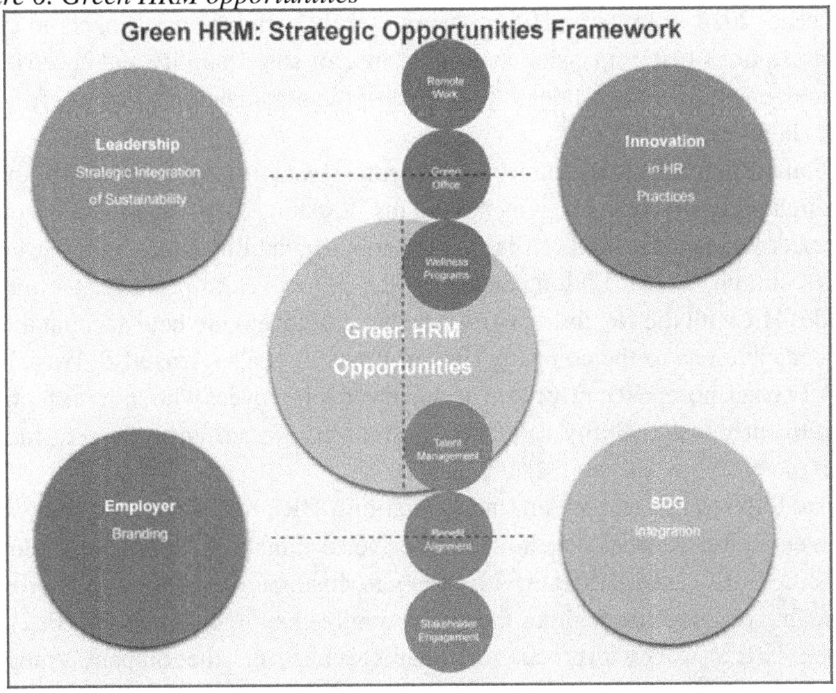

7.2.1 Leadership Role

As sustainability increasingly becomes a priority for businesses worldwide, HR professionals have a significant opportunity to take on leadership roles in driving sustainability-focused organizational changes. This leadership role involves adopting environmentally responsible practices within HR functions while also implementing a culture of sustainability throughout the entire organization (Roscoe et al., 2019). One of the most critical opportunities for HR professionals to lead sustainability efforts is through the strategic integration of sustainability into the organizational culture (Roscoe et al., 2019; Galpin et al., 2015). HR can champion sustainability by embedding it into the company's core values and mission, thereby setting the tone for all levels of operation (Jamali et al., 2015). Aligning sustainability goals with the overall organizational strategy positions HR in a driving role to ensure that every aspect of the business, from recruitment to performance management, reflects the organization's commitment to environmental stewardship (Holbeche, 2022; Buller & McEvoy, 2016). HR professionals can spearhead this cultural transformation by integrating sustainability into recruitment, selection, and onboarding processes (Singha, 2024). When hiring new employees, HR can prioritize candidates who share the company's sustainability values and have a passion for environmental initiatives (Holbeche, 2024). Similarly, HR can work closely with hiring managers to create job descriptions that emphasize the importance of sustainability and eco-friendly practices, ensuring that sustainability is part of the organizational identity from the outset (Jamil et al., 2023).

Another significant opportunity for HR professionals to lead sustainability efforts is through performance management systems (Saratun, 2016). HR can incorporate key performance indicators (KPIs) related to sustainability into employee evaluations (Saratun, 2016). Linking sustainability objectives to performance metrics provides HR with the flexibility to ensure that employees are held accountable for their contributions to the company's environmental goals (Arnaud & Wasieleski, 2014). Furthermore, HR can recognize and reward employees who show exceptional commitment to sustainability, further emphasizing the importance of green practices within the company culture (Mishra, 2017).

In addition to influencing internal operations, HR professionals can play a key role in engaging external stakeholders to drive sustainability initiatives (Adegoke et al., 2024). HR can collaborate with suppliers, customers, and partners to promote sustainable practices throughout the entire supply chain (Mishra et al., 2022). For example, HR can work with procurement teams to ensure that the company's suppliers follow environmentally responsible practices, or partner with local organizations to create community-based sustainability initiatives (Jackson et al., 2012). HR professionals also have the chance to influence organizational policies that support green initiatives (Mishra, 2017). By closely collaborating with top management, HR can advocate for policies that promote sustainability, such as reducing paper usage, implementing energy-saving technologies, or adopting green procurement practices (Viterouli et al., 2023). Additionally, HR can also lead the development of a sustainability policy that outlines the company's commitment to environmental responsibility and provides guidelines for employees to follow (Mandip, 2012).

7.2.2 Innovation in HR practices

Innovation in HR practices is a vital avenue through which HR professionals can drive sustainability and contribute significantly to green marketing strategies (Singh et al., 2020). As companies increasingly recognize the importance of sustainability in their operations, HR practices are evolving to not only meet organizational needs but also to implement a culture of environmental responsibility (Mishra, 2017). One notable innovation is the development of creative solutions such as remote work policies, which have the potential to significantly reduce an organization's carbon footprint (Geneidy et al., 2021).

Remote work, once viewed as a temporary solution to unforeseen circumstances like the COVID-19 pandemic, has now become a crucial part of many companies' sustainability strategies (Assaas & El-Adaway, 2021). HR professionals play a significant role in developing and implementing remote work policies that prioritize reducing environmental impact (Vahdat, 2022). Encouraging employees to work from home or from locations closer to their residences allows organizations to significantly cut down on commuting-related emissions, a major contributor to a company's carbon footprint (Tsairi & Martens, 2024). This approach benefits the environment and enhances employees' work-life balance, potentially leading to higher satisfaction and productivity (Tsairi & Martens, 2024). HR can also innovate by incorporating sustainability considerations into remote work policy design (Vahdat, 2022). For example, companies can invest in technology and digital tools that facilitate remote work, decreasing the need for physical office spaces and lowering energy consumption associated with heating, cooling, and lighting large office buildings (Abdullah & Lim, 2023). Additionally, HR can collaborate with IT departments to ensure the necessary infrastructure, such as reliable video conferencing tools and collaborative platforms, is established to support employees in remote work environments (Joseph, 2024). Furthermore, HR can provide guidelines on sustainable remote work practices, including reducing energy use at home, minimizing waste, and encouraging employees to adopt eco-friendly habits in their personal lives, like using renewable energy sources or recycling materials (Nagam & VidyaSagar, 2024).

Beyond remote work policies, HR can also innovate in other areas to promote sustainability. For instance, green office initiatives are gaining momentum, where HR professionals lead the charge in creating eco-friendly and energy-efficient office environments (Abdullah & Lim, 2023). This might include initiatives such as reducing paper usage, implementing digital document management systems and encouraging employees to reduce their consumption of single-use plastics (Nagam & VidyaSagar, 2024). Embracing green alternatives allows HR professionals contribute to sustainability efforts while ensuring that the workplace remains productive and functional (Nagam & VidyaSagar, 2024).

Additionally, HR can play an essential role in creating employee wellness programs that align with sustainability goals (Stahl et al., 2020). Programs that focus on healthy lifestyles, such as promoting walking or cycling to work or incorporating mindfulness practices that create an awareness of environmental impact, can further reduce a company's ecological footprint (Madan et al., 2023). Similarly, HR can collaborate with sustainability experts to design programs that educate employees about the environmental challenges the company is addressing and the steps they can take to contribute to sustainability initiatives (Jackson et al., 2012).

Furthermore, sustainability can be integrated into performance management systems in innovative ways (Saratun, 2016). Rather than solely measuring traditional business outcomes, HR professionals can create new metrics that capture the environmental impact of an employee's work (Dulebohn & Johnson, 2013). These metrics may encompass aspects related to energy efficiency, waste reduction, or contributions to the company's green initiatives. Such actions reinforce the idea that sustainability is a core value of the organization and that employees are expected to actively contribute to these goals actively (Jackson et al., 2012).

7.2.3 Strengthening Employee Branding

Strengthening employer branding through Green HRM practices is a powerful strategy for attracting top talent and enhancing a company's reputation in today's highly competitive job market (Yasin et al., 2023). Employer branding is increasingly important as job seekers, particularly those from younger generations, are placing a greater emphasis on environmental and social responsibility when choosing where to work (Hallova & Muller, 2023). Green HRM, which incorporates environmentally sustainable practices into human resource management significantly influences this aspect of a company's identity and can primarily contribute to its attractiveness as an employer of choice (Yasin et al., 2023). To strengthen employer branding, HR professionals can actively integrate sustainability into the company's values and culture (Cascio & Graham, 2016). Companies can position themselves as environmentally conscious organizations that care about the planet and their employee's well-being by promoting Green HRM initiatives such as eco-friendly recruitment processes, sustainability-focused employee benefits and green workplace initiatives (Anand, 2024). This perception is especially attractive to candidates who prioritise ethical work environments and want to work for companies that are actively contributing to solving global environmental challenges (Anand, 2024).

Also, creating opportunities for employees to be actively involved in environmental initiatives, both within and outside the workplace, strengthens employer branding by demonstrating the company's broader social responsibility (Stahl et al., 2020). HR can encourage employee participation in green volunteer programs, tree planting activities or local community projects that align with the organization's environmental values (Mishra, 2017). Consequently, the companies boost their employees morale and engagement and also build a positive reputation as a company that supports environmental causes (Mishra, 2017).

The role of Green HRM in strengthening employer branding extends to the digital space as well. In today's world, online presence and social media play are essential in shaping perceptions of an organization (Leonardi & Vaast, 2017). HR professionals can employ digital platforms to communicate the company's green initiatives, demonstrating sustainability-driven projects, employee engagement in environmental causes and the company's overall commitment to reducing its carbon footprint (Finnegan, 2024). Highlighting these efforts on the company website, social media channels and recruitment platforms can help reinforce the employer brand's association with environmental responsibility (Benitez et al., 2020). Additionally, creating content such as blogs, videos, or webinars about the company's green initiatives can further strengthen its reputation as a thought leader in sustainability and attract top talent who are passionate about working for a purpose-driven organization (Kaufman et al., 2023). Moreover, Green HRM practices can enhance employer branding by helping to foster a sense of CSR that both employees and customers can easily relate with (Kivinda et al., 2021). When HR integrates CSR efforts into the company's strategic vision, such as supporting environmental non-profits or participating in global environmental initiatives like the United Nations' Sustainable Development Goals (SDGs), the company's employer brand is perceived as being socially responsible (Ferdousi & Abedin, 2023). Such perception attracts top talent and contributes to consumer trust and loyalty, which are essential components of long-term business success (Mishra, 2017).

HR professionals can also emphasize the company's green certification or sustainability awards in recruitment efforts (Mishra, 2017). Recognized green certifications, such as LEED (Leadership in Energy and Environmental Design) for green buildings, or certifications from organizations like B Corp or ISO 14001, can serve as powerful signals to potential employees that the company adheres to high environmental and ethical standards (Jones et al., 2019). These certifications serve as a form of validation, giving the company credibility in its sustainability efforts and making it an attractive option for top-tier talent who value sustainability in the workplace (Jones et al., 2019).

7.2.4 Integration with Sustainable Development Goals (SDGs)

HR professionals have a pertinent role in aligning corporate goals with the SDGs, helping organizations not only meet their business objectives but also contribute to global sustainability efforts (Stahl et al., 2020). The SDGs, adopted by all United Nations member states in 2015, provide a universal framework for addressing the world's most pressing challenges, including poverty, inequality, environmental degradation, and climate change (Trends, 2017). For businesses, this represents an opportunity to demonstrate leadership in sustainability while enhancing their long-term viability and resilience (Mishra, 2017). Therefore, HR professionals can facilitate the integration of the SDGs by embedding sustainability into the organization's culture, values and strategic objectives (Stahl, 2020; Bilderback, 2024). This alignment begins with ensuring that the organization's mission and vision reflect a commitment to the SDGs (Bilderback, 2024). HR can contribute by drafting corporate policies that integrate SDGs into the core business strategy, ensuring that all departments, including HR, marketing, and operations, understand their role in advancing sustainability goals (Stahl, 2020). Through clear communication of these goals, HR helps employees at all levels understand how their roles and responsibilities contribute to broader environmental, social, and governance (ESG) outcomes (Ajayi, 2024).

One of the primary ways HR can support SDG integration is through talent management (Mujtaba & Mubarik, 2022). By focusing recruitment efforts on individuals who are passionate about sustainability, HR can attract employees whose values align with the SDGs (Adekoya, 2022). This includes promoting diversity and inclusivity (SDG 5: Gender Equality), hiring individuals from marginalised groups (SDG 10: Reduced Inequalities) and selecting candidates who are dedicated to environmental stewardship (SDG 13: Climate Action). HR can also ensure that job descriptions, advertisements, and interview processes reflect the organization's commitment to the SDGs, emphasising the importance of sustainability and corporate responsibility (Jamil et al., 2023). When HR are aligned with SDGs, they can build a workforce that is not only skilled but also motivated to contribute to global sustainability efforts (Bilderback, 2024). Beyond performance management, HR can play a significant role in aligning compensation and benefits packages with SDGs (Stahl, 2020). For instance, offering eco-friendly benefits such as subsidies for electric vehicles or promoting wellness programs that encourage healthy living aligns with several SDGs, including SDG 3 (Good Health and Well-Being) and SDG 12 (Responsible Consumption and Production). Similarly, HR can develop policies that promote work-life balance, equal pay, and family-friendly benefits, supporting SDG 5 (Gender Equality) and SDG 10 (Reduced Inequalities). Aligning compensation and benefits with SDGs not only strengthens the employer brand but also demonstrates the company's commitment to sustainability and social responsibility (Yasin et al., 2023).

In addition to internal policies and programs, HR can help organizations engage with external stakeholders to advance the SDGs (Chams et al., 2019). This could involve forming partnerships with NGOs, governments and other businesses that are also committed to sustainability (Chams et al., 2019). HR can facilitate employee involvement in CSR initiatives that directly support the SDGs (Ahmad, 2023). For instance, employees might volunteer for community projects focused on education (SDG 4: Quality Education), health (SDG 3), or environmental protection (SDG 13). Participating in these initiatives ensures that employees contribute to societal well-being and also gain a deeper understanding of the SDGs and their relevance to the company's mission (Jimenez et al., 2021).

Furthermore, HR can integrate SDGs into corporate governance by ensuring that the organization's leadership is accountable for sustainability outcomes (Bilderback, 2024). HR can influence how companies achieve their long-term sustainability objectives through its promotion of diversity in leadership (SDG 5) and ensuring that sustainability is embedded in decision-making processes (Chams et al., 2019). Board members and senior leaders who are committed to sustainability can help set the tone for the rest of the organization, ensuring that the SDGs remain at the forefront of business strategies (Rosati & Faria, 2019). More so, the integration of SDGs through HRM also enhances the organization's reputation and market position (Chams et al., 2019). As more consumers and investors seek out companies that align with the SDGs, HR plays an essential role in shaping the company's sustainability image (Chams et al., 2019). This alignment contributes to the company's long-term success while also helping to address the global challenges outlined in the SDGs (Bilderback, 2024).

8. CASE STUDIES OF SOLVED CHALLENGES FOR HRM IN GREEN MARKETING

Real-world instances of organizations addressing implementation challenges in integrating Green HRM with marketing strategies reveal both the obstacles encountered and the innovative solutions employed to overcome them (Viterouli et al., 2023). These examples underline the complexity of sustainable practices and also offer valuable insights into effective approaches for handling such challenges.

One notable instance is Unilever, a global consumer goods company that has consistently championed sustainability as part of its business ethos (Raja, 2021). While rolling out its *Sustainable Living Plan*, the company faced significant organizational resistance, particularly in aligning its sustainability goals with traditional operational practices across diverse regions (Raja, 2021). Employees and stakeholders were sceptical about the practicality of balancing profit and environmental stewardship. To address this, Unilever adopted a robust training and development initiative, embedding sustainability into leadership programs. The company trained over 160,000 employees in sustainability principles and integrated these values into its performance management systems (Raja, 2021). By creating "Sustainability Champions" within teams, Unilever bridged the gap between its HR and marketing departments, ensuring that sustainability messages became relatable with consumers (Adelusola, 2024). The outcome was a marked increase in consumer trust and a surge in demand for its eco-friendly products like Dove and Ben & Jerry's, illustrating how targeted training can drive both internal alignment and external marketing success (Vorecel, 2024).

Another instance is IKEA, which encountered significant resource constraints while implementing its *People & Planet Positive strategy* (Strategy, 2018). The company's ambitious goals to use 100% renewable energy and sustainable materials in its products required significant financial and operational investments (Elizaveta, 2021). Initially, there were concerns about cost implications and a lack of expertise among employees in sustainability practices (Elizaveta, 2021). IKEA tackled these challenges through a phased approach, emphasising collaboration and innovation (Alzghool, 2021). The company partnered with NGOs and academic institutions to develop cost-effective solutions, such as its investment in solar panel production (Lordan, 2024). Simultaneously, IKEA's HR team launched extensive green training programs for employees, equipping them with the skills needed to support sustainability initiatives (Anand, 2024). Integrating these practices into its employer branding strategy helped IKEA mitigate the resource challenges they were facing at the time (Wang, 2024). It also helped them attract top-talents passionate about environmental sustainability (Anand, 2024). The company's green marketing campaigns, including its *Live Lagom* initiative promoting sustainable living, aligned strongly with eco-conscious consumers, reinforcing its brand identity (Mahalakshmi, 2024).

In the tech industry, Google provides a compelling case of addressing cultural barriers to green initiatives (Google, 2024). As a multinational corporation operating in diverse markets, Google encountered varying levels of environmental awareness and acceptance of sustainability practices among its workforce (Google, 2024). This disparity created a challenge in implementing a cohesive green culture across global offices (Google, 2024). Google's HR team addressed this by tailoring its green initiatives to local contexts while maintaining a unified vision (Google, 2024). For instance, in regions with low environmental awareness, the company invested in community engagement programs to educate employees and local populations about the benefits of sustainability (Google, 2024). In tandem, it introduced green bonuses, such as bike-to-work schemes and renewable energy credits for employees, to make sustainable practices more accessible (Google, 2024). Consequently, Google successfully bridged cultural gaps and enhanced its sustainability credentials.

Additionally, Patagonia, the outdoor clothing company, exemplifies how organizations can address policy and regulatory issues while maintaining their sustainability commitments (Bosco, 2017). Operating in countries with diverse environmental regulations posed challenges for Patagonia in ensuring compliance while upholding its green values (O'Rourke & Strand, 2016). The company's solution lay in its proactive advocacy for stronger environmental policies and transparent reporting (Bosco, 2017). Patagonia's HR team played a key role in aligning its workforce with these goals through structured workshops on sustainability and compliance (Nishitha & Kavitha, 2024). Moreover, Patagonia's green marketing campaigns, such as its famous *Don't Buy This Jacket* initiative, which encouraged consumers to think critically about consumption, demonstrated the alignment between its HR-driven sustainability efforts and its marketing strategies (Allchin, 2013). This approach not only bolstered the company's brand reputation but also inspired industry-wide discussions on sustainable practices (Bosco, 2017).

Finally, Nestlé addressed the challenge of bridging the gap between green HRM policies and tangible marketing outcomes (Gyimah & Janisch, 2022). The company realized that while its HR policies promoted sustainability values, these were not consistently reflected in its marketing efforts (Gyimah & Janisch, 2022). To tackle this misalignment, Nestlé established cross-functional teams comprising HR, marketing, and operations personnel (Morshed, 2016). These teams were tasked with creating cohesive strategies that translated sustainability commitments into impactful marketing messages (Morshed, 2016). For instance, Nestlé's efforts to promote its sustainably sourced coffee under the Nescafé Plan involved both employee training on sustainability practices and consumer-facing campaigns that reflected the company's commitment to ethical sourcing (Nestle, 2024). Thus, Nestlé ensured that stakeholders were in agreement with its green initiatives, avoiding the pitfalls of greenwashing and enhancing consumer trust (Nestle, 2024).

These case studies demonstrate that while implementing Green HRM practices presents various challenges, organizations that adopt strategic, innovative, and collaborative approaches can effectively navigate these difficulties (Odulaja et al., 2023). This chapter proposes a framework for addressing the challenges associated with green HRM, derived from successful case studies.

Figure 7. Recommended solution framework for green HRM challenges

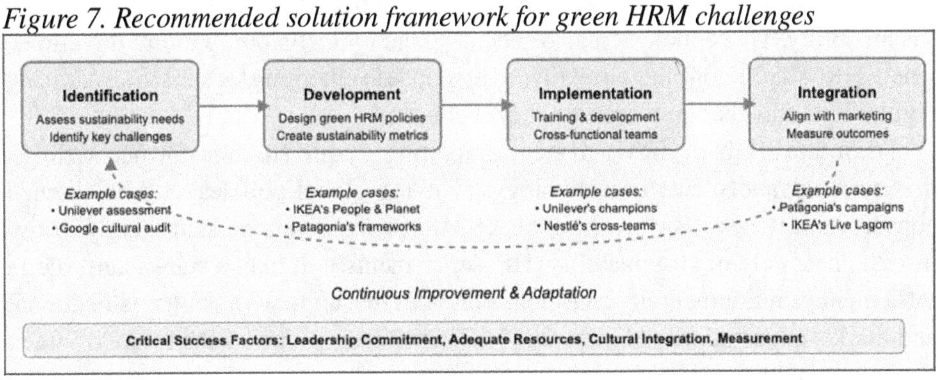

9. CONCLUSION

The conclusion draws together the critical discussions presented throughout the study, emphasising the central role of HRM in advancing green marketing strategies. The paper began by establishing the foundational concepts of Green HRM and green marketing, highlighting the increasing significance of sustainability in modern business practices. It positioned HRM as a significant force for driving green transformations, aligning corporate goals with environmental responsibility.

Subsequent discussions examined the theoretical foundations of Green HRM, demonstrating its potential to embed a culture of sustainability within organizations. Practical applications were explored, demonstrating how HR functions such as recruitment, training and performance management serve as key enablers for integrating sustainability into organizational practices. Case studies of companies like Unilever and IKEA underlined the tangible benefits of these strategies, illustrating their impact on market positioning and consumer engagement. The paper also explored the challenges organizations face, from regulatory and financial constraints to cultural resistance and interdepartmental misalignment. Despite these hurdles, the paper illuminated significant opportunities for HR professionals to lead innovation, enhance employer branding, and align with global Sustainable Development Goals (SDGs).

The synthesis of these insights reaffirms that aligning HRM with green marketing is not just a corporate responsibility but a strategic imperative. Organizations that invest in sustainable HR practices are poised to meet the demands of eco-conscious consumers, gain competitive advantage, and contribute to global environmental sustainability. This conclusion also sets the stage for envisioning future directions, where HRM's role continues to evolve in response to emerging technologies, shifting regulations, and changing consumer expectations.

The future of Green HRM and green marketing is poised for transformative shifts, driven by advancements in technology, evolving global policies, and heightened consumer awareness (Bashynska et al., 2024). As organizations increasingly recognise the necessity of sustainability, HR departments will play a significant role in influencing environmentally conscious practices that align with both organizational and market expectations (Mishra, 2017). This chapter proposes the future of green marketing and green HRM.

One of the most promising developments lies in the integration of advanced HR technologies, such as artificial intelligence (AI) and big data analytics, to enhance green hiring and workforce management (Lengnick-Hall et al., 2018). AI-driven recruitment tools can identify candidates whose values align with sustainability goals, ensuring a workforce committed to green initiatives (Chang & Ke, 2024). Big data analytics, on the other hand, can provide insights into employee behaviors and environmental impact, enabling organizations to fine-tune their HR practices (Sharma & Khan, 2022). For example, companies could use predictive analytics to design green training programs tailored to the specific needs of their employees, enhancing both engagement and efficacy (Viterouli et al., 2024).

Global HR policies are also expected to shift further toward sustainability as regulatory frameworks and corporate governance models emphasise the importance of environmental stewardship (Stahl et al., 2020). International agreements like the Paris Climate Accord and the United Nations' SDGs are likely to influence corporate strategies, prompting HR leaders to embed sustainability into their policies (Thida, 2024). This might include mandating green practices across supply chains, adopting carbon-neutral workplace policies or implementing sustainability-focused performance metrics for employees (Paul, 2024).

Furthermore, the growing demand for green products and services will also influence the future of HRM and marketing alignment (Ren et al., 2018). Eco-conscious consumers are increasingly prioritising brands that demonstrate genuine environmental responsibility (Liu & Jang, 2024). HR's role in fostering a sustainable organizational culture will become even more critical in meeting these expectations (Liu & Jang, 2024). The promotion of green initiatives within the workplace will ensure that HR can drive the authenticity of marketing campaigns (Mishra, 2017).

Figure 8. The future of green marketing and green HRM

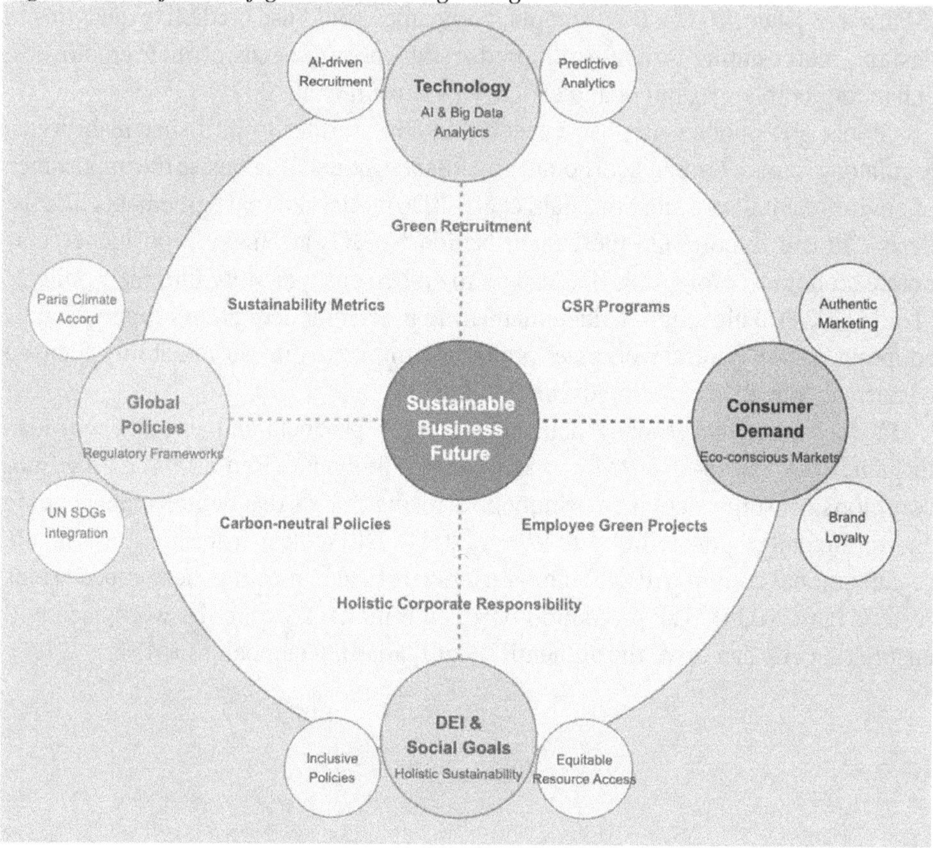

For instance, companies that actively involve employees in green projects, such as community clean-ups or sustainability-focused CSR programs, can use these initiatives in their branding efforts, creating a stronger emotional connection with their audience (Mishra, 2017). Moreover, the intersection of sustainability and diversity, equity, and inclusion (DEI) is likely to become a focal point. (Raskovic et al., 2024) Organizations will seek to align green objectives with broader social goals, such as equitable access to resources and opportunities (Sachs et al., 2019). HR professionals will play a critical role in designing inclusive policies that address both environmental and social sustainability, ensuring a holistic approach to corporate responsibility (Stahl et al., 2020).

As the corporate space continues to evolve, the challenge for HR professionals will be to stay ahead of these trends by embracing innovation and nurturing collaboration across departments (Ahmed, 2023). As Green HRM becomes a foundation of corporate strategy, its ability to drive effective green marketing will hinge on continuous adaptation to technological advancements, regulatory demands and shifting consumer priorities (Jamil et al., 2023). Through proactive engagement and strategic vision, HRM can lead the charge toward a more sustainable and socially responsible future (Jamil, 2023).

REFERENCES

Ababneh, O. M. A. (2021). How do green HRM practices affect employees' green behaviors? The role of employee engagement and personality attributes. *Journal of Environmental Planning and Management, 64*(7), 1204–1226. Advance online publication. DOI: 10.1080/09640568.2020.1814708

Abbas, Q. (2024). Sustainable Marketing in the Age of Environmental Consciousness. *JETIR, 11*.

Abdullah, N., & Lim, A. (2023). The Incorporating Sustainable and Green IT Practices in Modern IT Service Operations for an Environmentally Conscious Future. *Journal of Sustainable Technologies and Infrastructure Planning, 7*(3). https://publications.dlpress.org/index.php/JSTIP/article/view/33

Adegoke, A. A., Oyindamola, K. A., & Offonabo, N. (2024). The Role of HR in Sustainability Initiatives: A Strategic Review. *International Journal of Research in Engineering, Science and Management, 7*(5). https://journal.ijresm.com/index.php/ijresm/article/view/3025

Adekoya, O. (2022). *Responsible Management: Promoting Work-Life Balance through Social Sustainability and Green HRM* (Doctoral dissertation, University of East London). https://repository.uel.ac.uk/item/8qxvz

Adelusola, M. (2024). Sustainable Business Practices: Overcoming Barriers and Leveraging Enablers for Organizational Adoption. https://www.researchgate.net/profile/Michael-Adelusola/publication/385652688_Sustainable_Business_Practices_Overcoming_Barriers_and_Leveraging_Enablers_for_Organizational_Adoption/links/672df86b2326b47637d198eb/Sustainable-Business-Practices-Overcoming-Barriers-and-Leveraging-Enablers-for-Organizational-Adoption.pdf

Agnihotri, A., & Bhattacharya, S. (2023). *Wipro's Journey Towards Regaining a Market Leadership Position*. SAGE Publications: SAGE Business Cases Originals. https://doi.org/DOI: 10.4135/9781529621945

Ahmad, N., Samad, S., & Han, H. (2024). Charting new terrains: How CSR initiatives shape employee creativity and contribute to UN-SDGs in a knowledge-driven world. *Journal of Innovation & Knowledge, 9*(4), 100557. Advance online publication. DOI: 10.1016/j.jik.2024.100557

Ahmed, M. A. (2023). Innovations in Human Resource Management: A Contemporary Perspective. *Journal of Management & Social Science, 1*(1). http://www.rjmss.com/index.php/7/article/view/3

Ajayi, O. A. (2024). *Implementing Environmental, Social, and Governance (ESG) Principles in Organizations: The Role of Leadership and Impacts on Corporate Financial Performance* (Doctoral dissertation, Case Western Reserve University). https://rave.ohiolink.edu/etdc/view?acc_num=case171235193083631

Ali, M., Puah, C. H., Ali, A., Raza, S. A., & Ayob, N. (2022). Green intellectual capital, green HRM and green social identity toward sustainable environment: A new integrated framework for Islamic banks. *International Journal of Manpower*, *43*(3), 614–638. Advance online publication. DOI: 10.1108/IJM-04-2020-0185

Aliano, M., Cestari, G., & Madonna, S. (2024). Greenwashing. In *Sustainable Finance for SMEs: The Role of Capital for Sustainable and Inclusive Growth*. Springer Nature Switzerland., DOI: 10.1007/978-3-031-74193-7_7

Allchin, J. (2013). Case study: Patagonia;s ‘Don’t buy this jacket’ campaign. https://www.marketingweek.com/case-study-patagonias-dont-buy-this-jacket-campaign/

Alzghool, M. Z. (2021). Case study: IKEA’S organizational culture and rewards management. http://dx.doi.org/DOI: 10.13140/RG.2.2.30263.44969

Amir, T. S., & Sabri, R. (2023). *The Grass Is Greener Where You Water It!* Entrepreneurship and Green Finance Practices., DOI: 10.1108/978-1-80455-678-820231001

Anand, I. (2024). Unifying Green HRM With Sustainable Development Goals. *Implementing ESG Frameworks Through Capacity Building and Skill Development*, 237. https://books.google.com/books?hl=en&lr=&id=_9s2EQAAQBAJ&oi=fnd&pg=PA237&dq=Anand,+I.+(2024).+Unifying+Green+HRM+With+Sustainable+Development+Goals.+Implementing+ESG+Frameworks+Through+Capacity+Building+and+Skill+Development,+237.&ots=vjsOQfQDWH&sig=5fNAyLZfN2XcZd1QW0WKOc7sOEk

Arnaud, S., & Wasieleski, D. M. (2014). Corporate humanistic responsibility: Social performance through managerial discretion of the HRM. *Journal of Business Ethics*, *120*(3), 313–334. Advance online publication. DOI: 10.1007/s10551-013-1652-z

Arzo, S., & Hong, M. (2024). Resilient green infrastructure: Navigating environmental resistance for sustainable development, social mobility in climate change policy. *Heliyon*, *10*(13), e33524. Advance online publication. DOI: 10.1016/j.heliyon.2024.e33524 PMID: 39035491

Assaad, R., & El-Adaway, I. H. (2021). Guidelines for responding to COVID-19 pandemic: Best practices, impacts, and future research directions. *Journal of Management Engineering*, *37*(3), 06021001. Advance online publication. DOI: 10.1061/(ASCE)ME.1943-5479.0000906

Bashynska, I., Lewicka, D., Filyppova, S., & Prokopenko, O. (2024). *Green Innovation in Central and Eastern Europe*. Taylor & Francis., DOI: 10.4324/9781003492771

Benevene, P., & Buonomo, I. (2020). Green human resource management: An evidence-based systematic literature review. *Sustainability (Basel), 12*(15), 5974. Advance online publication. DOI: 10.3390/su12155974

Benitez, J., Ruiz, L., Castillo, A., & Llorens, J. (2020). How corporate social responsibility activities influence employer reputation: The role of social media capability. *Decision Support Systems, 129*, 113223. Advance online publication. DOI: 10.1016/j.dss.2019.113223

Berg, A., Chemlal Ärlemalm, S., & Flodin, F. (2023). Surviving Resource Scarcity: A qualitative study about how private firms can overcome obstacles in resource-scarce environments. https://www.diva-portal.org/smash/record.jsf?pid=diva2:1763484

Bhardwaj, A., Gupta, A., & Tawangar, S. (2024). CSR in engineering education: Evidences from India and abroad. *International Journal of Business Innovation and Research, 34*(1), 19–40. Advance online publication. DOI: 10.1504/IJBIR.2024.138139

Bilderback, S. (2024). Integrating training for organizational sustainability: The application of Sustainable Development Goals globally. *European Journal of Training and Development, 48*(7/8), 730–748. Advance online publication. DOI: 10.1108/EJTD-01-2023-0005

Blewitt, J. (2012). *Understanding sustainable development*. Routledge., DOI: 10.4324/9781849773645

Boiral, O. (2009). Greening the corporation through organizational citizenship behaviors. *Journal of Business Ethics, 87*(2), 221–236. Advance online publication. DOI: 10.1007/s10551-008-9881-2

Bosco, M. C. (2017). From Yosemite to a Global Market: How Patagonia, Inc. has Created an Environmentally Sustainable and Socially Equitable Model of Supply-Chain Management. https://scholarship.claremont.edu/pomona_theses/178/

Buller, P. F., & McEvoy, G. M. (2016). A model for implementing a sustainability strategy through HRM practices. *Business and Society Review, 121*(4), 465–495. Advance online publication. DOI: 10.1111/basr.12099

Carter, R. L., & Simmons, B. (2010). The history and philosophy of environmental education. *The inclusion of environmental education in science teacher education*. https://doi.org/DOI: 10.1007/978-90-481-9222-9_1

Cascio, W. F., & Graham, B. Z. (2016). New strategic role for HR: Leading the employer-branding process. *Organizational Management Journal, 13*(4), 182–192. Advance online publication. DOI: 10.1080/15416518.2016.1244640

Chams, N., & García-Blandón, J. (2019). On the importance of sustainable human resource management for the adoption of sustainable development goals. *Resources, Conservation and Recycling, 141*, 109–122. Advance online publication. DOI: 10.1016/j.resconrec.2018.10.006

Chang, Y. L., & Ke, J. (2024). Socially responsible artificial intelligence empowered people analytics: A novel framework towards sustainability. *Human Resource Development Review, 23*(1), 88–120. Advance online publication. DOI: 10.1177/15344843231200930

Chaudhary, R. (2020). Green human resource management and employee green behavior: An empirical analysis. *Corporate Social Responsibility and Environmental Management, 27*(2), 630–641. Advance online publication. DOI: 10.1002/csr.1827

Chen, W. H., Yang, Y. M., & Chen, H. N. (2024). Determinants of Carbon Inventory and Systematic Innovation Methods to Analyze the Strategies of Carbon Reduction: An Empirical Study of Green Lean Management in Electroplating an Factory. *Sustainability (Basel), 16*(19), 8301. Advance online publication. DOI: 10.3390/su16198301

Chen, Y., Tang, G., Jin, J., Li, J., & Paillé, P. (2015). Linking market orientation and environmental performance: The influence of environmental strategy, employee's environmental involvement, and environmental product quality. *Journal of Business Ethics, 127*(2), 479–500. Advance online publication. DOI: 10.1007/s10551-014-2059-1

Dulebohn, J. H., & Johnson, R. D. (2013). Human resource metrics and decision support: A classification framework. *Human Resource Management Review, 23*(1), 71–83. Advance online publication. DOI: 10.1016/j.hrmr.2012.06.005

Elemure, I., Dhakal, H. N., Leseure, M., & Radulovic, J. (2023). Integration of lean green and sustainability in manufacturing: A review on current state and future perspectives. *Sustainability (Basel), 15*(13), 10261. Advance online publication. DOI: 10.3390/su151310261

Elizaveta, S. (2021). Sustainable innovations of IKEA company. https://dspace.spbu.ru/bitstream/11701/30844/2/reviewSV_Otzyv_NR_2021_E.Safronova.pdf

Ericsson, A. (2018). Organizational Culture and Employee Loyalty: The Case of IKEA. https://www.diva-portal.org/smash/record.jsf?pid=diva2:1192802

Ferdousi, F., & Abedin, N. (2023). Strategic Human Resources Management for Creating Shared Value in Social Business Organizations. *Sustainability (Basel), 15*(4), 3703. Advance online publication. DOI: 10.3390/su15043703

Finnegan, A. (2024). The Essential Role of HR in Business Sustainability Initiatives. *CPA Ireland.* https://digital.cpaireland.ie/issue/march-2024/the-essential-role-of-hr-in-business-sustainability-initiatives/

Foly-Ehke, S. (2024). Sustainable living in the digital age: designing and evaluating an interactive mock-up of a carbon footprint tracker app for personal environmental awareness. https://urn.fi/URN:NBN:fi:amk-2024051612503

Galpin, T., Whitttington, J. L., & Bell, G. (2015). Is your sustainability strategy sustainable? Creating a culture of sustainability. *Corporate Governance (Bradford), 15*(1), 1–17. Advance online publication. DOI: 10.1108/CG-01-2013-0004

Gill, R. (2011). An integrative review of storytelling: Using corporate stories to strengthen employee engagement and internal and external reputation. https://figshare.swinburne.edu.au/articles/journal_contribution/An_integrative_review_of_storytelling_using_corporate_stories_to_strengthen_employee_engagement_and_internal_and_external_reputation/26226098

Goel, P., Mehta, S., Kumar, R., & Castaño, F. (2022). Sustainable Green Human Resource management practices in educational institutions: An interpretive structural modelling and analytic hierarchy process approach. *Sustainability (Basel), 14*(19), 12853. Advance online publication. DOI: 10.3390/su141912853

Gohain, T. T., & VS, S. (2023). The Imperative of Green Human Resource Management: Integrating Sustainability in HR Practices. *ASCI Journal of Management, 52*(2). https://search.ebscohost.com/login.aspx?direct=true&profile=ehost&scope=site&authtype=crawler&jrnl=02578069&AN=180144613&h=jPDkD20Dp9D4bYV6spFexh2LJ0FawPAKLlar8SRH790OnCi4UeSTz%2FM0WC%2BMBBmREiCAQx90E%2Ba2QJd%2FI62Dnw%3D%3D&crl=c

Google. (2024). How to be more sustainable. https://sustainability.google

Gyimah, I., & Janisch, T. (2022). Green Human Resource Development–Supporting Sustainable Economic Activity in Organizations. *Indiana Journal of Humanities and Social Sciences, 3*(6). https://indianapublications.com/articles/IJHSS_3(6)_22-31_62b44ed5033fb5.31872827.pdf

Halová, D., & Müller, M. (2023). Being an Employer of Choice: Attracting Generation Z to Work by Building Brand via Social Media. *Corporate Reputation Review.* Advance online publication. DOI: 10.1057/s41299-023-00172-0

Hammed, S. O. (2024). *The Impact of Green Talent Management Policies on Employer Branding: master's thesis* (Master's thesis). https://elar.urfu.ru/handle/10995/136231

Haque, S., Panda, D., & Ghosh, A. (2024). Gamifying sustainability with self-efficacy: Motivating green behaviors in large industrial firms. *The International Journal of Organizational Analysis*, *32*(11), 74–93. Advance online publication. DOI: 10.1108/IJOA-08-2023-3951

Heide, M. P., Prodan, S., Lazaroiu, G., Kreis-Engelhardt, B., & Ghigiu, A. M. (2024). Communication as a Key Performance Indicator in Employer Branding in the Context of the Social Economy—A Quantitative Study. *Behavioral Sciences (Basel, Switzerland)*, *14*(4), 303. Advance online publication. DOI: 10.3390/bs14040303 PMID: 38667099

Hennig, C. W. (2021). *Brand Activism as an Extension of Brand Identity and its Implications for Employer Branding* (Doctoral dissertation, Stuttgart Media University).

Holbeche, L. (2022). *Aligning human resources and business strategy*. Routledge., DOI: 10.4324/9781003219996

Hormes, J. (2024). *Claiming the Future of Greenwashing: enhancing trust and justice in the EU Green Claims Directive* (Master's thesis, University of Twente).

Hristov, I., Appolloni, A., Cheng, W., & Venditti, M. (2023). Enhancing the strategic alignment between environmental drivers of sustainability and the performance management system in Italian manufacturing firms. *International Journal of Productivity and Performance Management*, *72*(10), 2949–2976. Advance online publication. DOI: 10.1108/IJPPM-11-2021-0643

Hübscher, C., Susanne, H., & Jörg, H. (2022). Social marketing and higher education: Partnering to achieve sustainable development goals. *Journal of Social Marketing*, *12*(1), 76–104. Advance online publication. DOI: 10.1108/JSOCM-10-2020-0214

IDC, & Statista. (2024). *Spending on digital transformation technologies and services worldwide from 2017 to 2027 (in trillion U.S. dollars)*. Statista. Retrieved from https://www.statista.com/statistics/870924/worldwide-digital-transformation-market-size/

Islam, M. A., Hunt, A., Jantan, A. H., Hashim, H., & Chong, C. W. (2020). Exploring challenges and solutions in applying green human resource management practices for the sustainable workplace in the ready-made garment industry in Bangladesh. *Business Strategy & Development*, *3*(3), 332–343. Advance online publication. DOI: 10.1002/bsd2.99

Jackson, S. E., Ones, D. S., & Dilchert, S. (2012). *Managing human resources for environmental sustainability* (Vol. 32). John Wiley & Sons. https://books.google.com/books?hl=en&lr=&id=oPtRSNFQpHkC&oi=fnd&pg=PT8&dq=Jackson,+S.+E.,+Ones,+D.+S.,+%26+Dilchert,+S.+(2012).+Managing+human+resources+for+environmental+sustainability+(Vol.+32).+John+Wiley+%26+Sons.&ots=TeASMvQcN3&sig=sEwCY6NKALyDwSEI2sVZomJm3PI

Jamil, S., Zaman, S. I., Kayikci, Y., & Khan, S. A. (2023). The role of green recruitment on organizational sustainability performance: A study within the context of green human resource management. *Sustainability (Basel), 15*(21), 15567. Advance online publication. DOI: 10.3390/su152115567

Jay, J., & Gerard, M. (2015). Accelerating the theory and practice of sustainability-oriented innovation. https://doi.org/DOI: 10.2139/ssrn.2629683

Jimenez, D., Franco, I. B., & Smith, T. (2021). A review of corporate purpose: An approach to actioning the sustainable development goals (SDGs). *Sustainability (Basel), 13*(7), 3899. Advance online publication. DOI: 10.3390/su13073899

Johnstone, M. L., & Tan, L. P. (2015). Exploring the gap between consumers' green rhetoric and purchasing behavior. *Journal of Business Ethics, 132*(2), 311–328. Advance online publication. DOI: 10.1007/s10551-014-2316-3

Jones, J., York, J. G., Vedula, S., Conger, M., & Lenox, M. (2019). The collective construction of green building: Industry transition toward environmentally beneficial practices. *The Academy of Management Perspectives, 33*(4), 425–449. Advance online publication. DOI: 10.5465/amp.2017.0031

Joseph, A., & Jose, N. (2024). The Role of Incentives in Fostering Green Behavior Among the Emerging Workforce. In *Building Sustainable Human Resources Management Practices for Businesses*. IGI Global., DOI: 10.4018/979-8-3693-1994-9.ch018

Joseph, E. (2024). Resilient Infrastructure and Inclusive Culture in the Era of Remote Work. In *Infrastructure Development Strategies for Empowerment and Inclusion*. IGI Global., DOI: 10.4018/979-8-3693-2917-7.ch013

Joy, M. M., & Chiramel, M. J. (2017). *Fun is the future: A collection of compelling gamification success stories*. Educreation Publishing. https://books.google.com/books?hl=en&lr=&id=UU0oDwAAQBAJ&oi=fnd&pg=PA2&dq=Joy,+M.+M.,+%26+Chiramel,+M.+J.+(2017).+Fun+is+the+future:+A+collection+of+compelling+gamification+success+stories.+Educreation+Publishing.&ots=DSP3FCFay0&sig=C_NK6ZgEUjfW78tc5yBZaI8SxcQ

Kaufman, I., Horton, C., & Soltanifar, M. (2023). *Digital Marketing: Integrating Strategy, Sustainability, and Purpose*. Taylor & Francis. DOI: 10.4324/9781351019187

Kivinda, M. P., Su, Q., Hau, H. T., & Hashmi, H. B. A. (2021). Green HRM for employer branding: Evidence from ISO 14001 EMS certified firms. *Journal of Developing Areas*, *55*(3), 393–409. Advance online publication. DOI: 10.1353/jda.2021.0071

Lazarus, R. J. (2023). *The making of environmental law*. University of Chicago Press. https://books.google.com/books?hl=en&lr=&id=xPqgEAAAQBAJ&oi=fnd&pg=PR7&dq=Lazarus,+R.+J.+(2023).+The+making+of+environmental+law.+University+of+Chicago+Press.&ots=wMt_ek6erk&sig=WaHyV3Yct0NEhWOeN_4uvdh-dBc

Lengnick-Hall, M. L., Neely, A. R., & Stone, C. B. (2018). Human resource management in the digital age: Big data, HR analytics and artificial intelligence. In *Management and technological challenges in the digital age*. CRC Press., DOI: 10.1201/9781351238922-1

Leonardi, P. M., & Vaast, E. (2017). Social media and their affordances for organizing: A review and agenda for research. *The Academy of Management Annals*, *11*(1), 150–188. Advance online publication. DOI: 10.5465/annals.2015.0144

Leonidou, L. C., Fotiadis, T. A., Christodoulides, P., Spyropoulou, S., & Katsikeas, C. S. (2015). Environmentally friendly export business strategy: Its determinants and effects on competitive advantage and performance. *International Business Review*, *24*(5), 798–811. Advance online publication. DOI: 10.1016/j.ibusrev.2015.02.001

Li, J., Pan, Z., Sun, Y., Zheng, W., Zhang, Z., & Wang, Z. (2024). From Compliance to Strategy: Paradigm Shift in Corporate ESG Practices. *Academic Journal of Humanities & Social Sciences*, *7*(2). Advance online publication. DOI: 10.25236/AJHSS.2024.070225

Lindgren, E., & Österlind, L. (2018). Inclusion in a recruitment process. https://www.diva-portal.org/smash/record.jsf?pid=diva2:1483816

Lisniak, B. A. (2024). Global environmental problems and their impact on international business.

Liu, C., & Jiang, M. (2024). Green Messaging in the Fast-Food Industry: The Role of Responsibility, Obligation, and Values in Driving Eco-Conscious Behavior. *Sustainability (2071-1050), 16*(19). https://doi.org/DOI: 10.3390/su16198445

Lopess-Naglis, A. (2023). *Lean and green in SMEs: Practices for achieving sustainability goals key performance indicators* (Bachelor's thesis, University of Twente). http://essay.utwente.nl/100302/

Lordan, J. (2024). *'Low price. But not at any price' IKEA's engagement with social and environmental issues* (Doctoral dissertation, Institute of Art, Design+ Technology).

Madan, A., Gupta, A. K., & Goyal, M. K. (2023). Lifestyle for Environment: LiFE Mission and Synergies with Eco-restoration. In *Ecosystem Restoration: Towards Sustainability and Resilient Development*. Springer Nature Singapore. https://doi.org/DOI: 10.1007/978-981-99-3687-8_2

Mahalakshmi, S., Nallasivam, A., Kumar, S. H., Kalavathy, K. S., & Desai, K. (2024, February). Sustainability by Design: IKEA's Eco-Friendly Marketing Efforts. In *3rd International Conference on Reinventing Business Practices, Start-ups and Sustainability*. Atlantis Press. https://doi.org/DOI: 10.2991/978-94-6463-374-0_14

Mahesh, K. M., Aithal, P. S., & Sharma, K. R. S. (2024). Green HRM and Teaching Sustainability in higher education Institutions: For Promoting Sustainable Education and Sustainable Development Goals. *International Journal of Case Studies in Business* [IJCSBE]. *IT and Education*, *8*(1). Advance online publication. DOI: 10.47992/IJCSBE.2581.6942.0345

Malik, S. Y., Cao, Y., Mughal, Y. H., Kundi, G. M., Mughal, M. H., & Ramayah, T. (2020). Pathways towards sustainability in organizations: Empirical evidence on the role of green human resource management practices and green intellectual capital. *Sustainability (Basel)*, *12*(8), 3228. Advance online publication. DOI: 10.3390/su12083228

Mandip, G. (2012). Green HRM: People management commitment to environmental sustainability. *Research Journal of Recent Sciences*. https://www.academia.edu/download/43829709/38.ISCA-ISC-2011-18CLM-Com-03.pdf

Marrucci, L., Daddi, T., & Iraldo, F. (2024). Creating environmental performance indicators to assess corporate sustainability and reward employees. *Ecological Indicators*, *158*, 111489. Advance online publication. DOI: 10.1016/j.ecolind.2023.111489

Mishra, P. (2017). Green human resource management: A framework for sustainable organizational development in an emerging economy. *The International Journal of Organizational Analysis*, *25*(5), 762–788. Advance online publication. DOI: 10.1108/IJOA-11-2016-1079

Mishra, R., Singh, R. K., & Rana, N. P. (2022). Developing environmental collaboration among supply chain partners for sustainable consumption & production: Insights from an auto sector supply chain. *Journal of Cleaner Production, 338*, 130619. Advance online publication. DOI: 10.1016/j.jclepro.2022.130619

Miska, C., Szocs, I., & Schiffinger, M. (2018). Culture's effects on corporate sustainability practices: A multi-domain and multi-level review. *Journal of World Business, 53*(2), 263–279. Advance online publication. DOI: 10.1016/j.jwb.2017.12.001

Montgomery, A. W., Lyon, T. P., & Barg, J. (2024). No end in sight? A greenwash review and research agenda. *Organization & Environment, 37*(2), 221–256. Advance online publication. DOI: 10.1177/10860266231168905 PMID: 39091586

Morshed, M. (2016). The human resources department Nestle Bangladesh Limited its essential functions and activities. https://dspace.bracu.ac.bd/xmlui/handle/10361/8551

Mtembu, V. (2019). Does having knowledge of green human resource management practices influence its implementation within organizations? *Problems and Perspectives in Management, 17*(2), 267–276. Advance online publication. DOI: 10.21511/ppm.17(2).2019.20

Mtembu, V. N. (2017). *Green Human-Resource Management towards sustainable organizations: A case of KwaZulu-Natal higher education institutions* (Doctoral dissertation).

Mujtaba, M., & Mubarik, M. S. (2022). Talent management and organizational sustainability: Role of sustainable behavior. *The International Journal of Organizational Analysis, 30*(2), 389–407. Advance online publication. DOI: 10.1108/IJOA-06-2020-2253

Nagam, A. (2024). Mediating Role of Green Human Resource Management Practices on Employee Green Behavior in Wipro: A Review and Recommendations for Future Research. *Educational Administration: Theory and Practice, 30*(5), 5811–5817. Advance online publication. DOI: 10.53555/kuey.v30i5.3870

Nestle. (2024). Coffee Sourcing. https://www.nestle.com/sustainability/sustainable-sourcing/coffee

Nisar, Q. A., Haider, S., Ali, F., Jamshed, S., Ryu, K., & Gill, S. S. (2021). Green human resource management practices and environmental performance in Malaysian green hotels: The role of green intellectual capital and pro-environmental behavior. *Journal of Cleaner Production, 311*, 127504. Advance online publication. DOI: 10.1016/j.jclepro.2021.127504

Nishitha, K., & Kavitha, R. (2024). Exploring the Integration of Human Resource Management and Organizational Culture in Achieving Environmental Sustainability. In *Intersecting Human Resource Management and Organizational Culture for Environmental Sustainability*. IGI Global., DOI: 10.4018/979-8-3693-2699-2.ch001

O'Rourke, D., & Strand, R. (2016). *Patagonia: Driving sustainable innovation by embracing tensions*. The Berkeley-Haas Case Series. University of California, Berkeley. Haas School of Business. https://doi.org/DOI: 10.4135/9781526407610

Odhiambo, G. M., Waiganjo, E. W., & Simiyu, A. N. (2023). Incentivizing employee pro-environmental behavior: Harnessing the potential of green rewards. *African Journal of Empirical Research*, *4*(2), 601–611. Advance online publication. DOI: 10.51867/ajernet.4.2.60

Odulaja, B. A., Nnabugwu, O. C., Abdul, A. A., Udeh, C. A., & Daraojimba, C. (2023). HR'S role in organizational change within Nigeria's renewable energy sector: A review. *Engineering Science & Technology Journal*, *4*(5), 259–284. Advance online publication. DOI: 10.51594/estj.v4i5.615

Ogbu, A. D., Eyo-Udo, N. L., Adeyinka, M. A., Ozowe, W., & Ikevuje, A. H. (2023). A conceptual procurement model for sustainability and climate change mitigation in the oil, gas, and energy sectors. *World Journal of Advanced Research and Reviews*, *20*(3), 1935–1952. Advance online publication. DOI: 10.30574/wjarr.2023.20.3.2304

Olsson, O., & Storesund, J. (2015). Open-source Branding: How consumers develop a Corporate Brand Image through. https://lup.lub.lu.se/luur/download?func=downloadFile&recordOId=7862109&fileOId=7862114

Ottman, J. (2017). *The new rules of green marketing: Strategies, tools, and inspiration for sustainable branding*. Routledge., DOI: 10.4324/9781351278683

Palhau, M., Carlos Sá, J., Ávila, P., Dinis-Carvalho, J., Rodrigues, C., & Santos, G. (2024). Toyota Way-the Heart of TPS and its Impact on Sustainable Company Growth. *Quality Innovation Prosperity/Kvalita Inovácia Prosperita, 28*(3). https://doi.org/DOI: 10.12776/qip.v28i3.2073

Pathak, R. K., & Agarwal, S. (2024). Sustainability in Human Resources: Evaluating Competencies and Overcoming Challenges in India's Service Sector. *Library Progress International, 44*(3). https://bpasjournals.com/library-science/index.php/journal/article/view/1780

Paul, J. (2024). The Impact of Green Innovation on Financial and operational performance.

Peattie, K. (2001). Towards sustainability: The third age of green marketing. *The Marketing Review*, *2*(2), 129–146. Advance online publication. DOI: 10.1362/1469347012569869

Pham, N. T., Vo-Thanh, T., Shahbaz, M., Huynh, T. L. D., & Usman, M. (2020). Managing environmental challenges: Training as a solution to improve employee green performance. *Journal of Environmental Management*, *269*, 110781. Advance online publication. DOI: 10.1016/j.jenvman.2020.110781 PMID: 32560999

Potoski, M., & Callery, P. J. (2018). Peer communication improves environmental employee engagement programs: Evidence from a quasi-experimental field study. *Journal of Cleaner Production*, *172*, 1486–1500. Advance online publication. DOI: 10.1016/j.jclepro.2017.10.252

Prasanna, R. P. I. R., Jayasundara, J. M. S. B., Naradda Gamage, S. K., Ekanayake, E. M. S., Rajapakshe, P. S. K., & Abeyrathne, G. A. K. N. J. (2019). Sustainability of SMEs in the competition: A systemic review on technological challenges and SME performance. *Journal of Open Innovation*, *5*(4), 100. Advance online publication. DOI: 10.3390/joitmc5040100

Raja, S. (2021). *The neoliberal" do-good" spirit: a case study of Unilever digital communication of corporate social responsibility* (Doctoral dissertation, Rutgers University-School of Graduate Studies). https://rucore.libraries.rutgers.edu/rutgers-lib/65963/

Rašković, M. M., Hurd, F., & Onaji-Benson, T. (2024). Moving diversity, equity and inclusion research forward with (in) international business: Addressing blind spots through critical and reflexive management scholarship. *Critical Perspectives on International Business*. Advance online publication. DOI: 10.1108/cpoib-09-2024-0110

Ren, S., & Jackson, S. E. (2020). HRM institutional entrepreneurship for sustainable business organizations. *Human Resource Management Review*, *30*(3), 100691. Advance online publication. DOI: 10.1016/j.hrmr.2019.100691

Ren, S., Tang, G., & Jackson, E, S. (. (2018). Green human resource management research in emergence: A review and future directions. *Asia Pacific Journal of Management*, *35*. Advance online publication. DOI: 10.1007/s10490-017-9532-1

Rosati, F., & Faria, L. G. D. (2019). Business contribution to the Sustainable Development Agenda: Organizational factors related to early adoption of SDG reporting. *Corporate Social Responsibility and Environmental Management*, *26*(3), 588–597. Advance online publication. DOI: 10.1002/csr.1705

Roscoe, S., Subramanian, N., Jabbour, C. J., & Chong, T. (2019). Green human resource management and the enablers of green organizational culture: Enhancing a firm's environmental performance for sustainable development. *Business Strategy and the Environment*, *28*(5), 737–749. Advance online publication. DOI: 10.1002/bse.2277

Rotich, K. J. (2015). History, evolution and development of human resource management: A contemporary perspective. *Global Journal of Human Resource Management*, *3*(3).

Rouault, G. (2021). Sustainability Marketing and The Toyota Way. , *61*(2). https://shudo-u.repo.nii.ac.jp/record/3084/files/SG61216.pdf

Sachs, J. D., Schmidt-Traub, G., Mazzucato, M., Messner, D., Nakicenovic, N., & Rockström, J. (2019). Six transformations to achieve the sustainable development goals. *Nature Sustainability*, *2*(9), 805–814. Advance online publication. DOI: 10.1038/s41893-019-0352-9

Saratun, M. (2016). Performance management to enhance employee engagement for corporate sustainability. *Asia-Pacific Journal of Business Administration*, *8*(1), 84–102. Advance online publication. DOI: 10.1108/APJBA-07-2015-0064

Sarkar, M. K., Rao, A. C., & Singh, A. K. (2024). "Sustainability and Talent Management": A Two-Pronged Approach for the Evolution of E-commerce in India. *Circular Economy and Sustainability*, *4*(1), 267–285. Advance online publication. DOI: 10.1007/s43615-023-00282-1

Sarvaiya, H., Arrowsmith, J., & Eweje, G. (2021). Exploring HRM involvement in CSR: Variation of Ulrich's HR roles by organizational context. *International Journal of Human Resource Management*, *32*(21), 4429–4462. Advance online publication. DOI: 10.1080/09585192.2019.1660698

Sharma, P., & Khan, W. A. (2022). Revolutionizing Human Resources Management with Big Data: From Talent Acquisition to Workforce Optimization. *International Journal of Business Intelligence and Big Data Analytics*, *5*(1). https://research.tensorgate.org/index.php/IJBIBDA/article/view/64

Siemens. (2024). Sustainability Report 2024. https://assets.new.siemens.com/siemens/assets/api/uuid:32a7154d-edba-47bc-8e9b-9761617ba774/sustainability-report.pdf

Singha, S. (2024). Fostering a Culture of Sustainability Through Human Resources Practices. In *Building Sustainable Human Resources Management Practices for Businesses*. IGI Global., DOI: 10.4018/979-8-3693-1994-9.ch007

Stahl, G. K., Brewster, C. J., Collings, D. G., & Hajro, A. (2020). Enhancing the role of human resource management in corporate sustainability and social responsibility: A multi-stakeholder, multidimensional approach to HRM. *Human Resource Management Review, 30*(3), 100708. Advance online publication. DOI: 10.1016/j.hrmr.2019.100708

Story, J., Castanheira, F., & Hartig, S. (2016). Corporate social responsibility and organizational attractiveness: Implications for talent management. *Social Responsibility Journal, 12*(3), 484–505. Advance online publication. DOI: 10.1108/SRJ-07-2015-0095

Strategy, I. S. (2018). People & planet positive. *IKEA Sustainability Strategy*. https://solarthermalworld.org/sites/default/files/news/file/2021-05-13/people-and-planet-positive-ikea-sustainability-strategy-august-2020.pdf

Szabo, S., & Webster, J. (2021). Perceived greenwashing: The effects of green marketing on environmental and product perceptions. *Journal of Business Ethics, 171*(4), 719–739. Advance online publication. DOI: 10.1007/s10551-020-04461-0

Tahmasbi, E. (2024). Principles of Responsible Management. https://www.researchgate.net/profile/Ehsan-Tahmasbi-2/publication/380165279_Critically_evaluate_IKEA's_current_approach_to_responsible_management_and_propose_recommendations_for_further_action/links/662e8e26352430415351c606/Critically-evaluate-IKEAs-current-approach-to-responsible-management-and-propose-recommendations-for-further-action.pdf

The Body Shop. (2024). Open Hiring. https://www.thebodyshop.com/en-gb/about-us/open-hiring/a/a00060

The Body Shop. (2024). The Educational Programme: Buy for Good: Enriching the Future. https://www.thebodyshop.com/en-gb/about-us/open-hiring/a/a00060

Thida, S. M. (2024). *Integration of sustainable development goals in business strategies* (Doctoral dissertation, Vilniaus universitetas.).

Thummalapalli, U. S. (2019). The influence of green supply chain management on the competitive advantage: Case of Japanese auto manufacturing company (Toyota). (*Unpublished doctoral thesis. KwaZulu-Natal: Durban University of Technology*). https://ritsumei.repo.nii.ac.jp/record/12293/files/52117630.pdf

Trends, G. (2017). Challenges and opportunities in the implementation of the Sustainable Development Goals. *United Nations Development Programme& United Nations Research Institute for Social Development*. https://www.truevaluemetrics.org/DBpdfs/UN/Global-Trends-UNDP-UNRISD-Report-2017.pdf

Tsairi, Y., & Martens, K. (2024). Workplace responsibility for employee mobility? A review of sustainability reporting frameworks. *Transport Reviews*, *44*(5), 1077–1102. Advance online publication. DOI: 10.1080/01441647.2024.2356030

Usman, M., Rofcanin, Y., Ali, M., Ogbonnaya, C., & Babalola, M. T. (2023). Toward a more sustainable environment: Understanding why and when green training promotes employees' eco-friendly behaviors outside of work. *Human Resource Management*, *62*(3), 355–371. Advance online publication. DOI: 10.1002/hrm.22148

Vahdat, S. (2022). The role of IT-based technologies on the management of human resources in the COVID-19 era. *Kybernetes*, *51*(6), 2065–2088. Advance online publication. DOI: 10.1108/K-04-2021-0333

Viterouli, M., Belias, D., Koustelios, A., Tsigilis, N., & Bakogiannis, D. (2023). Fostering Sustainability Through the Integration of Green Human Resource Management and Change Management: Nurturing Eco-Conscious Organizational Practices. In *Managing Successful and Ethical Organizational Change* (pp. 241-278). IGI Global. https://doi.org/DOI: 10.4018/979-8-3693-0235-4.ch011

Vorecel. (2024). The impact of social responsibility on brand image and consumer preferences. *Vorecel.* https://psico-smart.com/en/blogs/blog-the-impact-of-social-responsibility-on-brand-image-and-consumer-preferences-166740

Wang, J., Tang, L., Zhang, T., Phillips, C., & Aldawish, L. S. (2024). The implementation and barriers of green recruitment: A qualitative study on green human resource management. *Businesses*, *4*(3), 411–425. Advance online publication. DOI: 10.3390/businesses4030025

Wang, S. (2024). An analysis of the problems and optimization strategies of employee relationship management in IKEA enterprises. In *Exploring the Financial Landscape in the Digital Age*. CRC Press., DOI: 10.1201/9781003508816-80

Wu, Y., & Tham, J. (2023). The impact of environmental regulation, environment, social and government performance and technological innovation on enterprise resilience under a green recovery. *Heliyon*, *9*(10), e20278. Advance online publication. DOI: 10.1016/j.heliyon.2023.e20278 PMID: 37767495

Yasin, R., Huseynova, A., & Atif, M. (2023). Green human resource management, a gateway to employer branding: Mediating role of corporate environmental sustainability and corporate social sustainability. *Corporate Social Responsibility and Environmental Management*, *30*(1), 369–383. Advance online publication. DOI: 10.1002/csr.2360

Zaid, A. A., Jaaron, A. A., & Bon, A. T. (2018). The impact of green human resource management and green supply chain management practices on sustainable performance: An empirical study. *Journal of Cleaner Production*, *204*, 965–979. Advance online publication. DOI: 10.1016/j.jclepro.2018.09.062

APPENDIX

Questions

1. How can organizations effectively overcome cultural barriers to implementing green HR practices across diverse global operations?
2. In what ways can technology and artificial intelligence be leveraged to enhance sustainability efforts in human resource management?
3. Discuss the potential long-term business advantages and challenges of aligning corporate strategies with the UN Sustainable Development Goals.
4. How might green HR practices contribute to improving an organization's employer branding and talent attraction strategies?
5. Compare and contrast the green HR approaches of two different companies discussed in the chapter. What unique strategies made each approach successful?
6. What role can individual employees play in driving sustainability initiatives within their organizations, beyond formal HR programs?

Chapter 8
Sustainable E-Commerce Platforms:
Integrating Green Marketing Strategies in Digital Marketplaces

Tinashe Mangudhla
https://orcid.org/0000-0003-4951-6617
University of Science and Technology of China, China

ABSTRACT

The rapid rise of e-commerce has inadvertently triggered an environmental crisis by promoting rapid deliveries, excessive over-packaging, and a "fast fashion" mentality that contributes to resource depletion, pollution, and ethical concerns in production, spurring transportation-related carbon emissions, creating significant amounts of non-recyclable waste. In response to this challenge, this chapter investigates how digital innovations and consumer behaviors facilitate circular economy practices in sustainable e-commerce while also evaluating digital marketing strategies that foster a greener future. Grounded in circular economy and sustainable development principles, the chapter examines how digital innovations and consumer behaviors can facilitate sustainable practices in e-commerce. Utilizing a conceptual framework supported by Patagonia, Etsy, and The RealReal case studies, the analysis explores how eco-friendly product curation, ethical sourcing, supply chain transparency, sustainable logistics, and AI-driven personalization are key drivers for promoting sustainable e-commerce.

DOI: 10.4018/979-8-3693-9831-9.ch008

1. INTRODUCTION

Amidst the rapid expansion of digital commerce, the absence of cohesive regulatory frameworks and robust digital compliance mechanisms threatens online marketplaces' sustainability and ethical integrity. Over the past two decades, the e-commerce sector has experienced unprecedented growth supported by increased internet penetration, the widespread of mobile devices, and advancements in digital infrastructure. According to Roszko-Wójtowicz et al. (2024), global e-commerce sales exceeded USD 5 trillion in 2022, and with over 63% of the global population now having access to the internet; thus, the use of e-commerce is expected to rise as digitalization and innovation continue to rise. Interestingly, this growth is evidenced in both developed and developing economies, demonstrating the sector's capacity to diversify and create new market opportunities worldwide. The COVID-19 pandemic further facilitated this shift to mobile commerce (m-commerce) as a vital segment that has rendered online retail and transactions more accessible and convenient (Khan et al., 2024). These advancements also enhanced payment infrastructures while positioning e-commerce activities as a key component of the circular economy by facilitating efficient utilization of resources, minimizing waste, and promoting the exchange of goods and services globally (Vyas et al., 2023). Moreover, reliable metrics and measurement frameworks have become pillars for quantifying and validating the sustainability efforts of these platforms, ensuring transparency and accountability in their operations.

Parallel to e-commerce's rise is a growing acknowledgment that long-term business viability is inextricably linked with sustainability. Thus, the pressing challenges of climate change, resource depletion, and pollution have necessitated a strategic reorientation. In response, governments and international organizations such as the United Nations have devised the Sustainable Development Goals (SDGs) to guide industries toward sustainable operations (Kwilinski et al., 2023). In this context, integrating green marketing strategies has become essential, as well as aligning environmental objectives of responsible consumption and production (SDG12) with commercial goals and reinforcing corporate social responsibility. Currently, regulations in many geographical locations require carbon reporting, sustainable packaging, and public disclosures of eco-friendly practices, compelling businesses to innovate and refine their process to meet these requirements while appealing to ethical consumers.

Green marketing surpasses meeting consumer preferences by differentiating brands, building consumer trust, and strengthening a firm's commitment to social and environmental responsibilities. Recent studies by (Roszko-Wójtowicz et al., 2024) and (Sharma et al., 2024) emphasized that ethical considerations and ecological awareness significantly influence purchasing decisions. Thus, consumers becoming more informed about product lifecycles and environmental impacts favor brands that champion eco-friendly practices (Borah et al., 2024). E-commerce platforms, therefore, have a role in transparently communicating their sustainability initiatives, ranging from using recycled packaging to enforcing ethical labor standards, thereby enhancing consumer loyalty and securing long-term market stability (Raihan, 2024).

Despite these advancements, sustainability-focused strategies face challenges such as greenwashing, high upfront investments in eco-friendly technologies, and the complexities of managing global supply chains that can hinder effective green marketing (Paul et al., 2023; Ren et al., 2019). Addressing these hurdles within the Triple Bottom Line theory framework, which evaluates social, environmental, and financial performance, this chapter examines the economic viability and the ecological and social challenges intrinsic to sustainability-focused strategies. In doing so, it considers regional and sectoral variations that shape the implementation of green marketing practices, as well as the regulatory inconsistencies that can hinder their effective adoption.

Furthermore, recognizing that sustainable transformation requires a collaborative effort from various stakeholders, this chapter emphasizes the importance of stakeholder engagement and cross-sector collaboration. In addition, this chapter delineates the issues and trends shaping the regulatory frameworks and digital compliance environment, offering novel insights into sustainable e-commerce. Businesses can share best practices and encourage innovation by promoting partnerships among policymakers, NGOs, and industry leaders, thereby catalyzing green e-commerce platforms. In addition, key terms such as "green marketing" and "sustainability" are clearly defined within the context of the triple bottom line theory, where "green marketing" refers to strategies that promote environmental benefits and ethical business practices, and "sustainability" encompasses ecological integrity, social equity, and economic prosperity. Therefore, this chapter addresses four key objectives: (1) examining the integration of green marketing strategies into e-commerce, (2) identifying challenges and opportunities inherent to sustainability in online marketplaces, (3) presenting case studies of successful green marketing implementations, and (4) proposing policy recommendations to ensuring that economic growth is harmoniously balanced with environmental preservation and social responsibility.

Following this introduction, Chapter 2 establishes the theoretical framework, drawing on the triple bottom line theory and green marketing principles. Section 3 reviews the global e-commerce environment; Section 4 explores sustainable business models; Section 5 examines sustainable supply chain management; Section 6 investigates digital marketing strategies; Section 7 analyzes consumer behavior related to green marketing; Section 8 discusses the challenges and opportunities in green e-commerce; Section 9 presents case studies of successful practices; and Section 10 concludes with strategic insights and policy recommendations.

2. THEORETICAL FRAMEWORK

2.1 Triple Bottom Line Theory

The Triple Bottom Line (TBL) Theory, introduced by John Elkington in the 1990s, fundamentally reshaped the understanding of corporate responsibility by advocating that businesses' success should not be measured solely by financial gains but also by social impact and environmental contributions (Zaharia & Zaharia, 2021). This framework promotes the integration of economic, social, and environmental factors into business decision-making, a concept often referred to as "people, planet, profit" (Liute & De Giacomo, 2022), which challenges traditional business paradigms by requiring e-commerce platforms to integrate economic efficiency with ethical labor practices, community engagement, and environmentally sustainable operations.

In reimagining the economic dimension, the TBL emphasizes long-term growth that extends beyond the immediate financial returns by promoting strategies such as optimized supply chains, energy-efficient operations, and innovative business models that deliver sustainable financial performance while aligning with broader social and environmental values (Paul et al., 2023). Additionally, e-commerce platforms are encouraged to implement sustainability metrics and key performance indicators (KPIs) to track progress, ensuring transparency and accountability in their financial practices. On the other hand, the social dimension of the TBL suggests that e-commerce platforms must commit to fair labor practices, ensure access to digital marketplaces, and actively support the community's well-being (Yu et al., 2025). This integration will foster inclusive digital environments that contribute to social progress and strengthen stakeholder trust. Moreover, to enhance these initiatives' social dimension and support continuous improvement, e-commerce platforms should actively engage various stakeholders, including employees, suppliers, local communities, and regulatory bodies.

The environmental aspect of TBL demands an assessment and the reduction of the ecological footprint associated with digital commerce. This process involves managing carbon emissions from transportation and logistics, minimizing packaging waste through adopting eco-friendly materials and practices, and prioritizing the responsible sourcing of products (Nogueira et al., 2023). Thus, by implementing these initiatives, organizations can effectively meet regulatory requirements and exceed the expectations of eco-conscious consumers. Furthermore, integrating circular economy practices, which include resource-efficient product lifecycle management and recycling initiatives, into digital marketplaces enhances environmental stewardship and promotes sustainable resource use (Ren et al., 2019).

Moreover, the integration of green marketing strategies further reinforces the TBL framework by promoting sustainable products such as ethical sourcing, sustainable packaging, fair-trade credentials, and e-commerce platforms that appeal to environmentally and socially conscious consumers while also creating a competitive advantage that supports the long-term profitability of the business. In this context, leveraging digital innovation and technology, such as blockchain for supply chain transparency and the Internet of Things (IoT) for operational efficiency, can facilitate these green marketing initiatives, ensuring that sustainability is embedded at every business level (Raihan, 2024). Thus, the TBL framework proves invaluable for organizations seeking pathways to sustainability, as it cultivates an environment of continuous improvement where transparency, accountability, and stakeholder engagement are essential for achieving sustainable development in digital commerce.

3. GLOBAL E-COMMERCE ENVIRONMENT

The e-commerce landscape is evolving rapidly, facilitated by technology, changing consumer behaviors, and increasing environmental concerns. As businesses and consumers adopt sustainable practices, market dynamics also shift. Therefore, understanding the role of the regional market, digital infrastructure, and the socioeconomic factors that influence e-commerce adoption is key for companies aiming to succeed.

3.1 Regional Market Dynamics and Growth Patterns

The growth of e-commerce varies across regions, influencing the adoption of green practices in online shopping. In developed areas, such as North America and Europe, e-commerce is advanced, with a focus on integrating sustainability into business practices, as consumers are concerned with environmental issues (D'Adamo et al., 2021). Green e-commerce platforms emphasizing ethical sourcing, carbon-neutral deliveries, and eco-friendly packaging are growing. Businesses in these markets face pressure to adopt sustainable practices to meet consumer demands and regulatory standards. For instance, the European Union has implemented stringent regulations on waste management and carbon emissions, pushing e-commerce companies to invest in greener logistics and energy-efficient technologies (Kannan et al., 2024).

In emerging markets, particularly in Asia, Latin America, and parts of Africa, e-commerce adoption is expanding rapidly; however, the focus on sustainability is still developing in these regions, with many consumers prioritizing convenience and price over environmental impact. The challenge in these regions lies in raising awareness of the ecological costs of e-commerce while developing the infrastructure needed to support sustainable practices (Putrevu & Mertzanis, 2024). Additionally, digital adoption rates are high; however, the supply chain infrastructure for green e-commerce, such as eco-friendly packaging and electric delivery fleets, is underdeveloped or costly (Muchenje, 2024). Hence, as digital infrastructure improves and consumer awareness increases, green e-commerce is likely to expand in developing regions.

3.2 Role of Digital Infrastructure in Sustainable E-Commerce

Digital infrastructure plays a pivotal role in the success of sustainable e-commerce, enabling the efficient delivery of products, waste reduction, and facilitating transparent supply chains. In sustainable e-commerce, integrating digital platforms with green technologies, such as cloud computing, artificial intelligence (AI), and data analytics, helps businesses optimize their operations while minimizing their environmental impact (Paul et al., 2023). For example, AI systems reduce their carbon footprint by optimizing inventory management delivery routes and minimizing overproduction (Suresh et al., 2024). Similarly, cloud computing facilitates data sharing across global networks, helping businesses to track sustainability metrics like carbon emissions and waste reduction more easily (Jayadeva et al., 2022).

Furthermore, digital infrastructure also allows businesses to improve logistics systems, especially in regions with limited traditional infrastructure, like some parts of Africa or Southeast Asia. Thus, mobile-based solutions bridge this gap by allowing consumers and suppliers to connect and transact virtually. For instance, mobile payment systems enable more consumers to access e-commerce platforms, while digital tracking systems improve transparency in the supply chain, ensuring that sustainable practices are being followed (Deng & Guo, 2024). However, despite the potential of digital infrastructure to support sustainability, accessibility and affordability remain major challenges to the growth of e-commerce. In less developed regions, the lack of reliable internet access and mobile technology infrastructure hinders sustainable e-commerce adoption (Putrevu & Mertzanis, 2024). Thus, investments in digital infrastructure are needed for greener e-commerce systems but require significant capital and strategic planning (Jayadeva et al., 2022).

3.3 Impact of Socioeconomic Factors on E-Commerce Adoption

Socioeconomic factors, such as income levels, education, and cultural attitudes, significantly influence e-commerce adoption and consumers' willingness to engage with sustainable products. In higher-income countries, where disposable incomes are higher, consumers are more willing to pay a premium for sustainable goods, valuing product certifications like organic labels, fair trade, and carbon-neutral certifications (Nakaishi & Chapman, 2024). Social factors, such as increasing emphasis on sustainability in public discussions, also increase demand for eco-friendly products.

Contrarily, in lower-income regions, price sensitivity dominates purchasing decisions, making consumers less likely to prioritize sustainability if eco-friendly products cost more. However, as environmental awareness grows, consumer preferences may shift towards sustainable options, especially when they are affordable. Cultural attitudes also influence e-commerce adoption. For instance, in some regions, traditional retail experiences hold cultural value, slowing the shift to online shopping compared to more digitally integrated societies (Faqih, 2022).

In developing economies, the recognition of sustainable development initiatives is positively influencing e-commerce adoption. Governments are adopting policies to promote sustainable consumption practices in e-commerce. However, for these initiatives to succeed, businesses must balance affordability with sustainability goals succeed. Hence, addressing regional disparities and socioeconomic challenges ensures the inclusive and accessible growth of green e-commerce.

4. SUSTAINABLE BUSINESS MODELS IN E-COMMERCE

As e-commerce continues to evolve, businesses are recognizing the importance of sustainability in shaping their operations and connecting with environmentally-conscious consumers. Sustainable business models in e-commerce integrate ecological, social, and economic sustainability principles into digital marketplaces, using green marketing strategies to promote environmental responsibility and secure competitive advantages.

Figure 1. Establishing a sustainable brand image online

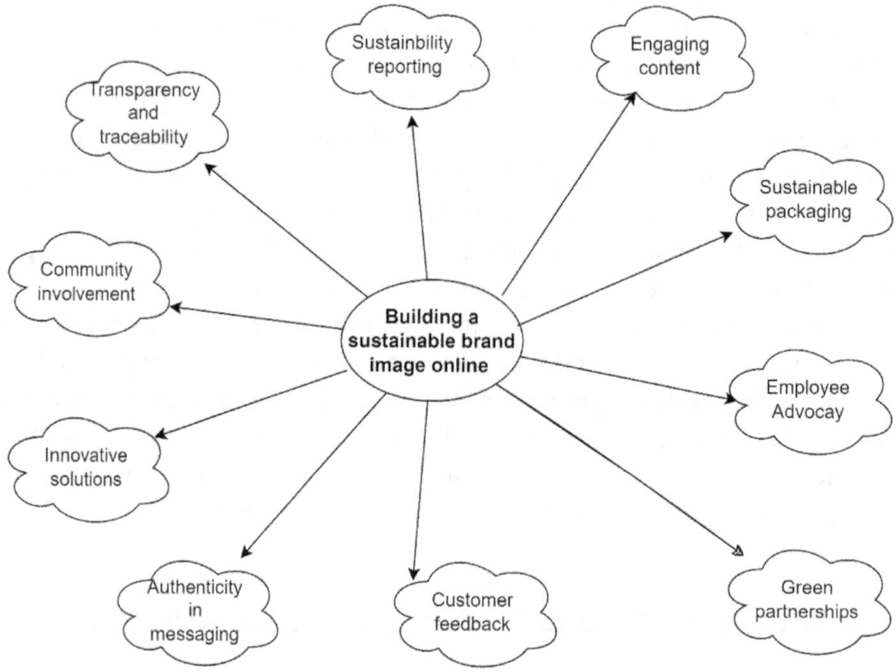

4.1 Eco-Friendly Product Curation and Promotion

The foundation of sustainable e-commerce is the promotion of eco-friendly products. Online platforms drive consumer behavior toward greener alternatives by curating products that adhere to sustainability criteria, such as renewable resources, recycled materials, or with minimal environmental impact throughout their lifecycle (Yang et al., 2023). Transparent labeling and certifications, such as organic or Fair-Trade labels, help consumers make informed choices aligned with their values (Selvakumar, 2025). Additionally, beyond product selection, eco-friendly promotion is key to influencing consumer behavior. Digital platforms are integrating green marketing strategies, such as eco-focused messaging, highlighting product sustainability to educate consumers on the environmental impact of their purchases. Research shows that consumers are more likely to support brands that promote sustainability (Khan et al., 2023; Nakaishi & Chapman, 2024). Thus, e-commerce businesses that emphasize their green credentials through targeted marketing campaigns can enhance brand equity and contribute to environmental goals.

Moreover, advanced algorithms and AI-driven recommendation systems are used to assist in the curation of eco-friendly products (Darban & Kabbaj, 2023). These technologies enable platforms to filter and rank products based on comprehensive sustainability criteria, improving user experience and fostering trust. By leveraging data analytics, systems can now predict consumer preferences and recommend products that meet their ecological standards and interests (Ren et al., 2019).

Additionally, integrating user-generated content reviews on environmental impact and sustainability practices increases credibility and transparency. The adoption of blockchain technology for supply chain verification provides a record of product sourcing and manufacturing processes that ensures that eco-friendly claims are substantiated (Messina et al., 2024). This transparency further reinforces consumer confidence in selecting sustainable products in the future. Furthermore, storytelling techniques are employed in marketing strategies to create a compelling narrative around a brand's commitment to sustainability. Thus, by embedding virtual tours of production facilities, "behind-the-scenes" look at sustainability or detailed lifecycle analyses of products, e-commerce platforms can raise awareness and emotionally engage consumers for sustainable consumption (Wongkitrungrueng et al., 2020). These initiatives highlight the importance of ethical sourcing and circular economy practices in reducing environmental footprints throughout the supply chain.

4.2 Ethical Sourcing and Supplier Partnerships

Ethical sourcing and supplier partnerships are vital components of sustainable e-commerce business models. E-commerce platforms are held accountable for not only the products they sell but also the origins of those products. Thus, ethical sourcing involves selecting suppliers who adhere to environmentally friendly practices, fair labor standards, and transparency throughout the supply chain. These partnerships prioritize selecting suppliers who minimize carbon footprints, use sustainable packaging, and adopt renewable energy sources in production. In this regard, digital marketplaces use technology to ensure supply chain traceability and transparency, boosting consumers' confidence in the ethically sourced products they purchase. Partnering with certifications like Fair Trade, Rainforest Alliance, and FSC enhances credibility and demonstrates a commitment to sustainability (Selvakumar, 2025). Thus, ethical sourcing mitigates reputational risks and builds a loyal customer base that values ethical consumption.

Moreover, innovative technologies such as blockchain and the Internet of Things (IoT) are increasingly leveraged to provide records of product origins, monitor environmental impact in real-time, and enforce compliance with ethical standards.

These technologies facilitate robust supplier audits, enabling businesses to verify claims regarding labor conditions and environmental practices, thus enhancing supplier accountability (Messina et al., 2024; Paul et al., 2023).

Additionally, forming long-term strategic partnerships with suppliers allows for collaborative innovation in sustainable practices, enabling shared investments in eco-friendly technologies, continuous improvement in production processes, and scaling of green initiatives across the supply chain (AlQudah et al., 2024). In fostering close relationships, e-commerce platforms influence suppliers to adopt circular economy principles, reduce waste, and implement energy-efficient practices that facilitate systemic change within industries (Yu et al., 2025). Also, beyond environmental concerns, socioeconomic factors drive companies to require suppliers to adhere to fair trade practices and social responsibility standards, thereby contributing to community development and enhancing workers' living standards. Hence, transparent reporting and sustainability dashboards provided by e-commerce platforms track supplier performance against ethical benchmarks, ensuring continuous commitment and improvement (Stefanovic et al., 2025).

4.3 Circular Economy Practices in E-Commerce

Circular economy practices are gaining recognition in e-commerce as businesses seek ways to reduce waste and extend product life cycles. Unlike the traditional linear model, where products are made, used, and discarded, circular economy principles focus on the reuse, recycling, and refurbishment of products to reduce environmental impact. E-commerce platforms are adopting circular strategies by promoting product take-back programs, offering refurbished goods, and facilitating the resale of second-hand items through their digital marketplaces. This shift to circularity is supported by innovative technologies like reverse logistics systems, which enable the efficient collection and redistribution of used products (Ren et al., 2019).

The integration of data analytics and AI technologies aids in forecasting demand for refurbished products and optimizing inventory management, ensuring that resources are allocated efficiently and waste is minimized (Yang et al., 2023). Additionally, platforms promote product longevity by encouraging manufacturers to design for durability and repairable items, with some businesses offering rental services for high-end products, allowing users to borrow fashion and electronics instead of owning them. These practices reduce waste and align with consumer preferences for sustainable consumption.

Furthermore, digital tools such as IoT and blockchain are utilized to track product lifecycle, certifying authenticity and quality in secondary markets (Ren et al., 2019). By providing transparent histories of product use and maintenance, these technologies build consumer trust in refurbished and second-hand items. Thus, integrating circular economy principles in business models allows e-commerce businesses to reduce their environmental footprint, minimize resource extraction, and promote sustainable consumption. The adoption of closed-loop supply chains and extended producer responsibility frameworks further reinforces the commitment to a circular approach, encouraging collaboration across stakeholders to improve sustainable packaging, refurbishing processes, and waste reduction strategies (Stefanovic et al., 2025).

5. SUPPLY CHAIN MANAGEMENT FOR SUSTAINABILITY

In e-commerce, the supply chain is key to determining the sustainability of business practices. As consumer demand for ethical and eco-friendly products grows, e-commerce platforms face pressure to adopt sustainable practices. Effective supply chain management for sustainability includes transparency and traceability, optimized logistics, and the adoption of eco-friendly packaging.

5.1 Transparency and Traceability in Supply Chains

A core aspect of sustainable supply chain management is transparency and traceability. Consumers increasingly want to know the origin, production methods, and conditions of their products. Transparency in the supply chain provides consumers with informed decisions and encourages businesses to enhance environmental and social responsibility. E-commerce platforms are using technologies like blockchain and the Internet of Things (IoT) to enhance supply chain transparency. Blockchain ensures product traceability, allowing businesses to record each step, from raw materials to delivery, securely (Paul et al., 2023; Stefanovic et al., 2025). This will enable customers to verify the ethical sourcing of products, from sustainable materials to fair labor practices, and build trust and loyalty. In addition, third-party certifications such as Fair Trade or B Corp further validate the credibility of a company's sustainability claims (Selvakumar, 2025). By embracing transparency, e-commerce businesses align with consumer demand for ethical consumption and enhance their brand reputation.

Moreover, the integration of data analytics and smart sensors within IoT frameworks enables real-time monitoring of environmental conditions and compliance across the supply chain. These tools facilitate quick identification of inefficiencies or breaches in ethical standards, allowing companies to promptly address issues before causing harm (Paul et al., 2023). Businesses are developing comprehensive digital dashboards that consolidate traceability data, certifications, and sustainability metrics, offering consumers a user-friendly interface to assess a product's performance. These dashboards empower consumers with knowledge while also providing businesses with insights to improve their supply chain practices continually.

5.2 Sustainable Logistics and Distribution

Sustainable logistics and distribution are key components of an eco-conscious e-commerce supply chain. Logistics, from transportation to warehousing, significantly contribute to a company's carbon footprint. As e-commerce expands, the environmental impact of delivery networks grows. To mitigate this, companies are adopting efficient and eco-friendly logistics practices, like optimized delivery routes, consolidated shipments, and low-emission transportation options (Yang et al., 2023). E-commerce businesses are also adopting local fulfillment centers to shorten delivery distances and reduce fuel consumption. This decentralized model minimizes transportation-related emissions and speeds up delivery times, offering a competitive advantage. Moreover, some platforms are partnering with third-party logistics providers that prioritize sustainability, using electric vehicles or alternative fuel sources in their fleets. For instance, the use of electric delivery vans or drones is gaining popularity in some urban areas to reduce reliance on gasoline-powered vehicles (Nakaishi & Chapman, 2024; Vyas et al., 2023). Sustainable distribution models also include crowdshipping, which is a system that leverages local networks for more resource-efficient deliveries. By aligning logistics and distribution with sustainable practices, e-commerce platforms reduce environmental impact and boost operational efficiency.

Furthermore, advanced technologies such as AI-driven route optimization and predictive analytics are being utilized to continually refine delivery schedules and reduce empty miles, which further minimizes emissions and energy usage (Vashishth et al., 2025). In addition, companies are investing in green warehouses powered by renewable energy sources, equipped with energy-efficient lighting, and optimized climate control systems. These facilities reduce carbon footprint in storage while promoting a holistic approach to supply chain sustainability.

5.3 Eco-Friendly Packaging Solutions

Packaging is a key area where e-commerce businesses can reduce environmental harm. Traditional packaging materials, such as plastic and Styrofoam, contribute to waste and pollution. In response to growing concerns about plastic waste and the need for sustainable practices, e-commerce businesses are adopting eco-friendly packaging alternatives, including biodegradable materials, recycled content, and packaging designed to be reusable or recycled (Escursell et al., 2021). Also, companies are reducing packaging waste by optimizing package sizes to fit products precisely, minimizing excess material. Innovative approaches such as minimalistic packaging and "right-sizing" packages minimize material use and reduce the carbon footprint related to shipping (Wang et al., 2022).

Moreover, some e-commerce businesses, like Loop and TerraCycle have introduced reusable packaging programs, allowing consumers to return packaging for reuse, creating closed-loop solutions that cut waste(Yang et al., 2023). By adopting eco-friendly packaging solutions, e-commerce businesses support a circular economy, reduce packaging waste, and meet growing consumer demand for sustainable practices. This also strengthens brand loyalty, as consumers favor companies that prioritize sustainable practices, offering a competitive advantage in the digital economy.

Furthermore, emerging technologies such as smart packaging that include sensors and QR codes enable consumers to access information on recycling instructions, material origins, and environmental impact, promoting responsible disposal (Yang et al., 2023). This integration educates consumers and encourages recycling and proper end-of-life management of packaged materials. In addition, collaboration with material scientists and packaging innovators is driving the development of alternative materials like mushroom-based packaging, seaweed-derived bioplastics, and paper foams that are compostable, reducing reliance on non-renewable resources (Wang et al., 2022). These materials can be sourced locally and produced with lower energy consumption, further minimizing the environmental footprint. To ensure cohesive implementation across operations, companies are adopting lifecycle assessments (LCA) of packaging solutions, evaluating environmental impacts from production to disposal. This holistic approach ensures continuous improvement, supports regulatory compliance, and aligns packaging strategies with corporate sustainability goals (Putrevu & Mertzanis, 2024; Wang et al., 2022).

6. DIGITAL MARKETING STRATEGIES FOR SUSTAINABILITY

In today's competitive, environmentally conscious e-commerce environment, digital marketing is crucial for promoting sustainability. As consumers demand eco-friendly products and practices, e-commerce platforms must adopt strategies that communicate their sustainability efforts. These strategies differentiate businesses from competitors and strengthen relationships with consumers who value environmental responsibility. The key strategy applied by companies is to educate consumers, build brand loyalty, and encourage sustainable consumption patterns.

6.1 Content Marketing and Consumer Education

Content marketing is a tool for communicating a company's sustainability values and practices to a wide audience (Krowinska et al., 2023); by sharing relevant content that educates consumers on the environmental and social impact of their purchasing decisions, businesses can foster awareness and engagement. Blogs, videos, infographics, and podcasts are usually used to showcase the brand's sustainability efforts, highlight eco-friendly product features, and practical offer tips for consumers to make greener choices.

Moreover, content marketing positions e-commerce businesses as thought leaders in sustainability. Through strategic storytelling that emphasizes real-world impacts, behind-the-scenes looks at sustainable production, and case studies of community initiatives, brands can connect emotionally with their audience (Khan et al., 2024). Educational content, such as "how-to" guides on sustainable living or insights into a product's environmental benefits, helps build trust with consumers wary of "greenwashing." Interactive content like webinars, virtual workshops, and quizzes can further engage consumers, encouraging active learning and deepening their understanding of sustainable practices. By providing transparency in their operations, companies can demonstrate authenticity and credibility, which are key factors in gaining consumer loyalty (Vashishth et al., 2025). Furthermore, integrating user-generated content and customer testimonials on sustainable experiences reinforces the brand's commitment and provides peer validation. Thus, content marketing promotes products while also fostering a culture of sustainability that is aligned with both business and customer values.

6.2 Influencer Collaborations and Advocacy

Influencer marketing is a key strategy of digital marketing that promotes sustainability. Influencers, particularly those focused on sustainability, provide e-commerce platforms with access to engaged, eco-conscious audiences (Sharma et al., 2024). Partnering with influencers who share the brand's values strengthens the sustainability message and builds authentic connections with consumers. When influencers advocate for sustainable products or practices, they foster trust and relatability, often lacking in traditional ads, by sharing their personal experiences with their followers, creating an emotional connection that encourages them to make more informed purchasing decisions. Studies show that consumers are more likely to trust recommendations from influencers they follow than traditional ads (Kwilinski et al., 2023; Liute & De Giacomo, 2022). This advocacy is particularly effective when influencers focus on highlighting the long-term environmental benefits of sustainable buying choices. Moreover, strategic collaborations with influencers can extend beyond mere product endorsements. For instance, co-creating content such as sustainability challenges, eco-friendly lifestyle tips, or behind-the-scenes looks at sustainable production can actively engage followers and generate community-driven movements. These campaigns often leverage multiple digital platforms to maximize reach and impact while using metrics and analytics to refine messaging and gauge audience response (Gao et al., 2023).

Influencer collaborations can drive social movements that create awareness and change. By hosting interactive webinars, live Q&A sessions, or community events, influencers can educate their audiences, debunk myths about green products, and mobilize consumer actions toward sustainable practices (Wongkitrungrueng et al., 2020). In doing so, influencers promote products while also championing systemic changes, partnering with brands to support sustainability, charitable initiatives, and sustainability-focused policy discussions. Thus, by engaging influencers in sustainability campaigns, e-commerce businesses enhance their credibility and promote a shared vision of a sustainable future.

6.3 Social Media Engagement and Community Building

Social media has become a central hub for engaging consumers in sustainability discussions. Through social media platforms like Instagram, Twitter, Facebook, and TikTok, e-commerce businesses directly connect with their target audience and build a community of shared values. Thus, social media engagement allows brands to respond to consumer concerns, share sustainability updates, and showcase their current environmental initiatives (Muchenje, 2024). Also, building a sustainability-focused community involves fostering meaningful conversations. Brands can encourage user-generated content, such as customers sharing photos of their sustainable purchases or using eco-friendly hashtags, offering social proof of the brand's commitment to sustainability while empowering consumers to join the brand's sustainability journey. This strengthens brand loyalty and deepens emotional connections with customers.

Additionally, leveraging analytics tools to monitor sentiment and engagement on sustainability topics enables brands to adjust content and strategies in real-time, ensuring that their messaging aligns with the community's values and concerns. Consistent social media engagement helps businesses stay aligned with consumer preferences and concerns, adapting marketing and product offerings accordingly. Interactive initiatives such as live Q&A sessions, polls on sustainable practices, and virtual events foster community involvement and empower consumers to influence brand decisions (Wongkitrungrueng et al., 2020). By doing so, e-commerce brands position themselves as sustainability leaders, cultivating a loyal, ethically-conscious customer base. Moreover, integrating social listening and transparent feedback mechanisms allows brands to address misinformation, clarify sustainability claims, and openly discuss challenges and progress. This openness builds trust in the community and promotes problem-solving in sustainable practices.

6.4 Personalization and AI in Green Marketing

As digital marketing evolves, artificial intelligence (AI) is playing a key role in driving sustainability. AI algorithms can be used to personalize marketing messages based on customer behavior, recommending sustainable products that align with individual preferences and past purchases (Haleem et al., 2022; Vashishth et al., 2025). These recommendations boost conversions and educate consumers about greener alternatives, promoting responsible consumption. In addition to product recommendations, AI also optimizes the customer journey, from the discovery phase to post-purchase engagement. Personalized communication through emails, social media ads, or app notifications highlights the environmental benefits of a consumer's choices, deepening the connection between the consumer and the brand. This kind of targeted marketing ensures that sustainability messages reach the right audience at the right time, influencing consumers' purchasing decisions.

Furthermore, AI-driven chatbots and customer service platforms provide real-time information on a brand's sustainability practices, guiding customers to more eco-friendly options (Ren et al., 2019). These intelligent systems leverage natural language processing to engage consumers in sustainability conversations, answer queries on product lifecycle, and even assist in making greener purchase decisions. Additionally, AI also optimizes marketing campaigns, directing resources to effective strategies. Machine learning models continuously refine targeting, content delivery, and channel selection, thereby reducing redundant ad placements and minimizing the environmental impact of digital advertising (Gao et al., 2023). This helps reduce the environmental impact of digital advertising by reducing wastage budgets related to marketing.

Moreover, advanced AI applications incorporate predictive analytics to forecast trends in sustainable consumption, allowing brands to proactively adjust their marketing strategies and inventory to meet consumer demands (Gao et al., 2023). By integrating ethical considerations and data privacy measures, AI personalization respects consumer data while delivering relevant eco-conscious content. Therefore, enhancing brand value promotes sustainable consumption and a greener future.

7. CONSUMER BEHAVIOR AND GREEN MARKETING

As the demand for sustainable products continues to rise, understanding the consumer behavior that facilitates these purchases is crucial for e-commerce businesses. Green marketing is central to this shift, as companies recognize the growing influence of environmental concerns on consumer decisions. Hence, sustainable purchasing is shaped by both internal factors, such as individual values, and external influences, including social dynamics and the perceived environmental impact of products. Personal values and environmental awareness are key drivers of sustainable consumption. Consumers with strong environmental responsibility are more likely to choose products that align with their values, believing that their purchasing decisions can contribute to positive environmental change (Kannan et al., 2024). These individuals often value brands committed to sustainability, such as those offering eco-friendly products, transparent supply chains, and ethical business practices.

Perceived product quality and price are also key factors that influence sustainable purchase. While many consumers are willing to purchase sustainable products, they often expect these items to meet the same quality standards as traditional products. This expectation can sometimes be a barrier, particularly if the sustainable alternatives are perceived as lower quality or overpriced (Khan et al., 2023; Kwilinski et al., 2023). However, as awareness of the environmental costs grows, many consumers are increasingly willing to pay more for certified sustainable, organic, or eco-friendly products. Additionally, trust in certifications and labels plays a crucial role, as consumers rely on third-party verifications to assess the authenticity of sustainability claims, further influencing their purchasing decisions (Selvakumar, 2025).

Social influence is a key determinant of sustainable purchasing. Consumers often look to others, especially those in their social circle or influencers they follow, to guide their purchasing behavior. Social norms and peer pressure heavily impact sustainable consumption decisions. For example, the increasing popularity of eco-friendly products on social media circles has spurred a cultural shift toward sustainability, with consumers seeking products that reflect their values and the behaviors of those they admire (Khan et al., 2023; Nakaishi & Chapman, 2024). Moreover, increased media visibility of sustainability issues fosters a collective consciousness, encouraging consumers to adopt sustainable consumption habits. Furthermore, cultural background, income levels, and accessibility to sustainable options also shape consumer behaviors, as socioeconomic factors can enable or constrain green product adoption. **Figure 2** shows how consumers can be engaged in green initiatives.

Figure 2. Engaging consumers with green initiatives

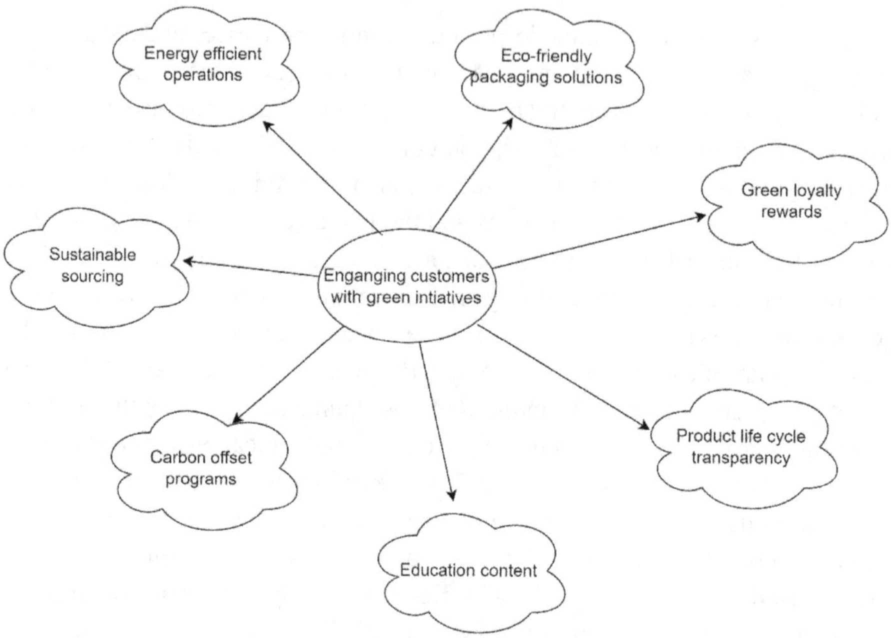

7.2 Role of Consumer Feedback on Sustainable Product Adoption

Consumer feedback is a vital component in promoting the adoption of sustainable products. In the digital age, online reviews, ratings, and social media platforms amplify consumers' voices, influencing purchasing decisions. Positive reviews and testimonials from other customers provide social proof of a product's sustainability claims, overcoming potential buyers' skepticism regarding the authenticity of green marketing. Conversely, negative feedback on product quality, environmental impact, or price can deter potential buyers from making similar purchases. The influence of consumer feedback is significant for sustainable products, where transparency and trust are essential. Potential buyers often rely on the experiences and opinions of others to assess if a product truly delivers on its sustainability promises. Platforms like Amazon Etsy and specialized sustainability-focused e-commerce websites feature reviews that validate green claims. As consumers' awareness of greenwashing grows, authentic feedback from real customers becomes vital in distinguishing genuinely sustainable products from misleading ones.

Additionally, the integration of sustainability rating systems and verified review badges on these platforms enhances credibility, allowing consumers to identify products that meet stringent environmental standards. Moreover, consumer feedback can help businesses improve their products and services. E-commerce brands that listen to consumer opinions can refine their sustainability goals, such as improving product packaging, sourcing sustainable materials, or clarifying sustainability claims (Park & Roome, 2017). By adapting to customer values, businesses strengthen loyalty and align marketing strategies with consumers' expectations.

Furthermore, advanced sentiment analysis tools enable companies to aggregate and analyze feedback at scale and trends and pinpoint areas for improvement in their sustainability initiatives. This data-driven approach refines product development cycles, optimizes supply chain processes, and tailors communication strategies to serve environmentally-conscious consumers better. Therefore, e-commerce platforms contribute to a shift toward sustainable consumption.

8. CHALLENGES AND OPPORTUNITIES IN GREEN E-COMMERCE

The rise of green e-commerce offers opportunities and challenges for businesses integrating sustainability into digital marketplaces. While the growing consumer demand for eco-friendly products creates a promising market success in sustainable e-commerce, it comes with obstacles. However, overcoming these barriers offers strategic opportunities for companies that innovate and use sustainability as a competitive advantage.

8.1 Logistical and Infrastructural Barriers

Logistics and infrastructure are major barriers in the transition to green e-commerce. As e-commerce businesses expand globally, transportation, warehousing, and delivery contribute significantly to carbon emissions. Traditional logistics systems are heavily reliant on fossil fuel-powered and centralized warehouses, harming the environment and leading to environmental degradation. To mitigate these effects, e-commerce businesses must invest in green logistics, which often requires the adoption of electric vehicles, sustainable packaging, and energy-efficient distribution centers.

However, implementing these changes is costly, and eco-friendly alternatives may be limited in some regions (Muchenje, 2024).

Additionally, there is a challenge in investing in technologies that enable sustainable supply chains. For example, managing carbon footprints across the supply chain requires advanced data systems, which may be out of reach for smaller businesses. The logistics sector, particularly in emerging markets, often lacks the infrastructure necessary to support sustainable practices, such as recycling facilities, low-carbon transportation networks, or renewable energy for warehouses (Kannan et al., 2024). As a result, companies may face difficulties in scaling green logistics systems that require investment and governmental support.

Furthermore, the lack of standardized regulations and incentives across different regions creates uncertainty and uneven adoption of green logistics. Variations in policy frameworks, tax incentives, and subsidies can hinder the widespread implementation of sustainable infrastructure. Also, fragmented supply chains and siloed operations complicate the integration of green practices. Coordinating among various stakeholders (suppliers, logistics providers, and retailers) to establish sustainability goals and share data transparently demands robust collaboration frameworks.

8.2 Market Penetration and Scalability Issues

While the demand for sustainable products is growing, market penetration and scalability remain challenging for many green e-commerce businesses. Although consumer interest in eco-friendly products is increasing, the market for sustainable goods is still relatively niche compared to traditional consumer goods markets (Kannan et al., 2024). Businesses that focus exclusively on sustainability often struggle to reach an audience, especially in markets where price sensitivity remains high, or consumers have a limited understanding of the environmental benefits of sustainable products (Kwilinski et al., 2023).

Scaling a sustainable e-commerce business presents additional challenges, particularly for companies striving to balance environmental goals with operational efficiency. For example, certified organic products, ethically sourced or produced with minimal environmental impact, may lead to higher production costs, posing a major barrier to market expansion. Additionally, smaller sustainable businesses may face difficulties competing with larger companies with more resources and established distribution channels (Takacs et al., 2022). On the other hand, market penetration is impeded by limited consumer awareness and skepticism regarding the authenticity of green claims. Effective marketing strategies, educational campaigns, and transparent communication are essential to bridge this gap. Despite these challenges, businesses that can effectively communicate the value of their green products and align their pricing strategies with consumer willingness to pay a premium for sustainability can benefit from the growing market (Yang et al., 2023). To overcome scalability issues, companies are exploring strategic partnerships, leveraging digital platforms to reach wider audiences, and investing in scalable sustainable practices that reduce costs over time. Economies of scale, improved supply chain coordination, and adaptive business models such as subscription services or circular economy initiatives enhance market reach while maintaining core environmental values.

8.3 Technological and Financial Constraints

The integration of sustainable practices into e-commerce operations requires significant technological innovation and financial investment, which can challenge businesses (AlQudah et al., 2024). For example, adopting green technologies such as renewable energy systems, carbon tracking software, and eco-friendly packaging requires substantial upfront capital, which may not be feasible for smaller companies or startups. Moreover, the technology necessary to support sustainable supply chains, such as blockchain for transparency or AI for optimized logistics, is prohibitively expensive for businesses with limited budgets (Messina et al., 2024).

Furthermore, sustainable technologies are often less available or mature than traditional ones, creating a gap that hinders their adoption. While larger companies can afford to develop and implement these technologies, smaller businesses struggle to keep up with innovation. This technological gap is worsened by the rapid evolution of green technologies, which often outpaces regulatory frameworks, making it challenging for businesses to remain compliant with environmental standards while adopting new solutions (AlQudah et al., 2024). Additionally, the costs of maintenance, system upgrades, and training personnel to operate new sustainable technologies add financial pressure on businesses. Continuous investment is required to stay current with advancing green technologies and the need to overhaul legacy IT systems, which can disrupt business operations.

8.4 Overcoming Barriers to Sustainable Technologies

Despite these challenges, businesses have numerous opportunities to overcome barriers and use sustainability as a strategic tool for gaining a competitive advantage. First, the integration of sustainable technologies can pave the way for operational efficiencies, leading to cost savings in the long term. For instance, investments in energy-efficient logistics networks or renewable energy sources can reduce operational costs over time, allowing businesses to maintain their commitment to sustainability (AlQudah et al., 2024). Additionally, the development of circular business models, such as product take-back programs or recycling initiatives, can create new revenue avenues while minimizing waste and environmental impact (Yu et al., 2025).

Another strategic opportunity lies in leveraging consumer demand for sustainability as a differentiating factor. By demonstrating a genuine commitment to green practices through transparent supply chains, eco-friendly products, and clear sustainability goals, businesses build brand loyalty and attract customers who prioritize sustainability. Studies show that consumers are willing to support brands that align with their sustainability values, particularly when these brands communicate the impact of their products on the environment (Darban & Kabbaj, 2023; Faqih, 2022). In this regard, adopting green marketing strategies that highlight a company's environmental efforts enhances its reputation and competitiveness in the market.

Furthermore, aligning sustainability initiatives with corporate strategy promotes innovation, improves employee morale, and attracts investors interested in environmental, social, and governance (ESG) criteria (Malhotra & Pachauri, 2023). Establishing measurable sustainability targets and key performance indicators (KPIs) ensures that green initiatives are effectively monitored and optimized over time. In overcoming the technological and financial constraints, businesses venture into partnerships with technology providers, government agencies, and non-governmental organizations that are experts in green practices. Collaboration reduces the financial burden of adopting sustainable technologies while enabling businesses to access innovative solutions. Moreover, government incentives and subsidies for adopting environmentally friendly technologies can make it feasible for businesses to transition to greener operations. By tapping into these partnership networks, companies can share resources, pool expertise, and accelerate the adoption of sustainable solutions. Hence, adopting sustainable practices positions e-commerce businesses position for long-term success and contributes to the global shift toward a sustainable economy.

9. CASE STUDIES OF LEADING SUSTAINABLE E-COMMERCE PLATFORMS

9.1 Patagonia Platform

Patagonia, a leader in sustainable business, embeds environmental stewardship into its e-commerce through innovative programs, ethical sourcing, and community engagement. The Worn Wear program encourages customers to trade in used Patagonia gear for credit. Repaired and resold items extend their lifecycle, reducing textile waste. In 2023, the Reno, Nevada, repair center serviced over 63,000 garments, significantly cutting waste and conserving resources. This circular economy initiative uses digital tools to streamline repairs and resale, enhancing customer engagement and transparency (Yu et al., 2025).

In September 2024, Patagonia joined Pack4Good, a Canopy initiative to eliminate forest-based fibers in packaging, opting for alternatives like agricultural waste. By incorporating blockchain verification, Patagonia ensures sustainable materials throughout its supply chain, boosting consumer trust and accountability (Takacs et al., 2022). Over 90% of Patagonia products are made in Fair Trade Certified™ factories, benefiting more than 85,000 workers. The company also supports 2,000+ farmers through its Regenerative Organic Certified Cotton program. Digital traceability systems let customers track products from raw materials to manufacture, reinforcing transparency and ethics (Raihan, 2024). These initiatives appeal to environmentally conscious consumers and set a benchmark for sustainable e-commerce. Patagonia proves that profitability and environmental responsibility can coexist, fostering brand loyalty and influencing industry standards. Data analytics monitor environmental impacts, enabling Patagonia to refine practices and share results, solidifying its leadership in sustainable e-commerce.

9.2 Etsy Platform

Etsy, a global online marketplace for handmade and vintage goods, consistently demonstrates a strong commitment to sustainability by embedding eco-friendly practices into its business model. This dedication to environmental responsibility is reflected in pioneering initiatives and strategic goals. In 2019, Etsy became the first major online shopping platform to offset 100% of shipping carbon emissions. The company invests in verified emissions reduction projects, such as renewable energy and forest preservation, to counterbalance the environmental impact of shipping. This carbon neutrality reduces Etsy's footprint and sets a precedent for sustainable shipping practices (Suresh et al., 2024).

Etsy aims to maintain sustainable operations by sourcing 100% of the electricity for its Etsy.com marketplace, Reverb, and Depop platforms from renewable sources. It also plans to achieve "Zero Waste" at offices under its control by the end of 2025. By investing in energy-efficient infrastructure and waste-reduction technologies, Etsy cuts costs and enhances its brand among eco-conscious consumers (Khan et al., 2023; Yang et al., 2023). To promote eco-friendly products, Etsy introduced sustainability attributes for listings, allowing sellers to highlight items made from environmentally conscious materials or designed for reusability. This feature helps buyers make informed choices and encourages sellers to adopt sustainable methods. Etsy's analytics tools track products' environmental attributes, offering insights into consumer preferences for sustainable goods and driving continuous improvement (Suresh et al., 2024).

Etsy also leverages its platform to advocate for policies supporting creative entrepreneurs and environmental sustainability. Engaging with policymakers, partnering with environmental NGOs, and participating in international sustainability forums, Etsy advances commitments to economic empowerment, equity, and ecological sustainability, reflecting its mission to "Keep Commerce Human" (Liute & De Giacomo, 2022). Also, through these initiatives, Etsy provides consumers with sustainable alternatives to mass-produced goods and fosters a community that values originality and environmental responsibility. This emphasis on sustainability reinforces brand loyalty and demonstrates that e-commerce platforms can integrate eco-friendly practices into their business models.

9.3 RealReal Platform

The RealReal has become a leader in luxury resale, pioneering a circular economy in high-end fashion. Thus, by offering a platform for buying and selling pre-owned luxury items, the company reduces waste linked to fast fashion. In 2024, it processed over 30 million items, diverting goods from landfills and extending their lifecycle. A unique aspect of The RealReal's model is its rigorous authentication process. In-house experts verify every item for authenticity and quality, upholding the integrity of luxury resale and building consumer trust. Advanced data analytics and machine learning streamline this process, reducing turnaround times and boosting accuracy.

Through marketing, The RealReal educates customers on the environmental benefits of buying second-hand luxury goods. For example, its 2025 Sustainability Calculator shows the carbon offset impact of purchases, emphasizing the value of resale over new production. This interactive tool provides personalized sustainability insights, motivating eco-friendly choices. Also, the RealReal has launched programs to foster sustainable practices. In partnership with Gucci, it introduced the "Circularity Program," encouraging customers to consign Gucci products for exclusive benefits. Such initiatives promote circularity and push brands toward sustainable models, often via innovation labs that develop joint strategies for reducing environmental impact.

The RealReal regularly publishes sustainability reports. In 2024, it claimed savings of 5.2 billion liters of water and a reduction of about 200,000 metric tons of carbon emissions, highlighting its environmental contribution. Future projections indicate continued growth, supported by scaling operations and integrating renewable energy in logistics. Appealing to eco-conscious, luxury-savvy consumers, The RealReal provides access to high-quality, authenticated goods while promoting the ethos of buying less but better. The platform continually refines the user experience by leveraging customer data and feedback, ensuring a seamless, sustainable shopping journey.

9.4 Identifying Success Factors and Applicability Across Markets

Several success factors emerge from leading sustainable e-commerce platforms in the case studies. First, consumer trust and transparency are critical. All the platforms discussed above emphasize transparency in their operations, whether through clear communication about sourcing practices, product certifications, or carbon offsetting efforts. Consumers who are concerned about the environmental and ethical implications of their purchases are more likely to engage with platforms that provide this transparency. Building consumer trust is a fundamental driver of success for sustainable e-commerce businesses. Advanced data analytics and blockchain-enabled traceability further enhance transparency, allowing consumers to verify product origins and sustainability claims in real-time (Gao et al., 2023).

Second, innovative business models focusing on sustainability, such as circular economy models and second-hand goods, are effective in driving sustainability and profitability. Offering eco-friendly products while reducing waste and resource consumption has become a competitive edge for many e-commerce businesses. The success of platforms like RealReal demonstrates growing consumer demand for resale and rental models that provide environmental benefits while capturing value from products that would otherwise be discarded. Moreover, integrating AI and machine learning to forecast demand for sustainable goods and personalize consumer experiences further strengthens these models, increasing customer satisfaction and loyalty.

Third, strong supply chain management is essential in aligning the supply chain with sustainability goals, a key success factor. Companies like Patagonia and Etsy collaborate with suppliers to ensure products meet strict sustainability standards, from sourcing to packaging and delivery. E-commerce platforms that reduce the environmental footprint in logistics and packaging can differentiate themselves in the market. Utilizing IoT sensors and digital twins within supply chains enables real-time monitoring and optimization of environmental performance, reinforcing the commitment to green practices (Gomes & Osman, 2019).

However, the applicability of these success factors across markets depends on contextual variables like regional economic conditions, consumer behavior, and infrastructure. For example, in markets where environmental awareness is less developed, platforms may need to invest heavily in consumer education and awareness campaigns before sustainable purchasing behaviors can take root. In developing regions, the infrastructure supporting sustainable e-commerce practices, such as reliable recycling programs or green delivery options, may be scarce, and implementation is more challenging (Escursell et al., 2021). Collaborative with local stakeholders, including NGOs and community organizations, can bridge this gap by fostering movements towards sustainability and building the necessary infrastructure.

Additionally, businesses must account for varying regulatory frameworks and sustainability standards across countries, affecting the implementation of green practices in different markets. For instance, Patagonia's sustainability practices, which focus on sourcing organic materials and offsetting carbon emissions, may be more easily adopted in eco-consciousness markets such as in Europe or North America. However, in emerging markets, such as Southeast Asia or Africa, local businesses often face supply chain transparency, logistics, and affordability challenges. Thus, companies seeking to expand sustainable e-commerce into these areas may need to tailor their models to local realities through partnerships with governments, NGOs, or other stakeholders to improve environmental standards. Adapting to local consumer preferences by offering region-specific sustainable products and leveraging prevalent mobile commerce can enhance market penetration and scalability.

10. CONCLUSION

The comprehensive exploration of green marketing in e-commerce platforms reveals the transformative potential of sustainability in the digital marketplace. First, the integration of green marketing strategies ranging from eco-friendly product curation, ethical sourcing, circular economy practices, and sustainable logistics shows that sustainability can be woven into every operational facet of an e-commerce business. These initiatives mitigate environmental impact, create strong brand differentiation, and enhance consumer trust in today's eco-conscious market.

The case studies examined in this chapter, including industry leaders like Patagonia, Etsy, and The RealReal, emphasize transparency and authenticity. These platforms build consumer trust and long-term loyalty by clearly communicating sourcing, production, and sustainability initiatives. Blockchain traceability, AI-driven personalization, and advanced data analytics provide verifiable sustainable practices and tailored consumer experiences.

Furthermore, the findings highlight that innovative business models such as circular economy, resale platforms, and sustainability-focused digital marketing are both environmentally beneficial and commercially viable. These models meet growing consumer demand for ethically sourced, eco-friendly products and contribute to competitive advantage by tapping into niche markets that prioritize sustainability. However, integrating these strategies faces challenges: logistical barriers, technological constraints, consumer education needs and regulatory compliance. Overcoming these challenges requires stakeholder collaboration, continuous innovation, and adaptability to regional markets.

10.1 Practical Implications

The integration of green marketing within e-commerce has significant strategic implications for stakeholders. For businesses, adopting sustainable practices is a regulatory or ethical necessity, a strategic imperative that drives innovation, differentiation, and long-term profitability. Companies can invest in green technologies and transparent supply chains; building brand trust and loyalty are essential assets in a competitive digital marketplace. This strategic shift demands embedding sustainability into core business models, marketing, and operations. Policymakers play a critical role, and the findings suggest that regulations, incentives, and standardized reporting are essential to accelerate green marketing. By fostering partnerships and cross-sector collaborations, policymakers can create an environment that reduces financial and technological barriers, especially for SMEs. These efforts facilitate industry sustainability, aligning commercial activities with environmental goals.

On the other hand, consumers emerge as active stakeholders whose preferences facilitate market transformation. Their demand for transparency, authentic sustainability, and eco-friendly products incentivizes businesses to refine sustainability practices. Hence, digital tools providing verified product and environmental impact information empower consumers as beneficiaries of sustainable e-commerce innovations. Also, technology providers are critical enablers of this transition. Hence, the need to develop affordable, transparent solutions is essential for green marketing. Strategic partnerships between e-commerce and tech firms can promote innovation development, cut costs, and create shared value across the value chain. Finally, these strategic implications show that sustainability and profitability are essential. Hence. stakeholders must collaborate transparently, embrace continuous improvement, and engage fully to realize green marketing benefits in e-commerce. Aligning interests and resources across the ecosystem has the potential to advance environmental goals, leading to the formation of resilient business models.

REFERENCES

AlQudah, M. Z., Samara, H., Qudah, H., Nazzal, R., Yousef Bani Hani, L., Radwan, R. A., & Alrahamneh, S. (2024). Financial technology's role in advancing social responsibility: a bibliometric review of research progress and future opportunities. *International Journal of Law and Management.*

Borah, P. S., Dogbe, C. S. K., & Marwa, N. (2024). Generation Z's green purchase behavior: Do green consumer knowledge, consumer social responsibility, green advertising, and green consumer trust matter for sustainable development? *Business Strategy and the Environment, 33*(5), 4530–4546. https://doi.org/https://doi.org/10.1002/bse.3714. DOI: 10.1002/bse.3714

D'Adamo, I., González-Sánchez, R., Medina-Salgado, M. S., & Settembre-Blundo, D. (2021). E-Commerce Calls for Cyber-Security and Sustainability: How European Citizens Look for a Trusted Online Environment. *Sustainability (Basel), 13*(12), 6752. DOI: 10.3390/su13126752

Darban, K., & Kabbaj, S. (2023). The Transformative Potential of AI in Green Marketing Strategies. *Traditional Journal of Law and Social Sciences, 2*(02), 14–38.

Deng, Z., & Guo, M. (2024). Research on the impact of the application of artificial intelligence technology on the sustainable development of mobile e-commerce. *Benchmarking, 31*(9), 3349–3372. DOI: 10.1108/BIJ-11-2022-0697

Escursell, S., Llorach-Massana, P., & Roncero, M. B. (2021). Sustainability in e-commerce packaging: A review. *Journal of Cleaner Production, 280*, 124314. DOI: 10.1016/j.jclepro.2020.124314 PMID: 32989345

Faqih, K. M. S. (2022). Internet shopping in the Covid-19 era: Investigating the role of perceived risk, anxiety, gender, culture, and trust in the consumers' purchasing behavior from a developing country context. *Technology in Society, 70*, 101992. https://doi.org/https://doi.org/10.1016/j.techsoc.2022.101992. DOI: 10.1016/j.techsoc.2022.101992

Gao, B., Wang, Y., Xie, H., Hu, Y., & Hu, Y. (2023). Artificial intelligence in advertising: Advancements, challenges, and ethical considerations in targeting, personalization, content creation, and ad optimization. *SAGE Open, 13*(4), 21582440231210759. DOI: 10.1177/21582440231210759

Gomes, R., & Osman, S. S. (2019). Managing Organizational Adoption of IoT: Revisiting Rogers' Diffusion of Innovation Theory. In.

Haleem, A., Javaid, M., Qadri, M. A., Singh, R. P., & Suman, R. (2022). Artificial intelligence (AI) applications for marketing: A literature-based study. *International Journal of Intelligent Networks, 3*, 119–132. DOI: 10.1016/j.ijin.2022.08.005

Jayadeva, S. M., Al Ayub Ahmed, A., Malik, R., Shaikh, A. A., Siddique, M. N.-E. A., & Naved, M. (2022). Roles of Cloud Computing and Internet of Things in Marketing Management: A Critical Review and Future Trends.

Kannan, S., Parashar, B., & Chaurasia, A. (2024). E-Commerce and Green Packaging: Sustainable Business Trends. In *Green Innovations for Industrial Development and Business Sustainability* (pp. 22-39). CRC Press.

Khan, M., Khan, N., Begum, S., & Qureshi, M. I. (2024). Digital future beyond pandemic outbreak: systematic review of the impact of COVID-19 outbreak on digital psychology. *foresight, 26*(1), 1-17. https://doi.org/DOI: 10.1108/FS-02-2021-0044

Khan, N. A., Hassan, S., Pravdina, N., & Akhtar, M. (2023). Drivers of sustainability: Technological and relational factors influencing young consumers' green buying intentions and green actual consumption behavior. *Young Consumers, 24*(6), 686–703. DOI: 10.1108/YC-09-2022-1610

Krowinska, A., Backhaus, C., Becker, B., & Bosser, F. (2023). *Digital Content Marketing: Creating Value in Practice*. Taylor & Francis. DOI: 10.4324/9781003346500

Kwilinski, A., Lyulyov, O., & Pimonenko, T. (2023). Environmental Sustainability within Attaining Sustainable Development Goals: The Role of Digitalization and the Transport Sector. *Sustainability (Basel), 15*(14), 11282. DOI: 10.3390/su151411282

Liute, A., & De Giacomo, M. R. (2022). The environmental performance of UK-based B Corp companies: An analysis based on the triple bottom line approach. *Business Strategy and the Environment, 31*(3), 810–827. https://doi.org/https://doi.org/10.1002/bse.2919. DOI: 10.1002/bse.2919

Malhotra, Y., & Pachauri, V. (2023). Employee Engagement in ESG Practices: A Way to Sustainability. *Digital Disruption and Environmental, Social & Governance, 34*.

Messina, M., Eslami, M. H., & Castilla, J. C. (2024). The use of blockchain in organisations for sustainable development: A systematic literature review and bibliometric analysis. *International Journal of Production Research*, •••, 1–28. DOI: 10.1080/00207543.2024.2432467

Muchenje, K. C. (2024). Green Logistics and Supply Chain Management. In *Contemporary Solutions for Sustainable Transportation Practices* (pp. 33–61). IGI Global. DOI: 10.4018/979-8-3693-3755-4.ch002

Nakaishi, T., & Chapman, A. (2024). Eco-labels as a communication and policy tool: A comprehensive review of academic literature and global label initiatives. *Renewable & Sustainable Energy Reviews*, *202*, 114708. https://doi.org/https://doi.org/10.1016/j.rser.2024.114708. DOI: 10.1016/j.rser.2024.114708

Nogueira, E., Gomes, S., & Lopes, J. M. (2023). Triple Bottom Line, Sustainability, and Economic Development: What Binds Them Together? A Bibliometric Approach. *Sustainability (Basel)*, *15*(8), 6706. DOI: 10.3390/su15086706

Park, J., & Roome, N. (2017). *The ecology of the new economy: sustainable transformation of global information, communications and electronics industries*. Routledge. DOI: 10.4324/9781351282048

Paul, S. G., Saha, A., Arefin, M. S., Bhuiyan, T., Biswas, A. A., Reza, A. W., Alotaibi, N. M., Alyami, S. A., & Moni, M. A. (2023). A Comprehensive Review of Green Computing: Past, Present, and Future Research. *IEEE Access : Practical Innovations, Open Solutions*, *11*, 87445–87494. DOI: 10.1109/ACCESS.2023.3304332

Putrevu, J., & Mertzanis, C. (2024). The adoption of digital payments in emerging economies: Challenges and policy responses. *Digital Policy. Regulation & Governance*, *26*(5), 476–500. DOI: 10.1108/DPRG-06-2023-0077

Raihan, A. (2024). A review of the potential opportunities and challenges of the digital economy for sustainability. *Innovation and Green Development*, *3*(4), 100174. https://doi.org/https://doi.org/10.1016/j.igd.2024.100174

Ren, S., Zhang, Y., Liu, Y., Sakao, T., Huisingh, D., & Almeida, C. M. V. B. (2019). A comprehensive review of big data analytics throughout product lifecycle to support sustainable smart manufacturing: A framework, challenges and future research directions. *Journal of Cleaner Production*, *210*, 1343–1365. DOI: 10.1016/j.jclepro.2018.11.025

Roszko-Wójtowicz, E., Deep Sharma, G., Dańska-Borsiak, B., & Grzelak, M. M. (2024). Innovation-Driven E-Commerce Growth in the EU: An Empirical Study of the Propensity for Online Purchases and Sustainable Consumption. *Sustainability (Basel)*, *16*(4), 1563. DOI: 10.3390/su16041563

Selvakumar, P. (2025). Social Sustainability Audits and Certifications. *Enhancing Social Sustainability in Manufacturing Supply Chains*, 221-248.

Sharma, A., Pandey, D. K., Girdharwal, N., & Charon, J. (2024). Global Culture of Eco-Friendly Products and Preference of Consumer in Digital Economy for Sustainable Development of G-20 Countries. In *Diversity, Equity And Inclusion* (pp. 368-380). Routledge. DOI: 10.4324/9781003487180-28

Stefanovic, N., Radenkovic, M., Bogdanovic, Z., Plasic, J., & Gaborovic, A. (2025). Adaptive Cloud-Based Big Data Analytics Model for Sustainable Supply Chain Management. *Sustainability (Basel), 17*(1), 354. DOI: 10.3390/su17010354

Suresh, P., Paul, A., Kumar, B. A., Ramalakshmi, D., Dillibabu, S. P., & Boopathi, S. (2024). Strategies for Carbon Footprint Reduction in Advancing Sustainability in Manufacturing. In *Environmental Applications of Carbon-Based Materials* (pp. 317–350). IGI Global. DOI: 10.4018/979-8-3693-3625-0.ch012

Takacs, F., Brunner, D., & Frankenberger, K. (2022). Barriers to a circular economy in small-and medium-sized enterprises and their integration in a sustainable strategic management framework. *Journal of Cleaner Production, 362*, 132227. DOI: 10.1016/j.jclepro.2022.132227

Vashishth, T. K., Sharma, K. K., Kumar, B., Chaudhary, S., & Panwar, R. (2025). Enhancing Customer Experience through AI-Enabled Content Personalization in E-Commerce Marketing. *Advances in Digital Marketing in the Era of Artificial Intelligence*, 7-32.

Vyas, S. K., Vyas, L., Singh, S., & Joshi, M. (2023). Future of E-Commerce: A Robust Review. In *Intelligent Sustainable Systems: Selected Papers of WorldS4 2022, Volume 2* (pp. 697-710). Springer. DOI: 10.1007/978-981-19-7663-6_66

Wang, L., Elahi, E., Zhou, Y., Wang, L., & Zhang, S. (2022). A review of packaging materials' consumption regulation and pollution control. *Sustainability (Basel), 14*(23), 15866. DOI: 10.3390/su142315866

Wongkitrungrueng, A., Dehouche, N., & Assarut, N. (2020). Live streaming commerce from the sellers' perspective: Implications for online relationship marketing. *Journal of Marketing Management, 36*(5-6), 488–518. DOI: 10.1080/0267257X.2020.1748895

Yang, Y., Habib, K., & Wood, M. O. (2023). Establishing best practices for E-commerce transport packaging waste management in Canada: A systematic review. *Journal of Cleaner Production, 429*, 139377. https://doi.org/https://doi.org/10.1016/j.jclepro.2023.139377. DOI: 10.1016/j.jclepro.2023.139377

Yu, P., Zhang, Z., Wong, S. K. M., Lu, S., Chen, Y., & Wang, Y. (2025). The Role of Technologies in Facilitating Circular Economy of China's E-Commerce Section. In *AI Strategies for Social Entrepreneurship and Sustainable Economic Development* (pp. 151–174). IGI Global Scientific Publishing.

Zaharia, R. M., & Zaharia, R. (2021). Triple bottom line. *The Palgrave Handbook of Corporate Social Responsibility*, 75-101.

Chapter 9
Regulatory Frameworks and Digital Compliance in Green Market Orientation

Courage Simon Kofi Dogbe
https://orcid.org/0000-0003-4658-4067
Jiangsu University, China

ABSTRACT

Green Market Orientation (GMO) integrates environmental sustainability into marketing and operations, balancing profit with responsibility. This chapter explores GMO's key components (green customer orientation, green competitor orientation, green inter-functional coordination, green innovation orientation, and green strategic orientation) and its drivers, including consumer demand, regulations, and competitive advantage. Benefits include brand reputation, cost savings, and innovation, while challenges involve high costs and supply chain issues. Case studies (Unilever, Patagonia, Tesla) and an implementation guide showcase adoption strategies. Regulatory frameworks (EU Green Deal, FTC Green Guides) and digital compliance tools (AI, blockchain, IoT) support GMO. The future of GMO lies in circular economies, data-driven sustainability, and climate resilience, making it essential for long-term success in an eco-conscious market.

1. INTRODUCTION

Green Market Orientation (GMO) is a strategic approach in which companies integrate environmental sustainability into their core marketing philosophies, practices, and processes (Borah et al., 2023b). It extends beyond traditional market orientation by emphasizing a commitment to environmental values, which includes

DOI: 10.4018/979-8-3693-9831-9.ch009

designing and delivering products and services with minimal ecological impact. GMO focuses on meeting the needs of environmentally conscious consumers, gaining a competitive advantage through sustainable practices, and proactively engaging in green innovation (Xie et al., 2023).

This orientation typically involves multiple components, including customer orientation towards green products, competitive monitoring of eco-friendly practices, and cross-functional coordination within the organization to ensure all departments align with green goals (Singh & Dhir, 2022). GMO also supports a long-term, proactive approach, considering both present market needs and future environmental impacts, rather than focusing solely on immediate profits (Kumar et al., 2023).

Companies adopting GMO aim to balance profit objectives with environmental responsibility, which increasingly resonates with the expectations of modern consumers, who prioritize sustainable options (Chowdhury et al., 2023). In this way, GMO not only benefits the environment but also enhances corporate image, boosts customer loyalty, and may lead to innovation and cost savings in the long term (Hao et al., 2022).

GMO should be differentiated from Green Marketing Orientation. Green Marketing Orientation (GMOt), though similar, is more specifically focused on the tactical aspects of marketing to promote eco-friendly values and products (Borah et al., 2022; Pomegbe et al., 2022). GMOt encompasses efforts to design, promote, and communicate environmentally sustainable products, emphasizing transparency and reducing environmental impact across the product life cycle (Hao et al., 2022). Key practices include green product development, eco-labeling, sustainable packaging, and targeted messaging that resonates with environmentally conscious consumers (Chowdhury et al., 2023). Unlike the broader focus of GMO, which integrates green values across all functions of the business, GMOt is concentrated on the marketing and promotional strategies that directly influence consumer perceptions and purchasing behavior (Bansal & Dhir, 2023).

Both concepts are critical for businesses aiming to capture environmentally conscious market segments, but while Green Market Orientation focuses on aligning all business functions toward sustainability, Green Marketing Orientation emphasizes the direct marketing and communication practices needed to build a green brand image.

2. COMPONENTS OF GREEN MARKET ORIENTATION

2.1 Green Customer Orientation

Green customer orientation focuses on understanding and addressing the environmental concerns and preferences of customers. It involves identifying the needs of eco-conscious consumers and aligning products and services accordingly. Key activities include conducting market research to understand customer attitudes toward sustainability, developing eco-friendly products and services that meet environmental standards, and communicating the environmental benefits of products to customers through green marketing campaigns. Companies that prioritize green customer orientation can build stronger relationships with environmentally conscious consumers, enhance brand loyalty, and differentiate themselves in the market. Patagonia, a leading outdoor apparel company, emphasizes its commitment to sustainability by using recycled materials and promoting fair trade practices. This resonates with its environmentally conscious customer base. Papadas et al. (2019) highlight that green customer orientation is critical for firms to align their offerings with the growing demand for sustainable products.

2.2 Green Competitor Orientation

Green competitor orientation involves monitoring and responding to the environmental strategies of competitors. It helps firms identify opportunities to differentiate themselves through superior green practices. Key activities include benchmarking competitors' green initiatives and performance, identifying gaps in the market where the firm can offer more sustainable solutions, and developing unique value propositions based on environmental performance. By staying aware of competitors' green strategies, firms can maintain a competitive edge and avoid being left behind in the transition to sustainability. Tesla for example has set a benchmark in the automotive industry by focusing on electric vehicles (EVs). Competitors like Ford and GM are now investing heavily in EVs to keep up with Tesla's green innovation. Leonidou et al. (2013) emphasize that green competitor orientation enables firms to adopt best practices and stay ahead in the market.

2.3 Green Inter-functional Coordination

Green inter-functional coordination refers to the integration of environmental sustainability across all departments within an organization. It ensures that sustainability is a shared responsibility and not limited to a single department. Key activities include aligning the goals of R&D, marketing, production, and other departments to support green initiatives, encouraging collaboration between departments to achieve environmental objectives, and establishing cross-functional teams to drive sustainability projects. Effective inter-functional coordination ensures that environmental considerations are embedded in all aspects of the business, leading to more cohesive and impactful green strategies. Unilever for example has integrated sustainability into its supply chain, product development, and marketing efforts. Its "Sustainable Living Plan" involves collaboration across departments to reduce environmental impact. Chang and Chen (2013) argue that inter-functional coordination is essential for the successful implementation of green strategies.

2.4 Green Innovation Orientation

Green innovation orientation involves a commitment to developing new products, processes, and technologies that reduce environmental impact (Borah et al., 2025). It focuses on continuous improvement in sustainability. Key activities include investing in R&D for sustainable technologies and materials, adopting green manufacturing processes, such as energy-efficient production methods, and developing innovative eco-friendly products that meet customer needs (Dalakishvili & Tchanturia, 2024). Green innovation is a key driver of long-term environmental and business performance. It allows firms to stay ahead of regulatory requirements and meet evolving customer expectations. IKEA for example has invested in green innovation by designing products that use renewable materials and developing circular business models, such as furniture recycling programs. Chen et al. (2012) emphasize that green innovation orientation is critical for achieving sustainable competitive advantage.

2.5 Green Strategic Orientation

Green strategic orientation involves integrating environmental sustainability into the overall strategic planning of the organization (Borah et al., 2023a). It reflects a long-term commitment to sustainability as a core business objective. Key Activities include setting long-term environmental goals, such as achieving carbon neutrality or zero waste, incorporating sustainability into the corporate mission, vision, & values, and aligning business strategies with environmental objectives, such as reducing resource consumption or improving supply chain sustainability. Green strategic orientation ensures that sustainability is not treated as a peripheral issue but as a central component of the firm's strategy. Microsoft for example has committed to becoming carbon negative by 2030 and has integrated this goal into its overall business strategy. Menguc and Ozanne (2005) suggest that green strategic orientation is vital for achieving a sustainable competitive advantage.

2.6 Green Cultural Orientation

Green cultural orientation involves fostering a corporate culture that values and prioritizes environmental sustainability (Kumari et al., 2025). It reflects the collective mindset and behaviors of employees toward sustainability. Key activities include promoting environmental awareness and education among employees, encouraging sustainable practices, such as reducing waste and conserving energy, and recognizing and rewarding employees for their contributions to green initiatives. A strong green culture enhances employee commitment to sustainability and ensures that environmental goals are embraced at all levels of the organization. Google for example has cultivated a green culture by encouraging employees to participate in sustainability programs, such as reducing energy consumption in offices and promoting recycling. Banerjee (2002) notes that a strong green cultural orientation can enhance employee commitment to environmental goals.

Figure 1. Components of Green Market Orientation

3. DRIVERS OF GREEN MARKET ORIENTATION

The drivers of Green Market Orientation (GMO) are diverse forces that encourage companies to incorporate environmentally sustainable practices within their marketing and business strategies. These drivers include both external pressures, such as regulatory and consumer demands, and internal motivations, such as cost savings and corporate social responsibility (CSR) objectives. Below is a detailed discussion of the primary drivers:

3.1 Consumer Demand for Sustainability

One of the most significant drivers of GMO is the increasing demand from consumers for sustainable and eco-friendly products (de Oliveira Lima et al., 2024). As awareness about environmental issues grows, consumers are more inclined to support companies that demonstrate environmental responsibility (Borah et al., 2024). Research indicates that environmentally conscious consumers actively seek out brands that prioritize sustainability, which has prompted companies to align their offerings with green values (Kumar et al., 2023). Companies that respond to this demand by adopting GMO can build loyalty with this segment of consumers and enhance their competitive advantage in the market (Xie et al., 2023).

3.2 Regulatory and Policy Pressures

Governments and regulatory bodies worldwide are implementing stricter environmental regulations and standards. Policies such as carbon emissions targets, waste management regulations, and sustainability reporting requirements are increasingly pressuring companies to adopt sustainable practices (Singh & Dhir, 2022). Compliance with these regulations often requires companies to align with GMO principles, including the adoption of green technologies and sustainable materials. Adopting GMO proactively can help companies mitigate risks associated with non-compliance, such as penalties, reputational damage, and legal challenges (Hao et al., 2022).

3.3 Competitive Advantage and Differentiation

GMO can provide companies with a distinct competitive advantage by differentiating them from competitors that lack a green focus. As environmental awareness becomes more mainstream, consumers are more likely to support brands that visibly and authentically incorporate sustainability into their strategies (Bansal & Dhir, 2023). Companies with strong GMO can leverage their green credentials to build a positive brand image, attract eco-conscious customers, and position themselves as leaders in sustainable practices within their industry (Chowdhury et al., 2023). This differentiation not only improves brand perception but can also lead to enhanced market share and profitability.

3.4 Corporate Social Responsibility (CSR) and Ethical Commitment

Corporate Social Responsibility (CSR) is another crucial driver of GMO. Companies today are under significant pressure to operate ethically and minimize their environmental impact as part of their broader CSR commitments (Hao et al., 2022). GMO aligns closely with CSR values by promoting ethical responsibility and environmental stewardship, which are increasingly important to stakeholders, including investors, employees, and customers. Companies that integrate GMO as part of their CSR strategy demonstrate a commitment to sustainability that goes beyond profit motives, potentially enhancing employee morale, investor confidence, and customer loyalty (Kumar et al., 2023).

3.5 Cost Savings and Operational Efficiency

Adopting GMO can lead to significant cost savings and operational efficiencies, particularly in areas such as energy consumption, waste reduction, and resource management. Sustainable practices like energy-efficient manufacturing, recycling, and waste minimization can reduce operating costs while also minimizing environmental impact (Singh & Dhir, 2022). For example, using sustainable materials or optimizing logistics to lower fuel consumption reduces costs, making GMO a financially viable strategy. As a result, the potential for cost savings serves as a powerful internal driver for companies to adopt GMO (Chowdhury et al., 2023).

3.6 Risk Management and Future-Proofing

Environmental risks, such as climate change, resource scarcity, and pollution, pose long-term threats to business operations and supply chains. Companies recognize that proactive environmental management through GMO can help them mitigate these risks and ensure long-term viability (Xie et al., 2023). By embedding green practices into their operations, companies can better navigate environmental disruptions, adapt to changing regulatory environments, and meet evolving consumer expectations. GMO acts as a form of future-proofing, helping companies anticipate and respond to environmental risks in a way that safeguards their longevity and resilience (Bansal & Dhir, 2023).

3.7 Innovation and Growth Opportunities

Finally, GMO encourages companies to pursue green innovation, which can open up new growth opportunities and markets. Developing sustainable products, exploring eco-friendly materials, and investing in green technologies can create additional revenue streams and attract environmentally conscious consumers (Bataineh et al., 2024). Companies driven by GMO are often at the forefront of green innovation, setting trends and leading the way in their industries (Hao et al., 2022). In this way, GMO enables companies to capitalize on emerging market opportunities, such as the growing demand for electric vehicles or renewable energy products, further driving business growth (Singh & Dhir, 2022).

Figure 2. Drivers of Green Market Orientation

4. BENEFITS OF GREEN MARKET ORIENTATION

Green Market Orientation (GMO) offers various benefits that enable companies to create value while contributing to environmental sustainability. As a strategic alignment with green principles, GMO improves brand reputation, drives customer loyalty, boosts innovation, and can lead to cost efficiencies, among other advantages. Here's a detailed look at the benefits:

4.1 Enhanced Brand Image and Reputation

One of the most immediate benefits of GMO is an enhanced brand image, as consumers increasingly favor companies committed to environmental responsibility. GMO aligns a company's practices with sustainability, which appeals to consumers, investors, and other stakeholders (Chowdhury et al., 2023). A strong green reputation can differentiate a company in a competitive market, making it more appealing to eco-conscious customers and enhancing brand loyalty (Hao et al., 2022). By proactively communicating their sustainability efforts, companies build trust with stakeholders and create a reputation that is more resilient to crises.

4.2 Increased Customer Loyalty and Market Share

GMO fosters customer loyalty by meeting the values and expectations of environmentally conscious consumers. By incorporating green principles into products and services, companies address consumer concerns around sustainability, which leads to stronger, more loyal customer relationships (Bansal & Dhir, 2023). Companies committed to GMO may capture a larger share of the eco-conscious market segment, potentially gaining an advantage over competitors who lack green practices (Xie et al., 2023). This loyalty is particularly important as younger consumers increasingly prioritize sustainable practices when making purchasing decisions.

4.3 Cost Savings and Operational Efficiency

Adopting GMO can lead to significant cost savings in areas like energy consumption, waste management, and resource efficiency. By optimizing operations to reduce waste and lower energy consumption, companies not only lessen their environmental impact but also reduce operational costs (Singh & Dhir, 2022). Sustainable practices such as recycling, energy-efficient manufacturing, and resource conservation are often financially beneficial, improving a company's bottom line while supporting its green commitments (Hao et al., 2022). Over time, these efficiencies contribute to a leaner and more cost-effective operation.

4.4 Innovation and Product Development Opportunities

GMO fosters a culture of innovation focused on developing environmentally friendly products and exploring sustainable business models. This focus on green innovation encourages companies to research and adopt new technologies, materials, and production methods that align with sustainability (Kumar et al., 2023). Innovation driven by GMO can lead to a competitive advantage, as companies that introduce eco-friendly products and solutions are well-positioned to capture emerging markets. For example, companies in the consumer goods sector that have developed biodegradable packaging or zero-waste products demonstrate the type of market opportunities enabled by GMO (Chowdhury et al., 2023).

4.5 Regulatory Compliance and Risk Mitigation

As governments increasingly impose environmental regulations, GMO helps companies comply with current and anticipated legislation. By aligning with green principles, companies can avoid penalties, reduce regulatory compliance costs, and stay ahead of potential future environmental laws (Xie et al., 2023). GMO also aids in risk mitigation by enabling companies to anticipate and manage risks associated with climate change, resource scarcity, and other environmental issues. Companies with a strong GMO strategy are often more resilient, as they have adapted to minimize the risks tied to environmental challenges (Bansal & Dhir, 2023).

4.6 Employee Engagement and Talent Attraction

Companies with a strong commitment to sustainability often see higher levels of employee engagement and are more successful in attracting top talent. Employees, particularly millennials and Gen Z, increasingly seek employers who prioritize environmental and social responsibility (Singh & Dhir, 2022). GMO enhances job satisfaction and engagement by fostering a workplace culture aligned with these values. Additionally, GMO helps attract talent with sustainability-focused skills, which can be beneficial for driving further innovation and achieving sustainability goals (Hao et al., 2022).

4.7 Long-term Resilience and Sustainable Growth

Finally, GMO contributes to a company's long-term resilience by building a foundation for sustainable growth. Companies that adopt GMO are better equipped to navigate environmental and economic challenges due to their proactive approach to resource management, regulatory compliance, and innovation (Kumar et al.,

2023). This resilience is particularly important in industries vulnerable to resource scarcity and environmental disruptions. By ensuring that their business practices are sustainable, companies can achieve steady, long-term growth that aligns with environmental and societal goals (Chowdhury et al., 2023).

Figure 3. Benefits of Green Market Orientation

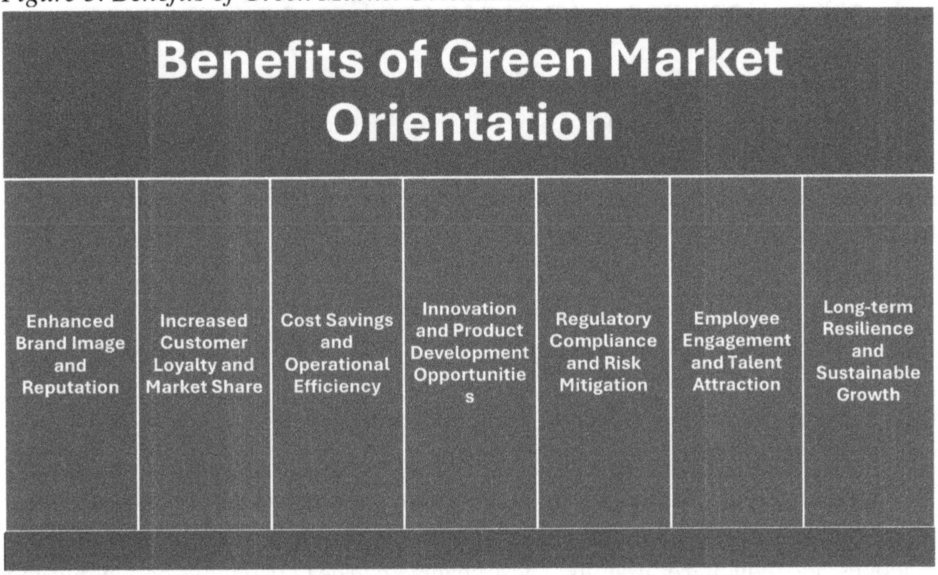

5. CHALLENGES IN IMPLEMENTING GREEN MARKET ORIENTATION

Implementing Green Market Orientation (GMO) comes with several challenges, ranging from financial and organizational barriers to consumer-related hurdles. Although GMO can offer competitive advantages and align businesses with sustainability goals, its implementation often requires navigating complex obstacles that can delay or complicate the integration of green practices. Below is a detailed discussion of the main challenges:

5.1 High Initial Costs and Financial Barriers

Implementing GMO typically requires significant upfront investment, which can be a deterrent, especially for small and medium-sized enterprises (SMEs). Companies may need to allocate funds for sustainable technologies, eco-friendly materials, or restructuring operational processes to align with environmental goals (Kumar et al., 2023). For instance, investing in renewable energy sources or sustainable packaging materials can be costly, and these expenses may not be immediately recouped (Chowdhury et al., 2023). Additionally, some companies face budget constraints that make it challenging to invest in R&D for green product development.

5.2 Lack of Consumer Awareness and Green Skepticism

While consumer demand for sustainable products is increasing, there remains a significant portion of the market that is either unaware of green products or skeptical of their benefits. This "green skepticism" stems from the phenomenon of greenwashing, where companies exaggerate or falsely claim their products are environmentally friendly (Singh & Dhir, 2022). As a result, even genuinely sustainable companies can struggle to gain consumer trust. Educating consumers about the value and authenticity of green products requires additional effort, resources, and marketing strategies, which can make implementing GMO more challenging (Xie et al., 2023).

5.3 Operational and Supply Chain Complexity

Integrating GMO into a company's operations often involves substantial changes in the supply chain, such as sourcing eco-friendly materials, ensuring ethical labor practices, and reducing emissions. These changes can be logistically challenging and may disrupt existing supplier relationships, particularly if the company's suppliers do not adhere to similar environmental standards (Hao et al., 2022). Additionally, ensuring sustainable practices across a global supply chain can be complex and costly, as it may require continuous monitoring and adjustments to meet regional environmental regulations (Bansal & Dhir, 2023). These complexities can slow down the implementation of GMO, as companies must balance environmental goals with supply chain efficiency.

5.4 Organizational Resistance to Change

Implementing GMO often involves transforming existing business practices, which can encounter resistance from employees and management who are accustomed to conventional methods. Organizational change toward green practices requires cross-departmental coordination and a shift in mindset, both of which may meet resistance from stakeholders who are focused on short-term profitability (Chowdhury et al., 2023). For example, senior executives and managers may be reluctant to divert resources toward sustainability initiatives if they perceive these efforts as compromising immediate financial performance. Overcoming this resistance requires strong leadership and a well-communicated vision of the long-term benefits of GMO (Kumar et al., 2023).

5.5 Challenges in Measuring and Reporting Environmental Impact

One of the key aspects of GMO is transparency in reporting environmental performance, but measuring the actual impact of green initiatives can be complex. For instance, calculating the carbon footprint, water usage, or waste reduction accurately across all stages of production and supply chain is challenging, especially for large organizations (Singh & Dhir, 2022). Additionally, companies may lack standardized metrics for evaluating their green performance, making it difficult to measure progress objectively or compare with industry standards (Xie et al., 2023). Inaccurate or incomplete data can undermine the credibility of green efforts, particularly in the eyes of consumers and regulators.

5.6 Balancing Profitability with Sustainability

GMO requires companies to take a long-term view that may initially conflict with traditional short-term profit motives. Balancing profitability with sustainability can be difficult, especially in industries where cost-sensitive consumers may not be willing to pay a premium for eco-friendly products (Hao et al., 2022). Additionally, certain green practices, such as sourcing ethically and sustainably, can increase costs, impacting profit margins. Companies must find ways to maintain financial performance while adhering to green practices, which may involve innovative pricing strategies, consumer education, and efficient resource management (Bansal & Dhir, 2023).

5.7 Difficulty in Establishing Green Culture and Values

A successful GMO implementation requires embedding green values into a company's culture, which can be challenging to achieve, especially in large organizations. Building a green culture means fostering an environment where sustainability is prioritized by all employees, from top executives to frontline staff. Achieving this alignment often requires comprehensive training, clear communication of sustainability goals, and incentives for employees to adopt green practices (Chowdhury et al., 2023). However, creating and maintaining a cohesive green culture can take time and effort, especially when employees may be more accustomed to traditional business practices focused on efficiency and profitability.

Figure 4. Challenges in Implementing Green Market Orientation

6. IMPLEMENTING GREEN MARKET ORIENTATION: A STEP-BY-STEP GUIDE

Implementing Green Market Orientation (GMO) requires a structured approach that integrates sustainable practices into a company's strategy, operations, and culture. Below is a step-by-step guide to effectively incorporate GMO principles.

Step 1: Conduct Market Research and Assess Environmental Expectations

Objective: Understand the environmental preferences, needs, and values of the target market.

Action: Conduct surveys, focus groups, and market analysis to gauge consumer interest in sustainability. Identify specific green trends and preferences relevant to your industry.

Outcome: Develop customer personas for environmentally conscious segments and identify the green practices and products that would meet these expectations.

Step 2: Set Clear Green Goals and Objectives

Objective: Define measurable, realistic sustainability goals aligned with your company's mission and market demands.
Action: Set targets for reducing carbon emissions, minimizing waste, sourcing sustainable materials, and creating eco-friendly products. Goals should be specific, measurable, achievable, relevant, and time-bound (SMART).
Outcome: Clear, actionable sustainability objectives that can guide all green initiatives, providing a basis for evaluation and improvement.

Step 3: Engage Stakeholders and Foster Internal Alignment
Objective: Ensure company-wide buy-in for green initiatives by engaging all departments and stakeholders.
Action: Educate employees and management on the benefits and goals of GMO. Encourage collaboration across departments such as marketing, product development, procurement, and logistics to foster a unified green strategy.
Outcome: An organizational culture aligned with green values, with employees and stakeholders committed to the company's sustainability goals.

Step 4: Develop Green Products and Services
Objective: Create products and services that meet eco-friendly standards and appeal to environmentally conscious consumers.
Action: Redesign products to use sustainable materials, reduce waste, and minimize environmental impact throughout the product life cycle. Invest in R&D to innovate eco-friendly alternatives.
Outcome: A portfolio of sustainable products or services that align with customer expectations and differentiate your brand in the green market.

Step 5: Optimize the Supply Chain and Implement Sustainable Practices
Objective: Incorporate sustainability into every step of the supply chain to reduce the overall environmental footprint.
Action: Work with suppliers who adhere to green standards, prioritize sourcing sustainable and ethically produced materials, and optimize logistics to reduce emissions. Implement waste management, recycling, and energy-efficient processes across operations.
Outcome: A more sustainable and efficient supply chain that supports GMO by minimizing waste, conserving resources, and reducing costs.

Step 6: Communicate and Market Green Initiatives Transparently

Objective: Build trust with consumers by promoting green initiatives transparently and authentically.

Action: Use clear and credible marketing messages to communicate sustainability efforts. Avoid greenwashing by providing accurate information about eco-friendly products and initiatives. Use eco-labels and certifications where applicable to enhance credibility.

Outcome: Increased brand trust and loyalty among consumers who value environmental transparency and appreciate the company's genuine green efforts.

Step 7: Measure, Track, and Report Environmental Performance

Objective: Continuously monitor and assess the impact of GMO efforts to ensure accountability and identify areas for improvement.

Action: Establish metrics to track environmental performance, such as energy savings, emission reductions, waste minimization, and resource efficiency. Publish sustainability reports regularly to communicate progress to stakeholders.

Outcome: A data-driven approach to sustainability that allows for continuous improvement, increased transparency, and accountability in green initiatives.

Step 8: Innovate and Adjust Based on Feedback and Trends

Objective: Foster an environment of ongoing innovation and adaptation to respond to changing consumer expectations and sustainability advancements.

Action: Regularly review GMO practices and seek feedback from consumers, employees, and industry trends. Invest in new technologies, sustainable materials, and improved processes as they emerge.

Outcome: A dynamic, responsive GMO strategy that remains relevant and competitive in the face of evolving environmental standards and consumer preferences.

Figure 5. Steps in the Implementation of Green Market Orientation

7. REGULATORY FRAMEWORKS FOR GREEN MARKET ORIENTATION

Regulatory frameworks ensure that businesses adhere to environmental standards, promote transparency, and prevent greenwashing.

7.1 International Regulatory Frameworks

7.1.1. United Nations (UN) Initiatives

- UN Sustainable Development Goals (SDGs) (2015)
    - *Relevance to GMO:* Encourages businesses to align with goals like SDG 12 (Responsible Consumption & Production) and SDG 13 (Climate Action).
    - *Key Regulations:*

Adoption of circular economy principles.
Reduction of carbon footprints in supply chains.

- UN Global Compact
    - o *Principles:* Covers environment (e.g., Principle 7: Precautionary approach to environmental challenges).
    - o *Compliance:* Businesses must report sustainability progress annually.

7.1.2. Paris Agreement (2015)

- *Key Focus:* National commitments to reduce greenhouse gas (GHG) emissions.
- *Impact on GMO:* Companies must align with national carbon reduction strategies (e.g., carbon pricing, renewable energy adoption).

7.1.3. OECD Guidelines for Multinational Enterprises

- *Environmental Due Diligence:* Requires firms to assess and mitigate environmental risks.
- *Green Marketing Standards*: Prevents misleading eco-claims.

7.2 Regional & National Regulatory Frameworks

7.2.1. European Union (EU) Regulations

- European Green Deal (2019)
    - o *Key Policies:*
        - ▪ *Circular Economy Action Plan:* Mandates sustainable product design (e.g., recyclability, durability).
        - ▪ *Corporate Sustainability Reporting Directive (CSRD):* Expands ESG disclosure requirements.
        - ▪ *EU Taxonomy Regulation:* Classifies sustainable economic activities.
- Ecodesign for Sustainable Products Regulation (ESPR)
    - o *Requirements:* Products must meet energy efficiency, repairability, and recyclability standards.
- Green Claims Directive (Proposed 2023)
    - o *Purpose:* Ensures all environmental claims (e.g., "carbon-neutral," "biodegradable") are scientifically verified.

7.2.2. United States Regulations

- Federal Trade Commission (FTC) Green Guides
    - *Objective:* Prevents deceptive environmental marketing.
    - *Key Rules:*
        - Clear definitions for terms like "compostable," "recyclable," and "non-toxic."
        - Requires proof for broad claims (e.g., "eco-friendly").
- Environmental Protection Agency (EPA) Regulations
    - *Energy Star Program:* Certifies energy-efficient products.
    - *Toxic Substances Control Act (TSCA):* Regulates harmful chemicals in products.
- California's Climate Corporate Accountability Act (2023)
    - *Mandate:* Large companies must disclose Scope 1, 2, and 3 emissions.

7.2.3. Asia-Pacific Regulations

- China's Dual Carbon Goals (2030 Peak Emissions, 2060 Carbon Neutrality)
    - *Key Policies:*
        - Mandatory carbon trading for key industries.
        - Green product certification system.
- India's Bureau of Energy Efficiency (BEE) Star Labeling
    - *Requirement:* Appliances must display energy efficiency ratings.
- Japan's Act on Promotion of Green Procurement
    - *Requires:* Government and businesses to prioritize eco-friendly products.

7.3 Industry-Specific Regulations

7.3.1. Energy Sector

- *Renewable Portfolio Standards (RPS):* Mandates minimum renewable energy usage (e.g., EU Renewable Energy Directive).

7.3.2. Automotive Sector

- *EU Emission Standards (Euro 7):* Stricter limits on vehicle emissions.
- *US Corporate Average Fuel Economy (CAFE) Standards*: Mandates fuel efficiency improvements.

7.3.3. Food & Agriculture

- *EU Organic Farming Regulation:* Defines organic labeling standards.
- *USDA Organic Certification:* Ensures compliance with organic farming practices.

7.3.4. Fashion & Textiles

- *EU Strategy for Sustainable Textiles:* Bans destruction of unsold textiles, enforces eco-design.
- *France's Anti-Waste Law (AGEC):* Requires transparency on environmental impact.

7.4 Compliance & Enforcement Mechanisms

- Mandatory ESG Reporting (e.g., EU CSRD, US SEC Climate Disclosure Rules).
- Third-Party Certifications (e.g., Fair Trade, LEED, Cradle to Cradle).
- Penalties for Greenwashing (e.g., fines under FTC Green Guides, EU Green Claims Directive).
- Carbon Pricing Mechanisms (e.g., EU Emissions Trading System, California Cap-and-Trade).

7.5 Emerging Trends in Green Market Regulation

- *Digital Product Passports (EU):* Tracks product lifecycle sustainability.
- *Extended Producer Responsibility (EPR) Laws:* Holds firms accountable for waste management.
- *Global Plastic Treaty (UN):* Potential ban on single-use plastics.

8. IMPACT OF REGULATORY FRAMEWORKS ON GREEN MARKET ORIENTATION

Regulatory frameworks define the rules for sustainable business operations, forcing companies to integrate GMO into their core strategies.

8.1 Compliance with Environmental Standards

Governments and regulatory bodies enforce environmental standards such as the EU Green Deal, Paris Agreement, and ISO 14001. Companies must adhere to these standards to operate legally, leading them to adopt green market strategies.

- Example: The European Union's Carbon Border Adjustment Mechanism (CBAM) encourages companies to lower their carbon footprint, pushing firms to integrate greener supply chain practices.

8.2 Market Access and Trade Regulations

Stringent environmental regulations can serve as either barriers or enablers for market entry. Companies that comply with green policies gain access to eco-conscious markets, while non-compliant firms may face restrictions.

- Example: The EU Battery Regulation mandates strict sustainability measures for battery manufacturers. Companies complying with these regulations gain a competitive edge in the European market.

8.3 Financial Incentives and Penalties

Many governments provide tax benefits, grants, and subsidies for companies investing in green technology. Conversely, non-compliance leads to penalties, such as carbon taxes or fines for excessive emissions.

- Example: The U.S. Inflation Reduction Act (2022) provides tax credits for businesses investing in clean energy, incentivizing a green market approach.

Figure 6. Impact of Regulatory Frameworks on Green Market Orientation

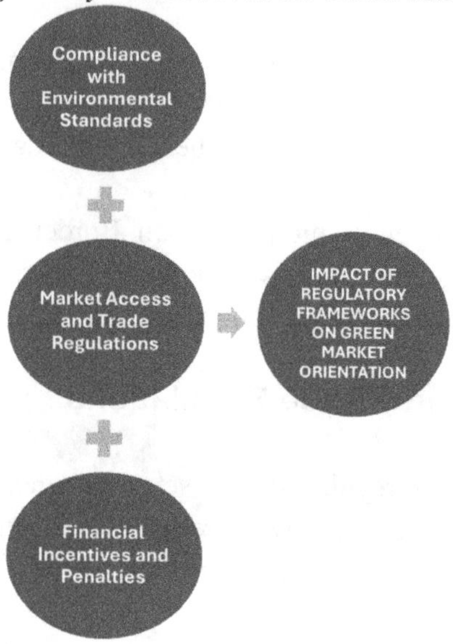

8.4 Key Impacts

Mandatory ESG Reporting (e.g., EU CSRD, SEC Climate Rules) → Forces firms to track & disclose sustainability metrics.
Carbon Pricing & Penalties (e.g., EU ETS, California Cap-and-Trade) → Incentivizes low-carbon innovation.
Bans on Greenwashing (e.g., FTC Green Guides, EU Green Claims Directive) → Ensures honest eco-marketing.
Extended Producer Responsibility (EPR) Laws → Holds firms accountable for product lifecycle waste.

9. DIGITAL COMPLIANCE FOR GREEN MARKET ORIENTATION

Digital compliance ensures that businesses adopting GMO adhere to environmental regulations, sustainability reporting standards, and anti-greenwashing measures through digital tools, data transparency, and automated governance (Dogbe & Marwa, 2024).

9.1 Key Digital Compliance Components for GMO

Table 1. Digital Compliance Components for GMO

Component	Description	Examples
Automated ESG Reporting	AI-driven tools for real-time sustainability data collection and disclosure.	SAP Sustainability Cloud, IBM Envizi
Blockchain for Traceability	Ensures transparent & tamper-proof supply chain tracking.	IBM Food Trust, VeChain
AI-Powered Carbon Accounting	AI models calculate Scope 1, 2, and 3 emissions.	Persefoni, Watershed
IoT for Energy Monitoring	Smart sensors track energy use, waste, and emissions in real time.	Siemens MindSphere, Schneider EcoStruxure
Digital Product Passports (DPPs)	QR codes/NFC tags with lifecycle environmental data.	EU's DPP initiative, Circularise
Green Cloud Computing	Sustainable data centers powered by renewables.	Google Carbon-Free Energy, Microsoft Circular Centers

9.2 Regulatory Frameworks Mandating Digital Compliance

9.2.1. European Union (EU) Regulations

1. Corporate Sustainability Reporting Directive (CSRD) (2024)
   Requires digitized ESG reporting using XBRL (eXtensible Business Reporting Language).
   Mandates AI-driven audit trails for sustainability claims.
2. Digital Product Passport (DPP) (2026 Enforcement)
   Applies to batteries, textiles, electronics.
   Requires blockchain/IoT-based tracking of materials.
3. EU Taxonomy Regulation
   AI tools must classify activities as "sustainable" per EU criteria.

9.2.2. United States Regulations

1. SEC Climate Disclosure Rule (2024)
   Public companies must disclose climate risks digitally (machine-readable formats).
   Requires AI-based carbon footprint calculations.
2. FTC Green Guides (2024 Update)

AI tools must verify environmental claims (e.g., "100% recyclable").
Automated compliance checks for green marketing.

9.2.3. Global Standards

1. Global Reporting Initiative (GRI) Digital Standards
   Requires cloud-based ESG data collection.
   APIs for automated sustainability reporting.
2. ISO 14090 (Climate Adaptation) & ISO 14064 (Carbon Accounting)
   AI-powered carbon credit verification.

9.3 Digital Tools for GMO Compliance

9.3.1. AI & Machine Learning

- *Carbon Footprint Tracking:* Tools like Persefoni, Normative.
- *Greenwashing Detection:* AI scans ads for misleading claims (e.g., EcoBot, TruthTagger).

9.3.2. Blockchain & IoT

- *Supply Chain Transparency:* IBM Blockchain, VeChain.
- *Smart Contracts for Carbon Credits:* Polygon Climate, Toucan Protocol.

9.3.3. Cloud & Big Data

- *ESG Data Lakes:* Salesforce Net Zero Cloud, Microsoft Cloud for Sustainability.
- *Real-Time Compliance Dashboards:* Siemens SiGREEN, Sphera.

9.3.4. Digital Product Passports (DPPs)

- *QR Code/NFC-Based:* Circularise, EON Product Cloud.
- *Lifecycle Assessment (LCA) Software:* SimaPro, GaBi.

9.4 Challenges in Digital Compliance for GMO

Table 2. Digital Compliance Challenges for GMO

Challenge	Solution
Data Silos	Unified ESG platforms (e.g., Workiva, Diligent ESG).
Greenwashing Risks	AI fact-checking tools (e.g., EcoChain, Greenly).
High Implementation Costs	Open-source tools (e.g., OpenLCA, Hyperledger).
Regulatory Fragmentation	Global ESG data standards (e.g., IFRS S1, SASB).

9.5 Future Trends in Digital GMO Compliance

1. AI-Powered Regulatory Forecasting (e.g., Google DeepMind for policy tracking).
2. Tokenized Carbon Credits (Blockchain-based trading).
3. Self-Auditing Smart Contracts (Auto-compliance with EU CSRD).
4. Generative AI for ESG Reporting (Automated sustainability narratives).

10. IMPACT OF DIGITAL COMPLIANCE ON GREEN MARKET ORIENTATION

Digital compliance refers to the use of technology-driven solutions to ensure adherence to environmental laws and standards. Digital compliance ensures real-time, auditable, and fraud-proof sustainability practices (Jaber, 2023). It directly impacts GMO through:

10.1 Data-Driven Environmental Reporting

Businesses must comply with environmental reporting regulations like the Corporate Sustainability Reporting Directive (CSRD) in the EU. Digital tools like blockchain, AI, and big data analytics enhance compliance by ensuring accurate emissions tracking, waste management, and carbon footprint calculations.

- Example: Companies use AI-powered Environmental, Social, and Governance (ESG) software to automate compliance with environmental laws.

10.2 Supply Chain Transparency and Compliance

Digital technologies like IoT sensors, blockchain, and cloud computing enable companies to monitor their supply chain sustainability, ensuring adherence to green regulations.

- Example: The Fashion Transparency Index encourages apparel brands to use digital compliance tools to track ethical sourcing and environmental impact.

10.3 Green Certification and Eco-Labeling

Firms use digital platforms for real-time compliance checks to obtain eco-certifications such as LEED (Leadership in Energy and Environmental Design) or Fair Trade. These certifications enhance green branding and consumer trust.

- Example: The EU Ecolabel certification requires businesses to provide digital compliance reports, ensuring adherence to strict sustainability standards.

Figure 7. Impact of Digital Compliance on Green Market Orientation

10.4 Key Impacts

AI & Big Data → Automates carbon accounting (e.g., Watershed, Persefoni).
Blockchain → Ensures supply chain transparency (e.g., IBM Food Trust).
IoT Sensors → Monitors energy/emissions in real time (e.g., Siemens MindSphere).
Digital Product Passports (DPPs) → Tracks product sustainability (e.g., EU's 2026 DPP mandate).

11. CASE STUDIES

Green Market Orientation (GMO) is increasingly implemented by organizations worldwide, aiming to reduce environmental impact while addressing the demands of eco-conscious consumers. Below are detailed examples of organizations with successful GMO practices, illustrating how they integrate sustainability into their business models.

11.1 Unilever's Sustainable Living Plan

Unilever, a global leader in consumer goods, has implemented GMO through its Sustainable Living Plan, which integrates environmental sustainability across its product portfolio and operations. The initiative, launched in 2010, has aimed to reduce the company's environmental footprint while increasing its positive social impact.

Key GMO practices include:

- *Green Product Innovation:* Unilever has reformulated products to be eco-friendly, using sustainable ingredients and minimizing packaging waste.
- *Supply Chain Optimization:* The company works with suppliers to ensure sustainable sourcing, such as sourcing 100% of palm oil from certified sustainable sources.
- *Consumer Engagement:* Unilever actively educates consumers on sustainability, encouraging water conservation and recycling through its products.

Unilever's Sustainable Living Plan has significantly contributed to its competitive advantage, enhancing brand loyalty and increasing its appeal to environmentally conscious consumers.

11.2 Patagonia's Environmental Activism and Product Lifecycle Initiatives

Patagonia, a clothing and outdoor gear brand, exemplifies GMO by integrating environmental responsibility into its core mission. Known for its advocacy for environmental causes, Patagonia has made sustainability a defining aspect of its brand, resonating strongly with eco-conscious consumers.

Key GMO practices include:

- *Worn Wear Program:* Patagonia encourages customers to repair, reuse, and recycle their products through its Worn Wear program. Customers can return used items to be refurbished or recycled, promoting a circular economy.
- *Sustainable Sourcing:* Patagonia uses recycled materials, such as polyester from plastic bottles, and organic cotton to reduce its environmental impact.
- *Environmental Activism:* Patagonia donates 1% of its annual sales to environmental causes and actively supports environmental movements, using its brand influence to raise awareness on climate change.

Patagonia's GMO practices have built a strong brand reputation and earned loyal customers who share its commitment to environmental activism.

11.3 IKEA's People & Planet Positive Strategy

IKEA, the global furniture retailer, has committed to sustainability through its People & Planet Positive strategy. This GMO-driven approach focuses on promoting resource efficiency, renewable energy, and sustainable products, helping IKEA mitigate its environmental impact.

Key GMO practices include:

- *Circular Product Design:* IKEA designs products to be durable, repairable, and recyclable, which reduces waste and maximizes product lifespan.
- *Sustainable Sourcing:* IKEA has committed to sourcing all of its cotton and wood from sustainable sources. It uses Forest Stewardship Council (FSC) certified wood and responsibly sourced cotton.
- *Renewable Energy Investments:* IKEA has invested heavily in renewable energy, with the goal of becoming climate-positive by 2030. It owns and operates wind farms and solar installations to power its stores and distribution centers.

IKEA's GMO initiatives enhance brand loyalty among consumers who value sustainability, positioning the brand as a leader in green retail practices.

11.4 Tesla's Commitment to Clean Energy

Tesla, an electric vehicle (EV) and clean energy company, has adopted GMO by positioning its products as sustainable alternatives to conventional vehicles and energy sources. Tesla's entire business model aligns with GMO principles, focusing on reducing emissions and promoting renewable energy.

Key GMO practices include:

- *Electric Vehicles (EVs):* Tesla's primary product line consists of zero-emission vehicles that reduce reliance on fossil fuels.
- *Renewable Energy Products:* Tesla produces solar panels and solar roofs for residential use, allowing consumers to generate renewable energy. It also offers energy storage solutions with its Powerwall and Powerpack products.
- *Supercharger Network:* Tesla has developed a global network of Superchargers to facilitate EV adoption, further reducing the carbon footprint associated with traditional fuel sources.

Tesla's GMO practices have established the brand as an industry leader in sustainable technology, appealing to consumers and investors who prioritize environmental impact.

11.5 The Body Shop's Community Trade Program and Cruelty-Free Commitment

The Body Shop, a global cosmetics and skincare brand, has integrated GMO into its business through ethical sourcing and cruelty-free product standards. The company is committed to protecting animal rights, sourcing sustainable ingredients, and supporting local communities.

Key GMO practices include:

- *Community Fair Trade:* The Body Shop sources raw materials through its Community Fair Trade program, which ensures fair wages and support for local suppliers.
- *Cruelty-Free Products:* The company has a long-standing commitment to animal welfare and offers a cruelty-free product line certified by the Leaping Bunny Program.
- *Recycling and Refill Initiatives:* The Body Shop encourages customers to recycle their product packaging and offers refill stations for popular products, reducing plastic waste.

These GMO practices have helped The Body Shop build a loyal customer base that values ethical and environmentally responsible products.

12. FUTURE DIRECTIONS IN GREEN MARKET ORIENTATION

The future of Green Market Orientation (GMO) is likely to be shaped by advancements in technology, changing regulatory landscapes, and evolving consumer expectations. As sustainability becomes increasingly central to business success, GMO will evolve to include more integrated, data-driven, and impactful strategies. Here's a look at some key future directions in GMO:

12.1 Digitalization and Data-Driven Sustainability

- *Impact:* The integration of digital technologies, such as artificial intelligence (AI), machine learning, and big data analytics, is transforming how companies manage and optimize their sustainability efforts.
- *Future Trends:*
    - *Predictive Analytics:* Companies can use predictive analytics to anticipate demand for sustainable products, manage resource use efficiently, and forecast environmental impacts based on consumer behavior.
    - *Real-Time Monitoring:* Through IoT sensors and digital twins, companies will be able to track energy consumption, emissions, and waste in real-time, allowing for quick adjustments to reduce environmental impact.
    - *AI-Driven Consumer Insights:* AI can analyze consumer sentiment on sustainability and tailor green marketing messages more effectively, increasing engagement and loyalty among eco-conscious consumers.
- *Outcome:* Digitalization enables companies to implement more efficient and responsive GMO strategies, enhancing transparency, operational efficiency, and customer satisfaction.

12.2 Increased Transparency and Enhanced Accountability

- *Impact:* As consumers and regulatory bodies demand more accountability, companies will need to provide verifiable and transparent reports on their sustainability practices.
- *Future Trends:*

Blockchain for Transparency: Blockchain technology can provide an immutable record of a product's lifecycle, from raw material sourcing to end-of-life disposal, allowing consumers and regulators to verify environmental claims.

Standardized Reporting and Certifications: With increased scrutiny on greenwashing, companies will adopt globally recognized sustainability standards, such as those from the Global Reporting Initiative (GRI) or the Science-Based Targets Initiative (SBTi), to provide consistent and credible data.

Public Disclosure Platforms: Future GMO strategies may include leveraging digital platforms where stakeholders can access real-time information on a company's sustainability progress, such as resource usage, emissions, and waste reduction.

- *Outcome:* Enhanced transparency will build consumer trust and solidify a brand's reputation as genuinely committed to sustainability, while ensuring compliance with emerging regulations.

12.3 Circular Economy Models and Product Lifecycle Management

- *Impact:* Companies are increasingly adopting circular economy models, which emphasize resource efficiency, waste reduction, and product reuse throughout the lifecycle.
- *Future Trends:*

  Product-as-a-Service (PaaS): Instead of selling products outright, companies may offer them as services (e.g., leasing or subscription models), which allows them to retain control over product lifecycles, encouraging recycling and reuse.

  Eco-Design for Longevity: GMO will focus more on designing products that are durable, repairable, and recyclable, minimizing waste and maximizing product lifespan.

  Reverse Logistics: Companies will develop reverse logistics systems to recover and recycle products, turning waste materials back into resources for new products, fostering a closed-loop system.
- *Outcome:* Circular economy models contribute to a significant reduction in waste, optimize resource use, and reduce dependency on raw materials, supporting long-term sustainability goals.

12.4 Collaboration for Sustainability

- *Impact:* The complexity of global supply chains and the scale of environmental issues have underscored the need for collaboration between businesses, governments, and NGOs.
- *Future Trends:*
  - *Cross-Industry Partnerships:* Companies will increasingly partner with other businesses to share resources, technologies, and best practices, helping to drive industry-wide sustainability improvements.
  - *Public-Private Partnerships:* Collaborations between businesses and governments can lead to the development of sustainable infrastructure, such as renewable energy facilities and waste management systems, benefiting the broader community.
  - *NGO Partnerships for Credibility:* Partnering with NGOs for certification, audits, and sustainability initiatives can lend credibility to a company's green claims and provide additional resources for GMO projects.
- *Outcome:* Collaborative efforts will allow companies to tackle complex sustainability challenges more effectively, pooling resources and expertise to create impactful, scalable solutions.

12.5 Focus on Social Sustainability and Ethical Practices

- *Impact:* The concept of sustainability is expanding to include social dimensions, such as ethical labor practices, community support, and economic equity.
- *Future Trends:*
  - *Social Impact Initiatives:* Companies will go beyond environmental impact, ensuring fair labor practices, diversity, and community engagement, especially within supply chains.
  - *Human Rights and Fair Trade:* GMO strategies will increasingly emphasize ethical sourcing, with companies taking responsibility for the social conditions under which their products are produced.
  - *Stakeholder-Centric Approach:* A broader definition of GMO will involve considering the needs of all stakeholders, not just consumers, thereby aligning sustainability practices with broader societal values.
- *Outcome:* By integrating social sustainability into GMO, companies can ensure that their green initiatives contribute positively to both people and the planet, meeting the expectations of ethically-minded consumers and investors.

12.6 Personalization and Hyper-Targeted Green Marketing

- *Impact:* Advances in data analytics enable companies to create highly personalized green marketing campaigns that resonate with individual consumer values.
- *Future Trends:*

  Customized Green Messaging: Companies will tailor green messaging based on specific consumer segments, enhancing the relevance and appeal of their sustainable products.

  Eco-Product Recommendations: Through AI-driven recommendation engines, companies can suggest products based on individual consumer preferences for sustainability.

  Behavioral Insights for Engagement: By understanding consumer behavior through data, companies can offer tips, rewards, and incentives that encourage sustainable actions, such as product recycling or energy conservation.
- *Outcome:* Hyper-targeted green marketing boosts customer engagement, creating stronger bonds with eco-conscious consumers and enhancing the effectiveness of GMO strategies.

12.7 Adaptation to Regulatory and Policy Changes

- *Impact:* Governments worldwide are setting increasingly stringent environmental regulations, prompting companies to be agile and adaptable in their GMO strategies.
- *Future Trends:*

  Compliance with Global Standards: Companies will need to align GMO efforts with international agreements, such as the Paris Agreement and regional carbon reduction mandates.

  Proactive Policy Engagement: Companies will engage in advocacy and policymaking to help shape sustainable regulations, aligning their GMO strategies with anticipated policy shifts.

  Internal Compliance Frameworks: To remain flexible, companies will develop internal compliance frameworks that allow them to adjust GMO practices in line with changing regulations.
- *Outcome:* Adapting to regulatory changes ensures that companies remain compliant and proactive, positioning them as leaders in sustainable practices and reducing the risk of penalties.

12.8 Investment in Renewable Energy and Carbon Neutrality

- *Impact:* With growing concerns over climate change, companies are committing to carbon neutrality and investing in renewable energy sources as part of their GMO strategies.
- *Future Trends:*
  - *Onsite Renewable Energy Production:* Companies will invest in solar, wind, and other renewable installations at their facilities to reduce reliance on fossil fuels.
  - *Carbon Offset Programs:* Companies unable to fully eliminate emissions may engage in carbon offset programs, such as reforestation and conservation projects, to achieve carbon neutrality.
  - *Supply Chain Decarbonization:* GMO strategies will increasingly involve suppliers in emissions reduction targets, extending carbon neutrality goals throughout the supply chain.
- *Outcome:* By investing in renewable energy and pursuing carbon neutrality, companies can significantly reduce their environmental footprint, positioning themselves as leaders in climate responsibility.

12.9 Resilience-Building for Climate Adaptation

- *Impact:* As climate risks intensify, GMO will encompass strategies for building resilience to environmental disruptions.
- *Future Trends:*
  - *Climate-Resilient Infrastructure:* Companies will invest in infrastructure that can withstand extreme weather events, minimizing disruption to operations and supply chains.
  - *Diversification of Resources:* To protect against resource scarcity, GMO will involve diversifying supply sources and investing in alternative materials.
  - *Risk Management Strategies:* Companies will adopt GMO strategies that prioritize risk assessment and adaptation planning, ensuring continuity and stability in the face of climate challenges.
- *Outcome:* By focusing on resilience, companies will be better equipped to navigate environmental risks, protecting both business continuity and long-term sustainability goals.

13. CONCLUSION

Green Market Orientation (GMO) emerges as a strategic imperative, enabling businesses to thrive in a sustainability-driven economy by aligning environmental responsibility with profitability. Through regulatory adherence, digital compliance, and innovative practices, companies can overcome challenges, build consumer trust, and secure competitive advantage. The future demands collaboration, technological integration, and adaptive strategies to meet evolving regulations and stakeholder expectations. By embedding GMO into their DNA, businesses not only future-proof their operations but also contribute meaningfully to global sustainability goals, proving that ecological stewardship and commercial success are inextricably linked. The journey toward GMO is not optional—it is the blueprint for resilient, relevant, and responsible business leadership in the 21st century.

REFERENCES

Bansal, P., & Dhir, A. (2023). Tactics and strategies in green marketing orientation: An analysis of best practices. *Journal of Sustainable Marketing*, *11*(2), 122–140.

Bataineh, M. J., Sánchez-Sellero, P., & Ayad, F. (2024). Green is the new black: How research and development and green innovation provide businesses a competitive edge. *Business Strategy and the Environment*, *33*(2), 1004–1023. DOI: 10.1002/bse.3533

Borah, P. S., Dogbe, C. S. K., Dzandu, M. D., & Pomegbe, W. W. K. (2023). Forging organizational resilience through green value co-creation: The role of green technology, green operations, and green transaction capabilities. *Business Strategy and the Environment*, *32*(8), 5734–5747. DOI: 10.1002/bse.3446

Borah, P. S., Dogbe, C. S. K., & Marwa, N. (2024). Generation Z's green purchase behavior: Do green consumer knowledge, consumer social responsibility, green advertising, and green consumer trust matter for sustainable development? *Business Strategy and the Environment*, *33*(5), 4530–4546. DOI: 10.1002/bse.3714

Borah, P. S., Dogbe, C. S. K., & Marwa, N. (2025). Green dynamic capability and green product innovation for sustainable development: Role of green operations, green transaction, and green technology development capabilities. *Corporate Social Responsibility and Environmental Management*, *32*(1), 911–926. DOI: 10.1002/csr.2993

Borah, P. S., Dogbe, C. S. K., Pomegbe, W. W. K., Bamfo, B. A., & Hornuvo, L. K. (2023b). Green market orientation, green innovation capability, green knowledge acquisition and green brand positioning as determinants of new product success. *European Journal of Innovation Management*, *26*(2), 364–385. DOI: 10.1108/EJIM-09-2020-0345

Borah, P. S., Pomegbe, W. W. K., & Dogbe, C. S. K. (2022). Mediating role of green marketing orientation in stakeholder risk and new product success relationship among European multinational enterprises in Ghana. *Society and Business Review*, *17*(4), 485–505. DOI: 10.1108/SBR-02-2021-0035

Chowdhury, S., Lau, H. S., & Zhang, D. (2023). Strategic approaches to green market orientation and consumer response. *Journal of Environmental Marketing Research*, *15*(3), 245–259.

Dalakishvili, R., & Tchanturia, N. (2024). Renewable energy for long-term, green progress. *Reviews of Modern Science*, (5).

de Oliveira Lima, L. A., da Silva, J. M. S., de Oliveira Santos, A., Marques, F. R. V., da Silva Leão, A. P., Carvalho, M. D. C. L., & Ferreira, A. B. S. (2024). The Influence of Green Marketing on Consumer Purchase Intention: A Systematic Review. *Revista de Gestão Social e Ambiental*, *18*(3), 1–11.

Dogbe, C. S. K., & Marwa, N. (2024). Digital Orientation and Manufacturing Firms' Green Innovation Performance: The Mediating Role of Green Competence. *Journal of Risk and Financial Management*, *17*(10), 430. DOI: 10.3390/jrfm17100430

Hao, F., Li, J., & Yang, T. (2022). Green market orientation: Impacts on competitive advantage and customer loyalty. *Sustainability*, *14*(12), 7465.

Jaber, M. (2023). IoT and machine learning for enabling sustainable development goals. *Frontiers in Communications and Networks*, *4*, 1219047. DOI: 10.3389/frcmn.2023.1219047

Kumar, R., Singh, B., & Gupta, A. (2023). The role of green market orientation in sustainable corporate performance. *International Journal of Marketing Studies*, *10*(1), 30–49.

Kumari, R., Dash, S. P., & Chatterjee, R. (2025). Green Human Resource Management: An Emerging Trend in HR Practices. *Examining Green Human Resources Management and Nascent Entrepreneurship*, 1-24.

Leonidou, C. N., Katsikeas, C. S., & Morgan, N. A. (2013). "Greening" the marketing mix: Do firms do it and does it pay off? *Journal of the Academy of Marketing Science*, *41*(2), 151–170. DOI: 10.1007/s11747-012-0317-2

Luzzini, D., Longoni, A., & Caniato, F. (2021). Environmental orientation in supply chain management: A systematic review and conceptual framework. *Sustainable Production and Consumption*, *27*, 238–256.

Papadas, K. K., Avlonitis, G. J., & Carrigan, M. (2017). Green marketing orientation: Conceptualization, scale development and validation. *Journal of Business Research*, *80*, 236–246. DOI: 10.1016/j.jbusres.2017.05.024

Pomegbe, W. W. K., Dogbe, C. S. K., Bamfo, B. A., Borah, P. S., & Novixoxo, J. D. (2022). Social risk, green market orientation, entrepreneurial orientation, and new product performance among European Multinational Enterprises operating in developing economies. *Business and Society Review*, *127*(4), 891–914. DOI: 10.1111/basr.12292

Singh, R., & Dhir, A. (2022). Exploring green market orientation: Emerging practices and strategic implications. *Environmental Business Review*, *12*(4), 333–348.

Xie, Q., Zhang, H., & Cao, S. (2023). Green market orientation: Drivers and outcomes in the global market. *Journal of Business Ethics*, *19*(2), 102–119.

Chapter 10
Practical Implications and the Future of Eco-Innovation, Digital Transformation, and Green Marketing:
Future of Sustainable Marketing

Prasad Siba Borah
https://orcid.org/0000-0002-4154-3373
School of Management, Jiangsu University, China

ABSTRACT

This chapter explores the intersection of eco-innovation, digital transformation, and green marketing, presenting these concepts as crucial pillars for sustainable business growth in a rapidly evolving global landscape. The chapter revises the concepts of eco-innovation, digital transformation, and green marketing, highlighting their interconnectivity and relevance in achieving sustainability goals. It then explains into future trends, discussing how firms can align digital and sustainability strategies, invest in green technologies, and enhance transparency to gain competitive advantages. Practical implications for managers are provided, including strategic recommendations, consumer trust-building approaches, and frameworks for setting measurable goals. Real-world examples of leading companies like Tesla, IKEA, and Patagonia are presented to illustrate how organizations integrate these concepts into their operations and marketing efforts.

DOI: 10.4018/979-8-3693-9831-9.ch010

1 INTRODUCTION

Eco-innovation, digital transformation, and green marketing are interconnected concepts shaping the future of sustainable business practices. Eco-innovation refers to the development of new or improved products, processes, and services that reduce environmental harm, enhance resource efficiency, and promote sustainability. It aims to address ecological challenges by integrating sustainability into innovation, fostering solutions like renewable energy technologies, circular economy models, and low-impact manufacturing. Digital transformation, on the other hand, involves integrating digital technologies into all aspects of a business, fundamentally altering how organizations operate and deliver value. It facilitates real-time data collection, automation, and connectivity, which can optimize resource use and reduce waste, playing a pivotal role in advancing eco-innovation (Shaukat et al., 2023).

Green marketing complements these efforts by promoting environmentally friendly products and services, influencing consumer behavior toward sustainability. It focuses on transparent communication of a product or brand's ecological benefits, often using digital platforms like social media, e-commerce, and online advertising to reach eco-conscious audiences effectively. Together, these concepts enable firms to innovate sustainably, operate more efficiently, and connect with consumers who value environmental stewardship. By embracing eco-innovation, firms can create products that align with global sustainability goals; through digital transformation, they can enhance efficiency and scalability; and with green marketing, they can build trust and awareness, driving a culture of sustainable consumption. These three pillars collectively contribute to a resilient and sustainable business ecosystem that addresses environmental, economic, and social challenges (Xu et al., 2023).

2 THE FUTURE RELEVANCE

In an era characterized by accelerating environmental degradation, technological advancement, and evolving consumer expectations, eco-innovation, digital transformation, and green marketing are becoming indispensable for firms across industries. Together, these concepts provide a holistic framework that not only addresses pressing ecological challenges but also positions companies for long-term success and customer trust in a rapidly transforming market. The future demands that firms integrate these approaches to remain competitive, achieve sustainable growth, and contribute to environmental protection.

2.1 Sustainable Innovation

Eco-innovation will be at the forefront of corporate strategies as the world grapples with climate change, resource scarcity, and stringent regulatory pressures. Firms will need to innovate sustainably, developing products, processes, and business models that minimize environmental impact while maximizing efficiency and profitability. For example, businesses in sectors like manufacturing, energy, and agriculture will increasingly turn to renewable energy technologies, waste-to-value systems, and bio-based materials to reduce carbon footprints. Companies failing to embrace eco-innovation risk being sidelined by consumers, investors, and regulators who prioritize sustainability. Moreover, the economic benefits of eco-innovation are undeniable, as it opens pathways to new markets, reduces operational costs, and enhances brand differentiation (Shaukat et al., 2023).

2.2 Digital Transformation: Crucial Enabler of Eco-Innovation

Simultaneously, digital transformation will be a crucial enabler of eco-innovation. Digital tools and technologies, such as artificial intelligence (AI), Internet of Things (IoT), blockchain, and big data analytics, empower firms to implement and scale sustainable practices effectively. For instance, AI-powered systems can optimize energy use in smart buildings, while IoT-enabled sensors provide real-time insights into supply chain inefficiencies, allowing companies to reduce waste and emissions. Blockchain technology is increasingly being used to ensure transparency in sustainable supply chains, verifying the authenticity of eco-friendly claims and building consumer trust. Additionally, digital platforms offer firms the agility to adapt quickly to changing environmental regulations and market demands. As the pace of technological innovation accelerates, firms that fail to digitize their operations may struggle to compete, particularly in global markets where agility and efficiency are paramount.

Similarly, the agriculture engineering in China think that it is necessary to improve the level of agricultural industrialization as agricultural enterprises have played an important role as market players. The impact mechanism reveals that digital transformation enhances risk-taking ability, alleviates information asymmetry, and decreases financing constraints, thereby promoting total factor productivity (TFP) (Cui et al., 2024). The researchers in the agricultural sector also found that the application of digital equipment helped to decrease the cost. On large-scale cotton farms, digital agriculture tends to be more economical than traditional agriculture. In the future, as the cost of fixed equipment decreases, and labor costs and water costs rise, the critical size of digital agriculture replacing traditional agriculture will get smaller, and the scope of the economic benefits of digital cotton field management will increase further (Shao et al., 2022).

2.3 Green Marketing: Bridging Consumers and Businesses

Green marketing, as the bridge between businesses and consumers, will play an equally critical role in the future. Consumers today are more environmentally conscious than ever, demanding transparency and accountability from brands they support. Green marketing allows firms to communicate their commitment to sustainability effectively, showcasing eco-friendly products and practices that resonate with eco-conscious customers. It is no longer sufficient for firms to merely produce green products; they must also educate and engage their audience through authentic and compelling narratives (Sun et al., 2021). Digital transformation enhances the reach and impact of green marketing efforts by focusing on data-driven insights to personalize messaging, utilize social media for storytelling, and create immersive experiences through augmented reality (AR) and virtual reality (VR). Companies that excel in green marketing will cultivate deep, long-lasting relationships with their customers, securing loyalty and advocacy in a competitive marketplace.

The integration of these three concepts will not only drive customer trust but also prepare firms for a future dominated by strict environmental policies and heightened stakeholder expectations. Governments and international bodies are increasingly introducing regulations aimed at curbing carbon emissions, reducing plastic waste, and promoting circular economies. Firms that proactively adopt eco-innovation and digital transformation to comply with these regulations will avoid penalties and gain a competitive edge. For instance, early adopters of renewable energy sources and energy-efficient technologies are already benefiting from subsidies, tax incentives, and reduced operating costs. These financial advantages are likely to grow as governments intensify efforts to meet global climate targets.

Moreover, investors and financial institutions are prioritizing sustainability in their decision-making processes. Environmental, Social, and Governance (ESG) criteria have become a standard for assessing corporate performance, and firms that demonstrate a commitment to eco-innovation and sustainability are more likely to attract investment. Digital transformation supports this by enabling transparent reporting and monitoring of sustainability metrics, while green marketing communicates these achievements to stakeholders effectively. As a result, firms that integrate these three pillars into their strategies will find it easier to access capital and maintain investor confidence.

From a consumer perspective, trust is increasingly linked to a company's environmental and social practices. Studies consistently show that consumers are more likely to support brands that demonstrate genuine efforts to reduce environmental harm and contribute positively to society. By embedding eco-innovation into their operations, firms can offer products that align with the values of conscious consumers. Digital transformation allows firms to deliver these products efficiently and sustainably, while green marketing ensures that these efforts are visible and credible. The synergy among these concepts fosters a virtuous cycle: consumers reward sustainable businesses with loyalty, which, in turn, incentivizes further innovation and environmental stewardship (Salnikova et al., 2022).

Small and medium-sized enterprises (SMEs) will also benefit significantly from adopting these principles. While SMEs may face resource constraints, digital transformation tools such as cloud computing, software-as-a-service (SaaS), and low-cost IoT devices make it feasible for them to implement eco-innovation at scale. Additionally, green marketing strategies tailored to niche audiences can help SMEs build strong community ties and differentiate themselves in crowded markets. The future will likely see a rise in collaborative ecosystems where SMEs and larger corporations work together to innovate sustainably, use shared digital platforms to reduce costs and maximize impact (Peredy & Feierzhati, 2023).

However, the path to integrating eco-innovation, digital transformation, and green marketing is not without challenges. Firms will need to overcome barriers such as technological limitations, high upfront costs, and resistance to change among stakeholders. Additionally, the risk of greenwashing, making exaggerated or false claims about sustainability, can damage a firm's reputation and erode consumer trust. To address these challenges, companies must prioritize transparency, invest in employee training, and adopt robust verification mechanisms. Partnerships with governments, NGOs, and academic institutions can also provide the support and expertise needed to navigate this complex landscape.

Looking ahead, the intersection of eco-innovation, digital transformation, and green marketing will shape the evolution of industries worldwide. As businesses move toward net-zero emissions, the integration of renewable energy systems, circular economy practices, and sustainable supply chains will become standard. Digital technologies will continue to evolve, offering advanced tools for monitoring and optimizing environmental performance. Green marketing will increasingly emphasize storytelling, community engagement, and co-creation with consumers to build strong emotional connections. There are certain priorities also mentioned that marketing professionals need to improve in the next years (Figure 1).

Figure 1. Marketers shifting toward sustainability[1]

Areas of Importance Marketing Professionals Worldwide Expect to Change in the Next 2 Years, July 2023
% of respondents

	More important	No change	Less important
Innovation and the adoption of new technologies	80%	17%	3%
Data, analytics, and measurement	75%	24%	1%
Agility and adaptability	73%	23%	3%
Customer retention	64%	32%	3%
Social impact and environmental sustainability	64%	29%	7%
Customer centricity	63%	35%	2%
Digital accessibility and inclusion	60%	36%	4%
Customer acquisition	58%	38%	4%
Organizational culture	52%	41%	7%
Brand purpose	51%	40%	9%
Long-term planning	47%	40%	13%

Note: n=611; numbers may not add up to 100% due to rounding
Source: Econsultancy, "Future of Marketing 2023," Sep 14, 2023
283409 Insider Intelligence | eMarketer

In conclusion, the future demands that firms embrace eco-innovation, digital transformation, and green marketing as integral components of their strategies. These concepts are not merely trends but essential drivers of sustainable growth, customer trust, and environmental protection. By preferring their combined potential, firms can address global challenges, meet stakeholder expectations, and secure a competitive advantage in an increasingly sustainability-focused world. The time to act is now, as the firms that lead this transformation will shape the future of business and leave a lasting positive impact on society and the planet.

3 POLICY AND REGULATORY IMPLICATIONS

As the global economy increasingly prioritizes sustainability, governments, international organizations, and regulatory bodies play a pivotal role in shaping the adoption and effectiveness of eco-innovation, digital transformation, and green marketing. Through carefully crafted policies, incentives, and standards, these authorities drive businesses to integrate sustainability into their operations while fostering accountability and transparency. These policy frameworks not only incentivize firms to embrace eco-friendly practices but also address challenges such as greenwashing and resource inefficiencies. This section explains how policies influence eco-innovation and digital transformation, the role of incentives in promoting green marketing, the growing importance of Corporate Social Responsibility (CSR), and the value of global standards and certifications.

3.1 Government and International Policies: Shaping Eco-Innovation and Digital Transformation

Governments and international organizations are key drivers of eco-innovation and digital transformation. They establish a regulatory environment that encourages or mandates the adoption of sustainable practices. Policies addressing climate change, energy efficiency, and waste management often set the stage for innovation by creating opportunities for firms to invest in greener technologies and processes.

Environmental Regulations and Compliance: Policies such as the European Green Deal, the Paris Agreement, and national emissions reduction targets compel firms to reduce their environmental impact. These frameworks promote eco-innovation by imposing limits on emissions, requiring the adoption of renewable energy, and incentivizing the development of sustainable materials. For instance, carbon pricing mechanisms, such as cap-and-trade systems or carbon taxes, encourage companies to innovate to reduce emissions and avoid financial penalties (Domorenok & Graziano, 2023).

Digital Transformation as a Policy Priority: Governments worldwide recognize the transformative potential of digital technologies in advancing sustainability. Policies supporting digital infrastructure development, such as the rollout of 5G networks and investments in AI research, enable firms to harness technology for eco-innovation. For example, smart grid technologies that optimize energy distribution rely on digital transformation facilitated by supportive policies.

Public-Private Partnerships: Collaborative initiatives between governments and businesses, such as clean energy funds or smart city projects, create a fertile ground for eco-innovation and digital transformation. These partnerships often combine public funding with private sector expertise, enabling the development and deployment of cutting-edge sustainable solutions.

3.2 Incentives for Firms Adopting Green Marketing

Green marketing thrives in a policy environment that rewards firms for their sustainability efforts. Governments use financial and non-financial incentives to encourage businesses to adopt environmentally friendly marketing strategies, driving the promotion of sustainable products and services.

Tax Incentives and Subsidies: Firms adopting green marketing strategies often benefit from tax breaks, grants, or subsidies. For instance, governments may offer financial incentives to companies that promote eco-labeled products or invest in renewable energy systems, reducing the cost burden of sustainability efforts. These incentives make green marketing a financially viable strategy, particularly for small and medium-sized enterprises (SMEs).

Access to Green Funds: International organizations and governments provide funding to support eco-innovation and sustainable marketing. Initiatives such as the Green Climate Fund or regional sustainability grants help firms develop and market products that align with environmental goals. By integrating green marketing with eco-innovation, companies can access these funds to finance their projects.

Market Access and Preferential Treatment: Regulatory frameworks often provide preferential treatment to firms engaging in green marketing. For example, government procurement policies may prioritize eco-friendly products, offering a competitive advantage to businesses that promote their green credentials.

Consumer Awareness Campaigns: Governments frequently collaborate with firms on public awareness campaigns to promote sustainable consumption. These initiatives encourage consumers to choose environmentally friendly products, indirectly incentivizing firms to adopt green marketing strategies to tap into this growing market demand (Roh et al., 2022).

3.3 Corporate Social Responsibility (CSR): Mandatory Disclosures and Sustainability Reporting

CSR has evolved from a voluntary practice to a mandatory requirement in many jurisdictions, significantly impacting how firms approach sustainability, transparency, and accountability. CSR policies increasingly emphasize mandatory disclosures and sustainability reporting as a means of holding businesses accountable for their environmental and social impacts.

Mandatory Disclosures: Governments and regulatory bodies now require firms to disclose their sustainability practices and environmental impacts. For instance, the European Union's Non-Financial Reporting Directive mandates large firms to report on issues such as greenhouse gas emissions, energy usage, and waste management.

These disclosures provide stakeholders with critical information, enabling them to assess a firm's commitment to sustainability.

Sustainability Reporting Standards: Frameworks such as the Global Reporting Initiative (GRI), Sustainability Accounting Standards Board (SASB), and Task Force on Climate-related Financial Disclosures (TCFD) guide firms in reporting their environmental and social performance. Adopting these standards not only ensures compliance but also enhances a firm's reputation among investors, customers, and regulators.

Integration with Green Marketing: Sustainability reporting supports green marketing by providing verified data that firms can use to substantiate their environmental claims. For example, a company can highlight its reduced carbon footprint or use of renewable energy in marketing campaigns, backed by credible reporting metrics.

Reputational Benefits: Beyond compliance, CSR reporting builds consumer trust by demonstrating a firm's commitment to transparency and accountability. Firms that excel in CSR practices often enjoy enhanced brand loyalty and customer advocacy, reinforcing the importance of sustainability in business strategies.

3.4 Global Standards and Certifications: Building Consumer Trust

Eco-labels and certifications play a crucial role in validating green marketing claims and fostering consumer trust. These standards provide a reliable benchmark for assessing products or company's environmental performance, enabling informed consumer choices.

Eco-Labels and Their Impact: Eco-labels, such as energy star, Fair Trade, and FSC (Forest Stewardship Council), help consumers identify products that meet specific environmental criteria. By displaying these labels, firms can differentiate their products in the market and appeal to eco-conscious customers. Studies show that certified products often enjoy a price premium, highlighting the value of eco-labels in building consumer trust.

Third-Party Verification: Independent certification bodies provide an unbiased assessment of a firm's environmental claims, reducing the risk of greenwashing. For instance, certifications like LEED (Leadership in Energy and Environmental Design) for buildings or support for products ensure that a company's claims are credible and meet stringent sustainability standards.

Global Standards Alignment: Internationally recognized standards, such as ISO 14001 for environmental management systems, enable firms to demonstrate their commitment to sustainability on a global scale. Compliance with these standards not only facilitates international trade but also enhances a firm's reputation as a responsible corporate citizen.

Consumer Education and Advocacy: Certifications and eco-labels also play a role in educating consumers about the environmental benefits of certain products or practices. By highlighting certified attributes, firms can engage customers in sustainability efforts, fostering a culture of responsible consumption.

Policies and regulations are essential for fostering the integration of eco-innovation, digital transformation, and green marketing into business strategies. Governments and international organizations shape the sustainability landscape through environmental regulations, digital infrastructure development, and financial incentives. Mandatory CSR disclosures and sustainability reporting ensure accountability, while global standards and certifications build consumer trust and mitigate greenwashing risks. For businesses, navigating these regulatory frameworks is not just about compliance, it is a strategic opportunity to align operations with sustainability goals, enhance reputation, and gain a competitive edge in an increasingly eco-conscious market. As policies continue to evolve, firms must proactively adapt to this regulatory environment to thrive in a sustainable future (Carrión-Bósquez et al., 2024).

4 CHALLENGES AND BARRIERS IN ECO-INNOVATION, DIGITAL TRANSFORMATION, AND GREEN MARKETING

Despite the growing recognition of the importance of eco-innovation, digital transformation, and green marketing, firms face significant challenges and barriers in adopting these practices. These obstacles, spanning technological, economic, cultural, and ethical domains, must be carefully addressed to ensure that businesses can effectively transition toward sustainable and innovative operations (Yordanova, 2023).

4.1 Technological Barriers

One of the primary challenges lies in the accessibility and deployment of advanced technologies, particularly for small and medium-sized enterprises (SMEs). These businesses often lack the financial resources and technical expertise to adopt cutting-edge technologies like artificial intelligence (AI), blockchain, and Internet of Things (IoT), which are instrumental in enabling eco-innovation and digital transformation. For instance, IoT sensors can provide real-time monitoring of energy use and emissions, but the cost and complexity of integrating such systems often deter smaller firms.

Cybersecurity risks further complicate the technological landscape. As firms embrace digital tools to optimize their operations and enhance sustainability efforts, they expose themselves to potential cyber threats. Digital systems, while valuable for monitoring supply chains, verifying sustainability claims, and automating processes, are vulnerable to data breaches, hacking, and other cyberattacks. These risks undermine consumer trust and can result in severe financial and reputational losses for companies. Addressing these challenges requires investment in secure technologies and robust training for employees to ensure compliance with cybersecurity protocols (Durst et al., 2024).

4.2 Economic Considerations

The economic challenges of adopting eco-innovation and digital transformation are significant, particularly the high upfront costs associated with these initiatives. Transitioning to renewable energy systems, retrofitting manufacturing plants for energy efficiency, or adopting digital supply technology often requires substantial capital investment. While these changes may yield long-term savings and operational benefits, the initial expenditure can be prohibitive, especially for smaller firms operating on tight margins.

Additionally, many firms struggle to justify these investments due to the perceived uncertainty of returns. For example, eco-innovation projects often involve research and development (R&D) activities that may not immediately translate into marketable products or services. Similarly, digital transformation efforts, such as implementing advanced analytics systems, may require time before tangible benefits, such as cost reductions or increased efficiency, become evident. This economic hesitation can delay or altogether prevent firms from pursuing necessary sustainable initiatives.

4.3 Cultural Resistance

Cultural resistance among stakeholders, whether internal or external, presents another formidable barrier to the adoption of eco-innovation and digital transformation. Internally, employees and management may resist changes to established workflows or business models, particularly if they do not fully understand the benefits of sustainability-focused initiatives. For instance, implementing new technologies often requires significant changes to existing practices, which can lead to apprehension among staff who may feel unprepared or unwilling to adapt (Nyamekye et al., 2024).

Externally, firms may face resistance from suppliers, partners, or even customers who lack awareness or understanding of the importance of sustainable practices. For example, suppliers accustomed to traditional production methods may be reluctant to invest in eco-friendly alternatives, while customers in certain markets may prioritize cost over sustainability, making it challenging for firms to justify their green marketing efforts. Overcoming this resistance requires targeted education and communication strategies to highlight the tangible benefits of sustainability, such as cost savings, regulatory compliance, and enhanced brand reputation.

4.4 Greenwashing Risks

As the demand for sustainable products and services grows, so does the risk of greenwashing misrepresenting or exaggerating the environmental benefits of a product, service, or practice. Greenwashing poses significant legal and reputational risks for firms, undermining consumer trust and potentially resulting in regulatory penalties. For instance, a company that falsely claims its product is "100% eco-friendly" without credible evidence may face backlash from watchdog organizations, consumers, and legal authorities.

Greenwashing risks are exacerbated by the lack of standardized definitions and frameworks for sustainability claims. Inconsistent certification processes and varying criteria across industries make it difficult for consumers to verify the authenticity of green claims. This not only harms firms that genuinely pursue sustainable practices but also erodes overall consumer confidence in green marketing. Addressing this challenge requires firms to prioritize transparency, adhere to recognized certification standards, and invest in third-party verification systems to substantiate their claims (Nisa et al., 2022).

4.5 Additional Challenges

Beyond the core barriers of technology, economics, culture, and greenwashing, firms also face operational and strategic hurdles in implementing eco-innovation, digital transformation, and green marketing. These include:

Resource Constraints: Limited access to skilled personnel, sustainable raw materials, or reliable renewable energy sources can hinder the adoption of eco-innovation practices.

Regulatory Complexity: Navigating a patchwork of environmental regulations across regions can be daunting, particularly for firms operating in global markets. Compliance costs and the risk of non-compliance add to the burden.

Short-Term Focus: Many businesses prioritize short-term financial performance over long-term sustainability goals, leading to underinvestment in eco-innovation and digital transformation.

4.6 Overcoming the Challenges

To address these barriers, firms can adopt a multifaceted approach that combines internal capacity-building, external collaboration, and strategic planning:

Investing in Technology and Training: Governments and industry associations can play a key role in supporting SMEs by providing subsidies, grants, and training programs to enable access to advanced technologies. Similarly, firms must prioritize employee training to build a workforce capable of using digital tools effectively.

Focus on Partnerships: Collaborations with technology providers, research institutions, and sustainability-focused organizations can help firms overcome technical and economic barriers. For example, public-private partnerships can facilitate the development and deployment of eco-innovative solutions on a scale.

Enhancing Transparency and Accountability: To mitigate greenwashing risks, firms should adopt internationally recognized sustainability standards, such as ISO 14001, and invest in third-party audits to validate their claims. Transparent reporting of environmental performance metrics can also build consumer and stakeholder trust.

Driving Cultural Change: Educational initiatives and targeted communication campaigns can help stakeholders understand the importance of sustainability and the long-term benefits of eco-innovation and digital transformation. Engaging employees in sustainability initiatives and aligning corporate values with environmental goals can foster internal cultural shifts.

Reducing Costs Through Innovation: Firms can explore cost-effective eco-innovation solutions, such as modular and scalable technologies, to minimize upfront investments. Additionally, adopting circular economic practices, such as recycling and remanufacturing, can reduce operational costs while supporting sustainability goals.

While the challenges and barriers to adopting eco-innovation, digital transformation, and green marketing are substantial, they are not insurmountable. By addressing technological, economic, cultural, and ethical obstacles, firms can position themselves for success in a rapidly evolving business landscape. The integration of these practices is not only essential for environmental protection but also a strategic imperative for building trust, securing competitive advantage, and achieving long-term sustainability. Businesses that proactively tackle these barriers will be well-equipped to thrive in a future shaped by ecological responsibility and technological advancement.

5 PRACTICAL IMPLICATIONS FOR FIRMS FOR FUTURE TRENDS

The convergence of eco-innovation, digital transformation, and green marketing is reshaping how firms operate in a world increasingly driven by sustainability and technological advancement. For firms to succeed in this rapidly evolving landscape, it is essential to adopt strategic recommendations, build consumer trust, and implement effective measurement and accountability frameworks. By doing so, businesses can align with future trends, strengthen their market position, and contribute positively to environmental goals. Below is a detailed exploration of the practical implications for firms across these key areas.

5.1 Strategic Recommendations

5.1.1 Aligning Digital and Sustainability Strategies

Integrated Planning: To align digital and sustainability strategies effectively, firms must develop comprehensive plans that integrate digital tools with sustainability objectives. For instance, using data analytics platforms can help companies monitor and optimize energy use, reduce waste, and identify areas for eco-innovation. By embedding sustainability into digital transformation projects, businesses can achieve greater efficiency and reduce their environmental footprint.

Smart Operations and Supply Chains: Digital technologies like the Internet of Things (IoT), blockchain, and AI can revolutionize operational processes and supply chains. IoT sensors enable real-time monitoring of resource usage, while AI algorithms can identify inefficiencies and suggest improvements. Blockchain technology ensures transparency and traceability in supply chains, helping firms verify the sustainability of raw materials and products.

Collaboration Platforms: Firms can align digital and sustainability strategies by adopting cloud-based collaboration platforms. These tools facilitate cross-functional teamwork, allowing sustainability and digital transformation teams to work together seamlessly. For example, project management software can track the progress of eco-innovation initiatives while ensuring alignment with digital goals.

Reducing the use of plastic: enterprises and business sector need to limit the use of plastic for the protection of ecosystem particularly in agriculture sector as suggested by the study of (Lakhiar et al., 2024)

Digital Twin Technology: Emerging technologies like digital twins, virtual replicas of physical systems, can support sustainability efforts. By simulating the impact of new eco-innovations or green processes, firms can test their feasibility and refine strategies without incurring unnecessary costs or waste.

Embedded computer control systems: An embedded computer-controlled, laser-guided, air-assisted, variable-rate precision sprayer developed can help to automatically adjust spray outputs on both sides of the sprayer to match the presence, size, shape, and foliage density of tree crops in real time (Shen et al., 2017).

5.1.2 Investing in Green Technology and Skills

Adopting Renewable Energy Solutions: Investing in renewable energy systems, such as solar panels, wind turbines, and energy storage solutions, is a critical step for firms aiming to reduce their carbon footprint. These technologies not only align with sustainability goals but also help firms reduce energy costs over time.

Green Infrastructure Upgrades: Firms should prioritize upgrading their infrastructure to support sustainable operations. For example, retrofitting buildings with energy-efficient systems, such as LED lighting, smart HVAC systems, and water-saving technologies, can significantly lower environmental impact while improving operational efficiency.

Upskilling and Reskilling Employees: As green technologies and digital tools evolve; firms must invest in training programs to equip employees with the necessary skills. Upskilling initiatives should focus on areas like data analytics for sustainability, managing AI-driven systems, and understanding green certifications and compliance requirements.

Partnerships for Innovation: Collaborating with universities, research institutions, and startups can accelerate the adoption of green technologies. Partnerships often provide access to cutting-edge innovations, such as biodegradable materials, carbon capture solutions, and circular economy models.

Modelling techniques for Greenhouse Microclimate (agriculture): Domestication of plants by man through greenhouse crop production has revolutionized agricultural farming systems worldwide. Selecting the appropriate greenhouse technology together with the user-friendly evapotranspiration model can optimize crop water use (Yan et al., 2021).

5.1.3 Building Consumer Trust

Clear Communication: Transparency is the cornerstone of building consumer trust. Firms must communicate their sustainability initiatives, eco-friendly products, and environmental impacts clearly and honestly. Avoiding vague terms like "green" or "sustainable" without substantiating claims ensures credibility.

Third-Party Certifications and Eco-Labels: Obtaining recognized certifications and displaying eco-labels validate sustainability claims and enhance consumer confidence. Certifications such as ENERGY STAR, Fair Trade, or ISO 14001 demonstrate a firm's commitment to sustainability and compliance with rigorous standards.

Consumer Education: Educating consumers about the environmental benefits of eco-innovations and green practices foster trust and engagement. Firms can create content, such as blogs, webinars, or infographics, to explain the science behind their sustainability initiatives and the impact of consumer choices.

Interactive Engagement: Utilizing digital platforms for interactive engagement, such as live Q&A sessions or behind-the-scenes virtual tours of sustainable facilities, can build stronger connections with consumers. Transparency in sharing processes, challenges, and achievements creates an authentic narrative.

Combatting Greenwashing: Firms must ensure that their marketing efforts are backed by credible data and verified practices to avoid greenwashing. Greenwashing not only damages a firm's reputation but also erodes overall consumer trust in sustainable products and services. Implementing third-party audits and adhering to global standards are effective ways to mitigate this risk.

5.1.4 Measurement and Accountability

Defining Relevant Metrics: Key Performance Indicators (KPIs) for eco-innovation, digital transformation, and green marketing should align with a firm's broader sustainability goals. Examples include carbon emissions reductions, energy savings, waste diversion rates, and customer engagement metrics related to green products.

Sustainability Dashboards: Firms should invest in digital dashboards to track and visualize sustainability performance in real-time. These tools provide a centralized view of KPIs, enabling managers to identify trends, make data-driven decisions, and communicate progress to stakeholders.

Regular Reporting: Transparent reporting on sustainability performance is essential for accountability. Annual sustainability reports, aligned with frameworks such as the Global Reporting Initiative (GRI) or the Task Force on Climate-Related Financial Disclosures (TCFD), provide stakeholders with detailed insights into a firm's achievements and areas for improvement.

Life Cycle Assessment (LCA): Conducting life cycle assessments helps firms measure the environmental impact of their products and processes from creation to disposal. LCA results can inform eco-innovation strategies and provide robust data for green marketing campaigns.

Consumer Feedback and Surveys: Measuring the effectiveness of green marketing campaigns requires direct input from consumers. Surveys, reviews, and social media engagement metrics can provide valuable insights into consumer perceptions and preferences, helping firms refine their strategies (Sun et al., 2021).

Benchmarking Against Industry Standards: Firms should benchmark their sustainability performance against industry standards to identify gaps and opportunities for improvement. Peer comparisons can inspire innovative approaches and highlight best practices.

5.2 Future Trends and Opportunities

Integration of Artificial Intelligence (AI): AI will play a critical role in future eco-innovation efforts. Predictive analytics can help firms anticipate sustainability challenges, while machine learning algorithms optimize resource allocation and reduce waste.

Circular Economy Models: The shift toward circular economy models will redefine production and consumption patterns. Firms adopting closed-loop systems, such as recycling and remanufacturing, will not only minimize waste but also create new revenue streams.

Digital Consumer Experiences: Digital technologies like augmented reality (AR) and virtual reality (VR) will revolutionize green marketing by offering immersive consumer experiences. For instance, virtual tours of sustainable supply chains or 3D visualizations of eco-friendly product designs can enhance consumer understanding and trust.

Decentralized Energy Systems: Digital transformation will enable firms to adopt decentralized energy systems, such as microgrids and peer-to-peer energy trading, to enhance energy efficiency and resilience.

Policy-Driven Innovations: Emerging regulations and incentives will create new opportunities for firms to innovate. For example, government mandates for carbon neutrality will drive the adoption of carbon capture technologies and renewable energy solutions.

The future success of firms depends on their ability to adapt to the growing demands for eco-innovation, digital transformation, and green marketing. By aligning digital and sustainability strategies, investing in green technologies and skills, and building consumer trust through transparency and authenticity, firms can secure a competitive edge while contributing to global sustainability goals. Additionally, setting up clear KPIs and using measurement tools ensure accountability and continuous improvement. Firms that embrace these practical implications will not only thrive in the evolving business landscape but also leave a lasting positive impact on the planet and society.

5.2.1 Organizations' Future Plannings

The following are examples of the organization who plan in future to use digital transformation for eco-innovation and green marketing developments.

Table 1. Tesla

Aspect	Details [2]
Eco-Innovation	Tesla is a pioneer in eco-innovation, primarily focusing on electric vehicles (EVs), renewable energy solutions, and energy storage technologies. Over the next five years, Tesla plans to expand its EV lineup with more affordable and energy-efficient models, including the Cybertruck and a new compact EV model. It also aims to scale its solar energy solutions and battery storage capabilities, such as the Powerwall and Megapack, to promote clean energy adoption globally. Tesla's innovations extend to material recycling, including lithium-ion battery recycling, to minimize environmental waste.
Digital Transformation	Tesla heavily integrates digital technology into its products and operations. The company's cars are equipped with advanced software that supports autonomous driving, over-the-air updates, and predictive maintenance. Over the next five years, Tesla plans to enhance its AI capabilities for self-driving technologies and optimize energy consumption in EVs through machine learning. Tesla's Gigafactories are also being automated and digitized to improve production efficiency and sustainability. The company's app and digital ecosystem will continue evolving to provide users with seamless energy management solutions.
Green Marketing	Tesla's marketing strategy revolves around its sustainability mission. The company uses digital platforms and direct consumer engagement to highlight its commitment to a zero-emissions future. Over the next five years, Tesla plans to focus on storytelling around its circular economy practices, renewable energy solutions, and global efforts to combat climate change. Tesla also uses its strong brand presence to educate consumers on the benefits of transitioning to sustainable technologies.
Future Goals	Tesla aims to produce 20 million EVs annually by 2030, significantly contributing to the reduction of global greenhouse gas emissions. In the next five years, it plans to double its manufacturing capacity, particularly in emerging markets. The company is also committed to achieving carbon neutrality in its operations by increasing reliance on renewable energy sources for its Gigafactories. Tesla is exploring innovative technologies, such as hydrogen fuel cells and advanced AI-driven energy optimization, to diversify its eco-innovation portfolio.
Key Initiatives	Key initiatives include expanding the EV charging network globally, increasing battery recycling programs, scaling solar energy adoption, and introducing new AI-driven energy management systems. Tesla is also investing heavily in R&D to improve battery efficiency and exploring partnerships to integrate renewable energy into regional grids worldwide.

Table 2. Unilever

Aspect	Details [3]
Eco-Innovation	Unilever's eco-innovation strategy is centered on creating sustainable consumer products. Its five-year plan includes innovating new biodegradable packaging solutions and reducing the environmental footprint of its products by 50% by 2030. It aims to develop new formulas using plant-based and recycled materials for its product lines, such as cleaning agents and personal care items. Unilever is also investing in circular economy models, focusing on waste reduction and sustainable sourcing practices for raw materials like palm oil and tea.
Digital Transformation	Unilever is embracing digital transformation to optimize its supply chain and improve sustainability tracking. Over the next five years, the company plans to use blockchain to ensure transparency in its sourcing practices and traceability of raw materials. It is also implementing AI-driven analytics to reduce waste in production and logistics. Additionally, Unilever is enhancing its e-commerce platforms to better serve environmentally conscious consumers with personalized product recommendations based on sustainability preferences.
Green Marketing	Unilever has committed to using green marketing to promote its sustainability initiatives. Over the next five years, the company plans to focus on storytelling around its efforts to eliminate fossil-fuel-derived chemicals in cleaning products and to transition to 100% recyclable packaging. Unilever's brands, such as Dove, Hellmann's, and Ben & Jerry's, will emphasize their eco-credentials through digital campaigns, influence partnerships, and sustainability certifications displayed prominently on packaging.
Future Goals	Unilever aims to become a fully net-zero companies by 2039 and halve its environmental impact by 2030. Its five-year targets include reducing greenhouse gas emissions across its operations, eliminating plastic waste, and ensuring 100% of its agricultural raw materials are sustainably sourced. It also plans to scale its water stewardship initiatives to mitigate water scarcity in areas where it operates.
Key Initiatives	Key initiatives include the "Clean Future" program, which focuses on developing sustainable formulations for home care products, and partnerships with technology providers to digitize its supply chain. Unilever is also expanding its reusable and refillable product systems in partnership with retail chains to reduce packaging waste. Investments in renewable energy projects and collaborations with environmental organizations to address biodiversity loss are integral to its strategy.

Table 3. Apple Inc.

Aspect	Details [4]
Eco-Innovation	Apple's commitment to eco-innovation is evident in its focus on renewable energy and product recycling. In the next five years, Apple aims to further enhance its circular economy practices by designing products with 100% recycled and renewable materials. It is also investing in advanced recycling technologies, such as its "Daisy" robot, to efficiently recover valuable components from old devices. Apple plans to expand its renewable energy projects to power all its facilities globally with clean energy.
Digital Transformation	Apple is preferring digital transformation to optimize its supply chain and manufacturing processes. Over the next five years, it plans to expand its use of AI and IoT to monitor energy use, reduce waste, and enhance production efficiency. Apple's digital ecosystem, including the App Store and iCloud, will further promote sustainable consumption by supporting apps and services designed to reduce energy consumption and carbon footprints. The company is also integrating blockchain to ensure transparency in its rare earth mineral sourcing.
Green Marketing	Apple's marketing strategy is heavily focused on its environmental commitment. It prominently showcases its sustainability milestones, such as carbon-neutral operations, through digital campaigns and product launch events. Over the next five years, Apple plans to enhance consumer awareness by integrating sustainability features into its products, such as detailed environmental impact reports for each product sold. It also aims to use augmented reality (AR) experiences to educate customers on recycling and product end-of-life management.
Future Goals	Apple aims to achieve carbon neutrality across its entire supply chain and product life cycle by 2030. In the next five years, the company plans to eliminate the use of plastics in packaging, introduce new energy-efficient technologies in its products, and support global initiatives to reduce electronic waste. It also aims to expand its renewable energy projects, including wind and solar farms, in collaboration with suppliers and local communities.
Key Initiatives	Key initiatives include expanding its recycling programs through trade-in and refurbishment services, collaborating with suppliers to reduce emissions, and investing in green energy projects worldwide. Apple is also exploring the use of AI-driven systems to optimize material use and improve product lifecycle management. Its "Restore Fund," dedicated to removing carbon from the atmosphere through reforestation projects, is a cornerstone of its sustainability efforts.

Table 4. Patagonia (USA)

Aspect	Details (Guerreiro et al., 2023)
Eco-Innovation	Patagonia, a medium-sized outdoor clothing company, is renowned for its commitment to environmental sustainability. The company focuses on eco-innovation by using recycled materials, such as polyester from plastic bottles, and organic cotton in its products. Over the next five years, Patagonia plans to expand its use of regenerative organic farming practices and innovate in textile recycling technologies to create fully circular apparel lines.
Digital Transformation	Patagonia uses digital tools to enhance its sustainability efforts and consumer engagement. It plans to expand its digital transformation by using blockchain for supply chain transparency, ensuring that raw materials are sustainably sourced. Additionally, the company is investing in AI-powered tools to optimize inventory management, reducing waste. Patagonia's e-commerce platform will further integrate educational content to inform consumers about sustainable practices and its products' environmental impacts.
Green Marketing	Patagonia's green marketing is built around its environmental activism. The company uses storytelling to connect with consumers, focusing on issues like climate change and biodiversity conservation. Over the next five years, Patagonia aims to amplify its messaging through digital campaigns and partnerships with environmental organizations. Its commitment to donating 1% of sales to environmental causes and its "Don't Buy This Jacket" campaign underscore its authenticity in promoting sustainable consumption.
Future Goals	Patagonia aims to achieve carbon neutrality by 2025 and transition all its products to renewable and recycled materials. It is committed to influencing industry standards through collaboration and advocacy. The company plans to expand its repair and reuse program, "Worn Wear," to reduce consumption and extend product lifespans.
Key Initiatives	Key initiatives include expanding regenerative agriculture projects, scaling up textile recycling technologies, increasing investment in renewable energy for operations, and growing the "Worn Wear" program. Patagonia is also collaborating with technology partners to innovate in supply chain transparency and consumer education.

6 CONCLUSION

Eco-innovation, digital transformation, and green marketing are not only interconnected but are also critical pillars for building a sustainable and successful business future. Together, they provide a pathway for firms to address pressing environmental challenges, align with shifting consumer demands, and stay competitive in an increasingly sustainability-conscious global market. Eco-innovation is no longer optional, it is a necessity for firms to thrive in a world facing the dual crises of climate change and resource scarcity. By developing sustainable products, processes, and business models, firms can reduce their environmental impact while meeting the demands of eco-conscious stakeholders. However, achieving eco-innovation at scale requires the support of digital transformation. Technologies such as artificial intelligence (AI), blockchain, and the Internet of Things (IoT) enable firms to optimize resource use, monitor supply chain sustainability, and enhance operational efficiency. Digital transformation not only accelerates the implementation of eco-innovations but also provides tools to measure their effectiveness and adapt to evolving regulatory and market conditions.

From these efforts, green marketing strategies naturally emerge. Green marketing is the bridge between a firm's sustainable practices and its consumers, fostering awareness and trust through transparent communication. Digital transformation enhances the effectiveness of green marketing by offering platforms to educate consumers, personalize experiences, and showcase sustainability credentials. For example, firms can use blockchain to verify and display the origin of sustainable products, AI to tailor marketing campaigns for eco-conscious audiences, and digital storytelling tools to engage customers emotionally and intellectually. Through these strategies, businesses can position themselves as leaders in sustainability, cultivating customer loyalty and advocacy.

To make these connections actionable, firms must integrate eco-innovation and digital transformation into their core strategies. This involves investing in sustainable technologies, upskilling employees, and aligning corporate values with environmental goals. Equally important is a commitment to transparency and accountability, as consumers increasingly demand verifiable evidence of sustainability claims. By setting clear sustainability metrics and adhering to global standards, firms can reinforce the credibility of their green marketing campaigns.

Moreover, collaboration is essential. Partnerships with governments, NGOs, and technology providers can help firms access the resources and expertise needed to implement these strategies effectively. By working together, businesses can drive systemic change, influencing industry standards and contributing to global sustainability goals. In conclusion, eco-innovation through digital transformation is not merely a response to environmental challenges, it is an opportunity for firms to redefine their value propositions, unlock new markets, and build lasting relationships with customers. Green marketing completes the cycle, transforming these efforts into compelling narratives that resonate with consumers and inspire action. By embracing these three interconnected concepts, businesses can achieve long-term success while playing a meaningful role in protecting the planet. The future belongs to companies that recognize the urgency of sustainability and harness the power of innovation and technology to lead the way.

7 CASES: (COMPILED BY AUTHOR)

7.1 Case Study 1: IKEA – A Sustainable Future Through Digital Transformation and Eco-Innovation

Case Overview

IKEA, the global leader in affordable home furnishings, has long been committed to sustainability. However, as consumer expectations evolve, the company faces increasing pressure to adopt deeper eco-innovation strategies and incorporate digital transformation to meet ambitious environmental goals. By 2030, IKEA aims to become a fully circular and climate-positive business. Despite these initiatives, the company must address several challenges, including waste reduction, sustainable sourcing, and scaling renewable energy use across its supply chain.

IKEA's future success depends on how its management plans to incorporate digital transformation and eco-innovation. Technologies such as artificial intelligence (AI), blockchain, and the Internet of Things (IoT) provide opportunities to track supply chain sustainability, optimize inventory, and enhance energy efficiency. Additionally, IKEA can explore 3D printing to manufacture furniture components on-demand, reducing waste and transportation emissions. Incorporating these digital tools will help IKEA achieve its circularity goals while enhancing operational efficiency.

In green marketing, IKEA has been effective at communicating its sustainability message, particularly through its campaigns highlighting renewable materials and energy-efficient products. However, future strategies must focus on increasing transparency. For instance, IKEA could use blockchain to provide customers with detailed information about product origins and lifecycle impacts. Moreover, digital storytelling through augmented reality (AR) and virtual reality (VR) can create immersive experiences that engage consumers and build trust in IKEA's sustainability efforts. To achieve these objectives, IKEA's management should prioritize investments in employee training on green technologies, collaboration with innovative startups, and partnerships with suppliers committed to sustainable practices. By integrating eco-innovation with digital tools and crafting compelling green marketing strategies, IKEA can strengthen its position as a sustainability leader in the home furnishing sector.

Discussion Questions

1. What role can AI and IoT play in helping IKEA achieve its circularity and climate-positive goals?

2. How can IKEA effectively use blockchain to enhance supply chain transparency and consumer trust?
3. What innovative approaches could IKEA adopt to reduce waste and emissions while maintaining affordability?
4. How can digital storytelling tools like AR and VR improve IKEA's green marketing campaigns?
5. What are the potential risks and barriers IKEA might face in adopting these digital and eco-innovation strategies?

7.2 Case Study 2: Tesla – Innovating Beyond Electric Vehicles

Case Overview

Tesla has established itself as a market leader in eco-innovation, with its electric vehicles (EVs) and renewable energy solutions revolutionizing the automotive and energy sectors. However, as competition grows and climate targets become more urgent, Tesla must expand its innovative efforts beyond its core EV products to remain a sustainability trailblazer.

Over the next decade, Tesla can explore integrating advanced AI and IoT technologies to create smart mobility ecosystems. For example, Tesla's self-driving technology could be combined with urban planning initiatives to optimize traffic flow and reduce emissions at a city-wide scale. Additionally, Tesla has the potential to innovate in energy storage by developing modular and scalable battery systems for homes, businesses, and public infrastructure.

In the realm of digital transformation, Tesla's over-the-air software updates are a major strength, allowing the company to continuously improve its vehicles and energy solutions. Building on this capability, Tesla could introduce blockchain technology to enhance supply chain transparency and ensure the ethical sourcing of materials like lithium and cobalt. Furthermore, Tesla can employ digital twin technology to simulate and optimize its Gigafactories, reducing waste and energy consumption during production. To enhance green marketing efforts, Tesla's management should focus on educating consumers about its circular economy practices, such as battery recycling programs and solar energy integration. Digital platforms, including Tesla's app and social media channels, can be used to showcase these initiatives, while partnerships with influencers and environmental organizations can amplify the message. By planning for these future initiatives, Tesla can reinforce its position as a leader in sustainability and innovation while addressing the growing expectations of regulators, investors, and environmentally conscious consumers.

Discussion Questions

1. How can Tesla expand its eco-innovation efforts beyond electric vehicles to address broader sustainability challenges?
2. What role does blockchain play in enhancing Tesla's supply chain transparency, particularly for critical materials?
3. How can digital twin technology be used to optimize Tesla's manufacturing processes and reduce waste?
4. What strategies should Tesla employ to educate consumers about its circular economic initiatives?
5. What are the ethical and operational challenges Tesla might face as it scales its energy solutions globally?

REFERENCES

Carrión-Bósquez, N. G., Ortiz-Regalado, O., Veas-González, I., Naranjo-Armijo, F. G., & Guerra-Regalado, W. F. (2024). The mediating role of attitude and environmental awareness in the influence of green advertising and eco-labels on green purchasing behaviors. *Spanish Journal of Marketing - ESIC*. Advance online publication. DOI: 10.1108/SJME-08-2023-0217

Cui, Y., Zhao, C., & Zhang, Q. (2024). Impact of digital transformation in agribusinesses on total factor productivity. *The International Food and Agribusiness Management Review*, *27*(5), 843–857. DOI: 10.22434/ifamr1064

Domorenok, E., & Graziano, P. (2023). Understanding the European Green Deal: A narrative policy framework approach. *European Policy Analysis*, *9*(1), 9–29. DOI: 10.1002/epa2.1168

Durst, S., Hinteregger, C., & Zieba, M. (2024). The effect of environmental turbulence on cyber security risk management and organizational resilience. *Computers & Security*, *137*, 103591. DOI: 10.1016/j.cose.2023.103591

Guerreiro, M., Muhs, C., Neves, M. C., Engel, L., & Cardoso, L. F. (2023). Green marketing: A case study of the outdoor apparel brand Patagonia. *Responsibility and Sustainability*, *8*(2), 49–57.

Lakhiar, I. A., Yan, H., Zhang, J., Wang, G., Deng, S., Bao, R., Zhang, C., Syed, T. N., Wang, B., Zhou, R., & Wang, X. (2024). Plastic pollution in agriculture as a threat to food security, the ecosystem, and the environment: An overview. *Agronomy (Basel)*, *14*(3), 548. DOI: 10.3390/agronomy14030548

Nisa, N. U., Mendoza, S. A. J., & Shamsuddinova, S. (2022). The Concept of Greenwashing and its Impact on Green Trust, Green Risk, and Green Consumer Confusion: A Review-Based Study. *JABS : Journal of Applied Biological Sciences*, *8*(3), 1–18.

Nyamekye, M. B., Martey, E. M., Agbemabiese, G. C., Preko, A. K., Gyepi-Garbrah, T., & Appah, E. (2024). Green marketing strategy, technology implementation and corporate performance: The role of green creative behaviour and institutional isomorphism. *Journal of Contemporary Marketing Science*, *7*(1), 84–109. DOI: 10.1108/JCMARS-09-2023-0038

Peredy, Z., & Feierzhati, F. (2023). Cloud Computing Solutions for Speeding-up the Small and Medium Sized Enterprise (SME's) Businesses in China. [EDUTUS]. *ACTA PERIODICA*, *27*(27), 14–33. DOI: 10.47273/AP.2023.1.14-33

Roh, T., Noh, J., Oh, Y., & Park, K.-S. (2022). Structural relationships of a firm's green strategies for environmental performance: The roles of green supply chain management and green marketing innovation. *Journal of Cleaner Production, 356*, 131877. DOI: 10.1016/j.jclepro.2022.131877

Salnikova, E., Strizhakova, Y., & Coulter, R. A. (2022). Engaging consumers with environmental sustainability initiatives: Consumer global–local identity and global brand messaging. *JMR, Journal of Marketing Research, 59*(5), 983–1001. DOI: 10.1177/00222437221078522

Shao, L., Gong, J., Fan, W., Zhang, Z., & Zhang, M. (2022). Cost comparison between digital management and traditional management of cotton fields—Evidence from cotton fields in Xinjiang, China. *Agriculture, 12*(8), 1105. DOI: 10.3390/agriculture12081105

Shaukat, F., Zaman, H. M. F., Nga, N. T. T., & Souvanhxay, P. (2023). The interplay of eco-innovation and market uncertainty on green marketing orientation and business performance. *Marketing i menedžment innovacij, 14*(4), 48-68.

Shen, Y., Zhu, H., Liu, H., Chen, Y., & Ozkan, E. (2017). Development of a laser-guided, embedded-computer-controlled, air-assisted precision sprayer. *Transactions of the ASABE, 60*(6), 1827–1838. DOI: 10.13031/trans.12455

Sun, Y., Luo, B., Wang, S., & Fang, W. (2021). What you see is meaningful: Does green advertising change the intentions of consumers to purchase eco-labeled products? *Business Strategy and the Environment, 30*(1), 694–704. DOI: 10.1002/bse.2648

Xu, J., Yu, Y., Zhang, M., & Zhang, J. Z. (2023). Impacts of digital transformation on eco-innovation and sustainable performance: Evidence from Chinese manufacturing companies. *Journal of Cleaner Production, 393*, 136278. DOI: 10.1016/j.jclepro.2023.136278

Yan, H., Acquah, S. J., Zhang, J., Wang, G., Zhang, C., & Darko, R. O. (2021). Overview of modelling techniques for greenhouse microclimate environment and evapotranspiration. *International Journal of Agricultural and Biological Engineering, 14*(6), 1–8. DOI: 10.25165/j.ijabe.20211406.3948

Yordanova, Z. (2023). Barriers to Organizations to Adopt Digital Transformation for Driving Eco-Innovation and Sustainable Performance. *International Conference on Optimization, Learning Algorithms and Applications*

ENDNOTES

1 https://www.emarketer.com/content/5-charts-marketers-sustainability

2 https://blog.disfold.com/innovation-sustainability-tesla/

3 https://www.unilever.com/

4 https://www.apple.com/environment/

Compilation of References

Ababneh, O. M. A. (2021). How do green HRM practices affect employees' green behaviors? The role of employee engagement and personality attributes. *Journal of Environmental Planning and Management*, *64*(7), 1204–1226. Advance online publication. DOI: 10.1080/09640568.2020.1814708

Abbas, Q. (2024). Sustainable Marketing in the Age of Environmental Consciousness. *JETIR, 11*.

Abdo, M. S., Ahmed, S. A., Awad, B. K., & Elsharnouby, M. H. (2023). Fostering green purchasing behavior: The moderated mediation role of customer disidentification. *Management & Sustainability: An Arab Review*, *2*(2), 155–176. DOI: 10.1108/MSAR-10-2022-0046

Abdullah, N., & Lim, A. (2023). The Incorporating Sustainable and Green IT Practices in Modern IT Service Operations for an Environmentally Conscious Future. *Journal of Sustainable Technologies and Infrastructure Planning*, *7*(3). https://publications.dlpress.org/index.php/JSTIP/article/view/33

Adebayo, T. S., & Özkan, O. (2024). Investigating the influence of socioeconomic conditions, renewable energy and eco-innovation on environmental degradation in the United States: A wavelet quantile-based analysis. *Journal of Cleaner Production*, *434*, 140321. DOI: 10.1016/j.jclepro.2023.140321

Adegoke, A. A., Oyindamola, K. A., & Offonabo, N. (2024). The Role of HR in Sustainability Initiatives: A Strategic Review. *International Journal of Research in Engineering, Science and Management, 7*(5). https://journal.ijresm.com/index.php/ijresm/article/view/3025

Adekoya, O. (2022). *Responsible Management: Promoting Work-Life Balance through Social Sustainability and Green HRM* (Doctoral dissertation, University of East London). https://repository.uel.ac.uk/item/8qxvz

Adelusola, M. (2024). Sustainable Business Practices: Overcoming Barriers and Leveraging Enablers for Organizational Adoption. https://www.researchgate.net/profile/Michael-Adelusola/publication/385652688_Sustainable_Business_Practices_Overcoming_Barriers_and_Leveraging_Enablers_for_Organizational_Adoption/links/672df86b2326b47637d198eb/Sustainable-Business-Practices-Overcoming-Barriers-and-Leveraging-Enablers-for-Organizational-Adoption.pdf

Adewole, O. (2022). "Issues emanating from business impact on climate, environmental sustainability and CSR (Corporate Social Responsibility): steps towards pragmatism in extant realities":"Brand translation to equity from 'CSR as a potential tool in climate change mitigation and enhancing financial performances in organizations" Brand translation to equity. *International Journal of Corporate Social Responsibility*, *7*(1), 6. DOI: 10.1186/s40991-022-00073-1

Adidas. (n.d.). Our targets. Adidas Group. Retrieved from https://www.adidas-group.com/en/sustainability/focus-on-sustainability/our-targets?utm_source=chatgpt.com

Adjei-Bamfo, P., Bempong, B., Osei, J., & Kusi-Sarpong, S. (2020). Green candidate selection for organizational environmental management. *International Journal of Manpower*, *41*(7), 1081–1096. DOI: 10.1108/IJM-10-2019-0480

Admin. (2023). The rise of green consumerism. ET2C International. Retrieved from https://et2c.com/news/the-rise-of-green-consumerism/

Admin. (2024). Overcoming barriers to sustainable consumer habits. Sustainable Living. Retrieved from https://sustainableliving.org.nz/overcoming-barriers-to-sustainable-consumer-habits/

Agnihotri, A., & Bhattacharya, S. (2023). *Wipro's Journey Towards Regaining a Market Leadership Position*. SAGE Publications: SAGE Business Cases Originals. https://doi.org/DOI: 10.4135/9781529621945

Ahmad, N., Samad, S., & Han, H. (2024). Charting new terrains: How CSR initiatives shape employee creativity and contribute to UN-SDGs in a knowledge-driven world. *Journal of Innovation & Knowledge*, *9*(4), 100557. Advance online publication. DOI: 10.1016/j.jik.2024.100557

Ahmed, M. A. (2023). Innovations in Human Resource Management: A Contemporary Perspective. *Journal of Management & Social Science*, *1*(1). http://www.rjmss.com/index.php/7/article/view/3

Ahmed, W., & Ahmed, I. H. (2022). Interconnection of Green Marketing and Green Human Resource Management Functions. *Macro Management & Public Policies*, *4*(3), 7–13. DOI: 10.30564/mmpp.v4i3.5063

Aiswarya, U. B., Harindranath, R. M., & Challapalli, P. (2024). Social Media Information Sharing: Is It a Catalyst for Green Consumption among Gen X and Gen Y Cohorts? *Sustainability (Basel), 16*(14), 6011. DOI: 10.3390/su16146011

Aivalis, C. J., Gatziolis, K., & Boucouvalas, A. C. (2016). Evolving analytics for e-commerce applications: Utilizing big data and social media extensions. *2016 International Conference on Telecommunications and Multimedia (TEMU)*

Ajayi, O. A. (2024). *Implementing Environmental, Social, and Governance (ESG) Principles in Organizations: The Role of Leadership and Impacts on Corporate Financial Performance* (Doctoral dissertation, Case Western Reserve University). https://rave.ohiolink.edu/etdc/view?acc_num=case171235193083631

Akhtar, S., Tian, H., Iqbal, S., & Hussain, R. Y. (2024). Environmental regulations and government support drive green innovation performance: Role of competitive pressure and digital transformation. *Clean Technologies and Environmental Policy, 26*(12), 1–21. DOI: 10.1007/s10098-024-02857-4

Akhtar, U. A., Muhammad, R., Bakar, L. J. A., Parameswaranpillai, V., Raj, B., & Khan, N. B. (2023). Green Human Resource Management Bibliometric Analysis of the Published Literature from 2008 to 2022. *International Journal of Professional Business Review: Int.J. Prof. Bus. Rev., 8*(4), 1.

Alboqami, H. (2023). Trust me, I'm an influencer! - Causal recipes for customer trust in artificial intelligence influencers in the retail industry. *Journal of Retailing and Consumer Services, 72*, 103242. DOI: 10.1016/j.jretconser.2022.103242

Alhamami, A., Petri, I., Rezgui, Y., & Kubicki, S. (2020). Promoting energy efficiency in the built environment through adapted bim training and education. *Energies, 13*(9), 2308. DOI: 10.3390/en13092308

Aliano, M., Cestari, G., & Madonna, S. (2024). Greenwashing. In *Sustainable Finance for SMEs: The Role of Capital for Sustainable and Inclusive Growth.* Springer Nature Switzerland., DOI: 10.1007/978-3-031-74193-7_7

Ali, B., Fatima, M., & Ahmed, Q. M. (2023). Examining the Theory of Planned Behaviour in Green Purchasing Behaviour – A Case of Millennial's Consumption of Organic Food. *Foundation University Journal of Business & Economics, 8*(1). Advance online publication. DOI: 10.33897/fujbe.v8i1.707

Ali, M., Puah, C. H., Ali, A., Raza, S. A., & Ayob, N. (2022). Green intellectual capital, green HRM and green social identity toward sustainable environment: A new integrated framework for Islamic banks. *International Journal of Manpower, 43*(3), 614–638. Advance online publication. DOI: 10.1108/IJM-04-2020-0185

Ali, W., Mahmood, Z., Wilson, J., & Ismail, H. (2023). The impact of sustainability governance attributes on comprehensive CSR reporting: A developing country setting. *Corporate Social Responsibility and Environmental Management, 31*(3), 1802–1817. DOI: 10.1002/csr.2677

Allchin, J. (2013). Case study: Patagonia;s 'Don't buy this jacket' campaign. https://www.marketingweek.com/case-study-patagonias-dont-buy-this-jacket-campaign/

AlQudah, M. Z., Samara, H., Qudah, H., Nazzal, R., Yousef Bani Hani, L., Radwan, R. A., & Alrahamneh, S. (2024). Financial technology's role in advancing social responsibility: a bibliometric review of research progress and future opportunities. *International Journal of Law and Management.*

Al-Swidi, A. K., Gelaidan, H. M., & Saleh, R. M. (2021). The joint impact of green human resource management, leadership and organizational culture on employees' green behaviour and organisational environmental performance. *Journal of Cleaner Production, 316*, 128112. DOI: 10.1016/j.jclepro.2021.128112

Alzghool, M. Z. (2021). Case study: IKEA'S organizational culture and rewards management. http://dx.doi.org/DOI: 10.13140/RG.2.2.30263.44969

Alzu'bi, R. M., & Kontor, E. (2023). The Impact of Green Marketing Strategies on Employees Green Performance: An HRM Perspective. *Economica, 14*(3-4), 83–92.

Amalfi India. (n.d.). About us. Amalfi India. Retrieved from https://www.amalfiindia.com/about-us

Amir, T. S., & Sabri, R. (2023). *The Grass Is Greener Where You Water It!* Entrepreneurship and Green Finance Practices., DOI: 10.1108/978-1-80455-678-820231001

Anand, I. (2024). Unifying Green HRM With Sustainable Development Goals. *Implementing ESG Frameworks Through Capacity Building and Skill Development*, 237. https://books.google.com/books?hl=en&lr=&id=_9s2EQAAQBAJ&oi=fnd&pg=PA237&dq=Anand,+I.+(2024).+Unifying+Green+HRM+With+Sustainable+Development+Goals.+Implementing+ESG+Frameworks+Through+Capacity+Building+and+Skill+Development,+237.&ots=vjsOQfQDWH&sig=5fNAyLZfN2XcZd1QW0WKOc7sOEk

Annan-Diab, F., & Molinari, C. (2017). Interdisciplinarity: Practical approach to advancing education for sustainability and for the Sustainable Development Goals. *International Journal of Management Education, 15*(2), 73–83. DOI: 10.1016/j.ijme.2017.03.006

Apaolaza, V., Policarpo, M. C., Hartmann, P., Paredes, M. R., & D'Souza, C. (2023). Sustainable clothing: Why conspicuous consumption and greenwashing matter. *Business Strategy and the Environment*, *32*(6), 3766–3782. DOI: 10.1002/bse.3335

Aranganathan, P. (2018). Green recruitment: A new-fangled approach to attract and retain talent. *International Journal of Business Management & Research*, *8*(2), 69–76. DOI: 10.24247/ijbmrapr20189

Aris, F., Ismail, K., & Mohezar, S. (2022). Fostering mobile payment adoption: A case of Near Field Communication (NFC). *International Journal of Business and Society*, *23*(3), 1535–1553.

Arnaud, S., & Wasieleski, D. M. (2014). Corporate humanistic responsibility: Social performance through managerial discretion of the HRM. *Journal of Business Ethics*, *120*(3), 313–334. Advance online publication. DOI: 10.1007/s10551-013-1652-z

Arulrajah, A. A., & Opatha, H. (2016). Analytical and theoretical perspectives on green human resource management: A simplified underpinning.

Arzo, S., & Hong, M. (2024). Resilient green infrastructure: Navigating environmental resistance for sustainable development, social mobility in climate change policy. *Heliyon*, *10*(13), e33524. Advance online publication. DOI: 10.1016/j.heliyon.2024.e33524 PMID: 39035491

Assaad, R., & El-Adaway, I. H. (2021). Guidelines for responding to COVID-19 pandemic: Best practices, impacts, and future research directions. *Journal of Management Engineering*, *37*(3), 06021001. Advance online publication. DOI: 10.1061/(ASCE)ME.1943-5479.0000906

Attah, R. U., Ogunsola, O., & Garba, B. (2023). Leadership in the digital age: Emerging trends in business strategy, innovation, and technology integration. *Iconic Research and Engineering Journals*, *6*(9), 389–411.

Bansal Gupta, A., & Agarwal, S. (2022). Green consumption: Awareness and purchase decisions. Management Journal for Advanced Research, 2(3), 10-17. Retrieved from https://ssrn.com/abstract=4315987

Bansal, P., & Dhir, A. (2023). Tactics and strategies in green marketing orientation: An analysis of best practices. *Journal of Sustainable Marketing*, *11*(2), 122–140.

Barker, L. (2021). Digital compliance and environmental advertising. *International Journal of Consumer Protection*, *34*(2), 78–99.

Barker, L. (2021). Navigating the FTC Green Guides. *Journal of Consumer Protection*, *45*(3), 67–82.

Bashynska, I., Lewicka, D., Filyppova, S., & Prokopenko, O. (2024). *Green Innovation in Central and Eastern Europe*. Taylor & Francis., DOI: 10.4324/9781003492771

Bass, S., Dalal-Clayton, B., & Pretty, J. (1995). Participation in strategies for sustainable development.

Bataineh, M. J., Sánchez-Sellero, P., & Ayad, F. (2024). Green is the new black: How research and development and green innovation provide businesses a competitive edge. *Business Strategy and the Environment*, *33*(2), 1004–1023. DOI: 10.1002/bse.3533

Beigi, M., Callahan, J., & Michaelson, C. (2019). A critical plot twist: Changing characters and foreshadowing the future of organizational storytelling. *International Journal of Management Reviews*, *21*(4), 447–465. DOI: 10.1111/ijmr.12203

Bell, J. (2024). 15 sustainability certifications for conscious consumption. Sustainable Jungle. Retrieved from https://www.sustainablejungle.com/sustainability-certifications/

Ben Schoon. (2019, December 24). *YouTubers successfully plant 20 million trees in less than 2 months w/ #TeamTrees*. https://9to5google.com/2019/12/24/youtube-teamtree-success-20-million/

Benevene, P., & Buonomo, I. (2020). Green human resource management: An evidence-based systematic literature review. *Sustainability (Basel)*, *12*(15), 5974. Advance online publication. DOI: 10.3390/su12155974

Benitez, J., Ruiz, L., Castillo, A., & Llorens, J. (2020). How corporate social responsibility activities influence employer reputation: The role of social media capability. *Decision Support Systems*, *129*, 113223. Advance online publication. DOI: 10.1016/j.dss.2019.113223

Berg, A., Chemlal Ärlemalm, S., & Flodin, F. (2023). Surviving Resource Scarcity: A qualitative study about how private firms can overcome obstacles in resource-scarce environments. https://www.diva-portal.org/smash/record.jsf?pid=diva2:1763484

Bhardwaj, A., Gupta, A., & Tawangar, S. (2024). CSR in engineering education: Evidences from India and abroad. *International Journal of Business Innovation and Research*, *34*(1), 19–40. Advance online publication. DOI: 10.1504/IJBIR.2024.138139

Bhukya, R., & Paul, J. (2023). Social influence research in consumer behavior: What we learned and what we need to learn? – A hybrid systematic literature review. *Journal of Business Research*, *162*, 113870. DOI: 10.1016/j.jbusres.2023.113870

Bilderback, S. (2024). Integrating training for organizational sustainability: The application of Sustainable Development Goals globally. *European Journal of Training and Development*, *48*(7/8), 730–748. Advance online publication. DOI: 10.1108/EJTD-01-2023-0005

Binnuri, A., & M, R. (2024). Consumerism, sustainable consumption, and consumer citizenship in the Indian context. *Cogent Business & Management*, *11*(1), 2428777. Advance online publication. DOI: 10.1080/23311975.2024.2428777

Blewitt, J. (2012). *Understanding sustainable development.* Routledge., DOI: 10.4324/9781849773645

Boçe, M. T., & Hoxha, J. (2024). Blockchain Technology as a Catalyst for Sustainable Development: Exploring Economic, Social, and Environmental Synergies. *Academic Journal of Interdisciplinary Studies, 13.*

Boerman, S. C., Meijers, M. H. C., & Zwart, W. (2022). The Importance of Influencer-Message Congruence When Employing *Greenfluencers* to Promote Pro-Environmental Behavior. *Environmental Communication*, *16*(7), 920–941. DOI: 10.1080/17524032.2022.2115525

Boiral, O. (2009). Greening the corporation through organizational citizenship behaviors. *Journal of Business Ethics*, *87*(2), 221–236. Advance online publication. DOI: 10.1007/s10551-008-9881-2

Bombiak, E. (2019). Green human resource management–the latest trend or strategic necessity? *Entrepreneurship and Sustainability Issues*, *6*(4), 1647–1662. DOI: 10.9770/jesi.2019.6.4(7)

Borah, P. S., Dogbe, C. S. K., Dzandu, M. D., & Pomegbe, W. W. K. (2023). Forging organizational resilience through green value co-creation: The role of green technology, green operations, and green transaction capabilities. *Business Strategy and the Environment*, *32*(8), 5734–5747. DOI: 10.1002/bse.3446

Borah, P. S., Dogbe, C. S. K., & Marwa, N. (2024). Generation Z's green purchase behavior: Do green consumer knowledge, consumer social responsibility, green advertising, and green consumer trust matter for sustainable development? *Business Strategy and the Environment*, *33*(5), 4530–4546. DOI: 10.1002/bse.3714

Borah, P. S., Dogbe, C. S. K., & Marwa, N. (2025). Green dynamic capability and green product innovation for sustainable development: Role of green operations, green transaction, and green technology development capabilities. *Corporate Social Responsibility and Environmental Management*, *32*(1), 911–926. DOI: 10.1002/csr.2993

Borah, P. S., Dogbe, C. S. K., Pomegbe, W. W. K., Bamfo, B. A., & Hornuvo, L. K. (2023b). Green market orientation, green innovation capability, green knowledge acquisition and green brand positioning as determinants of new product success. *European Journal of Innovation Management, 26*(2), 364–385. DOI: 10.1108/EJIM-09-2020-0345

Borah, P. S., Pomegbe, W. W. K., & Dogbe, C. S. K. (2022). Mediating role of green marketing orientation in stakeholder risk and new product success relationship among European multinational enterprises in Ghana. *Society and Business Review, 17*(4), 485–505. DOI: 10.1108/SBR-02-2021-0035

Bosco, M. C. (2017). From Yosemite to a Global Market: How Patagonia, Inc. has Created an Environmentally Sustainable and Socially Equitable Model of Supply-Chain Management. https://scholarship.claremont.edu/pomona_theses/178/

Boyce, M. E. (2017). Organizational story and storytelling: a critical review. *The Aesthetic Turn in Management*, 233-254.

Buller, P. F., & McEvoy, G. M. (2016). A model for implementing a sustainability strategy through HRM practices. *Business and Society Review, 121*(4), 465–495. Advance online publication. DOI: 10.1111/basr.12099

Burke, N. (2023). *Transforming sustainable food systems through transparency and digital inclusion*. https://blogs.cisco.com/our-corporate-purpose/transforming-sustainable-food-systems-through-transparency-and-digital-inclusion

Business Research Insights. (n.d.). Car pooling market growth, size, share and forecast [2033]. Retrieved from https://www.businessresearchinsights.com/market-reports/car-pooling-market-108249

Butar Butar, S., Ambarita, N., & Haniva, R. (2024). Green awareness and green product: A direction for sustainable consumption. *Applied Environmental Science, 1*(2). Advance online publication. DOI: 10.61511/aes.v1i2.2024.342

Caldevilla-Domínguez, D., Barrientos-Báez, A., & Padilla-Castillo, G. (2021). *COVID-19 as a Trigger for Sustainable Tourism and Eco-Influencers on Twitter*. DOI: 10.20944/preprints202101.0636.v1

Callan, V. J., Johnston, M. A., & Poulsen, A. L. (2015). How organisations are using blended e-learning to deliver more flexible approaches to trade training. *Journal of Vocational Education and Training, 67*(3), 294–309. DOI: 10.1080/13636820.2015.1050445

Cambridge Dictionary. (n.d.). Consumerism. Retrieved from https://dictionary.cambridge.org/dictionary/english/consumerism

Camilleri, M. A., Cricelli, L., Mauriello, R., & Strazzullo, S. (2023). Consumer perceptions of sustainable products: A systematic literature review. *Sustainability (Basel), 15*(11), 8923. DOI: 10.3390/su15118923

Cao, Y., Kou, F., Hu, H., & Wan, G. (2022). How gamified cooperation and com petition motivate low-carbon actions: An investigation of gamification in a popular online payment platform in China. *Journal of Environmental Management, 324*, 116259. DOI: 10.1016/j.jenvman.2022.116259 PMID: 36174473

Capital One Shopping Research. (2025, March 1). *Eco-Conscious Consumer Statistics*. https://capitaloneshopping.com/research/eco-conscious-consumer-statistics/

Capital One Shopping. (2025). Eco-conscious consumer statistics: Latest data & trends. Capital One Shopping. Retrieved from https://capitaloneshopping.com/research/eco-conscious-consumer-statistics/

Carbon Trust. (n.d.). Climate action plans & business sustainability. Retrieved from https://www.carbontrust.com/en-as

Carrión-Bósquez, N. G., Ortiz-Regalado, O., Veas-González, I., Naranjo-Armijo, F. G., & Guerra-Regalado, W. F. (2024). The mediating role of attitude and environmental awareness in the influence of green advertising and eco-labels on green purchasing behaviors. *Spanish Journal of Marketing - ESIC*. Advance online publication. DOI: 10.1108/SJME-08-2023-0217

Carter, R. L., & Simmons, B. (2010). The history and philosophy of environmental education. *The inclusion of environmental education in science teacher education*. https://doi.org/DOI: 10.1007/978-90-481-9222-9_1

Cascio, W. F., & Graham, B. Z. (2016). New strategic role for HR: Leading the employer-branding process. *Organizational Management Journal, 13*(4), 182–192. Advance online publication. DOI: 10.1080/15416518.2016.1244640

Castillo-Abdul, B., Romero-Rodríguez, L. M., & Fernández-Rodríguez, C. (2024). Lifestyle Eco-Influencers Advertising: Is Engagement Driven by Content or Fandom? *Comunicação e Sociedade, 45*, e024014. DOI: 10.17231/comsoc.45(2024).5629

CB. (2024). Business leader, climate and equality campaigner, co-author of "Net Positive: how courageous companies thrive by giving more than they take", a Financial Times Business Book of the Year. #3 Thinkers50; former CEO, Unilever. Retrieved from https://competentboards.com/faculty/paul-polman/#:~:text=Paul%20Polman%20works%20to%20accelerate,Goals%2C%20which%20he%20helped%20develop

Centric Software, Inc. (2025). The greener picture: Navigating the consumer goods sustainability landscape. Centric Software. Retrieved from https://www.centricsoftware.com/blog/the-greener-picture-consumer-goods-sustainability/

Chadee, D., Wiesner, R., & Roxas, B. (2011). Environmental sustainability change management in SMEs: Learning from sustainability champions. *International Journal of Learning and Change*, *5*(3-4), 194–207. DOI: 10.1504/IJLC.2011.045068

Chahal, A., Gulia, P., & Gill, N. S. (2022). Different analytical frameworks and bigdata model for internet of things. *Indonesian Journal of Electrical Engineering and Computer Science*, *25*(2), 1159–1166. DOI: 10.11591/ijeecs.v25.i2.pp1159-1166

Chaihanchanchai, P., & Anantachart, S. (2023). Encouraging green product purchase: Green value and environmental knowledge as moderators of attitude and behavior relationship. *Business Strategy and the Environment*, *32*(1), 289–303. DOI: 10.1002/bse.3130

Chams, N., & García-Blandón, J. (2019). On the importance of sustainable human resource management for the adoption of sustainable development goals. *Resources, Conservation and Recycling*, *141*, 109–122. Advance online publication. DOI: 10.1016/j.resconrec.2018.10.006

Chandrasekara, D. T. (2022). *Digital Social Influence: Reframing Social Influence for Online Social Networks*. 6648356 Bytes. DOI: 10.26180/19319933.V1

Chang, Y. L., & Ke, J. (2024). Socially responsible artificial intelligence empowered people analytics: A novel framework towards sustainability. *Human Resource Development Review*, *23*(1), 88–120. Advance online publication. DOI: 10.1177/15344843231200930

Chaudhary, R. (2020). Green human resource management and employee green behavior: An empirical analysis. *Corporate Social Responsibility and Environmental Management*, *27*(2), 630–641. Advance online publication. DOI: 10.1002/csr.1827

Chen, C., Li, Z., Yang, S., & Cao, D. (2024). Driving eco-friendly product purchases through social media: How does peer influence work? *Journal of Consumer Behaviour*, cb.2400. DOI: 10.1002/cb.2400

Chen, B., & Madni, G. R. (2023). Achievement of sustainable environment through effectiveness of social media in Z generation of China. *PLoS One*, *18*(11), e0292403. DOI: 10.1371/journal.pone.0292403 PMID: 37967117

Chen, C.-T., Chen, S.-C., Khan, A., Lim, M. K., & Tseng, M.-L. (2024). Big data analytics-artificial intelligence and supply chain ambidexterity impacts on corporate image and green communication. *Industrial Management & Data Systems, 124*(10), 2899–2918. DOI: 10.1108/IMDS-01-2024-0045

Chen, G., Sabir, A., Rasheed, M. F., Belascu, L., & Su, C.-W. (2024). Green marketing horizon: Industry sustainability through marketing and innovation. *Journal of Innovation & Knowledge, 9*(4), 100606. DOI: 10.1016/j.jik.2024.100606

Chen, M., & Liu, X. (2023). AI-driven compliance monitoring in sustainable marketing. *Journal of Marketing Ethics, 19*(4), 123–141.

Chen, M., Liu, X., & Wong, J. (2023). Digital Green Marketing and Consumer Perception. *Marketing & Sustainability Review, 15*(2), 90–112.

Chen, W. H., Yang, Y. M., & Chen, H. N. (2024). Determinants of Carbon Inventory and Systematic Innovation Methods to Analyze the Strategies of Carbon Reduction: An Empirical Study of Green Lean Management in Electroplating an Factory. *Sustainability (Basel), 16*(19), 8301. Advance online publication. DOI: 10.3390/su16198301

Chen, Y., Tang, G., Jin, J., Li, J., & Paillé, P. (2015). Linking market orientation and environmental performance: The influence of environmental strategy, employee's environmental involvement, and environmental product quality. *Journal of Business Ethics, 127*(2), 479–500. Advance online publication. DOI: 10.1007/s10551-014-2059-1

Cho, B.-K., Park, J.-Y., & Lee, Y.-K. (2023). Do green practices and green image promote consumers' participation in social network sites (SNS)? *Journal of Hospitality Marketing & Management, 32*(5), 631–648. DOI: 10.1080/19368623.2023.2191595

Choi, J., Kim, H., & Lee, S. (2021). Eco-labeling systems in Asia. *Sustainability Report, 18*(5), 233–251.

Chou, C.-J. (2014). Hotels' environmental policies and employee personal environmental beliefs: Interactions and outcomes. *Tourism Management, 40*, 436–446. DOI: 10.1016/j.tourman.2013.08.001

Chowdhury, S., Lau, H. S., & Zhang, D. (2023). Strategic approaches to green market orientation and consumer response. *Journal of Environmental Marketing Research, 15*(3), 245–259.

Christy Dawn. (n.d.). Regenerative, ethical & timeless dresses & accessories. Christy Dawn. Retrieved from https://christydawn.com/en-in

Chuchu, T., Maziriri, E. T., & Mototo, L. (2020). A review of the impact of consumerism, recycling and pollution: Evidence from Southeast Asia: 1999 to 2019. *Journal of Environmental Management and Tourism*, *11*(1), 23–28. https://repository.up.ac.za/bitstream/handle/2263/74316/Chuchu_Review_2020.pdf. DOI: 10.14505//jemt.v11.1(41).03

Clark, S., MacLachlan, M., Marshall, K., Morahan, N., Carroll, C., Hand, K., Boyle, N., & O'Sullivan, K. (2022). Including Digital Connection in the United Nations Sustainable Development Goals: A Systems Thinking Approach for Achieving the SDGs. *Sustainability (Basel)*, *14*(3), 1883. DOI: 10.3390/su14031883

Coca-Cola. (2018). World without waste strategy guidebook.

Costello, N. (2024). The best online stores for affordable secondhand & vintage clothing. Sustainably Chic. Retrieved from https://www.sustainably-chic.com/blog/thrift-shops-secondhand-vintage-clothing

Craig, C., & Allen, M. (2013). Sustainability information sources: Employee knowledge, perceptions, and learning. *Journal of Communication Management (London)*, *17*(4), 292–307. DOI: 10.1108/JCOM-05-2012-0035

Cronin, J. J.Jr, Smith, J. S., Gleim, M. R., Ramirez, E., & Martinez, J. D. (2011). Green marketing strategies: An examination of stakeholders and the opportunities they present. *Journal of the Academy of Marketing Science*, *39*(1), 158–174. DOI: 10.1007/s11747-010-0227-0

Cui, Y., Zhao, C., & Zhang, Q. (2024). Impact of digital transformation in agribusinesses on total factor productivity. *The International Food and Agribusiness Management Review*, *27*(5), 843–857. DOI: 10.22434/ifamr1064

D'Adamo, I., González-Sánchez, R., Medina-Salgado, M. S., & Settembre-Blundo, D. (2021). E-Commerce Calls for Cyber-Security and Sustainability: How European Citizens Look for a Trusted Online Environment. *Sustainability (Basel)*, *13*(12), 6752. DOI: 10.3390/su13126752

Dacin, M. T., Dacin, P. A., Greenwood, R., Oliver, C., Sahlin, K., & Suddaby, R. (2008). Traditions as institutionalized practice: Implications for deinstitutionalization. *The Sage handbook of organizational institutionalism, 327*, 352.

Dalakishvili, R., & Tchanturia, N. (2024). Renewable energy for long-term, green progress. *Reviews of Modern Science*, (5).

Dangelico, R. M., & Vocalelli, D. (2017). "Green Marketing": An analysis of definitions, strategy steps, and tools through a systematic review of the literature. *Journal of Cleaner Production*, *165*, 1263–1279. DOI: 10.1016/j.jclepro.2017.07.184

Darban, K., & Kabbaj, S. (2023). The Transformative Potential of AI in Green Marketing Strategies. *Traditional Journal of Law and Social Sciences*, *2*(02), 14–38.

de Oliveira Lima, L. A., da Silva, J. M. S., de Oliveira Santos, A., Marques, F. R. V., da Silva Leão, A. P., Carvalho, M. D. C. L., & Ferreira, A. B. S. (2024). The Influence of Green Marketing on Consumer Purchase Intention: A Systematic Review. *Revista de Gestão Social e Ambiental*, *18*(3), 1–11.

de Sio, S., Zamagni, A., Casu, G., & Gremigni, P. (2022). Green trust as a mediator in the relationship between green advertising skepticism, environmental knowledge, and intention to buy green food. *International Journal of Environmental Research and Public Health*, *19*(24), 16757. DOI: 10.3390/ijerph192416757 PMID: 36554638

Deng, Z., & Guo, M. (2024). Research on the impact of the application of artificial intelligence technology on the sustainable development of mobile e-commerce. *Benchmarking*, *31*(9), 3349–3372. DOI: 10.1108/BIJ-11-2022-0697

Departments, U. W. (2024). *International Student Carbon Footprint Challenge*. https://depts.washington.edu/i2sea/iscfc/index.php

Dhirani, L. L., Mukhtiar, N., Chowdhry, B. S., & Newe, T. (2023). Ethical dilemmas and privacy issues in emerging technologies: A review. *Sensors (Basel)*, *23*(3), 1151. DOI: 10.3390/s23031151 PMID: 36772190

Dionisio, M., De Souza, S. J.Junior, Paula, F., & Pellanda, P. C. (2023). The role of digital social innovations to address SDGs: A systematic review. *Environment, Development and Sustainability*, *26*(3), 5709–5734. DOI: 10.1007/s10668-023-03038-x PMID: 36855437

Dogbe, C. S. K., & Marwa, N. (2024). Digital Orientation and Manufacturing Firms' Green Innovation Performance: The Mediating Role of Green Competence. *Journal of Risk and Financial Management*, *17*(10), 430. DOI: 10.3390/jrfm17100430

Domorenok, E., & Graziano, P. (2023). Understanding the European Green Deal: A narrative policy framework approach. *European Policy Analysis*, *9*(1), 9–29. DOI: 10.1002/epa2.1168

Douglas, B. D., & Brauer, M. (2021). Gamification to prevent climate change: A review of games and apps for sustainability. *Current Opinion in Psychology*, *42*, 89–94. DOI: 10.1016/j.copsyc.2021.04.008 PMID: 34052619

Dudarenok, A. (2023). *The top social commerce trends in China that brands can learn from* [Https://www.campaignasia.com/article/the-top-social-commerce-trends-in-china-that-brands-can-learn-from/491480].

Dulebohn, J. H., & Johnson, R. D. (2013). Human resource metrics and decision support: A classification framework. *Human Resource Management Review*, *23*(1), 71–83. Advance online publication. DOI: 10.1016/j.hrmr.2012.06.005

Durst, S., Hinteregger, C., & Zieba, M. (2024). The effect of environmental turbulence on cyber security risk management and organizational resilience. *Computers & Security*, *137*, 103591. DOI: 10.1016/j.cose.2023.103591

Dyer, G., & Dyer, M. (2017). Strategic leadership for sustainability by higher education: The American College & University Presidents' Climate Commitment. *Journal of Cleaner Production*, *140*, 111–116. DOI: 10.1016/j.jclepro.2015.08.077

Elemure, I., Dhakal, H. N., Leseure, M., & Radulovic, J. (2023). Integration of lean green and sustainability in manufacturing: A review on current state and future perspectives. *Sustainability (Basel)*, *15*(13), 10261. Advance online publication. DOI: 10.3390/su151310261

Elizaveta, S. (2021). Sustainable innovations of IKEA company. https://dspace.spbu.ru/bitstream/11701/30844/2/reviewSV_Otzyv_NR_2021_E.Safronova.pdf

Ericsson, A. (2018). Organizational Culture and Employee Loyalty: The Case of IKEA. https://www.diva-portal.org/smash/record.jsf?pid=diva2:1192802

Escursell, S., Llorach-Massana, P., & Roncero, M. B. (2021). Sustainability in e-commerce packaging: A review. *Journal of Cleaner Production*, *280*, 124314. DOI: 10.1016/j.jclepro.2020.124314 PMID: 32989345

Essiz, O., & Mandrik, C. (2021). Intergenerational influence on sustainable consumer attitudes and behaviors: Roles of family communication and peer influence in environmental consumer socialization. *Psychology and Marketing*. Advance online publication. DOI: 10.1002/mar.21540

European Commission. (2023). Digital sustainability advertising: Green Claims Directive. *Journal of European Law*, *14*(2), 89–112.

European Commission. (2023). Green marketing and compliance: The evolution of digital sustainability regulations. *European Law Review*, *18*(2), 78–96.

European Commission. (2023). Proposal for a Directive on Green Claims. *European Law Journal*, *16*(1), 45–67.

European Commission. (2023). Proposal for a Directive on Green Claims. Retrieved from https://ec.europa.eu

Ewing, J. (2017). *Faster, Higher, Farther: The Volkswagen Scandal*. Random House.

Fagarasan, C., Cristea, C., Cristea, M., Popa, O., & Pisla, A. (2023). Integrating sustainability metrics into project and portfolio performance assessment in agile software development: A data-driven scoring model. *Sustainability (Basel), 15*(17), 13139. DOI: 10.3390/su151713139

Fahad, F. (2023). Green building materials: Aim, components, features, and list. Earth Reminder. Retrieved from https://www.earthreminder.com/green-building-materials/

Faqih, K. M. S. (2022). Internet shopping in the Covid-19 era: Investigating the role of perceived risk, anxiety, gender, culture, and trust in the consumers' purchasing behavior from a developing country context. *Technology in Society, 70*, 101992. https://doi.org/https://doi.org/10.1016/j.techsoc.2022.101992. DOI: 10.1016/j.techsoc.2022.101992

Farooq, H., Bilal Majid, M. B. M., & Ahmed, H. (2023). Impact of Green Packaging, Perceived Consumer Effectiveness, and Social Influence on Green Consumption Behavior: The Mediating Role of Green Satisfaction and the Moderating Role of Environmental Awareness. *Global Management Sciences Review, VIII*(I), 54–69. DOI: 10.31703/gmsr.2023(VIII-I).04

Farris, P. W., Bendle, N., Pfeifer, P., & Reibstein, D. (2020). *Marketing Metrics*. Pearson Education. https://books.google.com.pk/books?id=CtrPEAAAQBAJ

FasterCapital. (2024, June 3). *Leaderboards: Climbing the Ranks: How Leaderboards Drive Brand Loyalty in Gamification Marketing*. https://fastercapital.com/content/Leaderboards--Climbing-the-Ranks--How-Leaderboards-Drive-Brand-Loyalty-in-Gamification-Marketing.html

Fazel, H. (2024). Digital marketing and sustainability in the era of climate change: PLS-structural equation modeling approach. *Journal of Statistics Applications & Probability, 13*(1), 491–505. DOI: 10.18576/jsap/130134

Federal Trade Commission (FTC). (2022). Green Guides for Environmental Marketing Claims. Retrieved from https://ftc.gov

Ferdousi, F., & Abedin, N. (2023). Strategic Human Resources Management for Creating Shared Value in Social Business Organizations. *Sustainability (Basel), 15*(4), 3703. Advance online publication. DOI: 10.3390/su15043703

Fernández Galeote, D., Rajanen, M., Rajanen, D., Legaki, N.-Z., Langley, D. J., & Hamari, J. (2021). Gamification for climate change engagement: Review of corpus and future agenda. *Environmental Research Letters, 16*(6), 063004. DOI: 10.1088/1748-9326/abec05

Fibre2Fashion. (2024). *Italian firm Gucci achieves 78% reduction in greenhouse gas emissions*. https://www.fibre2fashion.com/news/apparel-news/italian-firm-gucci-achieves-78-reduction-in-greenhouse-gas-emissions-296755-newsdetails.htm#:~:text=Luxury%20fashion%20brand%20Gucci%20has%20achieved%20a%2078,scopes%201%2C%202%2C%20and%203%20compared%20to%202021

Finnegan, A. (2024). The Essential Role of HR in Business Sustainability Initiatives. *CPA Ireland*. https://digital.cpaireland.ie/issue/march-2024/the-essential-role-of-hr-in-business-sustainability-initiatives/

Foly-Ehke, S. (2024). Sustainable living in the digital age: designing and evaluating an interactive mock-up of a carbon footprint tracker app for personal environmental awareness. https://urn.fi/URN:NBN:fi:amk-2024051612503

Forever Against Animal Testing. (2019). *We Want to Ban the Cruel Practice of Animal Testing in Cosmetics. Forever.*https://www.thebodyshop.com.sa/east/en/forever-against-animal-testing

French, D., McKillop, D., & Stewart, E. (2021). The effectiveness of smartphone apps in improving financial capability. In *Financial literacy and responsible finance in the fintech era* (pp. 6–22). Routledge. DOI: 10.4324/9781003169192-2

Fuchs, C. (2008). The implications of new information and communication technologies for sustainability. *Environment, Development and Sustainability*, *10*(3), 291–309. DOI: 10.1007/s10668-006-9065-0

Galpin, T., Whitttington, J. L., & Bell, G. (2015). Is your sustainability strategy sustainable? Creating a culture of sustainability. *Corporate Governance (Bradford)*, *15*(1), 1–17. Advance online publication. DOI: 10.1108/CG-01-2013-0004

Gao, B., Wang, Y., Xie, H., Hu, Y., & Hu, Y. (2023). Artificial intelligence in advertising: Advancements, challenges, and ethical considerations in targeting, personalization, content creation, and ad optimization. *SAGE Open*, *13*(4), 21582440231210759. DOI: 10.1177/21582440231210759

Garcia, L., & Lee, M. (2021). Consumer trust in sustainability marketing. *Journal of Business Ethics*, *38*(3), 78–94.

García-Salirrosas, E. E., Escobar-Farfán, M., Gómez-Bayona, L., Moreno-López, G., Valencia-Arias, A., & Gallardo-Canales, R. (2024). Influence of environmental awareness on the willingness to pay for green products: An analysis under the application of the theory of planned behavior in the Peruvian market. *Frontiers in Psychology*, *14*, 1282383. DOI: 10.3389/fpsyg.2023.1282383 PMID: 38282852

Gasparin, M., Green, W., Lilley, S., Quinn, M., Saren, M., & Schinckus, C. (2021). Business as unusual: A business model for social innovation. *Journal of Business Research, 125*, 698–709. DOI: 10.1016/j.jbusres.2020.01.034

Geng, D., Lai, K., & Zhu, Q. (2021). Eco-innovation and its role for performance improvement among Chinese small and medium-sized manufacturing enterprises. *International Journal of Production Economics, 231*, 107869. DOI: 10.1016/j.ijpe.2020.107869

Gill, R. (2011). An integrative review of storytelling: Using corporate stories to strengthen employee engagement and internal and external reputation. https://figshare.swinburne.edu.au/articles/journal_contribution/An_integrative_review_of_storytelling_using_corporate_stories_to_strengthen_employee_engagement_and_internal_and_external_reputation/26226098

Global Forest Watch. (2024). *Global*. https://www.globalforestwatch.org/dashboards/global/

Global Risk Intel. (n.d.). Jakarta's air pollution crisis and concerns for future economic development. Retrieved from https://www.globalriskintel.com/insights/jakartas-air-pollution-crisis-and-concerns-future-economic-development

Glynn, M. A., & Abzug, R. (2002). Institutionalizing identity: Symbolic isomorphism and organizational names. *Academy of Management Journal, 45*(1), 267–280. DOI: 10.2307/3069296

Goel, P., Mehta, S., Kumar, R., & Castaño, F. (2022). Sustainable Green Human Resource management practices in educational institutions: An interpretive structural modelling and analytic hierarchy process approach. *Sustainability (Basel), 14*(19), 12853. Advance online publication. DOI: 10.3390/su141912853

Gohain, T. T., & VS, S. (2023). The Imperative of Green Human Resource Management: Integrating Sustainability in HR Practices. *ASCI Journal of Management, 52*(2). https://search.ebscohost.com/login.aspx?direct=true&profile=ehost&scope=site&authtype=crawler&jrnl=02578069&AN=180144613&h=jPDkD20Dp9D4bYV6spFexh2LJ0FawPAKLlar8SRH790OnCi4UeSTz%2FM0WC%2BMBBmREiCAQx90E%2Ba2QJd%2FI62Dnw%3D%3D&crl=c

Gomes, R., & Osman, S. S. (2019). Managing Organizational Adoption of IoT: Revisiting Rogers' Diffusion of Innovation Theory. In.

Google. (2024). How to be more sustainable. https://sustainability.google

Green Building Council of Australia. (n.d.). Exploring Green Star. Green Building Council of Australia. Retrieved from https://new.gbca.org.au/green-star/exploring-green-star/

Green, A., & Parker, D. (2021). The Role of Sustainability in Consumer Decision-Making. *Consumer Research Quarterly*, *14*(1), 18–36.

Guerreiro, M., Muhs, C., Neves, M. C., Engel, L., & Cardoso, L. F. (2023). Green marketing: A case study of the outdoor apparel brand Patagonia. *Responsibility and Sustainability*, *8*(2), 49–57.

Guest. (2024). The shift to a circular economy: How smart technology is driving sustainability in retail. Financial Express.

Guldal, E. (2019). Consumer skepticism: Attitude–behavior gap in green marketing and the role of ecopreneurs in the market.

Gutterman, A. S. (2020). Organizational Design and Sustainability. *Available atSSRN* 3813832.

Gyimah, I., & Janisch, T. (2022). Green Human Resource Development–Supporting Sustainable Economic Activity in Organizations. *Indiana Journal of Humanities and Social Sciences, 3*(6). https://indianapublications.com/articles/IJHSS_3(6)_22-31_62b44ed5033fb5.31872827.pdf

Haba, H. F., Bredillet, C., & Dastane, O. (2023). Green consumer research: Trends and way forward based on bibliometric analysis. *Cleaner and Responsible Consumption*, *8*, 100089. DOI: 10.1016/j.clrc.2022.100089

Habib, M. D., Attri, R., Salam, M. A., & Yaqub, M. Z. (2024). Bright and dark sides of green consumerism: An in-depth qualitative investigation in a retailing context. *Journal of Retailing and Consumer Services*, *82*, 104145. DOI: 10.1016/j.jretconser.2024.104145

Haleem, A., Javaid, M., Qadri, M. A., Singh, R. P., & Suman, R. (2022). Artificial intelligence (AI) applications for marketing: A literature-based study. *International Journal of Intelligent Networks*, *3*, 119–132. DOI: 10.1016/j.ijin.2022.08.005

Halová, D., & Müller, M. (2023). Being an Employer of Choice: Attracting Generation Z to Work by Building Brand via Social Media. *Corporate Reputation Review*. Advance online publication. DOI: 10.1057/s41299-023-00172-0

Hammed, S. O. (2024). *The Impact of Green Talent Management Policies on Employer Branding: master's thesis* (Master's thesis). https://elar.urfu.ru/handle/10995/136231

Hammedi, W., Leclercq, T., & Poncin, I. (2019). Customer engagement: The role of gamification. In *Handbook of research on customer engagement* (pp. 164–185). Edward Elgar Publishing. DOI: 10.4337/9781788114899.00014

Hamoudi, H., & Avilés-Palacios, C. (2023). Product Sustainability and Consumer Environmental Awareness in Differentiated Markets. *International Advances in Economic Research, 29*(4), 277–291. DOI: 10.1007/s11294-023-09881-y

Han, H. (2021). Consumer behaviour and environmental sustainability in tourism and hospitality: A review of theories, concepts, and latest research. *Journal of Sustainable Tourism, 29*(7), 1021–1042. DOI: 10.1080/09669582.2021.1903019

Hao, F., Li, J., & Yang, T. (2022). Green market orientation: Impacts on competitive advantage and customer loyalty. *Sustainability, 14*(12), 7465.

Hapuwatte, B. M., Seevers, K. D., & Jawahir, I. (2022). Metrics-based dynamic product sustainability performance evaluation for advancing the circular economy. *Journal of Manufacturing Systems, 64*, 275–287. DOI: 10.1016/j.jmsy.2022.06.013

Haque, S., Panda, D., & Ghosh, A. (2024). Gamifying sustainability with self-efficacy: Motivating green behaviors in large industrial firms. *The International Journal of Organizational Analysis, 32*(11), 74–93. Advance online publication. DOI: 10.1108/IJOA-08-2023-3951

Hayles, C. S. (2019). INSPIRE sustainability internships: Promoting campus greening initiatives through student participation. *International Journal of Sustainability in Higher Education, 20*(3), 452–469. DOI: 10.1108/IJSHE-03-2019-0111

Heide, M. P., Prodan, S., Lazaroiu, G., Kreis-Engelhardt, B., & Ghigiu, A. M. (2024). Communication as a Key Performance Indicator in Employer Branding in the Context of the Social Economy—A Quantitative Study. *Behavioral Sciences (Basel, Switzerland), 14*(4), 303. Advance online publication. DOI: 10.3390/bs14040303 PMID: 38667099

Heinemann, G. (2023). *The new online trade: Business models, business systems and benchmarks in e-commerce*. Springer Fachmedien Wiesbaden. https://books.google.com.pk/books?id=DOW2EAAAQBAJ

Hendrawan, S. A., Chatra, A., Iman, N., Hidayatullah, S., & Suprayitno, D. (2024). Digital transformation in MSMEs: Challenges and opportunities in technology management. *Jurnal Informasi dan Teknologi*, 141-149.

Hennig, C. W. (2021). *Brand Activism as an Extension of Brand Identity and its Implications for Employer Branding* (Doctoral dissertation, Stuttgart Media University).

Holbeche, L. (2022). *Aligning human resources and business strategy*. Routledge., DOI: 10.4324/9781003219996

Hoque, N. (2014). Analysing sustainable consumption patterns: A literature review. *Development, 57*(3-4), 431–439. https://link.springer.com/content/pdf/10.1057/dev.201

Horani, O. M., Al-Adwan, A. S., Yaseen, H., Hmoud, H., Al-Rahmi, W. M., & Alkhalifah, A. (2023). The critical determinants impacting artificial intelligence adoption at the organizational level. *Information Development, 02666669231166889*, 02666669231166889. Advance online publication. DOI: 10.1177/02666669231166889

Hormes, J. (2024). *Claiming the Future of Greenwashing: enhancing trust and justice in the EU Green Claims Directive* (Master's thesis, University of Twente).

Ho, V.-T., Nakamori, Y., Ho, T.-B., & Lim, C. P. (2016). Blended learning model on hands-on approach for in-service secondary school teachers: Combination of E-learning and face-to-face discussion. *Education and Information Technologies, 21*(1), 185–208. DOI: 10.1007/s10639-014-9315-y

Hristov, I., Appolloni, A., Cheng, W., & Venditti, M. (2023). Enhancing the strategic alignment between environmental drivers of sustainability and the performance management system in Italian manufacturing firms. *International Journal of Productivity and Performance Management, 72*(10), 2949–2976. Advance online publication. DOI: 10.1108/IJPPM-11-2021-0643

Hübscher, C., Susanne, H., & Jörg, H. (2022). Social marketing and higher education: Partnering to achieve sustainable development goals. *Journal of Social Marketing, 12*(1), 76–104. Advance online publication. DOI: 10.1108/JSOCM-10-2020-0214

IDC, & Statista. (2024). *Spending on digital transformation technologies and services worldwide from 2017 to 2027 (in trillion U.S. dollars)*. Statista. Retrieved from https://www.statista.com/statistics/870924/worldwide-digital-transformation-market-size/

IEA. (2024). Trends in electric cars – Global EV Outlook 2024. International Energy Agency (IEA). Retrieved from https://www.iea.org/reports/global-ev-outlook-2024/trends-in-electric-cars

Influencer Marketing New. (2024, June 14). *Sustainability in Influencer Marketing: Promoting Eco-Friendly Brands.* https://www.influencermarketingnews.co.uk/sustainability-in-influencer-marketing-promoting-eco-friendly-brands/#:~:text=Influencer%20marketing%20offers%20a%20powerful%20platform%20for%20promoting,authentic%20storytelling%2C%20brands%20can%20inspire%20positive%20environmental%20change

Irani, F., Kilic, H., & Adeshola, I. (2022). Impact of green human resource management practices on the environmental performance of green hotels. *Journal of Hospitality Marketing & Management, 31*(5), 570–600. DOI: 10.1080/19368623.2022.2022554

Islam, M. A., Hunt, A., Jantan, A. H., Hashim, H., & Chong, C. W. (2020). Exploring challenges and solutions in applying green human resource management practices for the sustainable workplace in the ready-made garment industry in Bangladesh. *Business Strategy & Development, 3*(3), 332–343. Advance online publication. DOI: 10.1002/bsd2.99

Iyengar, M. S., & Venkatesh, R. (2024). A Brief communication on Virtual Reality (VR) in Hospitality Industry & Global Travel and Tourism. *Gamification and Augmented Reality, 2*, 40. DOI: 10.56294/gr202440

Jaber, M. (2023). IoT and machine learning for enabling sustainable development goals. *Frontiers in Communications and Networks, 4*, 1219047. DOI: 10.3389/frcmn.2023.1219047

Jaciow, M., Rudawska, E., Sagan, A., Tkaczyk, J., & Wolny, R. (2022). The Influence of Environmental Awareness on Responsible Energy Consumption—The Case of Households in Poland. *Energies, 15*(15), 5339. DOI: 10.3390/en15155339

Jackson, S. E., Ones, D. S., & Dilchert, S. (2012). *Managing human resources for environmental sustainability* (Vol. 32). John Wiley & Sons. https://books.google.com/books?hl=en&lr=&id=oPtRSNFQpHkC&oi=fnd&pg=PT8&dq=Jackson,+S.+E.,+Ones,+D.+S.,+%26+Dilchert,+S.+(2012).+Managing+human+resources+for+environmental+sustainability+(Vol.+32).+John+Wiley+%26+Sons.&ots=TeASMvQcN3&sig=sEwCY6NKALyDwSEI2sVZomJm3PI

Jahidi, I. (2020). Style and Characteristics Transformational Leadership: How The Regional Head of Cimahi, Indonesia in Mobilizing Employees in Achieving Vision. *European Journal of Molecular and Clinical Medicine, 7*(7), 308–318.

Jairick. (2024). Patagonia Leadership & its Sustainable Values. Retrieved from https://humansofglobe.com/patagonia-leadership-in-environmental-and-social-responsibility/#:~:text=Environmentalism%20is%20intricately%20woven%20into,Patagonia's%20commitment%20to%20sustainable%20practices

Jamil, S., Zaman, S. I., Kayikci, Y., & Khan, S. A. (2023). The role of green recruitment on organizational sustainability performance: A study within the context of green human resource management. *Sustainability (Basel), 15*(21), 15567. Advance online publication. DOI: 10.3390/su152115567

Jawad, A. Q., Scott-Jackson, W., Jawad, A. Q., & Scott-Jackson, W. (2016). PACE: The Process of Active Committed Enthusiasm. *Redefining Well-Being in Nations and Organizations: A Process of Active Committed Enthusiasm*, 120-186.

Jaworski, B., & Cheung, V. (2023). Drucker Management Philosophy and Ten Principles. In *Creating the Organization of the Future: Building on Drucker and Confucius Foundations* (pp. 101-122). Emerald Publishing Limited. DOI: 10.1108/978-1-83753-216-220231009

Jayadeva, S. M., Al Ayub Ahmed, A., Malik, R., Shaikh, A. A., Siddique, M. N.-E. A., & Naved, M. (2022). Roles of Cloud Computing and Internet of Things in Marketing Management: A Critical Review and Future Trends.

Jay, J., & Gerard, M. (2015). Accelerating the theory and practice of sustainability-oriented innovation. https://doi.org/DOI: 10.2139/ssrn.2629683

Jha, A. K., & Verma, N. K. (2023). Social media sustainability communication: An analysis of firm behaviour and stakeholder responses. *Information Systems Frontiers, 25*(2), 723–742.

Jimenez, D., Franco, I. B., & Smith, T. (2021). A review of corporate purpose: An approach to actioning the sustainable development goals (SDGs). *Sustainability (Basel), 13*(7), 3899. Advance online publication. DOI: 10.3390/su13073899

Johnson, P. (2023). Regulatory enforcement in Australia. *Journal of Consumer Law, 15*(1), 32–48.

Johnstone, M. L., & Tan, L. P. (2015). Exploring the gap between consumers' green rhetoric and purchasing behavior. *Journal of Business Ethics, 132*(2), 311–328. Advance online publication. DOI: 10.1007/s10551-014-2316-3

Jones, J., York, J. G., Vedula, S., Conger, M., & Lenox, M. (2019). The collective construction of green building: Industry transition toward environmentally beneficial practices. *The Academy of Management Perspectives, 33*(4), 425–449. Advance online publication. DOI: 10.5465/amp.2017.0031

Jones, L., Smith, R., & Patel, D. (2022). The evolution of stakeholder theory. *Business Strategy Review, 24*(3), 78–95.

Jones, R., & Taylor, P. (2022). Regulating green marketing on digital platforms. *Consumer Protection Review*, *21*(1), 56–79.

Joseph, A., & Jose, N. (2024). The Role of Incentives in Fostering Green Behavior Among the Emerging Workforce. In *Building Sustainable Human Resources Management Practices for Businesses*. IGI Global., DOI: 10.4018/979-8-3693-1994-9.ch018

Joseph, E. (2024). Resilient Infrastructure and Inclusive Culture in the Era of Remote Work. In *Infrastructure Development Strategies for Empowerment and Inclusion*. IGI Global., DOI: 10.4018/979-8-3693-2917-7.ch013

Joy, M. M., & Chiramel, M. J. (2017). *Fun is the future: A collection of compelling gamification success stories*. Educreation Publishing. https://books.google.com/books?hl=en&lr=&id=UU0oDwAAQBAJ&oi=fnd&pg=PA2&dq=Joy,+M.+M.,+%26+Chiramel,+M.+J.+(2017).+Fun+is+the+future:+A+collection+of+compelling+gamification+success+stories.+Educreation+Publishing.&ots=DSP3FCFay0&sig=C_NK6ZgEUjfW78tc5yBZaI8SxcQ

Judijanto, L., Suarniki, N. N., & Muhtadi, M. A. (2024). Green Marketing and Consumer Environmental Awareness: A Bibliometric Review of Social Education and Campaigns. *West Science Social and Humanities Studies*, *2*(06), 948–959. DOI: 10.58812/wsshs.v2i06.972

Kannan, S., Parashar, B., & Chaurasia, A. (2024). E-Commerce and Green Packaging: Sustainable Business Trends. In *Green Innovations for Industrial Development and Business Sustainability* (pp. 22-39). CRC Press.

Kao, T.-F., & Du, Y.-Z. (2020). A study on the influence of green advertising design and environmental emotion on advertising effect. *Journal of Cleaner Production*, *242*, 118294. DOI: 10.1016/j.jclepro.2019.118294

Kapil, K. (2015). Green HRM: Trends & prospects. *International Journal of Management Research*, *3*(1), 43–55.

Karkera, A. (2023). *Role of the Chief Data Officer in Government*. University of Arkansas at Little Rock.

Karunia, R. L., Yanto, E., Prasetyo, J. H., Muthmainah, E., Hiswendari, L., Setiawan, P., & Saragih, M. A. P. (2024). Digital collaboration models for empowering SMEs: Enhancing public organization performance. *Emerging Science Journal*, *8*(4), 1492–1505. DOI: 10.28991/ESJ-2024-08-04-015

Kaufman, I., Horton, C., & Soltanifar, M. (2023). *Digital Marketing: Integrating Strategy, Sustainability, and Purpose*. Taylor & Francis. DOI: 10.4324/9781351019187

Kaur, G., & Srivastava, A. (2022). *Green Communication Technologies for Future Networks: An Energy-Efficient Perspective*. CRC Press. https://books.google.com.pk/books?id=3p8IEQAAQBAJ

Kaur, J., & Gupta, M. (2024). Exploration of factors of green marketing. International Conference on Communications and Cyber Physical Engineering 2018, Kumari, A. (2024). Transforming Business for a Sustainable Future Using Green Marketing. *Multidisciplinary Approach to Information Technology in Library and Information Science*, 132-150. DOI: 10.1007/978-981-99-7137-4_85

Khan, M., Khan, N., Begum, S., & Qureshi, M. I. (2024). Digital future beyond pandemic outbreak: systematic review of the impact of COVID-19 outbreak on digital psychology. *foresight, 26*(1), 1-17. https://doi.org/DOI: 10.1108/FS-02-2021-0044

Khan, N. A., Hassan, S., Pravdina, N., & Akhtar, M. (2023). Drivers of sustainability: Technological and relational factors influencing young consumers' green buying intentions and green actual consumption behavior. *Young Consumers, 24*(6), 686–703. DOI: 10.1108/YC-09-2022-1610

Kivinda, M. P., Su, Q., Hau, H. T., & Hashmi, H. B. A. (2021). Green HRM for employer branding: Evidence from ISO 14001 EMS certified firms. *Journal of Developing Areas, 55*(3), 393–409. DOI: 10.1353/jda.2021.0071

Kolding, M., Sundblad, M., Alexa, J., Stone, M., Aravopoulou, E., & Evans, G. (2018). Information management–a skills gap? *The Bottom Line (New York, N.Y.), 31*(3/4), 170–190. DOI: 10.1108/BL-09-2018-0037

Krasodomska, J., Zieniuk, P., & Kostrzewska, J. (2023). Reporting on Sustainable Development Goals in the European Union: What drives companies' decisions? *Competitiveness Review, 33*(1), 120–146. DOI: 10.1108/CR-12-2021-0179

Krowinska, A., Backhaus, C., Becker, B., & Bosser, F. (2023). *Digital Content Marketing: Creating Value in Practice*. Taylor & Francis. DOI: 10.4324/9781003346500

Kumar, H., & Raghavendran, S. (2015). Gamification, the finer art: Fostering creativity and employee engagement. *The Journal of Business Strategy, 36*(6), 3–12. DOI: 10.1108/JBS-10-2014-0119

Kumari, R., Dash, S. P., & Chatterjee, R. (2025). Green Human Resource Management: An Emerging Trend in HR Practices. *Examining Green Human Resources Management and Nascent Entrepreneurship*, 1-24.

Kumar, R., Singh, B., & Gupta, A. (2023). The role of green market orientation in sustainable corporate performance. *International Journal of Marketing Studies, 10*(1), 30–49.

Kunisch, S., Menz, M., & Langan, R. (2022). Chief digital officers: An exploratory analysis of their emergence, nature, and determinants. *Long Range Planning*, *55*(2), 101999. DOI: 10.1016/j.lrp.2020.101999

Kwilinski, A., Lyulyov, O., & Pimonenko, T. (2023). Environmental Sustainability within Attaining Sustainable Development Goals: The Role of Digitalization and the Transport Sector. *Sustainability (Basel)*, *15*(14), 11282. DOI: 10.3390/su151411282

Lakhiar, I. A., Yan, H., Zhang, J., Wang, G., Deng, S., Bao, R., Zhang, C., Syed, T. N., Wang, B., Zhou, R., & Wang, X. (2024). Plastic pollution in agriculture as a threat to food security, the ecosystem, and the environment: An overview. *Agronomy (Basel)*, *14*(3), 548. DOI: 10.3390/agronomy14030548

Landry, M. J., & Ward, C. P. (2024). Health benefits of a plant-based dietary pattern and implementation in healthcare and clinical practice. *American Journal of Lifestyle Medicine*, *18*(5), 657–665. Advance online publication. DOI: 10.1177/15598276241237766 PMID: 39309320

LaVan, H., Zilic, I., & Basappa, S. (2022). Attitudes of employees in green companies regarding CSR communication. *International Journal of Manpower*, *43*(6), 1301–1315. DOI: 10.1108/IJM-11-2020-0542

Lazarus, R. J. (2023). *The making of environmental law*. University of Chicago Press. https://books.google.com/books?hl=en&lr=&id=xPqgEAAAQBAJ&oi=fnd&pg=PR7&dq=Lazarus,+R.+J.+(2023).+The+making+of+environmental+law.+University+of+Chicago+Press.&ots=wMt_ek6erk&sig=WaHyV3Yct0NEhWOeN_4uvdh-dBc

Lee, J. (2005). Effects of leadership and leader-member exchange on commitment. *Leadership and Organization Development Journal*, *26*(8), 655–672. DOI: 10.1108/01437730510633728

Lee, K. (2010). The green purchase behavior of Hong Kong young consumers: The role of peer influence, local environmental involvement, and concrete environmental knowledge. *Journal of International Consumer Marketing*, *23*(1), 21–44. DOI: 10.1080/08961530.2011.524575

Lengnick-Hall, M. L., Neely, A. R., & Stone, C. B. (2018). Human resource management in the digital age: Big data, HR analytics and artificial intelligence. In *Management and technological challenges in the digital age*. CRC Press., DOI: 10.1201/9781351238922-1

Leonardi, P. M., & Vaast, E. (2017). Social media and their affordances for organizing: A review and agenda for research. *The Academy of Management Annals*, *11*(1), 150–188. Advance online publication. DOI: 10.5465/annals.2015.0144

Leonidou, C. N., Katsikeas, C. S., & Morgan, N. A. (2013). "Greening" the marketing mix: Do firms do it and does it pay off? *Journal of the Academy of Marketing Science*, *41*(2), 151–170. DOI: 10.1007/s11747-012-0317-2

Leonidou, L. C., Fotiadis, T. A., Christodoulides, P., Spyropoulou, S., & Katsikeas, C. S. (2015). Environmentally friendly export business strategy: Its determinants and effects on competitive advantage and performance. *International Business Review*, *24*(5), 798–811. Advance online publication. DOI: 10.1016/j.ibusrev.2015.02.001

Levi Strauss & Co. (2022). *Levi Strauss & Co. 2022 Sustainability Goals & Progress Update*. https://www.levistrauss.com/sustainability/report/

Li, D. (2025). Impact of green advertisement and environmental knowledge on intention of consumers to buy green products. *BMC Psychology*, *13*(1), 220. Advance online publication. DOI: 10.1186/s40359-025-02538-x PMID: 40059236

Ligorio, L., Venturelli, A., Rosato, P., & Campo, R. (2023). Fostering sustainable development goals through gamification. *Journal of Management & Organization*, •••, 1–22. DOI: 10.1017/jmo.2023.54

Li, J., Pan, Z., Sun, Y., Zheng, W., Zhang, Z., & Wang, Z. (2024). From Compliance to Strategy: Paradigm Shift in Corporate ESG Practices. *Academic Journal of Humanities & Social Sciences*, *7*(2). Advance online publication. DOI: 10.25236/AJHSS.2024.070225

Lindgren, E., & Österlind, L. (2018). Inclusion in a recruitment process. https://www.diva-portal.org/smash/record.jsf?pid=diva2:1483816

Lisniak, B. A. (2024). Global environmental problems and their impact on international business.

Liu, C., & Jiang, M. (2024). Green Messaging in the Fast-Food Industry: The Role of Responsibility, Obligation, and Values in Driving Eco-Conscious Behavior. *Sustainability (2071-1050), 16*(19). https://doi.org/DOI: 10.3390/su16198445

Liute, A., & De Giacomo, M. R. (2022). The environmental performance of UK-based B Corp companies: An analysis based on the triple bottom line approach. *Business Strategy and the Environment*, *31*(3), 810–827. https://doi.org/https://doi.org/10.1002/bse.2919. DOI: 10.1002/bse.2919

Li, Y., & Shan, B. (2025). Exploring the role of health consciousness and environmental awareness in purchase intentions for green-packaged organic foods: An extended TPB model. *Frontiers in Nutrition*, *12*, 1528016. DOI: 10.3389/fnut.2025.1528016 PMID: 40110167

Longo, D., & Magnusson, M. (2024). Combining Innovation and Sustainability: Exploring Green Marketing Strategies in SMEs. In.

Lopess-Naglis, A. (2023). *Lean and green in SMEs: Practices for achieving sustainability goals key performance indicators* (Bachelor's thesis, University of Twente). http://essay.utwente.nl/100302/

Lordan, J. (2024). *'Low price. But not at any price' IKEA's engagement with social and environmental issues* (Doctoral dissertation, Institute of Art, Design+ Technology).

Lossin, F., Kozlovskiy, I., Sodenkamp, M., & Staake, T. (2016). Incentives to Go Green: an Empirical Investigation of Monetary and Symbolic Rewards to Mo-Tivate Energy Savings.

Luu, T. T. (2020). Integrating green strategy and green human resource practices to trigger individual and organizational green performance: The role of environmentally-specific servant leadership. *Journal of Sustainable Tourism*, *28*(8), 1193–1222. DOI: 10.1080/09669582.2020.1729165

Luzzini, D., Longoni, A., & Caniato, F. (2021). Environmental orientation in supply chain management: A systematic review and conceptual framework. *Sustainable Production and Consumption*, *27*, 238–256.

Mabalay, A. A. (2025). Gamification for sustainability: A systematic review of applications, trends, and opportunities. *Computers in Human Behavior*, *165*, 108529. DOI: 10.1016/j.chb.2024.108529

Madan, A., Gupta, A. K., & Goyal, M. K. (2023). Lifestyle for Environment: LiFE Mission and Synergies with Eco-restoration. In *Ecosystem Restoration: Towards Sustainability and Resilient Development*. Springer Nature Singapore. https://doi.org/DOI: 10.1007/978-981-99-3687-8_2

Mahalakshmi, S., Nallasivam, A., Kumar, S. H., Kalavathy, K. S., & Desai, K. (2024, February). Sustainability by Design: IKEA's Eco-Friendly Marketing Efforts. In *3rd International Conference on Reinventing Business Practices, Start-ups and Sustainability*. Atlantis Press. https://doi.org/DOI: 10.2991/978-94-6463-374-0_14

Mahesh, K. M., Aithal, P. S., & Sharma, K. R. S. (2024). Green HRM and Teaching Sustainability in higher education Institutions: For Promoting Sustainable Education and Sustainable Development Goals. *International Journal of Case Studies in Business* [IJCSBE]. *IT and Education*, *8*(1). Advance online publication. DOI: 10.47992/IJCSBE.2581.6942.0345

Maheshwari, S., & Rai, A. (2022). Effective Leadership Attributes: Evidences from Indian Power Sector. *Indian Journal of Industrial Relations*, *58*(2).

Mahmoud, M. A., Tsetse, E. K. K., Tulasi, E. E., & Muddey, D. K. (2022). Green Packaging, Environmental Awareness, Willingness to Pay and Consumers' Purchase Decisions. *Sustainability (Basel)*, *14*(23), 16091. DOI: 10.3390/su142316091

Malhotra, Y., & Pachauri, V. (2023). Employee Engagement in ESG Practices: A Way to Sustainability. *Digital Disruption and Environmental, Social & Governance, 34.*

Malik, S. Y., Cao, Y., Mughal, Y. H., Kundi, G. M., Mughal, M. H., & Ramayah, T. (2020). Pathways towards sustainability in organizations: Empirical evidence on the role of green human resource management practices and green intellectual capital. *Sustainability (Basel)*, *12*(8), 3228. Advance online publication. DOI: 10.3390/su12083228

Mandip, G. (2012). Green HRM: People management commitment to environmental sustainability. *Research Journal of Recent Sciences*. https://www.academia.edu/download/43829709/38.ISCA-ISC-2011-18CLM-Com-03.pdf

Manoj Krishnan, C., & Arun, G. (2025). A study on environmental prosocial attitudes to green consumption values, openness to green communication, and its relationship with buying behavior. *Cogent Business & Management*, *12*(1), 2443050. DOI: 10.1080/23311975.2024.2443050

Marchington, M. (2015). The role of institutional and intermediary forces in shaping patterns of employee involvement and participation (EIP) in Anglo-American countries. *International Journal of Human Resource Management*, *26*(20), 2594–2616. DOI: 10.1080/09585192.2014.1003088

Marrucci, L., Daddi, T., & Iraldo, F. (2024). Creating environmental performance indicators to assess corporate sustainability and reward employees. *Ecological Indicators*, *158*, 111489. Advance online publication. DOI: 10.1016/j.ecolind.2023.111489

Measham, T. G., & Barnett, G. B. (2008). Environmental volunteering: Motivations, modes and outcomes. *The Australian Geographer*, *39*(4), 537–552. DOI: 10.1080/00049180802419237

Mefalopulos, P. (2005). Communication for sustainable development: applications and challenges. *Media and glocal change. Rethinking communication for development*, 247-260.

Messina, M., Eslami, M. II., & Castilla, J. C. (2024). Thc usc of blockchain in organisations for sustainable development: A systematic literature review and bibliometric analysis. *International Journal of Production Research*, •••, 1–28. DOI: 10.1080/00207543.2024.2432467

Mevoli, A., Leggett, K. L., & Davies, W. E. (2024). The Gamification of Circular Practices Using the SDGs. In Scholz, S. G., Howlett, R. J., & Setchi, R. (Eds.), *Sustainable Design and Manufacturing 2023* (Vol. 377, pp. 115–124). Springer Nature Singapore., DOI: 10.1007/978-981-99-8159-5_10

Mishra, P. (2017). Green human resource management: A framework for sustainable organizational development in an emerging economy. *The International Journal of Organizational Analysis*, *25*(5), 762–788. Advance online publication. DOI: 10.1108/IJOA-11-2016-1079

Mishra, R., Singh, R. K., & Rana, N. P. (2022). Developing environmental collaboration among supply chain partners for sustainable consumption & production: Insights from an auto sector supply chain. *Journal of Cleaner Production*, *338*, 130619. Advance online publication. DOI: 10.1016/j.jclepro.2022.130619

Mishra, R., Singh, R. K., & Rana, N. P. (2024). Digital orientation, digital eco-innovation and circular economy in the context of sustainable development goals. *Business Strategy and the Environment*, *33*(4), 2752–2770. DOI: 10.1002/bse.3619

Miska, C., Szocs, I., & Schiffinger, M. (2018). Culture's effects on corporate sustainability practices: A multi-domain and multi-level review. *Journal of World Business*, *53*(2), 263–279. Advance online publication. DOI: 10.1016/j.jwb.2017.12.001

Moberg, T. (2024). Enhancing Brand Image Through Sustainable Business Practices: How to Integrate and Market Sustainability, A Case Study of Pointman OY.

Mohd Suki, N., & Mohd Suki, N. (2019). Examination of peer influence as a moderator and predictor in explaining green purchase behaviour in a developing country. *Journal of Cleaner Production*, *228*, 833–844. DOI: 10.1016/j.jclepro.2019.04.218

Moni Omotoso. (2023). *"Who Made My Clothes" Movement – How it All Began.* https://fashioninsiders.co/features/inspiration/who-made-my-clothes-movement/

Montgomery, A. W., Lyon, T. P., & Barg, J. (2024). No end in sight? A greenwash review and research agenda. *Organization & Environment*, *37*(2), 221–256. Advance online publication. DOI: 10.1177/10860266231168905 PMID: 39091586

Morris, R., & Singh, P. (2023). Corporate accountability in sustainability branding. *Journal of Environmental Law*, *25*(2), 112–136.

Morshed, M. (2016). The human resources department Nestle Bangladesh Limited its essential functions and activities. https://dspace.bracu.ac.bd/xmlui/handle/10361/8551

Mtembu, V. N. (2017). *Green Human-Resource Management towards sustainable organizations: A case of KwaZulu-Natal higher education institutions* (Doctoral dissertation).

Mtembu, V. (2019). Does having knowledge of green human resource management practices influence its implementation within organizations? *Problems and Perspectives in Management*, *17*(2), 267–276. Advance online publication. DOI: 10.21511/ppm.17(2).2019.20

Muchenje, K. C. (2024). Green Logistics and Supply Chain Management. In *Contemporary Solutions for Sustainable Transportation Practices* (pp. 33–61). IGI Global. DOI: 10.4018/979-8-3693-3755-4.ch002

Mujtaba, M., & Mubarik, M. S. (2022). Talent management and organizational sustainability: Role of sustainable behavior. *The International Journal of Organizational Analysis*, *30*(2), 389–407. Advance online publication. DOI: 10.1108/IJOA-06-2020-2253

Mukonza, C., & Swarts, I. (2020). The influence of green marketing strategies on business performance and corporate image in the retail sector. *Business Strategy and the Environment*, *29*(3), 838–845. DOI: 10.1002/bse.2401

Murugesan, B., Jayanthi, K., & Karthikeyan, G. (2024). Integrating Digital Twins and 3D Technologies in Fashion: Advancing Sustainability and Consumer Engagement. In *Illustrating Digital Innovations Towards Intelligent Fashion: Leveraging Information System Engineering and Digital Twins for Efficient Design of Next-Generation Fashion* (pp. 1-88). Springer.

Nabieva, N. M. (2021). DIGITAL MARKETING: CURRENT TRENDS IN DEVELOPMENT. *Theoretical & Applied Science*, *94*(2), 333–340. DOI: 10.15863/TAS.2021.02.94.65

Nagam, A. (2024). Mediating Role of Green Human Resource Management Practices on Employee Green Behavior in Wipro: A Review and Recommendations for Future Research. *Educational Administration: Theory and Practice*, *30*(5), 5811–5817. Advance online publication. DOI: 10.53555/kuey.v30i5.3870

Nakaishi, T., & Chapman, A. (2024). Eco-labels as a communication and policy tool: A comprehensive review of academic literature and global label initiatives. *Renewable & Sustainable Energy Reviews*, *202*, 114708. https://doi.org/https://doi .org/10.1016/j.rser.2024.114708. DOI: 10.1016/j.rser.2024.114708

Napathorn, C. (2022). The development of green skills across firms in the institutional context of Thailand. *Asia-Pacific Journal of Business Administration*, *14*(4), 539–572. DOI: 10.1108/APJBA-10-2020-0370

Nestle. (2024). Coffee Sourcing. https://www.nestle.com/sustainability/sustainable -sourcing/coffee

Nguyen, D., & Taylor, M. (2022). The rise of consumer skepticism in green marketing. *Marketing & Ethics Review*, *20*(4), 45–67.

Nielsen, I. Q. (2023). Indian consumers' evolving priorities towards the environment and sustainability. NIQ. Retrieved from https://nielseniq.com/global/en/insights/ commentary/2023/indian-consumers-evolving-priorities-towards-the-environment -and-sustainability/

Nisa, N. U., Mendoza, S. A. J., & Shamsuddinova, S. (2022). The Concept of Greenwashing and its Impact on Green Trust, Green Risk, and Green Consumer Confusion: A Review-Based Study. *JABS : Journal of Applied Biological Sciences*, *8*(3), 1–18.

Nisar, Q. A., Haider, S., Ali, F., Jamshed, S., Ryu, K., & Gill, S. S. (2021). Green human resource management practices and environmental performance in Malaysian green hotels: The role of green intellectual capital and pro-environmental behavior. *Journal of Cleaner Production*, *311*, 127504. Advance online publication. DOI: 10.1016/j.jclepro.2021.127504

Nishitha, K., & Kavitha, R. (2024). Exploring the Integration of Human Resource Management and Organizational Culture in Achieving Environmental Sustainability. In *Intersecting Human Resource Management and Organizational Culture for Environmental Sustainability*. IGI Global., DOI: 10.4018/979-8-3693-2699-2.ch001

Nogueira, E., Gomes, S., & Lopes, J. M. (2023). Triple Bottom Line, Sustainability, and Economic Development: What Binds Them Together? A Bibliometric Approach. *Sustainability (Basel)*, *15*(8), 6706. DOI: 10.3390/su15086706

Novy, J. W., Banerjee, B., & Matson, P. (2021). A core curriculum for sustainability leadership. *Sustainability (Basel)*, *13*(19), 10557. DOI: 10.3390/su131910557

Nwabekee, U. S., Abdul-Azeez, O. Y., Agu, E. E., & Ignatius, T. (2024). Digital transformation in marketing strategies: The role of data analytics and CRM tools. *International Journal of Frontline Research in Science and Technology*, *3*(2), 055-072.

Nyamekye, M. B., Martey, E. M., Agbemabiese, G. C., Preko, A. K., Gyepi-Garbrah, T., & Appah, E. (2024). Green marketing strategy, technology implementation and corporate performance: The role of green creative behaviour and institutional isomorphism. *Journal of Contemporary Marketing Science*, *7*(1), 84–109. DOI: 10.1108/JCMARS-09-2023-0038

O'Rourke, D., & Strand, R. (2016). *Patagonia: Driving sustainable innovation by embracing tensions*. The Berkeley-Haas Case Series. University of California, Berkeley. Haas School of Business. https://doi.org/DOI: 10.4135/9781526407610

Odhiambo, G. M., Waiganjo, E. W., & Simiyu, A. N. (2023). Incentivizing employee pro-environmental behaviour: Harnessing the potential of green rewards. *African Journal of Empirical Research, 4*(2), 601–611-601–611.

Odhiambo, G. M., Waiganjo, E. W., & Simiyu, A. N. (2023). Incentivizing employee pro-environmental behavior: Harnessing the potential of green rewards. *African Journal of Empirical Research*, *4*(2), 601–611. Advance online publication. DOI: 10.51867/ajernet.4.2.60

Odulaja, B. A., Nnabugwu, O. C., Abdul, A. A., Udeh, C. A., & Daraojimba, C. (2023). HR'S role in organizational change within Nigeria's renewable energy sector: A review. *Engineering Science & Technology Journal*, *4*(5), 259–284. Advance online publication. DOI: 10.51594/estj.v4i5.615

oecd. (2009). Sustainable manufacturing and eco-innovation: Framework, practices and measurement. *Synthesis report*.

Office of Consumer Affairs. (2022, June 8). Environmental labels and claims. Retrieved from https://ised-isde.canada.ca/site/office-consumer-affairs/en/be-green-consumer/environmental-labels-and-claims#toc0

Ogbu, A. D., Eyo-Udo, N. L., Adeyinka, M. A., Ozowe, W., & Ikevuje, A. H. (2023). A conceptual procurement model for sustainability and climate change mitigation in the oil, gas, and energy sectors. *World Journal of Advanced Research and Reviews*, *20*(3), 1935–1952. Advance online publication. DOI: 10.30574/wjarr.2023.20.3.2304

Olaleye, D. S., Oloye, A. C., Akinloye, A. O., & Akinwande, O. T. (2024). Advancing green communications: The role of radio frequency engineering in sustainable infrastructure design. *International Journal of Latest Technology in Engineering* [IJLTEMAS]. *Management & Applied Science*, *13*(5), 113.

Oliveira, U. R., Gomes, T. S. M., de Oliveira, G. G., de Abreu, J. C. A., Oliveira, M. A., & César, A. S. (2022). Systematic literature review on sustainable consumption from the perspective of companies, people, and public policies. *Sustainability (Basel), 14*(21), 13771. DOI: 10.3390/su142113771

Olsson, O., & Storesund, J. (2015). Open-source Branding: How consumers develop a Corporate Brand Image through. https://lup.lub.lu.se/luur/download?func=downloadFile&recordOId=7862109&fileOId=7862114

Onesi-Ozigagun, O., Ololade, Y. J., Eyo-Udo, N. L., & Oluwaseun, D. (2024). Data-driven decision making: Shaping the future of business efficiency and customer engagement. *International Journal of Multidisciplinary Research Updates*, 7(2), 19–29. DOI: 10.53430/ijmru.2024.7.2.0031

Orecchia, C., & Zoppoli, P. (2007). Consumerism and environment: Does consumption behaviour affect environmental quality? CEIS Working Paper No. 261. Available at *SSRN*: https://ssrn.com/abstract=1719507 DOI: 10.2139/ssrn.1719507

Organisation for Economic Co-operation and Development. (2024). *Inclusive, green and digital transformation*. https://www.oecd.org/en/topics/sub-issues/inclusive-green-and-digital-transformation.html

Ottman, J. (2017). *The new rules of green marketing: Strategies, tools, and inspiration for sustainable branding*. Routledge., DOI: 10.4324/9781351278683

Ouariachi, T., Li, C.-Y., & Elving, W. J. L. (2020). Gamification Approaches for Education and Engagement on Pro-Environmental Behaviors: Searching for Best Practices. *Sustainability (Basel), 12*(11), 4565. DOI: 10.3390/su12114565

Pachar, S., Kishore, S. C., Karunakaran, N. B., Bhaskar, P., & Selvakumar, P. (2025). Green Job Design and Analysis. In *Examining Green Human Resources Management and Nascent Entrepreneurship* (pp. 317–342). IGI Global.

Palhau, M., Carlos Sá, J., Ávila, P., Dinis-Carvalho, J., Rodrigues, C., & Santos, G. (2024). Toyota Way-the Heart of TPS and its Impact on Sustainable Company Growth. *Quality Innovation Prosperity/Kvalita Inovácia Prosperita, 28*(3). https://doi.org/DOI: 10.12776/qip.v28i3.2073

Panagiotopoulou, V. C., Paraskevopoulou, A., Margaityte, M., Petkova, E. I., & Stavropoulos, P. (2024). *Customisable Training Programme on Best Industrial Practices for Sustainability, Circular Economy and Energy Efficiency.* Paper presented at the Conference on Learning Factories. DOI: 10.1007/978-3-031-65411-4_45

Panel, E. (2024). 17 sustainability initiatives of businesses that are going green. *Forbes*.

Pan, W., Cao, H., & Liu, Y. (2023). "Green" innovation, privacy regulation and environmental policy. *Renewable Energy, 203*, 245–254. DOI: 10.1016/j.renene.2022.12.025

Papadas, K. K., Avlonitis, G. J., & Carrigan, M. (2017). Green marketing orientation: Conceptualization, scale development and validation. *Journal of Business Research, 80*, 236–246. DOI: 10.1016/j.jbusres.2017.05.024

Park, J., & Roome, N. (2017). *The ecology of the new economy: sustainable transformation of global information, communications and electronics industries.* Routledge. DOI: 10.4324/9781351282048

Pathak, R. K., & Agarwal, S. (2024). Sustainability in Human Resources: Evaluating Competencies and Overcoming Challenges in India's Service Sector. *Library Progress International, 44*(3). https://bpasjournals.com/library-science/index.php/journal/article/view/1780

Pathak, R. K., & Agarwal, S. (2024). Sustainability in Human Resources: Evaluating Competencies and Overcoming Challenges in India's Service Sector. *Library Progress International, 44*(3), 7301–7313.

Patra, G. K., Rajaram, S. K., Boddapati, V. N., Kuraku, C., & Gollangi, H. K. (2022). Advancing Digital Payment Systems: Combining AI, Big Data, and Biometric Authentication for Enhanced Security. *International Journal of Engineering and Computer Science, 11*(08), 10.18535.

Paul, J. (2024). The Impact of Green Innovation on Financial and operational performance.

Paul, S. G., Saha, A., Arefin, M. S., Bhuiyan, T., Biswas, A. A., Reza, A. W., Alotaibi, N. M., Alyami, S. A., & Moni, M. A. (2023). A Comprehensive Review of Green Computing: Past, Present, and Future Research. *IEEE Access : Practical Innovations, Open Solutions, 11*, 87445–87494. DOI: 10.1109/ACCESS.2023.3304332

Peattie, K. (2001). Towards sustainability: The third age of green marketing. *The Marketing Review, 2*(2), 129–146. Advance online publication. DOI: 10.1362/1469347012569869

Peattie, K. (2016). Green marketing. In *The marketing book* (pp. 573–597). Routledge.

Peredy, Z., & Feierzhati, F. (2023). Cloud Computing Solutions for Speeding-up the Small and Medium Sized Enterprise (SME's) Businesses in China. [EDUTUS]. *ACTA PERIODICA, 27*(27), 14–33. DOI: 10.47273/AP.2023.1.14-33

Pham, N. T., Vo-Thanh, T., Shahbaz, M., Huynh, T. L. D., & Usman, M. (2020). Managing environmental challenges: Training as a solution to improve employee green performance. *Journal of Environmental Management, 269*, 110781. Advance online publication. DOI: 10.1016/j.jenvman.2020.110781 PMID: 32560999

Pittayachawan, S., Abareshi, A., Kam, B., & Teo, L. (2014). Green consumerism: A study on the prospect of consumers' participation in corporate environmental management programs. DOI: 10.13140/2.1.3238.3684

Podgorodnichenko, N., Akmal, A., Edgar, F., & Everett, A. M. (2022). Sustainable HRM: Toward addressing diverse employee roles. *Employee Relations, 44*(3), 576–608. DOI: 10.1108/ER-01-2019-0016

Pomegbe, W. W. K., Dogbe, C. S. K., Bamfo, B. A., Borah, P. S., & Novixoxo, J. D. (2022). Social risk, green market orientation, entrepreneurial orientation, and new product performance among European Multinational Enterprises operating in developing economies. *Business and Society Review, 127*(4), 891–914. DOI: 10.1111/basr.12292

Poornima, B., & Abishek, A. (2023). A study on consumer awareness towards eco-friendly products in Coimbatore city. [IJCRT]. *International Journal of Creative Research Thoughts, 11*(4), 772. https://ijcrt.org/papers/IJCRT2304772.pdf

Post, J. E., & Altman, B. W. (2017). Managing the Environmental Change Process: Barriers and Opportunities 1. In *Managing green teams* (pp. 84-101): Routledge.

Poston, R. S., & Dhaliwal, J. (2015). IS human capital: Assessing gaps to strengthen skill and competency sourcing. *Communications of the Association for Information Systems, 36*(1), 34. DOI: 10.17705/1CAIS.03634

Potoski, M., & Callery, P. J. (2018). Peer communication improves environmental employee engagement programs: Evidence from a quasi-experimental field study. *Journal of Cleaner Production, 172*, 1486–1500. Advance online publication. DOI: 10.1016/j.jclepro.2017.10.252

Prasanna, R. P. I. R., Jayasundara, J. M. S. B., Naradda Gamage, S. K., Ekanayake, E. M. S., Rajapakshe, P. S. K., & Abeyrathne, G. A. K. N. J. (2019). Sustainability of SMEs in the competition: A systemic review on technological challenges and SME performance. *Journal of Open Innovation, 5*(4), 100. Advance online publication. DOI: 10.3390/joitmc5040100

Pratap, S. (2018). A study on eco-friendly consumerism. *International Journal of Creative Research Thoughts, 6*(2), 940–941. https://ijcrt.org/papers/IJCRT1134708 .pdf

Putrevu, J., & Mertzanis, C. (2024). The adoption of digital payments in emerging economies: Challenges and policy responses. *Digital Policy. Regulation & Governance*, *26*(5), 476–500. DOI: 10.1108/DPRG-06-2023-0077

Qureshi, I. H., & Mehraj, D. (2022). Identifying the factors of internal green marketing: A scale development and psychometric evaluation approach. *International Journal of Manpower*, *43*(3), 786–804. DOI: 10.1108/IJM-06-2020-0276

Raihan, A. (2024). A review of the potential opportunities and challenges of the digital economy for sustainability. *Innovation and Green Development*, *3*(4), 100174. https://doi.org/https://doi.org/10.1016/j.igd.2024.100174

Raja, S. (2021). *The neoliberal" do-good" spirit: a case study of Unilever digital communication of corporate social responsibility* (Doctoral dissertation, Rutgers University-School of Graduate Studies). https://rucore.libraries.rutgers.edu/rutgers-lib/65963/

Ramus, C. A. (2001). Organizational support for employees: Encouraging creative ideas for environmental sustainability. *California Management Review*, *43*(3), 85–105. DOI: 10.2307/41166090

Rašković, M. M., Hurd, F., & Onaji-Benson, T. (2024). Moving diversity, equity and inclusion research forward with (in) international business: Addressing blind spots through critical and reflexive management scholarship. *Critical Perspectives on International Business*. Advance online publication. DOI: 10.1108/cpoib-09-2024-0110

Rathore, & Gangwar. (2024). Analyzing the benefits & challenges of eco mark rules & compliance. Lawrbit. Retrieved from https://www.lawrbit.com/article/analyzing-the-benefits-challenges-of-eco-mark-rules-compliance/

Recyclebank. (2024). *Pick up points for recycling and learning online*. https://recyclebank.com/

Reddy, K. P., Chandu, V., Srilakshmi, S., Thagaram, E., Sahyaja, C., & Osei, B. (2023). Consumers' perception of green marketing towards eco-friendly fast-moving consumer goods. *International Journal of Engineering Business Management*, *15*, 18479790231170962. Advance online publication. DOI: 10.1177/18479790231170962

Reeves, B., Ram, N., Robinson, T. N., Cummings, J. J., Giles, C. L., Pan, J., Chiatti, A., Cho, M., Roehrick, K., Yang, X., Gagneja, A., Brinberg, M., Muise, D., Lu, Y., Luo, M., Fitzgerald, A., & Yeykelis, L. (2021). Screenomics: A framework to capture and analyze personal life experiences and the ways that technology shapes them. *Human-Computer Interaction, 36*(2), 150–201. DOI: 10.1080/07370024.2019.1578652 PMID: 33867652

Reichheld, A. (2023). Research: Consumers' sustainability demands are rising. Harvard Business Review. Retrieved from https://hbr.org/2023/09/research-consumers-sustainability-demands-are-rising

Renault. (2024). *REFACTORY: THE FLINS SITE ENTERS THE CIRCLE OF THE CIRCULAR ECONOMY.* https://www.renaultgroup.com/en/magazine/sustainable-development/re-factory-the-flins-site-enters-the-circle-of-the-circular-economy

Ren, S., & Jackson, S. E. (2020). HRM institutional entrepreneurship for sustainable business organizations. *Human Resource Management Review, 30*(3), 100691. Advance online publication. DOI: 10.1016/j.hrmr.2019.100691

Ren, S., Tang, G., & Jackson, E, S. (. (2018). Green human resource management research in emergence: A review and future directions. *Asia Pacific Journal of Management, 35.* Advance online publication. DOI: 10.1007/s10490-017-9532-1

Ren, S., Zhang, Y., Liu, Y., Sakao, T., Huisingh, D., & Almeida, C. M. V. B. (2019). A comprehensive review of big data analytics throughout product lifecycle to support sustainable smart manufacturing: A framework, challenges and future research directions. *Journal of Cleaner Production, 210*, 1343–1365. DOI: 10.1016/j.jclepro.2018.11.025

Renwick, D. W., Redman, T., & Maguire, S. (2013). Green human resource management: A review and research agenda. *International Journal of Management Reviews, 15*(1), 1–14. DOI: 10.1111/j.1468-2370.2011.00328.x

Ritchie, H. (2021). *Deforestation and Forest Loss.* https://ourworldindata.org/deforestation

Ritchie, H., & Roser, M. (2020). *CO_2 emissions, How much CO_2 does the world emit? Which countries emit the most?*https://ourworldindata.org/co2-emissions

Riva, F., Magrizos, S., Basher Rubel, M. R., & Rizomyliotis, I. (2022). Green consumerism, green perceived value, and restaurant revisit intention: Millennials' sustainable consumption with the moderating effect of green perceived quality. *Business Strategy and the Environment, 31*(7), 2807–2819. DOI: 10.1002/bse.3048

Roh, T., Noh, J., Oh, Y., & Park, K.-S. (2022). Structural relationships of a firm's green strategies for environmental performance: The roles of green supply chain management and green marketing innovation. *Journal of Cleaner Production, 356*, 131877. DOI: 10.1016/j.jclepro.2022.131877

Rosati, F., & Faria, L. G. D. (2019). Business contribution to the Sustainable Development Agenda: Organizational factors related to early adoption of SDG reporting. *Corporate Social Responsibility and Environmental Management*, *26*(3), 588–597. Advance online publication. DOI: 10.1002/csr.1705

Roscoe, S., Subramanian, N., Jabbour, C. J., & Chong, T. (2019). Green human resource management and the enablers of green organizational culture: Enhancing a firm's environmental performance for sustainable development. *Business Strategy and the Environment*, *28*(5), 737–749. Advance online publication. DOI: 10.1002/bse.2277

Roszko-Wójtowicz, E., Deep Sharma, G., Dańska-Borsiak, B., & Grzelak, M. M. (2024). Innovation-Driven E-Commerce Growth in the EU: An Empirical Study of the Propensity for Online Purchases and Sustainable Consumption. *Sustainability (Basel)*, *16*(4), 1563. DOI: 10.3390/su16041563

Rotich, K. J. (2015). History, evolution and development of human resource management: A contemporary perspective. *Global Journal of Human Resource Management*, *3*(3).

Rouault, G. (2021). Sustainability Marketing and The Toyota Way. , *61*(2). https://shudo-u.repo.nii.ac.jp/record/3084/files/SG61216.pdf

Ruby's Organics. (n.d.). Ruby's Organics | Makeup that's good for you. Retrieved from https://rubysorganics.in/

Ryu, J., Park, S., Park, Y., Park, J., & Lee, M. (2021). Innovative culture and firm performance of medical device companies: Mediating effects of investment in education and training. *International Journal of Environmental Research and Public Health*, *18*(17), 8926. DOI: 10.3390/ijerph18178926 PMID: 34501515

Sachdeva, S., Jordan, J., & Mazar, N. (2015). Green consumerism: Moral motivations to a sustainable future. *Current Opinion in Psychology*, *6*, 60–65. Advance online publication. DOI: 10.1016/j.copsyc.2015.03.029

Sachs, J. D., Schmidt-Traub, G., Mazzucato, M., Messner, D., Nakicenovic, N., & Rockström, J. (2019). Six transformations to achieve the sustainable development goals. *Nature Sustainability*, *2*(9), 805–814. Advance online publication. DOI: 10.1038/s41893-019-0352-9

Salnikova, E., Strizhakova, Y., & Coulter, R. A. (2022). Engaging consumers with environmental sustainability initiatives: Consumer global–local identity and global brand messaging. *JMR, Journal of Marketing Research, 59*(5), 983–1001. DOI: 10.1177/00222437221078522

Samsudin, A., & Hotimah, R. A. D. N. H. (2024). The Influence of Green Product, Green Marketing, and Green Brand Image Towards Green Purchase Intention on Sensatia Botanicals Products in Surabaya. *Formosa Journal of Multidisciplinary Research, 3*(2), 241–260. DOI: 10.55927/fjmr.v3i2.8238

Sandionigi, C., Berrée, J.-F., Péralta, M., Piel, A., & Robin, B. (2024). *Sustainable technology and technology for sustainability: the paths towards eco-innovation. 2024 Electronics Goes Green 2024*. EGG.

Santos, P., Oliveira, R., & Silva, T. (2022). Blockchain Applications in Sustainability Reporting. *The Journal of Supply Chain Management, 58*(6), 493–510.

Saratun, M. (2016). Performance management to enhance employee engagement for corporate sustainability. *Asia-Pacific Journal of Business Administration, 8*(1), 84–102. Advance online publication. DOI: 10.1108/APJBA-07-2015-0064

Sarkar, M. K., Rao, A. C., & Singh, A. K. (2024). "Sustainability and Talent Management": A Two-Pronged Approach for the Evolution of E-commerce in India. *Circular Economy and Sustainability, 4*(1), 267–285. Advance online publication. DOI: 10.1007/s43615-023-00282-1

Sarvaiya, H., Arrowsmith, J., & Eweje, G. (2021). Exploring HRM involvement in CSR: Variation of Ulrich's HR roles by organizational context. *International Journal of Human Resource Management, 32*(21), 4429–4462. Advance online publication. DOI: 10.1080/09585192.2019.1660698

Saura, J. R., & Saura, J. R. (2023). *Big Data Marketing Strategies for Superior Customer Experience*. IGI Global. https://books.google.com.pk/books?id=nph5zwEACAAJ

SBToolkit. (2024). Eco-friendly transportation examples: Sustainable transport solutions. Sustainable Business Toolkit. Retrieved from https://www.sustainablebusinesstoolkit.com/eco-friendly-transportation-examples/

Sekhar, K. C., & Asio, J. M. R. (2022). Evaluation of Consumerism on Sustainability. *Technoarete Transactions on Advances in Social Sciences and Humanities, 2*(2), 1–6.

Selvakumar, P. (2025). Social Sustainability Audits and Certifications. *Enhancing Social Sustainability in Manufacturing Supply Chains*, 221-248.

Shahzad, M. F., Xu, S., Rehman, O. U., & Javed, I. (2023). Impact of gamification on green consumption behavior integrating technological awareness, motivation, enjoyment and virtual CSR. *Scientific Reports*, *13*(1), 21751. DOI: 10.1038/s41598-023-48835-6 PMID: 38066018

Shao, L., Gong, J., Fan, W., Zhang, Z., & Zhang, M. (2022). Cost comparison between digital management and traditional management of cotton fields—Evidence from cotton fields in Xinjiang, China. *Agriculture*, *12*(8), 1105. DOI: 10.3390/agriculture12081105

Sharma, A., Pandey, D. K., Girdharwal, N., & Charon, J. (2024). Global Culture of Eco-Friendly Products and Preference of Consumer in Digital Economy for Sustainable Development of G-20 Countries. In *Diversity, Equity And Inclusion* (pp. 368-380). Routledge. DOI: 10.4324/9781003487180-28

Sharma, A. P. (2021). Consumers' purchase behaviour and green marketing: A synthesis, review and agenda. *International Journal of Consumer Studies*, *45*(6), 1217–1238. DOI: 10.1111/ijcs.12722

Sharma, P., & Khan, W. A. (2022). Revolutionizing Human Resources Management with Big Data: From Talent Acquisition to Workforce Optimization. *International Journal of Business Intelligence and Big Data Analytics*, *5*(1). https://research.tensorgate.org/index.php/IJBIBDA/article/view/64

Sharma, R., & Gupta, N. (2015, January). Green HRM: An innovative approach to environmental sustainability. In *Proceeding of the Twelfth AIMS International Conference on Management* (pp. 2-5).

Shaukat, F., Zaman, H. M. F., Nga, N. T. T., & Souvanhxay, P. (2023). The interplay of eco-innovation and market uncertainty on green marketing orientation and business performance. *Marketing i menedžment innovacij*, *14*(4), 48-68.

Shaw, J. (2024). *Why Gen Z Values Sustainability: Tips for Marketing to the Eco-Conscious Generation.* https://kadence.com/en-us/why-gen-z-values-sustainability-tips-for-marketing-to-the-eco-conscious-generation/

Shen, Y., Zhu, H., Liu, H., Chen, Y., & Ozkan, E. (2017). Development of a laser-guided, embedded-computer-controlled, air-assisted precision sprayer. *Transactions of the ASABE*, *60*(6), 1827–1838. DOI: 10.13031/trans.12455

Sheoran, M., & Kumar, D. (2020). Benchmarking the barriers of sustainable consumer behaviour. *Social Responsibility Journal*. Advance online publication. DOI: 10.1108/SRJ-05-2020-0203

Siemens. (2021). *Siemens' MindSphere has been selected by TotalEnergies for IoT monitoring of its NGV stations.* https://newsroom.sw.siemens.com/en-US/totalenergies-selects-siemens-mindsphere-iot-monitoring/

Siemens. (2024). Sustainability Report 2024. https://assets.new.siemens.com/siemens/assets/api/uuid:32a7154d-edba-47bc-8e9b-9761617ba774/sustainability-report.pdf

Singh, S. (2022). National strategy for eco-tourism.

Singh, R., & Dhir, A. (2022). Exploring green market orientation: Emerging practices and strategic implications. *Environmental Business Review, 12*(4), 333–348.

Singh, R., & Taylor, P. (2023). Blockchain and transparency in sustainability advertising. *Consumer Protection Review, 21*(1), 56–79.

Smaniotto, C., Battistella, C., Brunelli, L., Ruscio, E., Agodi, A., Auxilia, F., Baccolini, V., Gelatti, U., Odone, A., Prato, R., Tardivo, S., Voglino, G., Valent, F., Brusaferro, S., Balzarini, F., Barchitta, M., Carli, A., Castelli, F., Coppola, C., & Sisi, S. (2020). Sustainable Development Goals and 2030 Agenda: Awareness, Knowledge and Attitudes in Nine Italian Universities, 2019. *International Journal of Environmental Research and Public Health, 17*(23), 8968. DOI: 10.3390/ijerph17238968 PMID: 33276530

Smith, J. (2023). Digital Ad Spending Trends. *Statista Reports.* Retrieved from https://statista.com

Smith, J. (2021). The impact of regulatory compliance on sustainable branding. *International Journal of Market Research, 36*(2), 94–118.

Smith, T. M. (1998). *The myth of green marketing: Tending our goats at the edge of apocalypse.* University of Toronto Press. DOI: 10.3138/9781442657427

Sohanda, M. K., Gupta, M., & Kalpana, A. (2024). Interactive E-Commerce: Addressing Cart Abandonment through Gamified User Engagement. 2024 International Conference on Communication, Computing and Internet of Things (IC3IoT), Theodorakopoulos, L., & Theodoropoulou, A. (2024). Leveraging big data analytics for understanding consumer behavior in digital marketing: A systematic review. *Human Behavior and Emerging Technologies, 2024*(1), 3641502.

Solina, A. M., & Ocampo, L. V. G. (2024). Driving Sustainable Change: Behavior and Environmental Awareness in the Case of the Philippines. In Prof. M. Turkmen (Ed.), *Research Advances in Environment, Geography and Earth Science Vol. 5* (pp. 23–31). B P International. DOI: 10.9734/bpi/raeges/v5/633

Staci, K. (2024). Top 5 eco-friendly transportation methods you can feel great about. Blue and Green Tomorrow. Retrieved from https://blueandgreentomorrow.com/transport/top-5-eco-friendly-transportation-methods-you-can-feel-great-about/

Stahl, G. K., Brewster, C. J., Collings, D. G., & Hajro, A. (2020). Enhancing the role of human resource management in corporate sustainability and social responsibility: A multi-stakeholder, multidimensional approach to HRM. *Human Resource Management Review*, *30*(3), 100708. Advance online publication. DOI: 10.1016/j.hrmr.2019.100708

Statista. (2025). *Annual carbon dioxide (CO_2) emissions worldwide from 1940 to 2024 (in billion metric tons).*

Stefanovic, N., Radenkovic, M., Bogdanovic, Z., Plasic, J., & Gaborovic, A. (2025). Adaptive Cloud-Based Big Data Analytics Model for Sustainable Supply Chain Management. *Sustainability (Basel)*, *17*(1), 354. DOI: 10.3390/su17010354

Story, J., Castanheira, F., & Hartig, S. (2016). Corporate social responsibility and organizational attractiveness: Implications for talent management. *Social Responsibility Journal*, *12*(3), 484–505. Advance online publication. DOI: 10.1108/SRJ-07-2015-0095

Strategy, I. S. (2018). People & planet positive. *IKEA Sustainability Strategy*. https://solarthermalworld.org/sites/default/files/news/file/2021-05-13/people-and-planet-positive-ikea-sustainability-strategy-august-2020.pdf

Sugandini, D., Susilowati, C., Siswanti, Y., & Syafri, W. (2020). Green supply management and green marketing strategy on green purchase intention: SMEs cases. [JIEM]. *Journal of Industrial Engineering and Management*, *13*(1), 79–92. DOI: 10.3926/jiem.2795

Sugiarto, A. B. (2024). The Leader's Role In Staff Mobilization To Realize The Goals Of Educational Institutions. *Tsaqofah: Jurnal Pendidikan Islam*, *9*(1), 269–298.

Sullivan, J. (2017). *Creating employee champions: How to drive business success through sustainability engagement training*. Routledge. DOI: 10.4324/9781351274609

Sun, Y., & Yoon, S. (2022). Determinants of green consumption: A systematic literature review using the triple bottom line framework. Frontiers in Sustainability. Retrieved from https://www.frontiersin.org/journals/sustainability/articles/10.3389/frsus.2024.1428764/full

Sun, Y., Luo, B., Wang, S., & Fang, W. (2021). What you see is meaningful: Does green advertising change the intentions of consumers to purchase eco-labeled products? *Business Strategy and the Environment*, *30*(1), 694–704. DOI: 10.1002/bse.2648

Suresh, P., Paul, A., Kumar, B. A., Ramalakshmi, D., Dillibabu, S. P., & Boopathi, S. (2024). Strategies for Carbon Footprint Reduction in Advancing Sustainability in Manufacturing. In *Environmental Applications of Carbon-Based Materials* (pp. 317–350). IGI Global. DOI: 10.4018/979-8-3693-3625-0.ch012

Swire Properties. (n.d.).. . *Sustainable Development.*

Szabo, S., & Webster, J. (2021). Perceived greenwashing: The effects of green marketing on environmental and product perceptions. *Journal of Business Ethics*, *171*(4), 719–739. Advance online publication. DOI: 10.1007/s10551-020-04461-0

Tahmasbi, E. (2024). Principles of Responsible Management. https://www.researchgate.net/profile/Ehsan-Tahmasbi-2/publication/380165279_Critically_evaluate_IKEA's_current_approach_to_responsible_management_and_propose_recommendations_for_further_action/links/662e8e26352430415351c606/Critically-evaluate-IKEAs-current-approach-to-responsible-management-and-propose-recommendations-for-further-action.pdf

Takacs, F., Brunner, D., & Frankenberger, K. (2022). Barriers to a circular economy in small-and medium-sized enterprises and their integration in a sustainable strategic management framework. *Journal of Cleaner Production*, *362*, 132227. DOI: 10.1016/j.jclepro.2022.132227

Team Experts. (2023). *Gamification: Feedback Loops Vs. Flow (Breaking it Down).* https://predictivethought.com/gamification-feedback-loops-vs-flow-breaking-it-down/

Team, S. (2023). 22 organic farming statistics that show its true power (2025). Soocial. Retrieved from https://www.soocial.com/organic-farming-statistics/

TerraChoice. (2022). The Seven Sins of Greenwashing. *Consumer Watch Report.*

Tesla. (2024). Impact. Retrieved from https://www.tesla.com/impact

Thakkar, R. (2021). Green marketing and sustainable development challenges and opportunities. *International Journal of Management. Public Policy Research*, *1*(1), 15–23.

Tharanatha, A., Shashidhar, R., Bharath, S., & Nagesh, P. (2023). The green behaviour role in relationship amid green human resource management and employer branding in green hospitals. *Indian Journal of Science and Technology*, *16*(14), 1062–1068. DOI: 10.17485/IJST/v16i14.247

The Body Shop. (2024). Open Hiring. https://www.thebodyshop.com/en-gb/about-us/open-hiring/a/a00060

The Body Shop. (2024). The Educational Programme: Buy for Good: Enriching the Future. https://www.thebodyshop.com/en-gb/about-us/open-hiring/a/a00060

The Conversation. (2020). *Fridays for Future: How the young climate movement has grown since Greta Thunberg's lone protest.* https://theconversation.com/fridays-for-future-how-the-young-climate-movement-has-grown-since-greta-thunbergs-lone-protest-144781

Thida, S. M. (2024). *Integration of sustainable development goals in business strategies* (Doctoral dissertation, Vilniaus universitetas.).

Thomas, R., & Brown, J. (2022). Balancing Compliance and Creativity in Green Marketing. *Business Horizons*, *65*(4), 459–469.

Thummalapalli, U. S. (2019). The influence of green supply chain management on the competitive advantage: Case of Japanese auto manufacturing company (Toyota). (*Unpublished doctoral thesis. KwaZulu-Natal: Durban University of Technology*). https://ritsumei.repo.nii.ac.jp/record/12293/files/52117630.pdf

Trends, G. (2017). Challenges and opportunities in the implementation of the Sustainable Development Goals. *United Nations Development Programme& United Nations Research Institute for Social Development.* https://www.truevaluemetrics.org/DBpdfs/UN/Global-Trends-UNDP-UNRISD-Report-2017.pdf

Trinh, T. L. M. (2021). Green Human Resources Management–Solutions to Enhance the Green Marketing Development of Enterprise. *International Journal of Research in Engineering. Science and Management*, *4*(8), 200–203.

TSAI, C.-W. (2023). Impacts of information channels on consumer decision journey: Evidence from an experience durable goods industry.

Tsairi, Y., & Martens, K. (2024). Workplace responsibility for employee mobility? A review of sustainability reporting frameworks. *Transport Reviews*, *44*(5), 1077–1102. Advance online publication. DOI: 10.1080/01441647.2024.2356030

UITP. (2024). 5 key public transport trends revealed in our global economic outlook 2024. UITP. Retrieved from https://www.uitp.org/news/5-key-public-transport-trends-revealed-in-our-global-economic-outlook-2024/

Ullah, A., Ahmad, S., & Sana, S. Leveraging Blockchain and Big Data-Optimized Supply Chain for Eco-Innovative Firm Performance. *Professor Qingyu and Ahmad, Sohail and Sana, Sana, Leveraging Blockchain and Big Data-Optimized Supply Chain for Eco-Innovative Firm Performance.*

Uniqode. (n.d.). QR code management platform for modern businesses. Retrieved from https://www.uniqode.com/

United Nations. (2024). *Sustainable Development Goals (SDGs)*. https://unosd.un.org/content/sustainable-development-goals-sdgs

Usman, M., Rofcanin, Y., Ali, M., Ogbonnaya, C., & Babalola, M. T. (2023). Toward a more sustainable environment: Understanding why and when green training promotes employees' eco-friendly behaviors outside of work. *Human Resource Management*, *62*(3), 355–371. Advance online publication. DOI: 10.1002/hrm.22148

Vahdat, S. (2022). The role of IT-based technologies on the management of human resources in the COVID-19 era. *Kybernetes*, *51*(6), 2065–2088. Advance online publication. DOI: 10.1108/K-04-2021-0333

Van Veldhoven, Z., & Vanthienen, J. (2022). Digital transformation as an interaction-driven perspective between business, society, and technology. *Electronic Markets*, *32*(2), 629–644. DOI: 10.1007/s12525-021-00464-5 PMID: 35602117

Vashishth, T. K., Sharma, K. K., Kumar, B., Chaudhary, S., & Panwar, R. (2025). Enhancing Customer Experience through AI-Enabled Content Personalization in E-Commerce Marketing. *Advances in Digital Marketing in the Era of Artificial Intelligence*, 7-32.

Vaz, N. (2021). *Digital Business Transformation: How Established Companies Sustain Competitive Advantage From Now to Next*. Wiley. https://books.google.com.pk/books?id=NQkLEAAAQBAJ

Vazquez Melendez, E. I., Bergey, P., & Smith, B. (2024). Blockchain technology for supply chain provenance: Increasing supply chain efficiency and consumer trust. *Supply Chain Management*, *29*(4), 706–730. DOI: 10.1108/SCM-08-2023-0383

Vitale, R., Blaine, T., Zofkie, E., Moreland-Russell, S., Combs, T., Brownson, R. C., & Luke, D. A. (2018). Developing an evidence-based program sustainability training curriculum: A group randomized, multi-phase approach. *Implementation Science : IS*, *13*(1), 1–12. DOI: 10.1186/s13012-018-0819-5 PMID: 30257695

Viterouli, M., Belias, D., Koustelios, A., Tsigilis, N., & Bakogiannis, D. (2023). Fostering Sustainability Through the Integration of Green Human Resource Management and Change Management: Nurturing Eco-Conscious Organizational Practices. In *Managing Successful and Ethical Organizational Change* (pp. 241-278). IGI Global. https://doi.org/DOI: 10.4018/979-8-3693-0235-4.ch011

Vorecel. (2024). The impact of social responsibility on brand image and consumer preferences. *Vorecel.* https://psico-smart.com/en/blogs/blog-the-impact-of-social-responsibility-on-brand-image-and-consumer-preferences-166740

Vyas, S. K., Vyas, L., Singh, S., & Joshi, M. (2023). Future of E-Commerce: A Robust Review. In *Intelligent Sustainable Systems: Selected Papers of WorldS4 2022, Volume 2* (pp. 697-710). Springer. DOI: 10.1007/978-981-19-7663-6_66

Walker, D. (2002). Enthusiasm, commitment and project alliancing: An Australian experience. *Construction Innovation, 2*(1), 15–31. DOI: 10.1108/14714170210814667

Wang, C., Ghadimi, P., Lim, M. K., & Tseng, M. L. (2019). A literature review of sustainable consumption and production: A comparative analysis in developed and developing economies. *Journal of Cleaner Production, 206*, 741–754. DOI: 10.1016/j.jclepro.2018.09.172

Wang, J., Tang, L., Zhang, T., Phillips, C., & Aldawish, L. S. (2024). The implementation and barriers of green recruitment: A qualitative study on green human resource management. *Businesses, 4*(3), 411–425. Advance online publication. DOI: 10.3390/businesses4030025

Wang, L., Elahi, E., Zhou, Y., Wang, L., & Zhang, S. (2022). A review of packaging materials' consumption regulation and pollution control. *Sustainability (Basel), 14*(23), 15866. DOI: 10.3390/su142315866

Wang, S. (2024). An analysis of the problems and optimization strategies of employee relationship management in IKEA enterprises. In *Exploring the Financial Landscape in the Digital Age*. CRC Press., DOI: 10.1201/9781003508816-80

Wang, S., Liu, M. T., & Pérez, A. (2023). A bibliometric analysis of green marketing in marketing and related fields: From 1991 to 2021. *Asia Pacific Journal of Marketing and Logistics, 35*(8), 1857–1882. DOI: 10.1108/APJML-07-2022-0651

Waqas, M., & Tan, L. (2023). Big data analytics capabilities for reinforcing green production and sustainable firm performance: The moderating role of corporate reputation and supply chain innovativeness. *Environmental Science and Pollution Research International, 30*(6), 14318–14336. DOI: 10.1007/s11356-022-23082-w PMID: 36152098

Wear, P. A. C. T. (n.d.). Sustainability, certified. Retrieved from https://wearpact.com/sustainability

White, K. (2024). The elusive green consumer. Harvard Business Review. Retrieved from https://hbr.org/2019/07/the-elusive-green-consumer

White, Z. (2022). *Introducing Koolboks: Pay-as-you-go solar refrigeration in Nigeria.* https://www.gsma.com/solutions-and-impact/connectivity-for-good/mobile-for-development/blog/introducing-koolboks-pay-as-you-go-solar-refrigeration-in-nigeria/

Wiradirja, I. R., Ras, H., Pranadita, N., Macmud, S., Anwar, H., & Haspada, D. (2020). Environmental Performance: Role Of Green Employee Involvement Practices, Green Training And Green Shared Vision. *Journal of Security & Sustainability Issues*, *10*(2), 721–733. DOI: 10.9770/jssi.2020.10.2(28)

Wongkitrungrueng, A., Dehouche, N., & Assarut, N. (2020). Live streaming commerce from the sellers' perspective: Implications for online relationship marketing. *Journal of Marketing Management*, *36*(5-6), 488–518. DOI: 10.1080/0267257X.2020.1748895

World Economic Forum. (2024). Renewable energy could power the world by 2050: Here's what that future might look like. Retrieved from https://www.weforum.org/stories/2020/02/renewable-energy-future-carbon-emissions/

World Economic Forum. (n.d.). How hydrogen-powered vehicles will help India reach its emissions targets. Retrieved from https://www.weforum.org/stories/2024/12/how-hydrogen-powered-vehicles-will-help-india-reach-its-emissions-targets/

World Health Organization. (2024). Electronic waste (e-waste). Retrieved from https://www.who.int/news-room/fact-sheets/detail/electronic-waste-%28e-waste%29

Wu, Y., & Tham, J. (2023). The impact of environmental regulation, environment, social and government performance and technological innovation on enterprise resilience under a green recovery. *Heliyon*, *9*(10), e20278. Advance online publication. DOI: 10.1016/j.heliyon.2023.e20278 PMID: 37767495

Xie, C., Wang, R., & Gong, X. (2022). The influence of environmental cognition on green consumption behavior. *Frontiers in Psychology*, *13*, 988585. DOI: 10.3389/fpsyg.2022.988585 PMID: 36237699

Xie, Q., Zhang, H., & Cao, S. (2023). Green market orientation: Drivers and outcomes in the global market. *Journal of Business Ethics*, *19*(2), 102–119.

Xu, J., Yu, Y., Zhang, M., & Zhang, J. Z. (2023). Impacts of digital transformation on eco-innovation and sustainable performance: Evidence from Chinese manufacturing companies. *Journal of Cleaner Production*, *393*, 136278. DOI: 10.1016/j.jclepro.2023.136278

Yang, Y., Habib, K., & Wood, M. O. (2023). Establishing best practices for E-commerce transport packaging waste management in Canada: A systematic review. *Journal of Cleaner Production, 429*, 139377. https://doi.org/https://doi.org/10.1016/j.jclepro.2023.139377. DOI: 10.1016/j.jclepro.2023.139377

Yan, H., Acquah, S. J., Zhang, J., Wang, G., Zhang, C., & Darko, R. O. (2021). Overview of modelling techniques for greenhouse microclimate environment and evapotranspiration. *International Journal of Agricultural and Biological Engineering, 14*(6), 1–8. DOI: 10.25165/j.ijabe.20211406.3948

Yasin, R., Huseynova, A., & Atif, M. (2023). Green human resource management, a gateway to employer branding: Mediating role of corporate environmental sustainability and corporate social sustainability. *Corporate Social Responsibility and Environmental Management, 30*(1), 369–383. Advance online publication. DOI: 10.1002/csr.2360

Yong, J. Y., Yusliza, M.-Y., Ramayah, T., & Fawehinmi, O. (2019). Nexus between green intellectual capital and green human resource management. *Journal of Cleaner Production, 215*, 364–374. DOI: 10.1016/j.jclepro.2018.12.306

Yordanova, Z. (2023). Barriers to Organizations to Adopt Digital Transformation for Driving Eco-Innovation and Sustainable Performance. *International Conference on Optimization, Learning Algorithms and Applications*

Yu, J., Hu, J. J., Liu, G. G., Jiang, W., & Walters, G. (2024). Not just a game: Understanding eco-gamification in sustainable destination development. *Journal of Hospitality and Tourism Management, 60*, 10–21. DOI: 10.1016/j.jhtm.2024.06.005

Yu, P., Zhang, Z., Wong, S. K. M., Lu, S., Chen, Y., & Wang, Y. (2025). The Role of Technologies in Facilitating Circular Economy of China's E-Commerce Section. In *AI Strategies for Social Entrepreneurship and Sustainable Economic Development* (pp. 151–174). IGI Global Scientific Publishing.

Zaccaro, S. J., Kemp, C., & Bader, P. (2004). Leader traits and attributes. *The nature of leadership, 101*, 124.

Zafar, A. U., Shahzad, M., Shahzad, K., Appolloni, A., & Elgammal, I. (2024). Gamification and sustainable development: Role of gamified learning in sustainable purchasing. *Technological Forecasting and Social Change, 198*, 122968. DOI: 10.1016/j.techfore.2023.122968

Zaharia, R. M., & Zaharia, R. (2021). Triple bottom line. *The Palgrave Handbook of Corporate Social Responsibility*, 75-101.

Zaid, A. A., Jaaron, A. A., & Bon, A. T. (2018). The impact of green human resource management and green supply chain management practices on sustainable performance: An empirical study. *Journal of Cleaner Production*, *204*, 965–979. Advance online publication. DOI: 10.1016/j.jclepro.2018.09.062

Zameer, H., & Yasmeen, H. (2022). Green innovation and environmental awareness driven green purchase intentions. *Marketing Intelligence & Planning*, *40*(5), 624–638. DOI: 10.1108/MIP-12-2021-0457

Zhao, H., Bai, R., Liu, R., & Wang, H. (2022). Exploring purchase intentions of new energy vehicles: Do "mianzi" and green peer influence matter? *Frontiers in Psychology*, *13*, 951132. DOI: 10.3389/fpsyg.2022.951132 PMID: 36176803

Zhao, S., Teng, L., & Ji, J. (2024). Impact of environmental regulations on eco-innovation: The moderating role of top managers' environmental awareness and commitment. *Journal of Environmental Planning and Management*, *67*(10), 2229–2256. DOI: 10.1080/09640568.2023.2184331

Zhou, C., Son, S.-B., Zhu, C., & Zhu, X. (2024). Research on the Application of Big Data Analysis in Green Marketing Strategies. 2024 3rd International Conference on Artificial Intelligence and Computer Information Technology (AICIT), Zreik, M. (2025). Digital Transformation and Organizational Relearning in China.

Zielinski, T., Sagan, I., & Surosz, W. (2018). *Interdisciplinary approaches for sustainable development goals*. Springer. DOI: 10.1007/978-3-319-71788-3

About the Contributors

Shamim Akhtar is a postdoctoral researcher at Jiangsu University, China in Management Science and Engineering. Currently, researching project related to green product innovation, entrepreneurship, innovation performance and digital transformation of SMEs. She has experience of teaching and research in the fields of Management, Leadership, Innovation performance, green product innovation, entrepreneurship and sustainability. She has publications in well reputed (SSCI) journals. She also published a book chapter "Digital Transformation in HRM - Using Social Media for Recruiting and Employer Branding, in Innovative Human Resources Management for SMEs" with IGI Global Publishing.

Prasad Siba Borah, Ph.D. and currently serving as an associate professor in the School of Management at Jiangsu University, China. In pursuit of academic excellence, Dr. Borah has published several scientific papers in top-notch academic journals SSCI/SCI Q1, A* level, including Business Strategy and the Environment, Energy Economics, and Technology in Society, among several others. He also edited a prestigious book titled "Selected Cases on Management" by Tsinghua University Press. He is also contributing his volunteer expertise as a reviewer and editorial board member for various peer-reviewed academic journals.

***

Aasim N. Gill is a seasoned educator, strategic leader, and corporate trainer with over 17 years of experience in academia and professional development. Currently serving as a Senior Assistant Professor and Deputy Head of BBA Programs at Lahore Business School, University of Lahore, Aasim specializes in teaching management, leadership, and strategic management courses. He is deeply involved in alumni relations, student counseling, and program development, contributing significantly to the institution's academic and administrative excellence. Aasim's expertise extends to AACSB accreditation processes, enhancing academic quality and international recognition. As a corporate and soft skills trainer, Aasim has delivered impactful workshops and seminars on leadership, communication, conflict resolution, team dynamics, and corporate ethics, empowering professionals and students to excel in their careers.

Shuja Iqbal has a Ph.D. from Jiangsu University, China, in Management Science and Engineering. Currently, serving as a postdoctoral researcher at Jiangsu University, China, focused on projects related to the innovation performance of SMEs, specifically researching digital transformation innovative and green human resources practices and related areas. Dr. Iqbal has experience in teaching and research in Human Resource Management, Organization Performance, Leadership, and innovation performance. He has more than 30 peer-reviewed publications in well-reputed journals. Additionally, he is serving as associate editor in two esteemed journals, including RAE-Revista de Administração de Empresas. Dr. Iqbal has also been reviewing scientific research papers for several high-quality journals. Dr. Shuja Iqbal's extensive academic and professional expertise, combined with his significant contributions to research and scholarly publishing, positions him as a leading figure in advancing knowledge and practices in Human Resource Management and organizational innovation, making impactful strides in the field.

Vishwanathan Iyer is a research enthusiast who is exploring finance, accounting, marketing, HR, and every other field of academics to the best of his abilities. His research is based on primary data as well as secondary data. Being consistent at research and providing quality research work is the ultimate aim of Dr Iyer. Collaborating with authors across spectrum is one of his strengths. Publishing articles and writing chapters are motivating factors for Dr Iyer to pursue his dream of becoming a Researcher to be recokned with.

Vishal Jain is presently working as Professor at Department of Computer Science and Engineering, School of Engineering and Technology, Sharda University, Greater Noida, U. P. India. Before that, he has worked for several years as an Associate Professor at Bharati Vidyapeeth's Institute of Computer Applications and Management (BVICAM), New Delhi. He has more than 15 years of experience in the academics. He obtained Ph.D (CSE), M.Tech (CSE), MBA (HR), MCA, MCP and CCNA. He has authored more than 100 research papers in reputed conferences and journals, including Web of Science and Scopus. He has authored and edited more than 45 books with various reputed publishers, including Elsevier, Springer, IET, Apple Academic Press, CRC, Taylor and Francis Group, Scrivener, Wiley, Emerald, NOVA Science, IGI-Global and River Publishers. His research areas include information retrieval, semantic web, ontology engineering, data mining, ad hoc networks, and sensor networks. He received a Young Active Member Award for the year 2012–13 from the Computer Society of India, Best Faculty Award for the year 2017 and Best Researcher Award for the year 2019 from BVICAM, New Delhi.

Benard Korankye is a PhD student pursuing Business Administration at Zhejiang Gongshang University, School of Business Administration. His research interests are Environmental, Social, and Governance (ESG), Corporate Social Responsibility (CSR), Consumer Behavior and Organizational Behavior. He has SSCI and several scientific publications to his name also a reviewer for some international journals. Email: benardkorankye31@outlook.com,Orcid number:

Tinashe Mangudhla is a PhD student at the School of Management, University of Science and Technology of China, Hefei. His research interests include environmental economics, development finance, and sustainable development across various countries. He has published in reputable journals in these fields and other related areas.

Archan Mitra is an Assistant Professor at School of Media Studies (SOMS) at Presidency University, Bangalore. He is the author of two book "Cases for Classroom Media and Entertainment Business" and "Multiverse and Media", he also has other several edited books to his credit. He has done his doctorate from Visva-Bharati Santiniketan, West Bengal in the field of "environmental informatics and communication for sustainability". In addition to that he is a certified Science Communicator and Journalism from Indian Science Communication Society (ISCOS), certified Corporate Trainer with Amity Institute of Training and Development, Certified Social Media Network Analyst. He has a strong interest in environmental communication. He was awarded certificate of merit by PRSI, Kolkata Chapter and Medal of Honor by Journalistic Club of Kolkata. He was working as a research assistant with the World Bank's "Environmental Capacity Building in Southeast Asia" project at IIM Kashipur. He was instrumental in launching the World Bank's Green MBA MOOC, he has also assisted in the research project on Uttarakhand disaster mitigation by ICSSR, the leading research on Uttarakhand disaster.

Pritesh Somani is working as an assistant professor at the Balaji Institute of International Business, Sri Balaji University, Pune with a widespread teaching experience of more than 11 years teaching subjects spread across general management and research. He specializes in research methodology and has good experience in operating SPSS. He has conducted sessions through faculty development programs on statistical analysis as an integral part of research methodology. He has published chapters across different disciples that are Scopus-indexed. Also, a few papers are published in ABDC-indexed journals. Many research articles are published in UGC care and peer-reviewed journals

Prachi Wani has over 18 years of experience in hospitality sales at Taj Lands' End, Mumbai, and Intercontinental the Grand, Mumbai, and with a hotel management college. Dr. Wani holds a PhD in Marketing. She is currently working with Sri Balaji University Pune, a prestigious university for management education in India. Dr. Wani has a passion to inspire, empower, and mentor the next generation of leaders and managers in the industry. She teaches various marketing courses to postgraduate students and supervises their research projects on relevant and emerging topics. Dr. Wani leverages the practical and industry-oriented insights from her industrial experience to enrich her teaching and research. Dr Wani has published multiple papers in reputed journals and presented a few at international conferences. She also has two patents in her name. Dr. Wani is always eager to learn new skills and stay updated with the latest trends and developments in my field of expertise.

Index

B

C

D

E

G

M

S

www.ingramcontent.com/pod-product-compliance
Lightning Source LLC
LaVergne TN
LVHW080343011026
849161LV00009B/2178
* 9 7 9 8 3 6 9 3 9 8 3 1 9 *